Cultural Pearls from the East

Studies on Performing Arts & Literature of the Islamicate World

Series Editors

Li Guo (*University of Notre Dame*)
Richard Jankowsky (*Tufts University*)
Margaret Litvin (*Boston University*)

Advisory Board

Walter Armbrust (*Oxford*)
Marvin Carlson (*CUNY-GC*)
Matthew Isaac Cohen (*Royal Holloway*)
Nacim Pak-Shiraz (*University of Edinburgh*)
Friederike Pannewick (*Marburg*)
Dwight Reynolds (*University of California Santa Barbara*)
Nehad Selaiha (*Cairo*)
Martin Stokes (*King's College, London*)
Andrew Weintraub (*University of Pittsburgh*)

VOLUME 11

The titles published in this series are listed at *brill.com/spal*

Portrait of Professor Shmuel Moreh

Cultural Pearls from the East

In Memory of Shmuel Moreh (1932–2017)

Edited by

Meir Hatina
Yona Sheffer

TUTA SUB AEGIDE PALLAS · 1683 ·

BRILL

LEIDEN | BOSTON

Cover illustration: وهي أول سني الملاحم العظيمة، والحوادث الجسيمة، والوقايع النازلة، والنوازل الهائلة، وتضاعف الشرور، وترادف الأمور، وتوالي المحن.
The opening passage of Egyptian historian ʿAbd al-Raḥmān al-Jabartī's description of the first year of the French occupation of Egypt (June 15, 1798–June 5, 1799). Al-Jabartī pronounced the occupation a grave disaster. Source: *The Marvelous Chronicles: Biographies and Events by ʿAbd al-Raḥmān b. Ḥasan al-Jabartī*, edited by Shmuel Moreh (Jerusalem: The Hebrew University, 2013), vol. 3, p. 1. [in Arabic].
Calligraphy and design by Nihad Nadam.

Library of Congress Cataloging-in-Publication Data

Names: Hatina, Meir, editor. | Sheffer, Yona, editor. | Moreh, Shmuel honoree.
Title: Cultural pearls from the East : in memory of Shmuel Moreh, 1932–2017 / edited by Meir Hatina, Yona Sheffer.
Description: Leiden ; Boston : Brill, 2021. | Series: Studies on performing arts & literature of the Islamicate world, 2214-6563 ; volume 11 | Includes bibliographical references and index.
Identifiers: LCCN 2021010839 (print) | LCCN 2021010840 (ebook) | ISBN 9789004448780 (hardback) | ISBN 9789004459120 (ebook)
Subjects: LCSH: Arabic literature—History and criticism. | Middle East—History. | Middle East—Historiography.
Classification: LCC PJ7510 .C85 2021 (print) | LCC PJ7510 (ebook) | DDC 892.7/09—dc23
LC record available at https://lccn.loc.gov/2021010839
LC ebook record available at https://lccn.loc.gov/2021010840

Typeface for the Latin, Greek, and Cyrillic scripts: "Brill". See and download: brill.com/brill-typeface.

ISSN 2214-6563
ISBN 978-90-04-44878-0 (hardback)
ISBN 978-90-04-45912-0 (e-book)

This book is printed on acid-free paper and produced in a sustainable manner.

Contents

Acknowledgments XI
A Note on Transliteration XII
Abbreviations XIII
Notes on Contributors XIV

Introduction: Shmuel Moreh (1932–2017): Scholar and Humanist 1
Meir Hatina

Shmuel Moreh's Scientific Achievements 18
Menahem Milson and Meir M. Bar-Asher

PART 1
Poetry

Narrative in Ancient Arabic Heroic Poetry: The Account of the Battle 31
Albert Arazi

An Unpublished Poem in Honor of the Prophet Moses 49
Joseph Sadan

An Anti-Jewish *Qaṣīda* by Sīdī Qaddūr al-ʿAlamī 57
Norman (Noam) A. Stillman

"To Choose Your Own Sky": Rootedness and Dislocation in the Poetry of Saʿdī Yūsuf 69
Yair Huri-Horesh

Intertextuality in Samīḥ al-Qāsim's Poetry: A Philosophy of Blending 91
Ibrahim Taha

PART 2
Prose and Drama

The Pimps' Maqāma: A Libertine Piece of Ornate Prose from a Manuscript of the Mamluk Period 109
Amir Lerner

Where Is the Holy Land? A Reading of Two Seventeenth-Century Arabic Manuscripts of *Virtues of the Holy Land* Literature 126
Ghaleb Anabseh

Samīr Naqqāsh: From One Universe to Another—Iraq to Israel 142
Geula Elimelekh

Representations of Women in the Literary Works of Egyptian Writer Jamāl al-Ghīṭānī 161
Yona Sheffer

Shared Passion: Imam Ḥusayn in Persian and Arabic Drama 179
Peter Chelkowski

Fūl, Egypt's National Food: A Key Component of Egyptian Identity and Its Reflections in Modern Egyptian Literature 194
Gabriel M. Rosenbaum

Contemporary Arabic Literature and Its Obsession with the Internet 224
Eman Younis

PART 3
Historiography

An Unknown Chronicle of Ottoman Egypt and Its Historiographical Implications 247
Jane Hathaway

The Sufi Personality of the Egyptian Historian ʿAbd al-Raḥmān al-Jabartī (1753–1825) 264
Michael Winter

Encountering Modernity in the Late Nineteenth Century: Two Egyptian Accounts 288
Meir Hatina

Shmuel Moreh's *Baghdad Mon Amour*: Autobiographical Works as Historical and Cultural Documents 315
Sigal Goorji

Index 333

Acknowledgments

This volume grew out of a collaborative endeavor by scholars from academic institutions in Israel and abroad who joined together to commemorate the work of Prof. Shmuel Moreh (1932–2017), an eminent scholar of Arabic culture. Their contributions correspond to Moreh's fields of interest: Arabic poetry, prose, drama, and historiography, and bring to the fore new materials, findings, and intriguing insights related to themes ranging from the classical period to modern times.

We would like to thank all those who contributed chapters to the book. Some of these chapters are the by-product of a conference on modern Arabic literature held at the Hebrew University of Jerusalem on March 19, 2018. We are grateful to Esther Meir-Glizenstein, Haya Bambaji-Sasportas, Orit Bashkin, Samīr al-Ḥājj, Raymond Moreh, and Fruma Zachs, who participated in the conference and provided valuable advice and critiques which enriched the discussions in this volume. Sadly, one of the volume's contributors, Professor Michael Winter, a renowned scholar of social history of the Middle East, passed away in September 2020 at age 86. He managed to complete his intriguing chapter on "The Sufi personality of the Egyptian historian ʿAbd al-Raḥmān al-Jabartī" before his death.

We are indebted to the Alice and Jack Ormut Chair in Arabic Studies at the Hebrew University of Jerusalem, which assisted us in the process of preparing this volume. An earlier draft of the work was completed while we were staying at the Institut für den Nahen und Mittleren Osten, Ludwig-Maximilians-Universität München, in 2019. We remain deeply grateful to Professors Ronny Vollandt and Andreas Kaplony for offering us a stimulating environment in which to pursue our work.

A special note of appreciation goes to the anonymous readers for their expertise and constructive comments. Thanks are also due to Belina Neuberger, who skillfully edited the book. Last but not least, we are deeply grateful to the editorial staff at Brill Publishers, especially Maurits van den Boogert, Teddi Dols and Pieter te Velde for their professional guidance and encouragement.

Meir Hatina and Yona Sheffer

A Note on Transliteration

In this volume, the English transliteration of Arabic words conforms to Brill's transliteration system. However, for the sake of convenience, and in order to make this volume more accessible to the non-specialist reader, the following letters were used: th (ث), dh (ذ), kh (خ), sh (ش), and gh (غ). Arabic names and terms used in English-language literature appear in their English form.

Arabic terms are written in italics except for those which recur often, such as Qur'an, Ḥadīth/ḥadīth, 'ulama', shari'a, qadi, or mufti. The letter *'ayn* is represented by ' and *hamza* by '. Conjunctions such as *wa* and *fī*, when followed by prepositions such as *li* and *bi*, are joined to the words which follow them by a hyphen. Anglicized place and corporate names are given in their familiar form (Cairo, Baghdad, Tehran, al-Sham) and dates are given according to the Hijri calendar, followed by the Western (i.e. AD) equivalent. From the seventeenth century onward, only the Western calendar is used.

Egyptian proper and last names, as well as book titles and place names, are written in J/j instead of G/g (Jamāl, Majīd, Najīb, *Mu'jam*). The transliteration of Turkish and Persian words and names, mainly in the essays of Jane Hathaway, Michael Winter, and Peter Chelkowski generally follows the system used in modern Turkish and Persian.

All translations of Qur'anic verses are those of M.A.S. Abdel Haleem, *The Qur'an: A New Translation* (Oxford: Oxford University Press, 2005), with occasional, slight alterations. Verses cited follow the numbering found in the common Egyptian edition.

Abbreviations

BRISMES	The British Society for Middle Eastern Studies
BSOAS	*Bulletin of the School of Oriental and African Studies*
*EI*²	*Encyclopedia of Islam*, second edition
EJIW	*Encyclopedia of Jews in the Islamic World*
HAEMA	*Journal of the Hellenic Society of Haematology*
IJMES	*International Journal of Middle East Studies*
JAL	*Journal of Arabic Literature*
JSAI	*Jerusalem Studies in Arabic and Islam*
ZDMG	*Zeitschrift der Deutschen Morgenländischen Gesellschaft*
Z.D.P.V.	*Zeitschrift des Deutschen Palästina-Vereins*

Notes on Contributors

Ghaleb Anabseh

is an associate professor of Arabic Language and Literature at Beit Berl Academic College. His research focuses on Holy Land literature (in Arabic), Sufism in the late Ottoman period, and anecdotes in classical Arabic literature. He is the author of *The Prophet David as Reflected in Early Muslim Tradition* (2016); *Acoustic Rhythm in al-Hareri's Maqamat* (2016); *A Look at the Sufi Orders in Historical Palestine* (2017); and *In the Inkwell of Words: Studies in Arab Literature and Culture* (2017).

Albert Arazi

is a professor emeritus in the Department of Arabic Language and Literature at the Hebrew University of Jerusalem. An eminent scholar in the field of pre-Islamic and classical Islamic poetry, poetics, love literature, and narratology Among his publications are *La réalité et la fiction dans la poésie arabe ancienne* (1989); *Amour divin et amour profane dans l'Islam médiéval à travers le Dīwān de Khālid al-Kātib* (1990); *Six Early Arab Poets* (1999, with S. Masalha [in Arabic]); *Le voyage de Saʿīd ibn Muhammad al-Suwaysī au Yaman* (2008, with Isaac Hasson); coeditor *In the Oasis of Pens: Studies in Arab Literature and Culture in Honour of Professor Joseph Sadan* (2013, with G. Anabseh and N. Masarwah).

Meir M. Bar-Asher

is Max Schloessinger Professor of Islamic Studies at the Hebrew University of Jerusalem and a member of the Department of Arabic Language and Literature at this university. His research interests include Qurʾanic exegesis and religious communities in Islam (especially Twelver Shiʿism and Nusayri-ʿAlawi religion), as well as historical encounters between Judaism and Islam. Among his publications are *Scripture and Exegesis in Early Shiʿism* (1999); *The Nusayri-ʿAlawi Religion: An Enquiry into its Theology and Liturgy* (2002, with A. Kofsky); *Les Juifs et le Coran* (2019); coeditor *Le Shiʿisme Imamite: quarante ans après: Hommage à Etan Kohlberg* (2009, with M.A. Amir-Moezzi and S. Hopkins); *Islam: History, Religion and Culture* (2017, with M. Hatina [in Hebrew]).

Peter Chelkowski

is professor emeritus in the Faculty of Arts and Science at New York University. Areas of research: literature, mysticism, Islamic studies, and performing arts in the Middle East. His numerous publications include: *Mirror of the Invisible*

World (1975); *Ta'ziyeh: Ritual and Drama in Iran* (1979); *Staging a Revolution: The Art of Persuasion in the Islamic Republic of Iran* (1999, with H. Dabashi); *Bir Devrimi Sahnelemek; Iran Islam Cumhuriyetinde Propaganda Sanati* (1999, with H. Dabashi) (in Turkish). He is also the editor of *Eternal Performance: Ta'ziyeh and Other Shi'ite Rituals* (2010); *The Gift of Persian Culture: Its Continuity and Influence in History* (2011); *Crafting the Intangible: Persian Literature and Mysticism* (2013); and *Ideology and Power in the Middle East: Studies in Honor of George Lenczowski* (2013, with R.J. Pranger).

Geula Elimelekh
is senior lecturer in the Department of Arabic at Bar-Ilan University. Her research field is modern Arabic literature, and focuses on Arabic political and prison literature. She has published a number of articles on related subjects, including "Existentialism in the Works of 'Abd al-Raḥmān Munīf," *Oriente Moderno* 94 (2014) 1–31; "Fantasy as 'Recovery, Escape and Consolation' in the Short Stories of Isaac Bar Moshe," *Middle Eastern Studies* 50/3 (2014): 426–441; "The Duality of the Victim and Torturer in Two works by Fadil al-Azzawi," *Journal of Semitic Studies* LXLL/2 (2017): 447–464. She is also the author of *Arabic Prison Literature: Resistance, Torture, Alienation, and Freedom* (2014).

Jane Hathaway
is Arts and Sciences Distinguished Professor of History at Ohio State University. She specializes in the Ottoman Empire before 1800, with a focus on the empire's Arab provinces, particularly Egypt and Yemen. Her publications include *A Tale of Two Factions: Myth, Memory, and Identity in Ottoman Egypt and Yemen* (2012); *The Chief Eunuch of the Ottoman Harem: from African Slave to Power-Broker* (2018); and *The Arab Lands under Ottoman Rule, 1516–1800* (2nd ed., 2020). She has also published four edited volumes and scores of articles on Ottoman eunuchs, Ottoman Egypt and Yemen, ethnoregional tensions in Ottoman provincial administration, and Jews under Muslim rule.

Meir Hatina
is professor in the Department of Islamic and Middle Eastern Studies at the Hebrew University of Jerusalem. His fields of research focus on the history of ideas and politics in the modern Middle East. His publications include *Martyrdom in Modern Islam: Piety, Power and Politics* (2014); *Arab Liberal Thought in the Modern Age* (2020). He is also the coeditor of *Martyrdom and Sacrifice in Islam: Theological, Political and Social Contexts* (2017, with M. Litvak); and *Muslims in a Jewish State: Religion, Politics and Society* (2018, with M. al-Atawneh [in Hebrew]).

Yair Huri-Horesh
is senior lecturer of Arabic literature and the former director of the Program of Arabic language Literature at Ben Gurion University of the Negev, Israel. His research focuses primarily on modern Arabic poetry, and his recent book entitled *Between Homeland and Exile* (2006). He is currently engaged in research on metapoetics in modern Arabic poetry.

Sigal Goorji
is lecturer in the Department of Middle Eastern Studies at Ben-Gurion University of the Negev. Her Ph.D. dissertation deals with existential elements in the literary works of the late Egyptian writer Anīs Manṣūr. Her fields of research and interest include aspects in modern Arabic literature, such as the relation between East and West, expressions of existentialism, youth in Arab society, minorities, women and gender, political criticism in modern Arabic literature, and literature of Iraqi Jews.

Amir Lerner
is senior lecturer at The Department of Arabic and Islamic Studies at Tel-Aviv University. He teaches medieval Arabic literature and classical *adab* literature, as well as literary materials that emerged and evolved among lower classes of society, such as the *One Thousand and One Nights*. He is the author of *The Juʿaydiyya Cycle: Witty Beggars' Stories from the Montague Manuscript—a Late Augmented Arabian Nights* (2014).

Menahem Milson
is professor emeritus of Arabic Literature at the Hebrew University of Jerusalem. His areas of interest include Sufi literature, modern Egyptian literature and Arabic lexicography. He is the author and director of the online edition of the Arabic-Hebrew dictionary, originally authored by David Ayalon and Pessah Shina. Among his publications are *A Sufi Rule for Novices: A Translation of the Kitab Adab al-Muridin* (1975); *Najib Mahfuz: The Novelist-Philosopher of Cairo* (1999).

Gabriel M. Rosenbaum
is a professor emeritus in the Department of Arabic Language and Literature at the Hebrew University of Jerusalem. He is also the director of the Israeli Academic Center in Cairo, and a visiting fellow at Wolfson College, Cambridge (UK). His fields of research focus on the language, literature, drama and popular culture of modern Egypt, as well as modern spoken Egyptian Judeo-Arabic. He also writes fiction, and has published some literary translations into

Hebrew. Among his recent publications: "Curses, Insults and Taboo Words in Egyptian Arabic in Daily Speech and in Written Literature," *Romano-Arabica* 19 (2019): 153–188; and "The Distinct Vocabulary of the Judeo-Arabic Spoken by the Karaites in Egypt in the Twentieth Century," *Massorot* 19–20 (2019): 183–208 (in Hebrew).

Joseph Sadan
is professor emeritus in the Department of Arabic and Islamic Studies at Tel-Aviv University. His research focuses on social and material culture (furniture, drinks), medieval Arabic literature, especially prose, and Jewish-Arab relations. He is the author of *Le mobilier au Proche-Orient médiéval* (1976); *Nouvelle source de l'époque bûyide* (1980), *Arabic Humoristic Literature and the Literary Genre "Anecdotes on Boring Persons"* (1984, in Arabic); *Yemenite Authorities and Jewish Messianism* (1990, with P. Sj. van Koningsveld and Q. al-Samarrai); *Et il y eut d'autres nuits* (2004); *al-Adab al-hāzil wa-nawādir al-thuqalā'* (2007, in Arabic).

Yona Sheffer
currently teaches at the Polis Institute of Languages and Humanities in Jerusalem and is Assistant Researcher for both the Departments of Islamic and Middle Eastern Studies, and of Arabic Language and literature at the Hebrew University of Jerusalem. His research focuses on modern Arabic literature. Recent publications include *The Individual and the Authority Figure in Egyptian Prose Literature* (2018); and translation from Arabic to Hebrew of two autobiographies by Meir Muallem, *A Piece of Life Memoirs from Iraq* (2011), and by Shmuel Moreh, *Baghdād ḥabībatī: Yahūd al-ʿIrāq, dhikrayāt wa-shujūn* (2020).

Norman (Noam) A. Stillman
is Schusterman/Josey Professor Emeritus at the University of Oklahoma and an internationally recognized authority on the history and culture of the Islamic world and on Sephardi Jewry. His books include *The Language and Culture of the Jews of Sefrou* (1988); *Sephardi Religious Responses to Modernity* (1995); *The Jews of Arab Lands: A History and Source Book* (1998); and *The Jews of Arab Lands in Modern Times* (2003).

Ibrahim Taha
is professor of literary semiotics and Arabic literature at the University of Haifa. His research areas include semiotics, anthroposemiotics and theory of literature, comparative literature, Arabic and Palestinian literature. Among his publications are *The Palestinian Novel: A Communication Study* (2002); *Arabic*

Minimalist Story: Genre, Politics and Poetics in the Self-colonial Era (2009); *Brevity in Rhetoric and Holy Quran* (2012, in Arabic); and *Heroizability: An Anthroposemiotic Theory of Literary Characters* (2015).

Michael Winter

(d. 2020), was a professor emeritus in the Department of Middle East and African History, Tel-Aviv University. He had published numerous articles on Egyptian society in Ottoman and modern times, as well as on contemporary educational problems in the Middle East. His publications include *Society and Religion in Early Ottoman Egypt* (Transaction Publishers, 1982); *Egyptian Society under Ottoman Rule 1517–1798* (1992); coeditor, *The Mamluks in Egyptian and Syrian Politics and Society* (2004, with A. Levanoni); coeditor, *The Encounter of Crusaders and Muslims in Palestine* as *Reflected in Arsuf, Sayyiduna 'Ali and Other Coastal Sites* (2007, with I. Roll and O. Tal [in Hebrew]).

Eman Younis

is head of the Department of Arabic Language and Literature at Beit-Berl College. Her research focuses on modern Arabic literature, learning and teaching Arabic language, and digital literacy. Among her publications: "Manifestations of the Arab Spring in Literature: "Video Clip Poems" on YouTube as a Model," *Journalism & Mass Communication Quarterly* 6/1 (February 2016): 33–42; "The Impact of the Internet on the Language of Literary Discourse," *The Islamic Quarterly* 61/4 (October 2017): 553–581; coauthor, *Artistic and Literary Interactivity in Digital Literature: The Poem 'Shajar al-Bughāz' as an Example* (2015, with ʾA. Nasrallah).

INTRODUCTION

Shmuel Moreh (1932–2017): Scholar and Humanist

Meir Hatina

Shmuel Moreh, professor emeritus in the Department of Arabic Language and Literature at the Hebrew University of Jerusalem, passed away on September 22, 2017. He was 85 years old. We mourn the passing of a gifted and creative scholar of Arab culture, a leading intellectual who worked incessantly to preserve the legacy of Iraqi Jewry. Regrettably, when I visited Moreh in his home after his discharge from the hospital in late July, I witnessed the first signs of the illness that had struck him so suddenly. On my last visit, about three weeks before his death, I found a man clear of mind but physically exhausted. I pleaded with him to return to his desktop and books, from which I hoped he would draw the strength to overcome the illness that had overtaken him. But he replied in a weak voice in Arabic: "I have no strength" (*ma biyya ḥayl*). His words deeply affected me. Could a man for whom knowledge and writing had always been his life's passion—even obsession—suddenly quit?

Moreh was a leading scholar of Arab culture. He was born in December 1932 to a respectable family in Baghdad. His grandfather, Ḥākhām Yeḥezkel Meir ben Muʿallim Raḥamim, was the author of *Liqquṭei Imrei El* (Collection of God's sayings). Moreh grew up in the prestigious al-Battāwīn neighborhood, where he lived with his parents, four brothers, and two sisters. His mother taught French at the Alliance School and his father was an accountant and businessman. Moreh studied at the Saʿdūn Exemplary School, which was attended by children of the Iraqi elite—ministers and senior government officials, army officers, and judges—and then at the Jewish Shammash school. While at school, he began publishing short stories and poems in the Baghdad newspapers. In 1951 he immigrated to Israel. He earned his BA and MA degrees from the Department of Arabic Language and Literature at the Hebrew University of Jerusalem. After completing his doctoral studies at the University of London in 1965, he continued his groundbreaking work in many fields of study: poetry and literature, theatre and drama, history and historiography. He had extensive knowledge, broad philological skills, and the capacity for lucid, in-depth analysis. Moreh's scholarship was multifaceted, crossing boundaries between classical, medieval, and modern Arabic culture, thus positioning his research subjects within a wide historical, social, and cultural context and paving the

 | DOI:10.1163/9789004459120_002

way for an exploration of their encounter with European culture. He was among the first scholars in the 1970s and 1980s to explore the *Nahḍa* (cultural renaissance) that took place in the Arab Middle East during the nineteenth and early twentieth centuries. The *Nahḍa* was an intense and ambitious project, whose proponents sought to invigorate Arab heritage and align it with scientific analysis, progress, and humanism.[1] Its manifestations in the fields of poetry, translation, and theatre were skillfully documented and discussed by Moreh. An important part of Moreh's academic research was devoted to the literary work of Jews from Iraq, the country of his birth and youth, and to their important contribution to general Arab culture.

The scope of his research yielded a rich variety of publications that were translated into several languages, including Arabic, and that conferred upon him status and an impeccable reputation in Israel and around the world. These publications have become cornerstones of the study of Arab culture. Moreh's name also gained prominence in Arab countries and his work has been widely cited by local intellectuals and academic institutions.[2] When the news of Moreh's death reached the Arab world, it led to dozens of eulogies and praise for his scholarly work.[3]

Moreh's academic credo was that anyone convinced of the validity of his or her research was obliged to prove the bona fides of original views and conclusions without bias or fear. "A good scholar must have scientific integrity," he stated. Adhering to this motto paved the way for new and creative ways of studying Arab culture. Three of Moreh's publications, which illustrate his varied fields of expertise, are considered groundbreaking: (1) *Modern Arab Poetry 1800–1970* (1976), analyzing the emergence of free verse (*al-shiʿr al-ḥurr*), which breaks fixed patterns and rules of grammar and style to give the poet more freedom in expressing his emotions; (2) *Live Theatre and Dramatic Literature in the Medieval Arabic World* (1992), demonstrating the existence of a medieval Arab theatre that lives and breathes, thus contradicting the prevailing scholarly approach that speaks only of an Arab shadow theatre and puppets (*khayāl*

1 For literature on the *Nahḍa*, see Albert Hourani, *Arabic Thought in the Liberal Age 1798–1939* (Oxford: Oxford University Press, 1962); Abdulrazzak Patel, *The Arab* Nahdah, *The Making of the Intellectual and Humanist Movement* (Edinburgh: Edinburgh University Press, 2013); Jens Hanssen and Max Weiss (eds.), *Arabic Thought Beyond the Liberal Age: Towards an Intellectual History of the Nahda* (Cambridge: Cambridge University Press, 2016); Tarek El-Ariss (ed.), *The Arab Renaissance: A Bilingual Anthology of the Nahda* (New York: Modern Language Association, 2018).

2 For Moreh's list of publications see pp. 23–28 of this book.

3 See for example *Elaph*, September 22, 2017; *al-Akhbār*, September 23, October 12, 2017; *al-Ḥiwār al-Mutamddin*, September 26, 2017; *al-Quds al-ʿArabī*, September 30, 2017.

al-ẓill); and (3) *ʿAjāʾib al-āthār fiʾl-tarājim waʾl-akhbār* (The marvelous chronicles: biographies and events, 2013), a scientific edition of the chronicle of the Egyptian historian ʿAbd al-Raḥmān al-Jabartī (d. 1825). The chronicle provides a fascinating glimpse into the history of Egypt in the eighteenth and early nineteenth centuries in the shadow of the charged encounter with colonial Europe and modern culture.[4]

These and other achievements earned Moreh a series of prizes during his lifetime; first and foremost the 1999 Israel Prize in Islamic and Middle Eastern Studies, which he saw not only as a source of pride for him and his family, but also for Iraqi Jewry and Mizrahi Jews in general.[5] His international reputation as a renowned scholar and the success of his publications, which became required reading at many universities, only fueled his intellectual curiosity and creativity as he continued to enrich our bookshelves with new works. At the same time, he kept on teaching, served as editor of important journals, and supervised advanced students. Many sought knowledge and guidance from him. Even after retiring, he continued to visit his office at the Hebrew University to study and to teach—a permanent presence that represented stability, perseverance, and devotion to his craft.

I met Moreh for the first time at the end of 2005, when I was appointed lecturer in the Department of Islamic and Middle Eastern Studies at the Hebrew University of Jerusalem, the twin department of the Department of Arabic Language and Literature where Moreh taught for many years and which he headed between 1979 and 1982. After our first meeting, we remained in close contact. We bridged gaps, narrowed distances, and soon moved from being professional colleagues to becoming soul friends, sharing personal experiences, family celebrations, and cultural events as well as conferences. My soul was tied to his despite the difference in our ages and despite our disagreements on various issues. I used to visit his office almost daily, and we had many conversations about his fields of interest and research, conversations which opened wide vistas of learning to me.

Moreh's passion for knowledge was ingrained in every fiber of his being and books were his close friends. I was struck by his endless intellectual curiosity, his extraordinary knowledge, and his command of Arabic language, literature, and poetry. I listened eagerly to stories about his life and about Jewish life in Iraq before his immigration to Israel. Together we read some of his poems,

---

4 On Moreh's innovative contribution to the study of poetry, theatre, and Arab historiography see also Menahem Milson and Meir Bar-Asher's chapter in this book.

5 The term Mizrahi refers to Jews who came to Israel from Arab-Muslim countries. Ella Shohat, "The Invention of the Mizrahim," *Journal of Palestinian Studies* 29/1 (1999), 5–20.

written by what proved to be a sensitive and humanist intellectual protesting against social oppression and class schisms, imbued with a strong sense of justice and advocating a cosmopolitan culture based on tolerance, freedom, and mutual solidarity.

Moreh's stories and poems eventually found their way into a volume of memoirs published in Arabic in 2012: *Baghdād ḥababtī: Yahūd al-ʿIrāq, dhikrayāt wa-shujūn* (Baghdad Mon Amour: The Jews of Iraq, memories and mourning).[6] Initially (2009–2010) some of the book's chapters were serialized in *Elaph*, an online Arabic journal based in London. *Elaph* defined itself as an independent journal unaffiliated with any ideology, political party, or state, and with a global and cosmopolitan orientation. The journal's goal, as stated by the editor, ʿUthmān al-ʿAmīr, was to serve as a bridge for Arabs to join the modern world and leave behind feelings of frustration, anger, and hostility.[7] Such a goal corresponded to that of Moreh's, so that his published chapters were well received by many Arab Iraqi readers who grieved for their lost community, hence creating a kind of intercultural dialogue.[8] Thus, for example, Samīr ʿĪd, depicting Moreh as his brother in humanity and patriotism (to Iraq), wrote:

فهل قبلت أخي شموئيل؟
فإن قبلت:
أدعوا [sic] الله أن يطيل بعمرك
وأن يقصّر عمر
الخراب
والظلم
والإحتلال [sic]
الذي حلّ ببلدي وبلدك
العراق

6 Moreh, *Baghdād ḥabībatī: Yahūd al-ʿIrāq, dhikrayāt wa-shujūn* (Haifa: Maktabat Kull Shay', 2012).

7 https://elaph.com/publishermessage.html.

8 There were also some readers who expressed their anger at Moreh and other Iraqi Jews who, they argued, had left Iraq of their own free will in order to expropriate Palestinian land. https://elaph.com/Web/ElaphWriter/2008/1/297034.html. See also Walīd al-Baʿāj, *Yahūd al-ʿImāra, ṣafaḥāt maṭwiyya min taʾrīkh Yahūd al-ʿIrāq* (Baghdad, Beirut: Wamaḍāt li'l-Tarjama wa'l-Nashr, 2018), 370–383.

Do you agree, Shmuel my brother [to be brothers in God and the motherland, and to strive for peace]?
If you agree,
I will pray to God to prolong your life
And to shorten the days of
The destruction,
The injustice,
And the occupation
That befell my country and yours
Iraq[9]

Moreh's *Baghdad Mon Amour* reveals longing and desire (*ashwāq*) for a beloved, all-embracing, and tolerant Iraq. The reign of King Fayṣal (1920–1933), during which Muslims, Christians, and Jews studied and worked together, and during which Jews held senior positions, earned special praise. The government ministries were guided by "the principles of the French Revolution: freedom, justice, and equality," to which Faisal added another: "religion belongs to God, and the homeland to the people (*al-dīn li'l-lāh wa'l-waṭan li'l-jamīʿ*)."[10] This motto, which was also a key concept of the nineteenth-century *Nahḍa*—cultural renaissance, also prevailed among the Jewish intelligentsia in Iraq. Its members, at least until the riots of June 1941, known as the *Farhūd*, truly believed that there was nothing to prevent Jews from holding onto their religion. Iraq was their only homeland and their language and culture were Arabic.[11]

While yearning for Fayṣal's tolerant Iraq, Moreh mourned the later Iraq, ungrateful, tearful, and bleeding in the shadow of erupting ethnic and religious

9 ʿĪd quoted in al-Baʿāj, *Yahūd al-ʿImāra*, 382.

10 Moreh, *Baghdād ḥabībatī*, 34.

11 Reuven Snir, *Arabness, Jewishness, Zionism: A Clash of Identities in the Literature of Iraqi Jews* (Jerusalem: Ben-Zvi Institute, 2005), 47–42. In the *Farhūd* events, at least 179 Jews were killed, businesses looted, and houses pillaged. There is a fierce dispute among Iraqi Jewish scholars and intellectuals about the *Farhūd*: Was it sporadic incidents instigated by a handful of Muslims, or perhaps a massacre initiated and directed by the authorities and fueled by waves of radical Arab nationalism and pro-Nazi influences? See, for example, Moreh, *Baghdād ḥabībatī*, chapter 7; Shmuel Moreh and Zvi Yehuda (eds.), *al-Farhud: The 1941 Pogrom in Iraq* (Jerusalem: Magnes, Press, 2010); Sasson Somekh, *Baghdad, Yesterday: The Making of an Arab Jew* (Jerusalem: Ibis Editions; 2007), chapter 17; Orit Bashkin, *New Babylonians: A History of Jews in Modern Iraq* (Redwood City: Stanford University Press, 2012), 105–140.

conflicts. Moreh likened Baghdad to "a traitorous woman that had expelled him" and that had caused—on a much greater scale—the mass exodus of 1951.[12]

Moreh, as his memoirs indicate, did not spare his criticism of Arab leaders who had expelled Jews as punishment for the 1948 displacement of the Palestinian refugees from their land (*Nakba*). Particularly harsh accusations were leveled at Iraqi society, which he called arrogant and hypocritical, and its corrupt and greedy state institutions. Moreh also debated with second-generation Jewish intellectuals who defined themselves as "Arab Jews," a defiant term aimed at the State of Israel which, guided by a sense of superiority and patronage, sought to erase their separate identity, ostensibly in the name of a deceptive concept of "melting pot."[13] "The fact that I write in Arabic and like to listen to Arabic music and speak with the generation that came from Iraq in the Arab-Jewish dialect, does not make me an Arab," Moreh argued, thus seeking to fortify his Jewish-national identity.[14]

However, alongside differentiation and alienation from the Arab landscape, Moreh also displayed empathy and admiration for Arab language and culture and for many of its classic and modern literates. For him, Arabic was the cornerstone of a shared Middle Eastern culture, of which Iraqi Jewish were an organic component. He also praised modern Arab poets who, while influenced by Western currents, did not imitate them blindly. Their broad education, understanding of poetry, and sensitivity to social and political problems enabled some of them to translate local poetry into a dynamic and evolving art form.[15]

Moreh perceived poetry and literature as a bridge to mutual intellectual coexistence. His affinity for Western culture did not detract from his love for Arabic culture. He lived on the seam between West and East, between Jeruslaem, London, and Baghdad, seeking to harmonize them and in this way, to find tranquility for his own soul. He also sought to reach out to Arab intellectuals who were open-minded and critical of what was happening in their countries, and whom he regarded as the moral leaders of their communities.

---

12 Moreh in a book event on his memoirs, Hebrew University of Jerusalem, Mt. Scopus, January 21, 2013.

13 Yehouda Shenhav, *The Arab Jews: A Postcolonial Reading of Nationalism, Religion, and Ethnicity* (Redwood City: Stanford University Press, 2006); Reuven Snir, *Who Needs Arab-Jewish Identity? Interpellation, Exclusion, and Inessential Solidarities* (Leiden: Brill, 2015).

14 Moreh's interview from November 13, 2008. See https://www.articles.co.il/article/29151.

15 Moreh, "Basic Outlines in the Development of Modern Arabic Literature," in *The Tree and the Branch: Studies in Modern Arabic Literature and Contributions of Iraqi-Jewish Writers*, edited by Olga Bramson (Jerusalem: Magnes Press, 1997), 24–25, 38–39 (in Hebrew).

He encountered some of them in European capitals, and in Cairo and Amman.[16] In contrast, Moreh expressed an aversion towards Western intellectuals, both Christians and Jews, whose main goal in life, he argued, was the pursuit of money, luxuries, and entertainment instead of spirituality, and who rarely showed sympathy for their Middle Eastern counterparts.[17]

Moreh even positioned himself as an "alarm sounder," directing constructive criticism at the Arabs that emphasized the urgent need for them to interact with the surrounding world lest they descend into the abyss. He aspired to an Arab renaissance and the restoration of the glory of the East, rather than its relinquishment to the pages of history books. The inner tension between alienation and closeness, between dislike and inclusion, that pervaded Jewish-Arab relations was built into his worldview and writings, as well as those of many of Iraqi Jews, hence turning their circle of identities into a fluid and hybrid one.[18]

The painful chapters about his youth in Baghdad reflect Moreh's feelings of sadness and bitterness (intertwined with the emotional trauma of the *Farhūd*),[19] while the happy chapters, with their places, smells, and tastes (set in Baghdad's central Jewish neighborhood of al-Battāwīn), reveal his sense of belonging, hope, and optimism. In his memories, he admitted that alongside frustrations, "we had loyal friends from all communities and religions, and we shared with them joy and sadness and spent beautiful nights with them on the Tigris River."[20]

Indeed, Iraq was deeply entrenched in the soul and mind of Moreh, who remained unable to slip away or divert his gaze from it. The young man, who had successfully assimilated in his new country, was still attached to the country from which he had been exiled. "Iraq is haunting me like fate (*qadar*)," he wrote in his memoirs. To his "misfortune," the street on which he lived in Mevaseret Zion (a town near Jerusalem) was called the Euphrates River, an everlasting testament to the bonds that tied him to his country of birth.[21]

In his poem "Longings for Baghdad" (*al-ḥanīn ilā Baghdād*), dedicated to a friend who went to visit Iraq, Moreh wrote:

---

16 Ibid., 38–39; Moreh, *Baghdād ḥabībatī*, chapters 46–50.

17 Moreh, *Baghdād ḥabībatī*, 21.

18 On the identity struggle among Iraqi Jewry, see Snir, *Arabness*.

19 Moreh was a survivor of the *Farhūd*. He wrote extensively on this episode and was active in the campaign to have the *Farhūd* recognized as a Holocaust event. Moreh, *Baghdād ḥabībatī*, chapter 7.

20 Ibid., 144–145.

21 Ibid., 135, 142.

يا ليتني كنت معك،
لأرى بغداد صبايا وأحلامي
قبل الرحيل
ولكن آمالي، تتحطم
على جدران أوهامي
فقد تعبت مهجتي من طول انتظاري
فاذهب أنت إلى بغداد
واطلب من البواب أن يفتح الباب
فقد طال الانتظار، والعمر يمضي

I wish I were with you
To see Baghdad of my youth and dreams
Before setting on the final journey
But my hopes are shattered
On the walls of my imaginations
For my soul is wearied from my long-lasting waiting
So, you go to Baghdad
and ask the porter to open the gate
Too much has the waiting lasted, and life is fading away.[22]

Moreh's personal account, which became an official and detailed autobiography in 2012, was closely intertwined with the history of an entire community, its hardships and its hopes. Moreh himself turned it into a Gordian knot, as can be deduced from the subtitle of his memoirs: *The Jews of Iraq, Memories and Mourning*. I had the privilege to have known a sharp, disciplined, and diligent scholar and intellectual. I view him as the soundtrack of an entire generation that experienced the trauma of estrangement from its birthplace and the pains of resettlement in a new country, and of its impressive integration into a variety of fields and institutions, from commerce, economics, and banking to academia, literature, and poetry.

Moreh, like many Iraqi Jewish immigrants, expressed anger at the cool and arrogant attitude adopted by officials in Israel who were supposed to facilitate the immigrants' absorption but instead left "everyone to his own destiny and

22 *Elpah*, December 5, 2011.

his ability to survive, facing a strange new world."[23] Still, Moreh and others like him represented proud and staunch Sephardi/Mizrahi Jews who, despite a life of poverty in transit camps, language difficulties, and social marginality, did not remain helpless or captive in the rhetoric of deprivation. On the contrary, they took the initiative, shook off the initial shock of the assimilation experience, and integrated into their new environment, learning its language while taking advantage of the cultural capital they had accumulated in their country of origin. Most of them, members of the Jewish *effendiyya*, or bourgeoisie, tended to embrace the process of Israelization and adopt the modern secular lifestyle, but at the same time, did not turn their backs on the heritage of the past, on the knees of which they had grown up and been educated.[24] Some, however, never recovered from the shock of being thrown into a new country and remained alienated from their new cultural environment. Their sense of uprootedness and dislocation was channeled into a literature of exile, and they insisted on speaking and writing in their native Arabic.[25]

In a reference to the hardships his family experienced upon arriving in Israel, Moreh praised his mother (a key figure in his life), who—earning that the family's property in Baghdad had been frozen—rose from her mourning over their exile. While her husband was still in Baghdad, she built her new home in the holy city of Jerusalem, in the Talpiot transit camp and afterwards in the Meqor Hayim transit camp. As Moreh wrote in his poem "The Holy City" (October 17, 2008):

> The tin house turned into a castle
> Where [my mother] gathered her sons
> And said to them:
> "Now all we need to do is to implement the verse's imperative
> 'From Zion Torah will go out
> And God's word from Jerusalem'
> And all her sons repeated after her,
> Amen."[26]

---

23 Moreh, *Baghdād ḥabībatī*, 62.

24 Ibid., 349. See also the autobiography of Sasson Somekh, *Baghdad, Yesterday*.

25 The case study of Samīr Naqqāsh is featured in Geula Elimelekh's chapter in this volume. On exile literature, see a special volume of *JAL* 47 (2016).

26 For the full Hebrew text, see http://www.news1.co.il/Archive/0022-D-32557-00.html?t=201648. On Moreh's accounts of life in the transit camps, see his *Baghdād ḥabībatī*, 60–65.

For Moreh, therefore, immigration to Israel and the hardship, anguish, and stress it brought in its wake were not the shattering of a dream, but the fulfillment of one: the ingathering of the exiles, the victory of the Zionist dream, the establishment of the State of Israel as a technological and military power, and the creation of a free, multicultural, democratic society. As far as he was concerned, it was also a personal victory, as he forged a path from the muck of the transit camps to the peak of the academic world.[27]

Moreh was not only a towering scholar specializing in Arabic Studies, but also one of the custodians of Iraqi Jewry, the guardian of its culture and identity, documenting its history in the country of the Euphrates and Tigris and in the State of Israel.

Moreh's academic activities were interwoven with his extensive public service. He was an involved intellectual who enlisted his vast knowledge and scholarly authority in his fight to attain a legitimate place for Arabic- and Jewish-Iraqi heritage within Israeli society, and hence to shape that society's aesthetic development.[28] While still a new immigrant, he was one of the founders of the Arab Poets' Association in 1956. He was involved in molding the image of the Babylonian Jewry Heritage Center in Or-Yehuda, inaugurated in 1973, and also served as chairman of the Association of Jewish Academics from Iraq, which he established in 1980. Under his leadership, the association championed the publishing, editing, and distribution of research, manuscripts, memoirs, and works relating to Iraqi Jewry, as well as the development of research and teaching in the field of Babylonian cultural heritage. Faithful to the founder's path, the association has yielded a rich and diverse crop of publications (sixty-four books so far).[29] The association defined itself first and foremost as a cultural forum that strove to preserve and nurture the legacy of Babylonian Jewry, and positioned itself as a bridge between Jews and Arabs in Israel and between Israel and the Arab world.

Moreh's life was full and rich. He celebrated his eightieth birthday, embraced five lovely grandchildren, and kept on creating and writing. For many of us, he was a "mentor of the generation" (*ustādh al-jīl*) for his research accomplishments, and a "crown of our heads" (*tāj rāsna*) for his unique contribution to the commemoration of Babylonian Jewry. His death cut off the thread of creation from this intriguing intellectual, and his office on Mount Scopus, which served as his second home for decades, was left orphaned. The scholarly world

27 *Baghdād ḥabībatī*, chapter 8; also quoted in https://www.articles.co.il/article/29151.

28 On involved intellectuals see Pierre Bourdieu, "Fourth Lecture, Universal Corporatism: The Role of Intellectuals in the Modern World," *Poetic Today* 12/4 (1991): 655–669.

29 See also http://www.jmemories.co.il/jewish-academics-iraq.

of Arabic literature and culture, for which Moreh had served as a compass, lost a gifted scholar possessed of rare knowledge and great achievements. His legacy will live on in the pages of his numerous works and the products of his rich public activity.

About the Book

Cultural Pearls from the East is dedicated to Shmuel Moreh's scholarly legacy. What should have been a Festschrift in honor of Moreh's eightieth birthday in 2012 became a memorial volume following his death in 2017.

The present volume, whose contributors are well-known scholars in their fields, some of which were close colleagues and students of Moreh, explores three themes that reflect Moreh's own fields of research and are true to his blueprint: Arab poetry, prose and drama, and historiography. These issues have been overshadowed to a large degree by the preoccupation of Middle Eastern historians with politics and society, authoritarian regimes, or radical ideologies and movements. However, a well-established premise is that literary works hold a mirror up to society's ebbs and flows, frequently tackling fraught religious and politics issues, while positioning authors as intellectuals deeply involved in public debates and speaking truth to power.[30] Hence, literate works (poems, novels, novellas, short stories) interact in a sociocultural context. They are not just designed to provide comfort and an escape from a difficult and miserable reality: they also challenge this reality by defying corruption and the suppression of human rights, and they serve as the impetus for social change.[31]

By focusing on selected themes of Arab culture throughout the ages, this volume aims at providing additional prisms through which we can look at the history of Arab society and its intellectual evolution and artistic achievements. It offers a thematic, as well as chronological, discussions of the affinity between literature and poetry, society and politics. Among the topics examined in depth: Arabic poetry of warfare at the dawn of Islam; medieval poems about venerated sites and saints; Ottoman and Egyptian chronicles portraying the socioreligious landscapes of Egypt and the Fertile Crescent under the

30 Edward Said, *Representations of the Intellectual* (New York: Vintage Books, 1996), chapter 5.

31 See for example Yona Sheffer, *The Individual and the Authority Figure in Egyptian Prose Literature* (New York and London: Routledge, 2018). On literary works and their wider framework and intersystemic interactions, see Reuven Snir, *Modern Arabic Literature: A Theoretical Framework* (Edinburgh: Edinburgh University Press, 2017), mainly 1–7.

Ottoman Empire and in the shadow of growing European encroachment; and Arab-Jewish literature dealing with suppression, exile, and identity.

The book explores these issues through three dimensions: an historical framework linking the classical and middle periods up to the modern era, thereby allowing us to trace patterns of continuity and dynamics of change on an array of issues related to Arabic literature; an integrative discussion of cross-sectional themes; and, lastly, a comparative perspective of, among others, countries and ethnoreligious sects (Arabs and Jews, Shiʿis and Sunnis). By intertwining these three dimensions—the historic, the integrative, and the comparative—this book offers a major contribution to a better understanding of the evolution of Arabic culture and thereby inspires future research.

Introduced by Menahem Milson and Meir M. Bar-Asher's review of Shmuel Moreh's scientific achievements, which reveal an innovative and trailblazing scholar, each part of this volume discusses selected sociocultural aspects of Middle Eastern life, from early and medieval periods to contemporary times. The chapters are based on textual analysis and criticism of texts, some of which are yet unexplored.

Part 1 focuses on poetry, its historical contexts and close affinity to politics, identity, and power struggles between clans and sects, and consists in essence of three translations of and commentaries on poems. The poem (*qaṣīda*), as shown also by Moreh,[32] was an ideal tool for ruling elites and high government officials to mark holidays and periods of mourning and to celebrate heroic battles; these poems strengthened group identity and solidarity, and distinguished it from the "other," the adversary. The two opening chapters deal with classical Arabic poetry, characterized by a uniform weight, rhythm, and epic style. Two further chapters analyze modern Arabic poetry, which breaks free of the conventional form of the *qaṣīda* with its monorhyme and monometre to reflect the poet's distress and hopes, and the problems of society.

Albert Arazi's opening chapter discusses a *qaṣīda* fragment from the early days of Islam in the Arab Peninsula that was composed by Unayf b. al-Ḥakam, who belonged to a Ṭayyi' clan, Banū Nabhān b. 'Amr b. Aws. Ibn al-Ḥakam's poem links the causes and stakes that led the Ṭayyi' to take up arms against the rival Asad clan after the establishment of the caliphate of Medina under Abū Bakr (42/622). Religion, and not just agricultural-economic interests, was a major cause as the Ṭayyi' embraced Islam and supported the Prophet Muḥammad, while the Asads sided with his rivals. The strong religious component in the poet's tale contradicts the common view regarding the supposed

32 Shmuel Moreh, "Ideological Trends in Modern Arab Poetry," *Hamizrah Hehadash*, 19/1–2 (1969), 31–49 [in Hebrew].

predominance of pre-Islamic values in the poetry of the first decades following the death of the Prophet. The poem's structure and its detailed narrative, Arazi argues, constitute a significant and useful tool for historians, but also for literary scholars who study the influx of nascent and triumphant Islam on poetry.

Moving from tribal feuds to religious competitions, Joseph Sadan discusses an unpublished poem in which the author, Shams al-Dīn b. Ṭūlūn (d. 953/1546)—probably in an attempt to flatter the then-governor of Damascus—expresses the opinion that Moses' tomb is in Greater Syria, of which Damascus is the capital. Alongside the general historical background about the question of Moses' tomb, the chapter describes how the literary work in question emerged and discusses its literary merits and flaws. Norman Stillman shifts the focus away from Damascus to North Africa by examining an anti-Jewish poem attributed to Sīdī Qaddūr al-ʿAlamī (d. 1850), a Sufi from the town of Sefrou, Morocco. The poem's vitriolic barbs were aimed at Muslims of Jewish ancestry, who were accused not only of sharing the negative traits of their Jewish ancestors but were also depicted as having remained faithful to their former religion. Such poetry, Stillman points out, is of particular interest, since Sefrou, with its large Jewish community, was known for its good Muslim-Jewish relations.

Modern times brought about not only technical, administrative, and military changes, but also changes in the social and literary aspects of Middle Eastern lives. Arabic poetry was less epic or commissioned to promote ideologies and regimes, and more individualist and critical in fleshing out sensitive socio-political issues. Yair Huri-Horesh's discussion of the poetry of the exiled Iraqi Saʿdī Yūsuf (b. 1934) demonstrates how Yūsuf's writings witnessed a gradual shift from "narrative of exile," which is underpinned by a distinct elegiac mode, to "narrative of counter-exile," which tends toward integration and universalism. A similar shift to individual self-experience and concerns with humanity can be traced in the poetry of the Palestinian Samīḥ al-Qāsim (d. 2014). As Ibrahim Taha argues in his chapter, from the 1970s onward, al-Qāsim gradually emancipated himself from the powerful burden of history, politics, and national identity to move towards individualism and humanism. This, according to Taha, forms the essence of al-Qāsim's intertextual writing: to make global history an individual concern.

Part 2 is devoted to prose and drama, and highlights—in their voices—the inner world of lowly or subaltern groups, such as pimps, women, and exiles, as well as the exalted status of martyrs and cultural icons and new modes of literate production. Amir Lerner's chapter looks at a literary genre (*maqāma*) from the Mamluk period of Egypt (1250–1517); it describes an amusing literary salon of pimps belonging to the lower strata of society, and presents them as professional craftsmen. The language of the work deviates from standard

Arabic and brings to the fore the spoken language and voice of the masses. Moving from the profane to the sacred and from Mamluk Egypt to Ottoman Syria, Ghaleb Anabseh uses two seventeenth-century manuscripts to shed new light on the evolving Holy Land literature. The two accounts provide a prism through which the role played by local traditions in determining the essence of the Holy Land can be examined—the specific issue explored in the chapter is whether Damascus should be considered part of the Holy Land.

The other essays in Part 2 deal with identity and symbolism in modern Arabic and Persian literature. Geula Elimelekh discusses the theme of exile in the writings of Samīr Naqqāsh (d. 2004), who embodied a "double-diasporic" person. He left the diaspora, the Iraq he loved, and came to Israel, where—as Mizrahi or Oriental Jews—he and his peers were reviled as backward by an Ashkenazi (chiefly European) majority. Throughout his life and writings, Naqqāsh conveyed the anguish of the unsettled persona living between two worlds. His colleague, the Egyptian novelist Jamāl al-Ghīṭānī (d. 2015), was also caught between two worlds: in his case, between tradition and modernity with regard to the status of women. As Yona Sheffer points out in his chapter, it is precisely the women of the patriarchal environment who gained a place of honor in al-Ghīṭānī's work: they were strong and assertive characters and the central pillar of the Egyptian family. In contrast, al-Ghīṭānī displayed aversion to careerist and provocative women.

The status of women, Islam in the state, and social and patriarchal norms were (and still are) controversial in Egyptian (and Arabic) society and hence, are widely discussed in modern Arabic literature. Another issue that has gained a broad consensus and captured the public imagination is the figure of Imam Husayn, as reflected in Persian and Arabic dramas. Peter Chelkowski's chapter focuses on the *ta'ziya*, the Shi'i mourning rituals observed in Iran, which originated in the tragedy of the battle of Karbala (61/680), when Imam Ḥusayn was brutally killed along with family members and companions. In line with Moreh's bold thesis, Chelkowski argues that, just as modern Arabic theatre has its roots in Arabic culture, the roots of contemporary Persian drama are to be found in Iran rather than in the West. The essay highlights Ḥusayn's profound impact on a wide spectrum of Muslim society. Whether acted by *ta'ziya* performers or written by Arab playwrights, various aspects of Ḥusayn's character and sacrifice are used to motivate audiences religiously, socially, politically, and emotionally.

The last two chapters of Part 2 deal with two additional neglected fields of research that should guide scholars dealing with modern Arabic literature: culinary and digital media. Gabriel M. Rosenbaum examines the representations of *fūl* (fava or broad beans) in literary works, both fiction and non-fiction. His findings, based on fieldwork and personal observations, demonstrate the dominant role of *fūl* in Egyptian society and daily life. The essay identifies and describes *fūl* terminology and expressions used in Egypt today and, no less important, the connection between *fūl* and Egyptian identity. Eman Younis, for her part, explores the intriguing yet hotly debated issue of the digital sphere, mainly the internet, as it appears in contemporary Arabic literature. On the one hand, Arab writers acknowledge the importance of virtual reality in crossing over the barriers of time and place to go beyond the obstacles of religion, race, and ethnicity. On the other hand, the digital media harbors fallacies and trumps up dangers, thus deceiving young adolescent men and women by dismantling their family connections and destroying their social values and norms.[33] Through an analysis of selected literary texts, the chapter shows how Arabic literature has perceived and dealt with the new media.

Part 3 of the volume shifts the focus from *adab* to *ta'rīkh*, from literature to historiography. Its first three chapters shed light on Arab self-perceptions of the religious and social landscape of Egypt and the Fertile Crescent under the Ottoman Empire and in the shadow of a growing European encroachment. Jane Hathaway's chapter analyzes an unknown chronicle of Ottoman Egypt (covering events between 1517–1714) and its historiographical implications. Comparative notes to later, better-known chronicles of Ottoman Egypt, in particular those dealing with the treatment of the 1711 "civil war" among Egypt's military cadres, lead Hathaway to argue that the discussed chronicle followed a standard official calendar of events (*taqwīm*). Furthermore, she contends that the "civil war" was the culminating event of the early eighteenth-century chronicles and may even have inspired their composition. One of the compared chronicles in Hathaway's chapter is ʿAbd al-Raḥmān al-Jabartī's *ʿAjā'ib al-āthār fi'l-tarājim wa'l-akhbār* (The marvelous chronicles: biographies and events), written in the early nineteenth century, which is also the hero in Michael Winter's chapter.

While Hathaway focuses on al-Jabartī's accounts of military and political events, mainly the 1711 revolution, Winter focuses on al-Jabartī's accounts of religious life in Egypt, mainly Sufism. Winter sets out to explore the Sufi

33 On the impact of the new media on the Arab discourse, see e.g. Dale Eickelman and Jon W. Anderson (eds.), *New Media in the Muslim World: The Emerging Public Sphere* (Bloomington: Indiana University Press, 1999); Naomi Sakr (ed.), *Arab Media and Political Renewal* (London: I.B. Tauris, 2007); Deborah L. Wheeler, *Digital Resistance in the Middle East: New Media Activism in Everyday Life* (Edinburgh: Edinburgh University Press, 2017).

personality of al-Jabartī, how he regarded Sufism as it was in his time, and which aspects he supported and which he opposed and despised. Al-Jabartī (d. 1825) was an eyewitness to the European encroachment into the Muslim heartland with the French occupation of Egypt (1798–1801) and recorded its events and their implications on the modernized reforms of local elites in Cairo and Istanbul. He was enchanted by Europe's modern science and technology but as a religious scholar, he displayed an aversion to its "secular" values. Such duality between tradition and modernity continued to guide Egyptian and Muslim writers throughout nineteenth and early twentieth centuries. Some were keen to preserve indigenous norms, while others challenged them in the name of science, enlightenment, and progress.

A further glance at the impact of modernity on Middle Eastern perceptions is offered by Meir Hatina's chapter, which deals with two late-nineteenth-century Egyptian accounts by authors who were in Syria and closely documented the local society's human makeup and landscape. Beyond the rich information contained in them, the two compositions provide an important and comparative prism through which to monitor the impact and challenges of modernity in the Middle East under growing European colonialism and the gradual transition from the Ottoman imperial era to the national era. The discussed texts also depict the vivid rivalry between *ʿulamaʾ* and modern Westernizers over cultural identity and moral authority.

A Jewish angel provides a comparative perspective by analyzing Shmuel Moreh's own account and memoirs on the Jewish-Arab legacy and modern dilemmas. Sigal Goorji's chapter, in lines with cultural history theories, treats Moreh's *Baghdad Mon Amour* (2012) and other memoirs of Iraqi Jews as cultural and historical documents. Such autobiographies enrich our knowledge of the Iraq Jewry's ways of thinking and behaving in the crucial period from the 1930s to their immigration to Israel during the early 1950s. A current theme in these narratives is love of the homeland and hatred of its betrayal.

⁘

Without being definitive, this volume offers persuasive insights that suggest areas for future research on the evolving manifestations and historical settings of Arabic culture. The opening and closing sections, which deal with Shmuel Moreh's scholarship, as well as various other chapters citing his works, highlight his vast knowledge and valuable contributions to Arabic studies. The obituary written for Moreh by the Iraqi poet Jabbār Jamāl al-Dīn seems appropriate:

وهنيئا لك عمر عشته
مر في جود وبذل وهبات
فكرك الوضاء يبقى بيننا

Your life was kind to you.
You lived it by showing generosity and giving.
Your enlightened and shining ideas are forever with us.[34]

34 Jabbār Jamāl al-Dīn, "ʿAwāṭif fī ʿīd mīlādika," December 22, 2017.

Shmuel Moreh's Scientific Achievements

Menahem Milson and Meir M. Bar-Asher

Few academic scholars manage to break truly new paths.* While many have added useful and important details to human knowledge, only seldom are scholars able to enrich their own field of knowledge or blaze a new trail and develop something completely original, never before seen or properly understood. People who break new ground in their research can justifiably be proud of their achievement. Shmuel Moreh was an innovator and trailblazer in three important fields of research in Arabic culture: (1) the study of modern Arabic poetry; (2) the history of theatre in Arabic, both medieval and modern; (3) Arabic historiography: the project of editing al-Jabartī's monumental chronicle *ʿAjāʾib al-āthār fiʾl-tarājim waʾl-akhbār* (The marvelous chronicles: biographies and events).

1 The Study of Modern Arabic Poetry

Moreh published important books and many articles on modern Arabic poetry, some of which have become classics in their field. His first contributions on this subject were related to the dissertation he submitted to SOAS University of London, in 1965, and whose revised and expanded version appeared ten years later as *Modern Arabic Poetry 1800–1970: The Development of its Forms and Themes under the Influence of Western Literature*. The book aroused so much interest in the Arab world that just ten years after the publication of the English original in 1986, it was translated into Arabic by two Egyptian scholars, both lecturers at Cairo University. A revised and updated edition was prepared by Ms. Lubnā Ṣafadī-ʿAbbāsī and published by *Kull Shayʾ* Press of Haifa in 2004. Even before writing his book, Moreh published two articles on the development of modern Arabic poetry in the *Bulletin of the School of Oriental*

* This text, published here jointly in memory of our friend and colleague Shmuel Moreh, is based on speeches given by both of us on different occasions honoring him: the talk given by Menahem Milson at the evening launching Moreh's book *Baghdād ḥabībatī: Yahūd al-ʿIrāq, dhikrayāt wa-shujūn* (Baghdad Mon Amour: The Jews of Iraq, memories and mourning) on March 29, 2012; and the address given by Meir Bar-Asher at the book launch of the critical edition of *ʿAjāʾib al-āthār* by al-Jabartī on January 7, 2013, and at Moreh's funeral on September 24, 2017.

 | DOI:10.1163/9789004459120_003

and African Studies; they were subsequently included in a volume edited by Dr. Saʿd Maṣlūḥ of Cairo University. The volume was published in Cairo in 1969, under the title *Ḥarakat al-tajdīd fi'l-shiʿr al-ʿArabī al-ḥadīth*. Moreh's book, which deals mainly with the development of strophic poetry, and in particular the *murabbaʿāt* genre, is a cornerstone of research on modern Arabic poetry. Indeed, it is difficult to conceive of any study in the field that does not have recourse to this book.

Moreh's main contribution was his identification of the classical *qaṣīda* as the source of inspiration for change, and the time period in which this change took place. It is worth recalling that the *qaṣīda* has been considered the most admired form of Arabic poetry. Other forms, such as the *zajal* (colloquial strophic poetry) and the *muwashshaḥ* ("girdled" strophic poems), were considered less prestigious. A major change occurred in the middle of the twentieth century, when important poets began to write free verse (*al-shiʿr al-ḥurr*), i.e. poetry that had freed itself of the shackles of the meter-and-rhyme schemes of the classical and neoclassical *qaṣīda*, and imitated a type of verse current in European poetry, which had lines of undetermined length and a changing rhyme. There was a longstanding debate in the research concerning the identity of the first poet to write in this manner. Was it the Iraqi poetess Nāzik al-Malāʾika (1923–2007) or her countryman Badr Shākir al-Sayyāb (1926–1964), both of whom were considered among the greatest Arab poets of the twentieth century? In his exhaustive and meticulous work, Moreh showed, by means of solid textual evidence, that neither could claim to be the first writer of free verse in Arabic. Both were preceded by nineteenth-century Christian-Arab translators of hymns and liturgies, who made extensive use of free-verse techniques. Thus, the penetration of Western forms, which have dominated modern Arabic poetry since the mid-twentieth century, already began in the nineteenth century, and the standard-bearers of this revolutionary change were Christian-Arab writers, not as original poets, but as translators of liturgical poetry from various tongues into Arabic.

In retrospect, we may say that there is poetic justice in the fact that Moreh, at heart a poet, made a unique contribution to the understanding of the development of modern Arabic poetry.

2 The History of Theatre in Arabic, in Medieval and in Modern Times

Professor Moreh devoted many years of research to the study of theatre, and his efforts bore fruit in 1992 with the publication of his important book *Live Theatre and Dramatic Literature in the Medieval Arab World*. This book, too, was translated into Arabic, at the initiative of the Academy for the Arts and Translations in Egypt. The book shows that in the Middle Ages, live theatre existed in the Arab world, and not merely in the form of shadow plays and puppet theatre, as had been assumed by many scholars in the West and subsequently by Arab scholars who did not devote much research to the subject.

Moreh showed that previous scholars had not properly understood the basic terminology of the dramatic arts and had interpreted it incorrectly in accordance with its usage in other fields. A salient example that Moreh discussed at length is the word *khayāl*. Its usual meaning, as is well known, is "imagination," but in classical Arabic it also signified, among other things, "acting." This meaning was forgotten, and when shadow plays reached the Arab world from the Far East, the Arabs added the word *ẓill* ("shadow") to the original term. *Khayāl ẓill* became the term for acting. Moreh justifiably argued that had the scholars understood that the term *khayāl* was used in the cultural world of classical Arabic to mean "acting," there would have been no need for them to create the artificial compound *khayāl ẓill*. As was his wont, Moreh adduced a wealth of examples from classical Arabic literature and unpublished manuscripts, proving that *khayāl* was used in the meaning of acting. He thereby highlighted the vital importance of sources from early Arabic literature for understanding the terminology and content of modern Arabic literature. The depth of Moreh's research derived, inter alia, from his command of both classical and modern Arabic literature.

Moreh made another important contribution to the study of theatre with his book *The Jewish Contribution to Nineteenth-Century Arabic Theatre: Plays from Algeria and Syria. A Study and Texts* (Oxford and Manchester, 1996), published together with his colleague Dr. Philip Sadgrove of Manchester University. In this groundbreaking work, the two authors pointed to the close connections between Sephardi-Jewish playwrights from Amsterdam, who wrote in Hebrew, and Jewish playwrights from North Africa. They discovered that the first play in Arabic, printed in lithograph already in 1847, had been written by Abraham Daninos, a Jew from Algiers. In their book, Moreh and Sadgrove discuss the story of the Binding of Isaac, which underwent a modern adaptation and was dramatized. The Binding appears in the play as an expression of the suffering and nostalgia of parents who agree to send their sons to study in faraway places; thus the Binding of Isaac was interpreted as the willingness of parents and children to make sacrifices in order to acquire knowledge and higher education.

Among Moreh's important contributions to the study of medieval literature, mention should be made of the *Kitāb al-ghurabā': The Book of Strangers, Medieval Arabic Graffiti on the Theme of Nostalgia. Attributed to Abu'l Faraj al-Isfahani*, the fruit of a collaboration with the renowned scholar of early Islam Patricia Crone. The book was published in 2000 by Princeton University Press and has since been translated into Danish, Crone's mother tongue. As its title indicates, this book, whose purported author was a Shiʿi historian and one of the greatest medieval *adab* authors, deals with the theme of nostalgia. The author collected, described, and analyzed graffiti written by strangers on the walls of buildings, fortresses, and inns. These passersby wrote of their homesickness, their beliefs, the meaning of wandering and the meaning of life, and their longing for their homeland. The words of those anonymous medieval men were expertly translated, described, and analyzed by these two learned and talented scholars.

3 Arabic Historiography: The Project of Editing al-Jabartī's Chronicle *ʿAjāʾib al-āthār*

There is no doubt that the crowning achievement of Shmuel Moreh's scientific work is his exemplary critical edition of the monumental *ʿAjāʾib al-āthār fiʾl-tarājim waʾl-akhbār*, the magnum opus of the historian ʿAbd al-Raḥmān al-Jabartī (1752–1825). This edition is the culmination of Moreh's lifework, as he devoted close to thirty years to its preparation. Moreh's interest in al-Jabartī's chronicle began during his MA studies, when he wrote a thesis on this topic under the supervision of Prof. David Ayalon. The thesis eventually came out as a book and was the first in a long string of writings that Moreh dedicated to this subject. The book, bearing the title *Al-Jabarti's Chronicle of the First Seven Months of the French Occupation of Egypt (Muḥarram—Rajab 1213/15, June–December 1798)*, comprised a critical edition of the Arabic text, an English translation, and a comprehensive and enlightening introduction.

David Ayalon, like many other historians, was aware of the great value of al-Jabartī's vast chronicle. There is no doubt that had he lived to see the edition prepared by his pupil Shmuel Moreh, he would have been pleased with it. In Ayalon's comprehensive article, "The Historian al-Jabarti and His Background," based on a lecture given at a conference held at the School of Oriental and African Studies in London in 1958, he rightly included part of Moreh's introduction to al-Jabartī's work.

Ayalon, who pioneered research on the history of the Mamluk dynasties and was also an authority on other periods of Islamic history, delineates in this article al-Jabartī's character, describes his chronicle and explains its immense importance, and emphasizes al-Jabartī's unique and extraordinary status as a historian. Ayalon writes thus:

> Of the local historians of Ottoman Egypt, al-Jabartī stands out as a giant among dwarfs. Moreover, but for his chronicle, the chronicles of the other historians of that period would have been of very limited value, because it is mainly as supplementary sources to his chronicle that they acquire considerably added importance.[1]

And he adds:

> But to compare al-Jabartī with the historians of Egypt under the Ottomans is to do him a great injustice, for he has an importance far transcending the period and the country with which his chronicle deals. In my opinion, al-Jabartī should be considered one of the greatest historians of the Muslim world of all times, and by far the greatest historian of the Arab world in modern times.[2]

Shmuel Moreh was not the first scholar to retrieve al-Jabartī's great chronicle from the depths of oblivion, since it was published in at least nine editions before his own; yet his edition—in four volumes plus an index volume—is far superior to all its predecessors. In the first place, it is based on no less than thirty-eight manuscripts (although some of these are more prominent and central than others). Secondly, it is the only edition based on al-Jabartī's autograph copy, which Moreh discovered in Cambridge University Library and identified positively as such. It was, in fact, the discovery of the autograph that persuaded David Ayalon of the necessity of preparing a new critical edition, and he set to work together with Shmuel Moreh. Sadly, Ayalon's death cut short this collaboration, leaving Moreh to continue the project by himself, with considerable help from devoted research assistants.

Last but not least, we must mention Moreh's contribution to the study of the heritage of Iraqi Jewry. Moreh not only wrote important studies in this field, but also encouraged many others to undertake further research on the subject. Space does not allow us to list the many books and articles by Moreh and the scores of researchers whose work he encouraged. This aspect of his research is not always known to those familiar only with his career as a scholar and teacher

1 David Ayalon, "The Historian al-Jabartī and His Background," BSOAS 23 (1960): 217–249, at p. 218; reprinted in ʿAbd al-Raḥmān b. Ḥasan al-Jabartī al-Zaylaʿī al-Ḥanafī, *ʿAjāʾib al-āthār fiʾl-tarājim waʾl-akhbār*, edited by Shmuel Moreh (Jerusalem: The Hebrew University of Jerusalem, 2013), 1: 21.

2 Ibid.

of Arabic literature at the Hebrew University and at Bar-Ilan University. Moreh conducted his studies of Iraqi Jewry within the framework of the Babylonian Jewry Heritage Center in Or-Yehuda, of which he was one of the main driving forces.

In addition to Professor Moreh's research, he was actively engaged as a lecturer and graduate supervisor. Over the course of decades of academic teaching at the Hebrew University and at Bar-Ilan University, Moreh raised many pupils. He knew how to identify those interested and talented enough to succeed in research, and nurtured them with love and devotion. Many of his best students now hold important research and teaching positions at academic institutions in Israel and abroad.

Beyond Moreh's important contributions as a scholar of poetry, prose, and drama; his stellar edition of al-Jabartī's chronicle; and his tireless efforts to promote the heritage of Iraqi Jewry in every shape and form, he was also, as already mentioned, a poet. Some of his poems (all in Arabic) were collected in his book *Tilka ayyām al-ṣibā*. Mention should finally be made of his memoir *Baghdād ḥabībatī: Yahūd al-ʿIrāq, dhikrayāt wa-shujūn* (Baghdad Mon Amour: The Jews of Iraq, memories and mourning) which evoked numerous moving reactions in Iraq and beyond.[3]

A source of great pride and inspiration for Moreh was his grandfather, Ḥākhām Yeḥezkel Meir ben Muʿallim Raḥamim ben Avraham Shalom (1865–1939). He often mentioned him and his seven-volume work, *Liqquṭei Imrei El*.

Those who were only superficially acquainted with Professor Moreh probably saw only the serious man of elegant appearance, who even on an ordinary day was smartly dressed, always wearing a suit and tie; a man of few words, reserved and rather distant. But those who knew him well were deeply aware of his unique and irrepressible sense of humor, including the ability to laugh at himself, usually in his mother tongue, the Judeo-Arabic dialect of Baghdad, and his fount of jokes and unstoppable bursts of laughter. His passing is a grievous loss.

Selected Works of Shmuel Moreh

Books

Modern Arabic Poetry 1800–1970: The Development of Its Forms and Themes under the Influence of Western Literature. Leiden: Brill, 1976.

Studies in Modern Arabic Prose and Poetry. Leiden: Brill, 1988.

3 See also Meir Hatina's introduction and Sigal Goorji's chapter in this book.

Live Theatre and Dramatic Literature in the Medieval Arab World. Edinburgh: Edinburgh University Press, 1992.

The Jewish Contribution to Nineteenth-Century Arabic Theatre: Plays from Algeria and Syria. A Study and Texts. Oxford-Manchester: Oxford University Press, 1996 (with P. Sadgrove).

The Tree and the Branch: Studies in Modern Arabic Literature and Contributions of Iraqi-Jewish Writers, edited by Olga Bramson. Jerusalem: Magnes Press, 1997 [in Hebrew].

The Book of Strangers: Medieval Arabic Graffiti on the Theme of Nostalgia, Attributed to Abu'l Faraj al-Isfahani. Princeton: M. Wiener Publishers, 2000 (with Patricia Crone).

The Egyptian Historian ʿAbd al-Raḥmān al-Jabartī: His Life, Works, Autographs, Manuscripts and the Historical Sources of ʿAjāʾib al-Āthār. Manchester-Oxford: Oxford University Press, 2012.

Translated Books

Al-Jabarti's Chronicle of the First Seven Months of the French Occupation of Egypt, (Muharram-Rajab 1213/15, June–December 1798), edited and translated by Shmuel Moreh. Leiden: Brill, 1975.

Napoleon in Egypt. al-Jabarti's Chronicle of the French Occupation, 1798, translated by Shmuel Moreh with an introduction by R.L. Tignor. Princeton and New York: Marcus Wiener Publishing, 1993; an expanded edition: Princeton and New York: Marcus Wiener Publishing, 2004.

Edited Books

Muntakhabāt min al-shiʿr al-ʿArabī al-muʿāṣir (Selections of modern Arabic poetry), edited by Shmuel Moreh. Tel Aviv: Dār al-Nashr al-ʿArabī, 1968.

Al-Naqd al-ʿArabī al-ḥadīth li'l-funūn al-adabiya wa'l-shiʿriyya fi'l-adab al-ʿArabī al-muʿāṣir (Modern Arabic criticism of prose and poetic genres in modern Arabic literature), edited by Shmuel Moreh. Tel Aviv: Dār al-Nashr al-ʿArabī, 1968.

Maṣādir li-dirāsat al-adab fi'l-ʿālam al-ʿArabī al-ḥadīth 1800–1970 (Sources for the study of literature in the modern Arab world 1800–1970), edited by Shmuel Moreh, Menahem Milson, and Joseph Zaydān. Jerusalem: The Hebrew University, 1970.

Fihris al-maṭbūʿāt al-ʿArabiyya allatī allafahā wa-nasharahā al-udabāʾ wa'l-ʿulamāʾ al-Yahūd (Catalogue of publications in Arabic written and published by Jewish intellectuals and scholars), edited by Shmuel Moreh. Jerusalem: Ben-Zvi Institute, 1973.

Fihris al-maṭbūʿāt al-ʿArabiyya fī Isrāʾīl, 1948–1972 (Catalogue of publications in Arabic in Israel, 1948–1972), edited by Shmuel Moreh. Jerusalem: The Hebrew University, 1974.

Al-Kutub al-ʿArabiyya allatī ṣadarat fī Isrāʾīl, 1948–1977 (Arabic books published in Israel, 1948–1977), edited by Shmuel Moreh and Maḥmūd ʿAbbāsī. Haifa: Beit Ha'Gefen, 1977.

On the Other Bank: A Collection of Modern Egyptian Stories, edited and translated by Menahem Milson and Shmuel Moreh. Jerusalem: 'Idanim, 1980 [in Hebrew].

Al-Qiṣṣa al-qaṣīra 'inda Yahūd al-'Irāq, 1922–1978 (The short story by Iraqi Jews, 1922–1978), edited by Shmuel Moreh. Jerusalem: Magnes Press, 1981.

Studies on the History of the Iraqi Jewry and Their Culture, edited by Shmuel Moreh. Or-Yehuda: Babylonian Jewry Heritage Center, Institute for Research on Iraqi Jewry, 1981 [in Hebrew].

Tarājim wa-āthār fi'l-adab al-'Arabī fī Isrā'īl, 1948–1986 (Biographies and chronicles in Arabic literature in Israel, 1948–1986), edited by Shmuel Moreh and Maḥmūd 'Abbāsī. 3rd ed. Jerusalem-Haifa: Truman Institute and Beit Ha'Gefen, 1987.

Mālṭī, Ḥabīb Ablā. The Quick-Tempered Simpleton (al-Aḥmaq al-basīṭ), edited by S. Moreh and Mūsā Shawārba. Haifa: The Department of Arabic Language and Literature and The Institute of Middle Eastern Studies at the University of Haifa, 1997.

Al-Farhud: The 1941 Pogrom in Iraq, edited by Shmuel Moreh and Zvi Yehuda. Jerusalem: Magnes Press, 2010.

Al-Jabartī, 'Abd al-Raḥmān b. Ḥasan al-Zayla'ī al-Ḥanafī. *'Ajā'ib al-āthār fi'l-tarājim wa'l-akhbār*, edited by Shmuel Moreh. Jerusalem: The Hebrew University of Jerusalem, 2013. 5 vols.

Articles

"Arabic Literature in Israel," *Hamizrah Hehadash* 9/33–34 (1958): 26–40 [in Hebrew].

"The Arab Literary Revival in Israel," *Ariel, A Quarterly Review of the Arts and Sciences in Israel* 2 (Spring 1962): 14–28.

"The Iraqi Poet Nāzik al-Malā'ika and Free Verse in Modern Arabic Poetry," *Hamizrah Hehadash* 16/3–4 (1966): 319–338 [in Hebrew].

"Arabic Literature in Israel," *Middle Eastern Studies* 3 (1968): 283–294.

"Blank Verse (*al-Shi'r al-mursal*) in Modern Arabic Literature," *BSOAS* 31/1 (1968): 28–51.

"The Influence of Western Poetry, and that of T.S. Eliot in Particular, on Modern Arabic Poetry (1947–1964)," *Hamizrah Hehadash* 18/1–2 (1968): 3–41 [in Hebrew].

"Nāzik al-Malā'ika and *al-Shi'r al-ḥurr* in Modern Arabic Literature," *Asian and African Studies* 4 (1968): 57–84.

"Poetry in Prose (*al-Shi'r al-manthūr*) in Modern Arabic Literature," *Middle Eastern Studies* 4/4 (July 1968): 330–360.

"Ideological Trends in Modern Arab Poetry," *Hamizrah Hehadash* 19/1–2 (1969): 31–49 [in Hebrew].

"The Influence of Western Poetry and Particularly T.S. Eliot on Modern Arabic Poetry," *Asian and African Studies* 5 (1969): 1–50.

"On Arabic Literature after the 1967 War," *Hamizrah Hehadash* 19/4 (1969): 386–389 [in Hebrew].

"Prose as a Medium for the New Perception of Modern Arabic Poetry," *Keshet* 12/3 (Spring 1970): 151–160 [in Hebrew].

"Basic Development in Modern Arabic Literature," in *Arabic and Islamic Studies*, edited by Jacob Mansour. Ramat Gan: Bar-Ilan University, 1973, 1: 95–122 [in Hebrew].

"The Neoclassical *Qasida*, Modern Poets and Critics," in *Arabic Poetry: Theory and Development*, edited by G.E. von Grunebaum. Wiesbaden: Otto Harassowitz, 1973, 155–179.

"Five Writers of *Shiʿr manthūr* (prose-poem) in Modern Arabic Literature," *Middle Eastern Studies* 10/3 (1974): 229–233.

"The Arabic Theatre in Egypt in the Eighteenth and Nineteenth Centuries," *Etudes Arabes et Islamiques*, II—Langue et Littérature 3, Paris, L'Asiatheque, Actes du XXIX Congres International des Orientalistes (1975): 109–113.

"An Outline of the Development of Modern Arabic Literature," *Orient Moderno Anno* 55/1–2 (Fennaio–Febbraio 1975): 8–28.

"Demutu Shel Hyisre'li Ba-Sifrut Ha-ʿArvit Me-Az Qom Ha-Medina [The Character of the Israeli in Arabic Literature since the Founding of the State of Israel]," in *The Arab-Israeli Conflict as Reflected by Arab Literature*, edited by Yehoshafat Harkabi, Yehoshua Porath and Shmuel Moreh. Jerusalem: The Van Leer Jerusalem Foundation, 1975, 25–52 [in Hebrew].

"The Jew and the Israeli in Modern Arabic Literature," *The Jerusalem Quarterly* 2 (Winter 1977): 119–136.

"Technique and Form in Modern Arabic Poetry up to World War II," in *Studies in Memory of Gaston Wiet*, edited by Myriam Rosen-Ayalon. Jerusalem: The Hebrew University of Jerusalem, 1977, 415–434.

"Arabic Literary Creativity of Jewish Writers in Iraq," in *Arabic and Islamic Studies*, edited by J. Mansour. Ramat Gan: Bar-Ilan University, 1978, 2: 60–68 [in Hebrew].

"The Arabic Novel between Arabic and European Influence during the Nineteenth Century," in *Studea Orientalea Memoria D.H. Baneth*, edited by Joshua Blau et al. Jerusalem: Magnes Press, 1979, 367–394.

"The Jewish Theatre in Iraq in the First Half of the Twentieth Century," *Peʿamim* 23 (1985): 64–98 [in Hebrew].

"Town and Country in Modern Arabic Poetry," *Asian and African Studies* 18/2 (July 1984): 161–185.

"Live Theatre in Medieval Islam," in *Studies in Islamic History and Civilization in Honour of Professor David Ayalon*. Leiden: Brill, 1986, 565–611.

"The *'Farhud'*—the Pogrom of Shavuot 1941—as reflected in the Literary Works of Jewish Writers from Iraq," in *Misgav Yerushalayim Studies in Jewish Literature*, edited by Ephraim Hazan. Jerusalem: Misgav Yerushalayim, 1987, 143–151 [in Hebrew].

"The Shadow Play (*Khayāl al-Ẓill*) in the Light of Arabic Literature," *JAL* 18 (1987): 46–61.

"Yaʿqūb Ṣanūʿ: His Religious Identity and Work in the Theatre and Journalism According to the Family Archive," in *The Jews of Egypt*, edited by Shimon Shamir. Boulder: Westview Press, 1987, 111–129.

"Shining Heart in the East—and Absurd in the Uttermost West," *Moznaim* 62/2–3 (May–June 1988): 73–78 [in Hebrew].

"The Background of Medieval Arabic Theatre: Hellenistic-Roman and Persian Influences," *JSAI* 13 (1990): 294–329.

"The Hobby-Horse, a Cultural Tradition between Asia and Africa," in *BRISMES Proceedings of the 1991 International Conference on Middle Eastern Studies*. Exeter: University of Exeter, 1991, 57–60.

"The Hobby-Horse and Masks in Medieval Arabic Theatre: Aspects of Contacts between Arabic and Persian Cultures," in *Contacts between Cultures*, edited by A. Harrak. *West Asia and Africa*. New York: The Edwin Mellenn Press, 1992, I: 369–373.

"The '*Khayal*' as a Medieval Arabic Theatre," in *Proceedings of the 32 International Congress for Asian and North African Studies*. Hamburg, August 25–30, 1986. Stuttgart: Steiner, 1992, 445–446.

"Hebrew Words and Baghdadi Judeo-Arabic Dialect in the Poetry of the Iraqi Poet Mulla ʿAbbūd al-Karkhī (1861–1946)," in *Hebrew and Arabic Studies in Honour of Joshua Blau*. Tel Aviv and Jerusalem: Tel Aviv University and the Hebrew University of Jerusalem, 1993, 351–373 [in Hebrew].

"Masks in Medieval Arabic Theatre," *Assaph: Studies in the Theatre* C/9 (1993): 89–94.

"The Meaning of the Term *Kharja* in the Arabic Andalusian *Muwashshah*," in *Circa 1492: Proceedings of the Jerusalem Colloquium: Litterae Judaeorum in Terra Hispanica*, edited by Isaac Benabu. Jerusalem: The Hebrew University, 1993, 134–144.

"New Light on Yaʿqūb Sanua's Life and Editorial Work through His Paris Archive," in *Writer, Culture, Text: Studies in Modern Arabic Literature*, edited by Ami Elad. Fredericton: York Press, 1993, 101–115.

"The Algerian Playwright Abraham Daninos and His Play *Nazāhat al-Mushtāq (1847)*," in *Between Fuṣha and ʿĀmmiyya, Studies in Canonical and Popular Arabic Literature*, edited by Shimon Ballas and Reuven Snir. Toronto: York Press, 1998, 37–45.

"The Nineteenth-Century Jewish Playwright Abraham Daninos as a Bridge between Muslim and Jewish Theatre," in *Judaism and Islam: Boundaries, Communication and Interaction*, edited by Benjamin H. Hary et al. Leiden: Brill, 2000, 409–416.

"Arabic Poetics from the Eighteenth to the Twentieth Centuries," in *Studies in Arabic and Islamic Culture*, edited by Benjamin Abrahamov. Ramat Gan: Bar-Ilan University, 2000, vii–lxvii.

"Al-Jabartī's Method of Composing His Chronicle: *ʿAjāʾib al-Āthār fī al-Tarājim wa-'l-Akhbār*," *JSAI* 25 (2001): 346–373.

"The Egyptian Scholar Hasan al-ʿAttar (d. 1834) and His Journey from Cairo to Izmir," in *Expressions et représentations littéraires de la Méditerranée: Iles et ports, XVIᵉ–XXᵉ siècles*, Actes du Colloque, Centre Culturel Européen de Delphes, November 5–6, 1999, edited by Z.I. Siaflekis and Rania Polycandioti. Athens: The Greek General &

Comparative Literature Association & Association International de Littérature Comparée, 2002, 19–32.

"Evolution of the Jewish Theatre and Cinema in Iraq," in *Studies in the History and Culture of the Jews in Babylonia, Proceedings of the Second International Congress for Babylonian Jewry Research (June 1998)*, edited by Yitzhak Avishur and Zvi Yehuda. Or-Yehuda: The Babylonian Jewry Heritage Center, 2002, Hebrew Section, 39–59 [in Hebrew].

"Jewish Periodicals in Hebrew and Arabic," in *Jewish Communities in the East in the Nineteenth and Twentieth Centuries: Iraq*, edited by Haim Saadoun. Jerusalem: Ministry of Education and Ben-Zvi Institute, 2002, 108–114 [in Hebrew].

"The Palestinians' Role in the 1941 *Farhūd* Riots in Iraq," in *Zion and Zionism among Sepharadi and Oriental Jews*, edited by W. Zeev Harvey et al. Jerusalem: Misgav Yerushalayim, 2002, 419–441 [in Hebrew].

"Poetry and Belles Lettres," in *Jewish Communities in the East in the Nineteenth and Twentieth Centuries: Iraq*, edited by Haim Saadoun. Jerusalem: Ministry of Education and Ben-Zvi Institute, 2002, 101–107 [in Hebrew].

"Theatre," in *Jewish Communities in the East in the Nineteenth and Twentieth Centuries: Iraq*, edited by Haim Saadoun. Jerusalem: Ministry of Education and Ben-Zvi Institute, 2002, 132–138 [in Hebrew].

"Napoleon and the French Impact on Egyptian Society in the Eyes of al-Jabarti," in *Napoleon in Egypt, Proceedings of the Conference on Two Hundred Years to the French Occupation of Egypt*, UCLA, May 9–10, 1997. Oxford: Ithaca, 2003.

"Al-Jabarti's Attitude towards the 'Ulama' of His Time," in *Guardians of Faith in Modern Times: 'Ulama' in the Middle East*, edited by Meir Hatina. Leiden: Brill, 2009, 47–63.

Translated Works

Ḥarakāt al-tajdīd fī mūsīqā al-shiʿr al-ʿArabī al-ḥadīth. Translated by Saʿd Maṣlūḥ. 1st ed. Cairo: ʿĀlam al-Kutub, 1969; 2nd ed. Tel Aviv: Dār al-Nashr al-ʿArabī, 1970.

Al-Shiʿr al-ʿArabī al-ḥadīth 1800–1970, taṭawwur ashkālihi wa-mawḍūʿātihi bi-taʾthīr al-adab al-gharbī. Translated by Shafīʿ al-Sayyid and Saʿd Maṣlūḥ. Cairo: Dār al-Fikr al-ʿArabī, 1986.

Athar al-tayyārāt al-fikriyya wa'l-shiʿriyya al-gharbīyya fī al-shiʿr al-ʿArabī al-ḥadīth 1800–1970. Translated by Shafīʿ al-Sayyid and Saʿd Maṣlūḥ. Revisions, corrections, and compilation of a name index by Lubnā Ṣafadī-ʿAbbāsī. 2nd ed. Haifa: Maktabat Kull Shayʾ, 2004.

De fremmedes bog: Arabisk nostalgisk graffiti fra middelalderen. Translated by Sune Haugbølle. Copenhagen: Vandkunsten, 2005.

PART 1

Poetry

Narrative in Ancient Arabic Heroic Poetry: The Account of the Battle

Albert Arazi

1 Introduction*

History and war have long made fine bedfellows. A great number of history books have endeavored to study wars, describe battles, and sort out the mechanisms and the various stages of armed conflicts. Literature as well takes war as an essential source of inspiration. Heroic and epic poetic texts have expressed the quintessential character of nations, their aspirations, and values—in brief, the best of their heritages. The need to analyze this material made itself felt early on, as seen in large portions of Aristotle's *Poetics*, which expound, discuss, and analyze the epic and heroic poetry of the Greeks. This work thus laid the groundwork for a new branch of human knowledge, the study of poetics. Orientalist studies have likewise taken similar paths: chivalric and heroic conduct has long been examined and numerous studies have elucidated the constituent elements of *murūʾa* (the sum of the physical and moral qualities of a man) in its altruistic and charitable aspects. That said, no work—or next to no work—has studied the form of narrative found in this kind of poetry.

It is true that the historical framework from which battle poetry sprang, the *Ayyām al-ʿArab*, has aroused and continues to arouse a good deal of interest and inspires research of great merit. It will suffice to mention the most noteworthy examples, those that have taken new paths and distinguished themselves from the works of the pioneers who preceded them. Muḥammad al-Yaʿlāwī, in his very important study *Adab Ayyām al-ʿArab* (Literature of *Ayyām al-ʿArab*), devotes an entire section to the narrative characteristics of these prose tales of battle, before going on to an analysis of the characters, the plot, and the spatial-temporal framework of this work from a decidedly modern perspective.[1] He argues further, and repeatedly, that the materials contained in these texts are literary and not historical. Issues 3 and 4 of the 1999 volume of the journal

* This article was originally written in French; I would like to thank Dr. Daniel Lav from the Hebrew University of Jerusalem for translating it into English.

1 Muḥammad al-Yaʿlāwī, "Adab Ayyām al-ʿArab," *Ḥawliyyāt al-Jāmiʿa al-tūnisiyya* xx (March 1982): 57–135.

 | DOI:10.1163/9789004459120_004

Arabica, which are devoted to new readings of Arabic literature, include two studies on the *Ayyām*. In the first of these, Albert-Louis de Prémare analyzes the evolution of narrative structures in the prose texts that accompany the *Ayyām* and the *Maghāzī* in Ṭufayl b. ʿAmr al-Dawsī's transmission.[2] In the second, Muḥammad al-Qāḍī examines the narrative of another transmitter of the *Ayyām* in the commentary on the *al-Naqāʾiḍ* of Jarīr and al-Farazdaq, namely, Abū ʿUbayda, and remarks that the style is one characteristic of folk legends.[3]

The poetry that sings the exploits of certain combatants and their heroism in the face of their enemies, and fixes them in the collective memory by relating the events in verse, appears to have been of no interest to scholars. In this study, I intend to lay some groundwork for those who would like to address this topic in the future. To this end, I intend to examine fragment no. 33 in the *ḥamāsa* (valor) section of Abū Tammām's *Dīwān al-ḥamāsa* (Collection of valor poems). The fragment is ascribed to Unayf b. Ḥakam al-Nabhānī.

2 Broken Time in Unayf b. Ḥakam al-Nabhānī

Fragment no. 33 of Abū Tammām's *Ḥamāsa* tells the tale of a battle as narrated by Unayf b. Ḥakam (or b. Ḥakīm) of the Banū Nabhān b. ʿAmr b. Aws, a clan of the Ṭayyiʾ.[4] The various commentaries on the *Ḥamāsa* include an excerpt of ten lines compiled by Abū Tammām. Nine are ascribed to Unayf; verse four should probably be attributed to the anthologist himself, who is known to have slipped verses of his own into the poetry of other poets, on more than one occasion. Ibn Maymūn (529–597/1135–1201), who transmitted the poem in its complete version of thirty-seven verses, does not include this verse at all.[5] The complete text is a true bipartite *qaṣīda* that revels in summoning up all the commonplaces of the genre, with a *nasīb* of the "missed rendezvous" type and a bellicose *gharaḍ*: the love-struck poet, come to meet his mistress Ḥubbā, is present for the relocation of the entire clan to a new camp (v. 1–7). He recounts that the new camp is very distant and only a sturdy she-camel can take him to

2 Alfred-Louis de Prémare, "Ayyām al-ʿArab—Ayyām al-Islām: Ṭufayl b. ʿAmr al-Dawsī," *Arabica* 46/3–4 (1999): 347–357.

3 Muḥammad al-Qāḍī, "La composante narrative des 'Journées des Arabes' (*Ayyām al-ʿArab*)," *Arabica* 46/3–4 (1999): 358–371.

4 ʿAbd al-Qādir Ḥarfūsh, *Qabīlat Ṭayyiʾ fī'l-Jāhiliyya wa'l-Islām* (Beirut: Dār al-Bashāʾir, 1995), 39–74.

5 Muḥammad b. al-Mubārak b. Maymūn, *Muntahā al-ṭalab min ashʿār al-ʿarab*, edited by Muḥammad Nabīl Ṭarīfī (Beirut: Dār Ṣādir, 1999), 7: 71–78.

his beloved. This is followed by the *gharaḍ* (v. 8–37), which is just as conventional. In the *gharaḍ* we are dealing with pure tribal bluster, though in Unayf this is somewhat tempered by the major psychological transformations that follow the advent and triumph of a new faith, Islam, in the first stages of taking root. In addition, let us not forget that the enemy in the poem is a coreligionist and that the hostility between the two stems from religious causes. All of this explains the importance of this section's religious aspect; the next part will attempt to show it.

Let us add, before commencing the analysis, that the complete *qaṣīda* relates the causes and the stakes that led the Ṭayyi' to take up arms against the Asad after the establishment of the caliphate in Medina. Our poet, a true chronicler, meticulously situates certain events recounted in the poem, ones that shed light on intertribal relations in this epoch, in their geographical, chronological, and psychological context. We find ourselves in Medina (v. 8).[6] The city and its surroundings are repeatedly invoked. In the opening *nasīb* we find mention of Rammān, where the love that tied the poet to Ḥubbā bloomed; the region was among the Asad territories occupied by the Ṭayyi' in their fight against the Asad, who had been the original inhabitants of the region in the pre-Islamic period.[7] Further on, the poet relates that he and his relations came to Medina spurred on by faith and motivated by a declared desire to act in accordance with the precepts of religion and with a concern for achieving peace. He adds that they have banished from their actions all trace of violence or tribal prejudice (v. 8). These assertions largely contradict the common view regarding the supposed predominance of pre-Islamic values in the poetry of the first decades following the death of the Prophet. The poet proclaims at the opening

6 This ought not surprise us: the chroniclers relate that the Ṭayyi', as soon as they arrived from Yemen, occupied a good portion of the region to the west of Medina and controlled several places on the Medina-Mecca route: Ibn Saʿīd al-Andalusī, *Nashwat al-ṭarab fī ta'rīkh al-ʿarab*, edited by Naṣrat ʿAbd al-Raḥmān (Amman: Maktabat al-Aqṣā, 1982), 1: 222: "… *nazalat ḥīna kharajat min al-Yaman baʿda sayl al-ʿArim ʿalā banī Asad fa-ḥārabathā ilā an iṣṭalaḥatā ʿalā al-jiwār fa-ḥallat Ṭayyi' bi-jabalay Aja' wa-Salmā min Najd al-Ḥijāz ilā al-yawmi wa'ntasharat fi'l-aqṭār*" (after leaving Yemen [the Tayyi' tribe] camped [in the region] after the ʿAram flooded in and fought against the Asad until they conquered them, forcing upon them an agreement of protected status [and thus as accepted neighbors], the Ṭayyi' took up residence on Mounts Aja' and Salmā on the Hijaz plateau, and have remained there, and in the surrounding environs into which they expanded, to this day).

7 Abū ʿUbayd al-Bakrī, *Muʿjam mā ʿstuʿjim min asmā' al-bilād wa'l-mawāḍiʿ*, edited by Jamāl Ṭalba (Beirut: Dār al-Kutub al-ʿIlmiyya, 1998), 2: 264–265 (with references from poetic sources); Aḥmad Mūsā al-Jāsim, *Shiʿr Banī Asad fi'l-Jāhiliyya* (Beirut: Dār al-Kunūz al-Adabiyya, 1995), 28 and n. 2, citing Muḥammad b. ʿAbdallāh al-Najdī's *Ṣaḥīḥ al-akhbār ʿammā fī bilād al-ʿArab min āthār*.

of his *gharaḍ* that the entry of the three Ṭayy'ite clans—ʿAmr, Ghawth, and Mālik—into the city of the Prophet was motivated by these religious concerns. Furthermore, these verses (8, 9, and 11) are suffused with religiosity:

ألا هل أتى أهل المدينة عرضنا / خلالاً من المعروف يعرف حالها
على عاملينا والسيوف مصونة / بأغمادها ما زايلتها نصالها
عرضنا كتاب الله والحق سنّة / هي النصف ما يخفى علينا اعتدالها

Have not the Medinans received our licit proposal / the benefits of which are plain to see?
Through our representatives, while our swords are well-kept / their blades sheathed;
Our goal was [in accordance with] God's Book and His precepts; / These constitute the half part of [religion] whose justice has not escaped us.[8]

In the same vein, the strong presence and predominance of religion is attested by the poet's affirmation that his tribe had chosen to remain loyal to the shariʿa and that this attachment remains unwavering. Thus, he states in the poem that he and his clan arrived at Firtāj as loyal subjects in order to give the *zakāt*; at Fayd they paid the *ṣadaqa* at a time when numerous tribes had taken advantage of Muḥammad's passing to renege on these obligations. He states in this regard:

وجئنا إلى فرتاج سمعًا وطاعة / نؤدي زكاة حين حان عقالها
وفي فيد صدّقنا وجاءت وفودنا / إلى فيد حتى ما تُعَدُّ رجالها

We arrived in Firtāj out of duty and obedience / to give the annual *zakāt* in its own time;
And at Fayd we gave our *ṣadaqa*, and our delegates there, they are innumerable.[9]

Fayd, as al-Bakrī tells us, was situated in the region that separated the Asad from the Ṭayyi' in the area of the pre-Islamic Yathrib. When the Ṭayyi' delegation arrived to embrace Islam, the Prophet Muḥammad offered it to Zayd al-Khayl, one of the Ṭayyi' tribal heads.[10]

8 Muḥammad b. al-Mubārak Ibn Maymūn, *Muntahā al-ṭalab min ashʿār al-ʿarab*, edited by Muḥammad Nabīl Ṭarīfī (Beirut: Dār Ṣādir, 1999), 7: 72–73, v. 8–10.
9 Ibid., 73, v. 11–12.
10 Al-Bakrī, *Muʿjam*, 4: 283–285.

A number of other details in the poem situate the recounted events and place them in a well-defined spacio-temporal entity: the beginning of the reign of Abū Bakr in the region of Medina. All these particulars are indispensable for an understanding of the nature, stakes, and import of the combat between these two great tribes, Asad and Ṭayyi', over possession of the agricultural areas of Medina and its environs. Other tribes also intervened in the dispute, an intervention that was quite foreseeable. At the time, the region had experienced an agricultural and economic boom with the acquisition of numerous latifundia by the *ṣaḥāba* (the Prophet's companions) and their descendants among the Meccan aristocracy. The great clans, which had been long established in the region, involved themselves in these quarrels so as to defend their own interests. Unayf's *qaṣīda* mentions the Banū Jarm (Quḍā'a), who mobilized their forces to prevent the Ṭayyi' delegation from accomplishing its mission of supporting the caliphal regime in the city:

وسارت إلى جرم من القوم عصبة / فأدّت بنو جرم وجاءت رجالها
فلم ندرِ حتى راعنا بكتيبة / تروع ذوي الألباب والدين خالها
دعا كل ذي تبل وصاحب دمنة / قبائل من شتى غضابًا سبالها
فقالوا أَغِرْ بالناس تعطك طيئ / إذا وطئتها الخيل واجتيح مالها

A number of our men made their way towards Jarm / They gave [their *zakāt*], and a large number of them faced off against us,
In the blink of an eye a large troop of Jarm / blocked our way, a troop that throws the pious and the wise into a state of turmoil
They [Jarm] called up all those who hated us and harbored hidden enmity to us / a throng of tribes issuing threats
They said: Attack Ṭayyi', they will pay you / when the riders crush them and their herds are decimated.[11]

These details, garnered from the complete version of the poem, are significant and useful not only for the historian, but also for the specialist in the history of literature who seeks to study the influence of an emergent Islam on poetry. They are much less so for the expert in narratology, who is far less interested in ultimate causes than in the course of the battles. Abū Tammām's editing

11 Ibn Maymūn, *Muntahā al-ṭalab*, 7: 73–74, v. 13–16. Jarm, as Ibn Ḥazm tells us, held territory in al-'Aqīq and got on well with their Asad neighbors. Ibn Ḥazm relates that the Companion al-Ḥārith b. Rifā'a requested the Prophet's arbitration against the Banū 'Uqayl regarding al-'Aqīq: Abū Muḥammad 'Alī b. Aḥmad b. Sa'īd b. Ḥazm, *Jamharat ansāb al-'Arab*, edited by 'Abd al-Salām Hārūn (Cairo: Dār al-Ma'ārif, 1971), 451.

retained only the details regarding the battle and foregrounded them. By isolating them, he brought them into relief, sharpened their impact, and accorded them a much more profound meaning. In essence, he forged them into a tale. It is for this reason that the fragment is much more interesting than the full poem from the perspective of narrative, because it tells a story. We will thus focus our attention on the text from the *Ḥamāsa*.

We have opted to enter naively into the poet's game and pay no heed to his propensity for exaggeration as regards numbers of fighters, arms, or victim counts. In short, we will take him at his word, knowing full well that Unayf's inflationary tendency is found in early poetic texts in general.

From the schematic perspective, the story included in the poem stretches over three episodes that are quite distinct one from another, yet nonetheless complementary, and which moreover fit together to form a whole. These episodes are described in the order of their appearance:

1. The two camps face off against one another: One gets the impression that the battle is imminent (v. 1–4). What follows is a narration of the different stages of the armed conflict, articulated through use of the temporal adverb *lammā* (when) that is placed at the beginning of each of the episodes retained by Unayf. This division holds numerous advantages in terms of the structure of the poem: it allows us to clearly distinguish the different episodes in the mêlée and establish a chronology, and in addition it intimates the existence of lacunae in the narrative regarding the times in between. Furthermore, this division offers the audience a favorable vantage point for following the development of the action.
2. The Ṭayyi' maneuver that sets off the conflict: With the first *lammā*, the Ṭayyi' army leaves the strategic positions it had occupied (on the mountain summit) and spreads into the plains of Ḥā'il, where the Asad are arrayed. The second *lammā* encapsulates an account of the battle in a single verse:

فلما التقينا بيّن السيف بيننا / لسائلة عنا حفيّ سؤالها

> When the face-to-face combat was engaged in/was initiated/commenced, the sword distinguished between them and us [opting for one of us] / [in the eyes of] a woman who never ceased to inquire after us.[12]

12 Al-Khaṭīb al-Tibrīzī, *Sharḥ Dīwān al-Ḥamāsa*, edited by Gharīd al-Shaykh (Beirut: Dār al-Kutub al-ʿIlmiyya, 1421/2000), 130 (no. 34). This version seems preferable to the one in Ibn Maymūn, *Muntahā al-ṭalab*, 26: 76: *fa-lammā ʿrtamaynā bayyana ʿr-ramyu baynanā* ("When we set to firing our arrows the firing separated out the ranks"). Ibn Maymūn's version pays more attention to the battle sequence, but it nonetheless lacks a major narrative clause—the summary, with all the charge that it carries.

This procedure has been widely employed by narrators and has been termed "Summary" by Gérard Genette. (Here "Summary" is capitalized in order to indicate that the narratological sense of the term is intended.)[13] It should be remarked that there exists a similarity between the role Genette attributes to Summary and its actual use by narrators since the beginnings of Islam. Summary, according to Genette, entails beyond doubt a dramatic charge. It is an exceptionally powerful moment of action in the full sense of the term: in verse 7 of Unayf's poem, five words suffice to convey the slaughter committed by the Ṭayyi'. The poet composed a Summary that expresses the dramatic destruction wreaked by swords through the very brevity of the wording and the decisive nature of the content, so that thenceforth it is not difficult to distinguish between the victorious Ṭayyi' and the Asad, who are on the verge of being routed. The image is quite eloquent: the tight ranks of the former face off against their adversaries' sparse lines. The laconic wording adopted by the poet expresses better than a hundred speeches the significance of what has transpired—Ṭayyi' arms have inflicted serious carnage. Moreover, the image of the Ṭayyi' woman who has sneaked into the ranks, despite the dangers and impropriety involved, indicates the poet's anxiety for the fate of his fellow tribe members. When seen in this light, the Summary, though composed of one single verse, makes for one of the most intense moments in the poem. If we are to follow Genette's analyses, it turns out that the integration of narrative and descriptive elements lends these passages a dramatic—and hence narrative—structure.[14] Even a superficial examination of the verse shows that the Ṭayyi' narrator gives the scene an acute, dramatic dimension precisely because it is transmitted from a feminine perspective.

3. The two final *lammās*, the third and the fourth, are purely narrative. The former relates the defeat of the Asad (v. 9: the Ṭayyi' sabers soak up the blood of their enemies), whereas the latter *lammā* portrays them in flight, pursued by the spears and arrows of the Ṭayyi'. In Abū Tammām's version, the narrative ends as follows:

ولما تدانوا بالرماح تضلعت / صدور القنا منهم وعُلّت نهالها
ولما عصينا بالسيوف تقطعت / وسائل كانت قبلُ سلمًا حبالها
فولّوْا وأطراف الرماح عليهم / قوادر مربوعاتها وطوالها

13 See Gérard Genette, *Discours du récit* (Paris: Éditions du Seuil (Collection Points), 2007), 91.

14 Ibid., 107–110.

When the [two camps'] spears approached one another, our spearheads were repeatedly glutted with their [the enemies'] blood.
And when we battered them with our swords / the connections that had established ties of peace between us were ruptured,
They fled, at the mercy of our spearheads and arrows / both the long and the short ones reaching them.[15]

One sees clearly that the poet, in accordance with the age-old narratological conventions of Arabic poetry, from its origins up to the dawn of the modern age, adopts a linear chronology of events, following the order in which they transpired. This technique was a necessity, since Unayf played the role of chronicler and had to be immediately understood by his fellow tribe members as well as by all Arabs of his time. Moreover, to be effective, the text had to be simple, lucid, and well organized. Thus conceived and constructed, it could serve as a deterrent to other tribes and serve the interests of his own.

Before broaching the study of the various meanings of this narrative, we need to examine the beginning of the story in Abū Tammām's version, since generally speaking, the excerpt outweighs the full text of the poem from the narrative perspective, as previously noted. The beginning of the story bears an unmistakably descriptive emphasis. Unayf relates, but also describes, how the sizeable Ṭayyiʾ troops arrayed themselves in order of battle. The anthologist thus chose to open with a descriptive pause that is worth examining more closely. It should be noted that this passage, despite the "descriptive" qualifier, never leads to a pause in the narrative or to a suspension of the story or the action; in other words, the action certainly slows down, but never ceases entirely. In fact, in this episode in which the armies face off, the poet only lingers over a given object or sight when this pause corresponds with a pause on the part of the protagonists or shows that their movement has not yet commenced. Let us allow the poet to speak in order to better grasp this mixed character of description and action. The Ṭayyiʾ *katāʾib* (troops), he asserts, stand at the ready for the attack on the Nizār (Asad):

15 Abū ʿAlī Aḥmad b. Muḥammad b. al-Ḥasan al-Marzūqī, *Sharḥ Dīwān al-Ḥamāsa*, eds. Aḥmad Amīn and ʿAbd al-Salām Hārūn (Beirut: Dār al-Jīl, 1411/1991), 1: 172–173; al-Aʿlam al-Shantamarī, *Sharḥ Ḥamāsat Abī Tammām*, edited by ʿAlī al-Mufaḍḍal Ḥammūdān (Dubai: Markaz Jumʿa al-Mājid and Beirut: Dār al-Fikr al-Muʿāṣir, 1413/1992), 1: 278; al-Tibrīzī, *Sharḥ al-Ḥamāsa* [already added above], 1: 89–90; Ibn Maymūn, *Muntahā al-ṭalab*, 7: 76, v. 26–27; ibid., 77, v. 31.

جمعنا لهم من حي عوف بن مالك / كتائب يردي المقرفين نكالها
لهم عجز بالحزن فالرمل فاللوى / وقد جاوزت حي جديس رعالها
وتحت نحور الخيل حرشف رجلة / تتاح لغرات القلوب نبالها
أبى لهم أن يعرفوا الضيم أنهم / بنو ناتق كانت كثيرًا عيالها

We have gathered against them troops from the clan of ʿAwf b. Mālik, /
fear of whose retribution scares the "metis" to death;
Our rear lies in wait for the Ḥazan, there where the sands make detours, /
whereas our front has traversed the gathering site of the two clans of Jadīs.[16]
Near the horses numerous are our foot soldiers / and their arrows strike
their enemies in the heart;
They haughtily reject all tyranny, for they are / born of a mother who
birthed many.

The first three lines in this quotation depict three scenes of psychological warfare. It is quite possible that these lines were meant to dissuade potential enemies by recalling the fate that awaits those who attack the Ṭayyiʾ. To this aim, the author slips in three episodes based on acts of belligerence and extols the military know-how of his side. These are well-seasoned troops, of formidable efficacy and motivated by an unwavering desire for victory, as reflected in the second hemistich of line 1: "[troops] fear of whose retribution scares the half-breeds to death." Line 2 in its entirety depicts the Ṭayyiʾ deploying throughout an immense terrain, thus showing how numerous they were. The third line describes the positioning of the troops in ranks of battle order waiting to attack. The troops are still stationary, but one may assume that it will not be long before the fighting begins. Thus, this is not a description in the sense of contemplation, as for example when one stops to admire the countryside. In the case of Unayf, the description encompasses an entire story, one that this passage relates to us. To paraphrase Genette, we can conclude this descriptive overture by saying that in Unayf's "pause," the description is absorbed into the narration [...]—and is anything but a pause in the narrative.[17]

Unayf says nothing whatsoever about the phase of mobilization. He is completely silent on the ultimate causes that conceivably revived hostilities between the two tribes, such as the stark divergence of options posed to them

16 According to the commentators these were Ṭasam and Jadīs.
17 Genette, *Discours du récit*, 103.

by the Prophet's death and the *ridda* wars. We know that the Asad sided with Musaylima, whereas the Ṭayyi', who lived near Medina and were led by 'Adī b. Ḥātim and Zayd al-Khayl, had given the *bay'a* to Abū Bakr, paid the *zakāt*, and sent troops to fight against the rebels.[18] In most cases, Unayf's tribespeople sided with the legitimate rulers. As it happens, the full *qaṣīda* contains numerous mentions of this state of affairs and constitutes a heretofore untapped historical document on the *ridda* in Medina and its environs. Silence is likewise kept regarding the arrival of the combatants at the theatre of operations and the mutual invectives hurled between the adversaries, whose aim was to rouse the warriors' zeal. Nor is anything said on the topic of the traditional prebattle, one-on-one duels.[19] This ellipsis, which often narrates events covering several days, constitutes a rift in the continuity of the story and signifies an elision of undetermined length. In narratology, this is known as an "implicit ellipsis," which Genette defines as one "whose presence is not stated in the text, and which the reader can only infer from some chronological lacuna or from solutions regarding narrative continuity."[20]

The construction and deployment of the various narratives is carried out masterfully by the poet. In the first verse, Unayf sets down, within the confines of the poetic format, the semantic ties that join the diverse episodes. In so doing, he produces a unitary and well-constructed text. Let us take a closer look at the opening line according to its semantic components:

1. *Jamaʿnā* + *katāʾiba* ("we gathered troops") + *yurdī al-muqrifīna nakāluhā* ("fear of whose [the suffix -*hā* = the troops'] retribution scares the half-breeds to death");
2. -*nā* ("we," from *jamaʿnā*) + *ḥayyi ʿAwfi bni Mālikin* ("[from] the clan of 'Awf b. Mālik").

18 On these events, in addition to classic sources such as al-Ṭabarī and the various chronicles, it is worth consulting al-Wāqidī, who devoted an independent work to them: Muḥammad b. 'Umar al-Wāqidī, *Kitāb al-ridda maʿa nubdha min futūḥ al-ʿIrāq*, edited by Yaḥyā al-Jubūrī (Beirut: Dār al-Gharb al-Islāmī, 1990). Regarding modern studies one may mention the two major studies by Ella Landau-Tasseron: "The Participation of Ṭayy in the *Ridda*," *JSAI* 5 (1984): 53–71; and idem, "Asad from Jāiliyya to Islam," *JSAI* 6 (1985): 1–28.

19 Such details have been discussed at length in the various Arabic-language studies of *Ayyām al-ʿarab*. See, for example, Mundhir al-Jubūrī, *Ayyām al-ʿArab wa-atharuhā fi'l-shiʿr al-jāhilī* (Baghdad: Dār al-Shu'ūn al-Thaqāfiyya al-ʿĀmma, 1986), in particular section two, where he lists and attempts to determine the characteristics: pp. 99–113 and 114–175; Rāshid Fāliḥ, "al-Baṭal fī shiʿr al-ḥamāsa," *Majallat ādāb al-Rāfidayn* (September 14, 1981): 241–267; 'Alī al-Jundī, *Shiʿr al-ḥarb fi'l-ʿaṣr al-jāhilī*, 2nd ed. (Cairo: Maktabat al-Anglo, 1963), and the sources cited therein, n. 1–3; as well as the contribution of an historian, Saʿd 'Abbūd Sammār, on these early phases of the battle, "'Ādāt al-ḥarb ʿind al-ʿArab qabla al-Islām," *Majallat kulliyat al-tarbiya—Wāsiṭ* 13 (April 2013): 173–199.

20 Genette, *Discours du récit*, 105.

A quick reading suffices to show that this overture is built on the interaction of the double semantic axis provided by the words *katāʾib* and *yurdī*. I will next demonstrate that the entire narrative of the combat rests on this double semantic axis—the troop of warriors who sow death—which is already put in place in the first line of the poem.

Line 2 specifies that the term *katāʾib* refers to the Ṭayyiʾ troops and, more specifically, to those of the clan of ʿAwf b. Mālik, already mentioned in line 1. Emphasis is placed on their large numbers, in accordance with a model that will earn a fixed place in Arabic poetry: the troops occupy an area that stretches between two distant places that mark the forward positions and the rear of the army. In our poem, Unayf accords the company a mythological dimension in that it extends through the region that separates the Ḥazn from the land of the two clans of Jadīs.[21] The mythical element is in the mention of Jadīs, an archaic tribal confederation dating from time immemorial, before the *jāhiliyya*.

In my view, line 3 is a perfect example of the interaction of the double semantic axis *katāʾib-yurdī*. The first hemistich develops a new aspect in relation to the armed contingent, as it discusses the positioning of the foot soldiers and the cavalry placed alternately in the same row. The second hemistich informs us of the destructive power of the infantry corps, which is one aspect of the superiority of the Ṭayyiʾ *katāʾib*; it likewise suggests what the outcome of the battle will be. The narration of this episode, devoted to the time preceding the battle, concludes with an inopportune intervention on the part of the transmitter-anthologist—a practice not rare for the period under discussion—who appears to have slipped in an important explanatory element of his own device regarding the intransigence of the Ṭayyiʾ fighters and their desire to outdo themselves. Their refusal to accept humiliation and their tenacity in saving their honor are rooted in genetic hereditary traits: they were born to a mother who gave birth to a large number of male children, and they are thus a powerful clan that cannot submit to the dictates of other tribes. This is the human element that made up the *katāʾib*. Incidentally, in his commentary on this line, al-Marzūqī considers it to be a characteristic literary trope of the

---

21 The commentators on the *Ḥamāsa* are not unanimous on the identity of these two clans (*ḥayyay*). Al-Marzūqī, *Sharḥ*, 1: 170 at first mentions Ṭasm (or Ṭasam), then identifies them as Ḥadas and Jadīs, with the front lines of the army covering al-Ḥazn and the rear extending to Ḥadas and Jadīs. Other commentators name them as Ṭasm and Jadīs, two Arabian tribes that were established in Yamāma and disappeared before the advent of Islam: *Al-Mawsūʿa al-ʿArabiyya* (Damascus: Hayʾat al-Mawsūʿa al-ʿArabiyya, 1998–), 12: 546 (also available online at arab-ency.com/ar); Ḥusayn Khalaf Khazʿal, *Ḥayāt al-shaykh Muḥammad ʿAbd al-Wahhāb* (Beirut: Maṭābiʿ Dār al-Kutub, 1968), 26.

katā'ib (*hādhā al-kalām min ṣifat al-katā'ib*).[22] On the other hand, they are so touchy when it comes to their own self-esteem that they respond to any slight with the greatest violence, sowing death.

Once the positioning of the Ṭayyi' forces is completed the rhythm, accelerates and the movement becomes faster and faster, building toward the climax at the end of the narrative. At that point, the Asad fighters flee, harried by the spears of their enemies. The text suggests to us that their situation is desperate: the buffer zone between them and their pursuers shrinks continually, and their survival depends on the goodwill or the clemency of the Ṭayyi' warriors:

فولّوا وأطراف الرماح عليهم / قوادر مربوعاتها وطوالها

> They fled under the barrage of our spearheads / both our long and short spears reaching them

It is worth noting that the narration takes care to adhere to the chronological order of the various episodes in the battle, through the four *lammā*s mentioned above. The episodes of which we are told—that is, the ones retained by the poet—are: (1) The Ṭayyi' warriors descend from their gathering place on the mountain to the valley of Ḥā'il where the Asad are amassed. The two parties, once on the battlefield, raise their battle cries. The battle begins (v. 5–6). Notably, the poet invites his public to see this as the beginning of the combat proper thanks to the introduction of a semantic segment that associates *iqdām* (a forward charge) and *nizāl* (a sword duel; parenthesis of the second stanza): *ka-usd al-Sharā iqdāmuhā wa-nizāluhā*—the Tayyi' fighters are "like the lions of al-Sharā in their forward charge and in their one-to-one duels". (2) The phase of individual combat, when the cavalrymen of both camps dismount and engage in duels, ends with the enemy's defeat (v. 7). (3) The episode of individual combats ends with the enemy's defeat (v. 8). (4) The final mêlée ensues, with the Asad fleeing and the Ṭayyi' cavalry hot on their heels (v. 9–10).

The basic narrative structure evident in this fragment is also found in other poems of war, and may be set out schematically as follows:

1. Preliminary phase:
   - the arrival of the troops
   - the deployment of the fighters
2. The Summary: the entire narrative condensed into a single verse uniting description and action—to great effect, due to its dramatic charge;
3. Selected episodes from the combat, separated by ellipses;
4. Defeat of the enemy

---

22 Al-Marzūqī, *Sharḥ*, 1: 171, commentary on line 4.

Between each of these phases is a narrative gap, clearly discernible because of the chronological lacuna announced by the *lammā* that opens each of the five episodes chosen by the narrator. These *lammā*s are markers of the suspension of narrative continuity. In other words, we are in the presence of four ellipses whose nature and content it is impossible for us to determine. As noted above, these are indeterminate or implicit ellipses of the kind one encounters in almost all narratives. The role of the narrator is to compress the length of the event. The role of the ellipsis is essential to the story since it serves to elide the downtime in the action or to plug certain chronological lacunae that the narrator could not fill with the sources at his disposal.[23] The use of ellipses helps to reinforce the coherence of the story and preserves the validity of temporal analysis.

These considerations regarding the role of ellipses can help us better understand the battle story and its literary characteristics. The text, as arranged by Abū Tammām, tells the tale of a past event that has been related to us, divided up by as many cuts as there are ellipses. In a sense the narrator, by choosing certain episodes and remaining silent regarding others, has made a choice. He could not do otherwise, given that the length (*durée*) of the narration diverges from that of the action. The narration is necessarily briefer, lasting only the time taken to read or listen. The author is thus breaking up to the extreme the time that he had at his disposal and presenting us with its quintessence, or most meaningful parts.

A number of examples of verses following this narrative structure are to be found in the *ḥamāsa* chapter of Abū Tammām's anthology. Here we will mention one example, the second entry for the *jāhilī* al-Find al-Zimmānī (aka Shahl b. Shaybān), which is constructed according to the same narrative plan; references to other examples will be given in the notes.

1\. The preliminary phase does not merely mention the deployment of the Rabīʿa troops; the poet also gives us the anterior reasons why the Rabīʿa decided to carry out their campaign against the Dhuhl. For brevity's sake we will cite here only the operational details [*hajaz*]:

فلما صرّح الشر / فأمسى وهو عريان
ولم يبق سوى العُدوا / نِ دنّاهم كما دانوا
مشينا مشية الليث / غدا والليث غضبان

23 See the section that Genette devotes to the ellipsis: *Discours du récit*, 103–106.

When evil showed its true colors / and appeared naked
And nothing was left but injustice[24] / we paid them back in kind
We advanced with the prowl of a lion / who has been angered.

2. The Summary, or mixed verse, combines description with action; in a way it summarizes the story:

بضرب فيه توهين / وتخضيع وإقران

[Striking] with spear blows that sow weakening, degradation, and defeat.[25]

3. As an early poet, but also due to the strictures of his chosen poetic meter, al-Find's motifs include episodes that, though mentioned, are not yet developed. The main reason why he focuses on developing just one motif is the extent and gravity of the wounds inflicted on the enemy—as well as the blood of the Dhuhl, which flowed freely.

A number of other examples are attested,[26] especially those that valorize the kind of tribal heroism from which individual bluster is absent and in which the spaces [normally] devoted to aggrandizing the person of the poet can be better employed in recounting the bravery of all.

A distinction ought to be made here between that which pertains to the factual aspect of the events and that which pertains to humans. Time, as it appears in the factual narrative, is fragmented and does not form a whole. As far as the fortunes of the protagonists are concerned, time is broken up. An empirical observation will help us explain this characteristic of time in archaic war poetry: Unayf transmits this narrative part by part, never as a whole. He proceeds by distinguishing that which is worth mentioning from what is to be relegated to an ellipsis, narrative poetry's realm of silence. As concerns the events or the action, it is a strictly poetic calculus that determines which are worth being spoken and which must be passed over in silence.

24 Cf. al-Marzūqī, *Sharḥ*, 1: 35, commentary on line 4: *al-ʿudwān al-ẓulm.*

25 The meaning of *iqrān* is not clear due to the paucity of details supplied by the text. Three readings are possible: weakness (L.A. Jamāl al-Dīn Muḥammad b. Mukarram b. Manẓūr, *Lisān al-ʿArab* (Beirut: Dār Ṣādir, 1410/1990), 13: 340: *aqrana ʿan al-shayʾ = ḍaʿufa*); to spread copiously, said of blood (ibid.); and to vanquish (*al-iqrān = al-ghalaba*).

26 Al-Marzūqī, *Sharḥ*, no. 18 (Waddāk b. Numayl al-Māzinī, 1:127–130), no. 35 (ʿAmr b. Maʿdīkarib, 1:181–183), no. 42 (anonymous, *rajul min banī ʿUqayl*, 1:199–201), no. 111 (*rajul min banī Ḥimyar*, 1:330–335), no. 133 (al-Ḥusayn b. al-Ḥumām, 1:386–393)—a remarkable example, no. 194 (Iyās b. Mālik al-Ṭāʾī, 2:595–600), no. 214 (ʿAmr b. Mikhlāt al-Kalbī, 2:646–649), and no. 224 (Zāhir Abū Kirām al-Taymī, 2: 672–674).

Now this partition between that which is said and that which is unsaid can reach existential dimensions when the consequences of the combat touch on the human sphere. Thrice the narrative alludes to victims: at the end of episode 2 after the one-on-one duels (verse 7); at the end of episode 3, when Ṭayyi' arms ravage the ranks of their adversaries and repeatedly spill their blood (verse 8); and likewise in verse 10, when the Asad take flight, pursued by the spears and lances of their enemies, who are liable to fell them at any instant. These *fityān* (combatants killed in battle) were in the flower of youth, strong and hale; they could have lived long lives. Their time was brutally cut short by enemy arms. One single message emanates from these passages: the victims' lifetimes were cut short by force. Broken time is undeniably present in any battle narrative. We owe this expression, "broken time," to the contemporary philosopher Pierre Bouretz in his analyses of Manès Sperber's (autobiographical) trilogy,[27] which relates how the lifetimes of an entire generation of young intellectuals was cut short by the genocidal atrocities of the Shoah and the great Stalinist purges.[28]

Closer to our topic, modern Arabic literature as well alludes to this "broken time" (*al-zaman al-maksūr*) in a context identical to the scheme outlined by Bouretz. The contemporary Palestinian poet Maḥmūd Darwīsh (1941–2008) recalls with a bucolic hue the trajectory of the Palestinian people before the *nakba*. With the advent of the *nakba*, this tranquil trajectory—and the ancestral tie between the Palestinian people and its history—were broken by a brutal war that brings about the exodus of the overwhelming majority of the people:

نحن أوراق الشجر،
كلمات الزمن المكسور، نحن
الناي إذ يبتعد البيت عن الناي

27 Pierre Bouretz, "Le temps brisé de l'espérance: Messianisme et philosophie de l'histoire dans la trilogie Romanesque de Manès Sperber," *Esprit* 214/8–9 (August–September 1995): 187–204. Sperber was born into a Galician Hasidic family; at a young age he lost his faith, joined the Communist party, and moved to France. During the German occupation, his life was saved by André Malraux and he reclaimed his Jewish identity, though not his religious faith.

28 Jennifer Aileen Orth-Veillon, *Ignazio Silone, Albert Camus and Manès Sperber: Writing between Stalinism and Fascism* (unpublished Ph.D. dissertation, Emory University, 2011), 133–190. Accessible online at: https://docplayer.net/94701341-Signature-jennifer-aileen-orth-veillon.html.

We are the tree leaves,
Words of the broken time, we are
The flute when home grows different from the flute.[29]

The second and third lines clearly express the elements of "broken time" as they have been treated in our prior discussion.

3 Conclusion

I would like to raise two important points in conclusion:

1. The narrative structure of heroic songs, as treated in this article, applies only to poems that celebrate collective valor, that of the clan or the tribe. In these poems, the narrator effaces himself to yield primacy to his people. One could say that the artist's approach is a "figural" one in which the hero-narrator-poet effaces himself completely and yields center stage to other protagonists, while playing the role of the "witnessing I." In other words, the me is completely integrated into the us, and is content to play the role of one fighter among many, observing and relating the exploits of the fighters of his clan. In other poems—and they are quite numerous—the hero-narrator-poet celebrates his own acts of courage and limits himself to relating his own boldness, his mastery of the arts of war, and his generosity in distributing the spoils in which he himself refuses a share. He monopolizes the entire narrative space devoted to the battle in order to glorify himself. He acts and moves, easily visible to the public, the poem's hearers and later, its readers. This is a well-known type of narrative which, according to Franz Stanzel's definition, is known as "authorial."[30]

This duality reflects in a faithful manner the complexity of relations between the hero (*al-fatā*) and his tribe. At those junctures, where the predominance of the clan is contested, the *fatā*, if he possessed any poetic talent, would loudly complain about the exaggerated demands from his clan to attack their adversaries, regardless of the dangers to which he himself would thus be exposed. He accuses them of selfishness and of prioritizing their own interests over potentially fatal risks.

2. The collective warrior narrative, as described in this article, fulfills its role well. The (optional) narrative descriptions of the preliminary phase, the

29 Maḥmūd Darwīsh, *Dīwān Maḥmūd Darwīsh* (Beirut: Dār al-ʿAwda, 1994), 2: 148.

30 See the masterful article by Franz Stanzel, "Teller-Character and Reflector-Character in Narrative Theory," *Poetics Today* 2/2 (Winter 1981): 1–14.

Summary, which gives in one verse the narrative of the battles and the episodes chosen by the narrator to be the only ones retained, a narrative divided up by ellipses whose elided narrative content remains obscure—all of this results in a succinct and well-demarcated text, which nonetheless gives the impression of having said all there is to say of the battle. It must be recalled that the points of contact between reality and its literary expression are few indeed, and invisible to the naked eye. In these conditions it would be imprudent to consider archaic heroic poetry as animated by an epic spirit.

Bibliography

Al-Aʿlam al-Shantamarī. *Sharḥ Ḥamāsat Abī Tammām*, edited by ʿAlī al-Mufaḍḍal Ḥammūdān. Dubai: Markaz Jumʿa al-Mājid and Beirut: Dār al-Fikr al-Muʿāṣir, 1992. 2 vols.

Al-Andalusī, Ibn Saʿīd. *Nashwat al-ṭarab fī taʾrīkh al-ʿArab*, edited by Naṣrat ʿAbd al-Raḥmān. Amman: Maktabat al-Aqṣā, 1982. 2 vols.

Al-Bakrī, Abū ʿUbayd. *Muʿjam mā* ʿstuʿjim min asmāʾ al-bilād wa*ʾl-mawāḍiʿ*, edited by Jamāl Ṭalba Beirut: Dār al-Kutub al-ʿIlmiyya, 1998. 3 vols.

Bouretz, Pierre. "Le temps brisé de l'espérance: Messianisme et philosophie de l'histoire dans la trilogie Romanesque de Manès Sperber," *Esprit* 214/8–9 (August–September 1995): 187–204.

Darwīsh, Maḥmūd. *Dīwān Maḥmūd Darwīsh*. Beirut: Dār al-ʿAwda, 1994. 2 vols.

De Prémare, Alfred-Louis. "Ayyām al-ʿArab—Ayyām al-Islām: Ṭufayl b. ʿAmr al-Dawsī," *Arabica* 46/3–4 (1999): 347–357.

Fāliḥ, Rāshid. "al-Baṭal fī shiʿr al-ḥamāsa," *Majallat ādāb al-Rāfidayn* (September 14, 1981): 241–267.

Genette, Gérard. *Discours du récit*. Paris: Éditions du Seuil (Collection Points), 2007.

Ḥarfūsh, ʿAbd al-Qādir. *Qabīlat Ṭayyiʾ fīʾl-jāhiliyya waʾl-islām*. Beirut: Dār al-Bashāʾir, 1995.

Ibn Ḥazm, Abū Muḥammad ʿAlī b. Aḥmad b. Saʿīd. *Jamharat ansāb al-ʿArab*, edited by ʿAbd al-Salām Hārūn. Cairo: Dār al-Maʿārif, 1971.

Ibn Manẓūr, Jamāl al-Dīn Muḥammad b. Mukarram. *Lisān al-ʿArab*. Beirut: Dār Ṣādir, 1990. 15 vols.

Ibn Maymūn, Muḥammad b. al-Mubārak. *Muntahā al-ṭalab min ashʿār al-ʿarab*, edited by Muḥammad Nabīl Ṭarīfī. Beirut: Dār Ṣādir, 1999. 9 vols.

Al-Jāsim, Aḥmad Mūsā. *Shiʿr Banī Asad fīʾl-Jāhiliyya*. Beirut: Dār al-Kunūz al-Adabiyya, 1995.

Al-Jubūrī, Mundhir. *Ayyām al-ʿArab wa-atharuhā fīʾl-shiʿr al-jāhilī*. Baghdad: Dār al-Shuʾūn al-Thaqāfiyya al-ʿĀmma, 1986.

Al-Jundī, ʿAlī. *Shiʿr al-ḥarb fī l-ʿaṣr al-jāhilī*. 2nd ed. Cairo: Maktabat al-Anglo, 1963.

Al-Khaṭīb al-Tibrīzī. *Sharḥ Dīwān al-Ḥamāsa*, edited by Gharīd al-Shaykh. Beirut: Dār al-Kutub al-ʿIlmiyya, 1421/2000.

Khazʿal, Ḥusayn Khalaf. *Ḥayāt al-Shaykh Muḥammad ʿAbd al-Wahhāb*. Beirut: Maṭābiʿ Dār al-Kutub, 1968.

Landau-Tasseron, Ella. "The Participation of Ṭayy in the Ridda," *JSAI* 5 (1984): 53–71.

Landau-Tasseron, Ella. "Asad from Jāhiliyya to Islam," *JSAI* 6 (1985): 1–28.

Al-Marzūqī, Abū ʿAlī Aḥmad b. Muḥammad b. al-Ḥasan. *Sharḥ Dīwān al-Ḥamāsa*, edited by Aḥmad Amīn and ʿAbd al-Salām Hārūn. Beirut: Dār al-Jīl, 1411/1991. 4 vols.

Al-Mawsūʿa al-ʿArabiyya. Damascus: Hay'at al-Mawsūʿa al-ʿArabiyya, 1998. 24 vols.

Orth-Veillon, Jennifer Aileen. *Ignazio Silone, Albert Camus and Manès Sperber: Writing between Stalinism and Fascism*. Unpublished Ph.D. dissertation. Emory University, 2011.

Al-Qāḍī, Muḥammad. "La composante narrative des 'Journées des Arabes' (Ayyām al-ʿArab)," *Arabica* 46/3–4 (1999): 358–371.

Sammār, Saʿd ʿAbbūd. "ʿĀdāt al-ḥarb ʿind al-ʿArab qabla al-Islām," *Majallat kulliyat l-tarbiya—Wāsiṭ* 13 (April 2013): 173–199.

Stanzel, Franz. "Teller-Character and Reflector-Character in Narrative Theory," *Poetics Today* 2/2 (Winter 1981): 1–14.

Al-Wāqidī, Muḥammad b. ʿUmar. *Kitāb al-ridda maʿa nubdha min futūḥ al-ʿIrāq*, edited by Yaḥyā al-Jubūrī. Beirut: Dār al-Gharb al-Islāmī, 1990.

Al-Yaʿlāwī, Muḥammad. "Adab Ayyām al-ʿArab," *Ḥawliyyāt al-Jāmiʿa al-tūnisiyya* (March 1982): 57–135.

An Unpublished Poem in Honor of the Prophet Moses

Joseph Sadan

Overt rivalries and latent competitions over Muslim shrines, especially the tombs of venerated saints, were common from the Middle Ages to the end of the Ottoman period, and in fact continue to our day. Competition over locations—that is, between several sites, each of which claims to be the location of the *same* saintly person's resting place—were also quite prevalent. We can find such competition between countries or regions, each of which lays claim to a number of holy shrines. This is the case despite the fact that already at the dawn of Islamic history, traditions emerged that reflected a measure of opposition to pilgrimages to venerated tombs (*ziyāra*). In later periods, the popular custom of visitation and veneration of graves, known in every human civilization, enjoyed a strong revival. Custom thus overcame the objection to such veneration, at least in most Muslim schools of religious thought.

The present author deals with the polemics concerning the location of Moses's tomb and the various shrines identified as his "authentic" burial place, as published in a number of papers as of 1979.[1] These essays, which deal with the Ottoman period, analyze previously unpublished manuscripts that teach us quite a lot about rites practiced at the time—hence the need to publish some of these debates and epistles. Out of the 54 sources (most of them manuscripts) displayed in our 1979 and 1981 articles, we have chosen to publish the

1 J. Sadan, "The Holy Site (Maqām) of Nabī Mūsā, between Jericho and Damascus: A History of a Competition between Sacred Places," *Hamizrah Hehadash* 27/1–2 (1979): 22–38 (in Hebrew). We use here the French version: Sadan, "Le tombeau de Moïse, à Jéricho et à Damas; une compétition entre deux lieux saints," *Revue des Etudes Islamiques* 49/1 (1981): 59–99, based on many manuscripts, but unfortunately the poem in honor of the prophet Moses is neither mentioned nor translated in the French version; for the preparation of the present article, we have returned to one of the manuscripts. Studies with less relevance to the present article on the poem in honor of Moses: Shmuel Tamari, "Maqām Nabī Mūsā," *Assaph: Studies in Art History* (Tel Aviv) section B, 1 (1980): 167–190; Amikam Elad, "Some Aspects of the Islamic Traditions Regarding the Site of the Grave of Moses," *JSAI* 11 (1988): 1–15; Kāmil J. ʿAsalī, *Mawsim al-Nabī Mūsā fī Filasṭīn* (Amman: Dār al-karmil, 1990), passim; ʿAwaḍ Ḥalabī is about to publish an article in English on Moses's grave and its modern aspects. In our notes below, we shall mainly refer to Sadan, "Le Tombeau," since it is this study that is richest in sources (about 54, most of which are manuscripts).

 | DOI:10.1163/9789004459120_005

full text of four epistles (or treatises) which are now ready to be sent to the press as a book in Arabic.[2] In this article, however, we would like to focus on a specific case that has literary implications as well. Most noticeable is the direct competition between Damascus (the city and its suburbs) and Jerusalem, while Jericho can also be presumed to belong to the Jerusalem group of holy sites.

Various books and manuscripts mention that in springtime, a well-known festival in honor of the prophet Moses took place, consisting of a procession from Jerusalem to Jericho, which was said to be "four-and-a-half hours distant from Jerusalem." However, it is somewhat disproportionate to focus solely on these two centers—Jerusalem and Damascus—since other tombs ascribed to Moses exist outside these centers, even at a considerable distance (as we shall see below). Furthermore, in Damascus and its environs, at least two tombs were ascribed to Moses.[3] This is also due to practical considerations; after all, a Muslim living, say, in northern Palestine would have to decide how many days (of walking or riding) he was willing to spend on a pilgrimage to Damascus or on a journey southward to Jericho (by way of Jerusalem) in order to participate in the festival.[4]

We shall now discuss the position taken by Muḥammad b. Ḥabīb (d. 1649) on the question of Moses's tomb. Although his name testifies to a connection with Damascus, Ibn Ḥabīb was also associated with the city of Nablus in Palestine. What little is known about him is derived from his short composition *Durr al-niẓām fī maḥāsin al-Shām* (Pearls of the necklace on the merits of al-Sham),[5] in which he describes an encounter between the governors of Nablus and Damascus in the latter's court. It is noteworthy that the governor of Damascus was directly responsible to the Ottoman authorities, while the governor of Nablus was subject to the governor of Damascus. During their meeting, some traditions (ḥadīths) were quoted that were not widely accepted by Islamic scholars, including one that claimed that God was the God of Damascus

2 Joseph Sadan, Ghālib ʿAnābsa, and Nādir Maṣārwa, *Arbaʿ rasāʾil ḥawla masāʾil tataʿallaqu bihā abʿād muqaddasa* (Four treatises on questions concerning sanctity), at the al-Qāsimī College (forthcoming).

3 Sadan, "Le tombeau," passim; v. the example of al-Rabaʿī, and of the "Merits of Syria" literature, 61, note 3 and 66, 82–83. 88, among our 53.

4 Though in a sense *ziyāra* means pilgrimage, Muslims like to preserve the term *ḥajj*—the "great" and "real"—to denote the pilgrimage of all Muslims to Mecca. This does not mean that in some cases, the distinction between the two terms is not emphasized in rare poetical (metaphorical) cases or in rare colloquial talk.

5 Sadan, "Le tombeau," 64–66.

or al-Sham. This is clearly a local tradition that deviates from the framework of what was generally acceptable in Islam, but it was of a kind that pleased the governor of Damascus even though those present at the meeting rejected it. The sycophantic governor of Nablus decided to ask the scholar Shams al-Dīn b. Ṭūlūn (d. 953/1546) to compose the above-mentioned work on the merits of Damascus.

Although the intention of *Durr al-niẓām* was to flatter the governor of Damascus by providing some appealing arguments explaining his predilection for officially unrecognized, local traditions, the author is not consistent. On the one hand, he praises Damascus, but on the other, he includes a sentence that implies that Jerusalem is superior to Damascus.[6] Even on the issue of Moses's burial in Damascus (as already noted, in later times two different locations in Damascus were revered as Moses's sepulchers), it takes a scholarly and ostensibly neutral position. An anonymous writer who tried to encompass traditions and impressions of both Damascus and Jerusalem in a small book (MS) with the pretentious title "History of Jerusalem and Damascus" mentions all the traditions about Moses's tomb with which he is familiar—a total of seven different variations, that is, seven distinct burial places.[7]

The tombs are enumerated in the prose part and, again, in verse. Here is a list of the tombs ascribed to Moses, with some minor changes in their order:
- Al-Maydān (nowadays called Mīdān);[8]
- Lydda (al-Lidd), a town in Palestine;
- The Sinai Desert;
- Damascus (Dimashq, al-Sham);
- Bosra (Buṣrā; other spellings are also used) in southern Syria, near the present border with Jordan;
- Al-Balqā', today in Jordan;
- The monument near Jericho.

After presenting these data and localities to the reader in prose, our anonymous author turns them into a versified and rhymed text. However, the present study deals mainly with a seven-times-longer, unpublished poem excelling in

6 Ibid., 66.

7 Ibid., 67–68, Sadan, "Le tombeau" contains *more* than seven variations.

8 A suburb of Damascus, but in earlier periods, when the traditions about its location were written down, it was considered an independent town next to Damascus. See Brigitte Marino, *Le faubourg du Mīdān à Damas à l'époque ottomane* (Damascus: Institut Français de Damas, 1997).

the elegance of its style, and written, or copied, by Ibn Ṭūlūn.[9] It is included in his book *Tuḥfat al-ḥabīb bi-akhbâr al-kathīb* (The masterpiece of the beloved on the traditions concerning the (red) hill). The "hill" in this title is *al-Kathīb*, which canonical Islamic traditions describe as "the red hill" and which certain Islamic traditions localize as the hill where Moses was buried.[10]

The fact that such a poem in honor of a prophet or a saint appears in various compositions (mostly in manuscripts) can be explained in a number of ways:

- The author received his inspiration to create the poem on a pilgrimage to one of the sites that tradition identified with the holy person's tomb. The poem is an expression of thanks for the visit and the experience of proximity to the revered deceased. Possibly the pilgrims also used other expressions (of a more popular nature).
- The author composed the poem when he jotted down his impressions from the visit.
- The author heard the poem or found a written copy, and decided to quote from it.

From a literary perspective these issues may hint at the differences between degrees of immediate oral identification with a holy site and written testimonies composed at a later date—that is, between the literary-philological level of scholarly clerical writings and the folklore of holy places and pilgrimages. Although there are some errors in the version that has come down to us (for example in the poem's prosody, or its patterns of rhythm and sound), this does not imply that the work is entirely lacking in literary qualities. It also contains much religious knowledge acquired by clerics. Ibn Ṭūlūn is not a very gifted poet, especially not when he composes (or copies from written or oral sources) a text on religious matters.

The poem we are publishing here contains several imprecisions in terms of poetic meter and rhyme—at least in Nādir Maṣārwa's draft, and I am very thankful for his efforts. In fact, Ibn Ṭūlūn's version contains a list of the very few scholars who transmitted the poem, from its original creator to the author of the present work. It is worth mentioning that one of the links in the chain of transmission is a woman, who obtained the poem from her grandfather. While the poem thus does not typify fine literary poetry, but is the product of the kind of creativity one finds among clerics, it does have qualities that raise it above

9 Sadan, "Le tombeau," 88, ff. (§ 34). The poem appears in MS Leiden, Or. 2512. The author, Ibn Ṭūlūn, indicates that this poem reached him after being circulated among pious people for over two or three generations. Such circles, including our most erudite author Ibn Ṭūlūn himself and the copyists of the text, were not always "professional" poets in matters of prosody.

10 Ibid., 73, note 73, relying on J. Sourdel-Thomine and passim.

the folkloristic perspective of the shrines of saints and prophets and above the measured cries uttered by the masses at the rites near Moses's tomb.[11]

The poem's creator could perhaps have used the word al-Sham in an older, more comprehensive sense (already in use in the Middle Ages) of "Bilād al-Shām" that encompasses Lebanon and Palestine in addition to today's Syria, and could, in certain more restricted contexts, refer to Damascus only. But he did not do so, because he was commissioned to write a work on the merits of Damascus with which the client intended to flatter the governor of that city. Ibn Ṭūlūn was known as a local patriot of Damascus. Other views are also worth mentioning, such as that of Mujīr al-Dīn al-ʿUlaymī al-Ḥanbalī,[12] which is based on the statement in Holy Scripture that Moses's burial place is not known. However, Mujīr al-Dīn argues, there is no contradiction between this statement and the tomb's identification. He goes on to explain that at the time of Moses's death, God refused to let the Jews know the tomb's location (probably so that it would not become a shrine), but that now, at the time of Islam, believers are permitted to know where it is located. He is, of course, of the opinion that Moses's sepulcher is the one near Jericho.

Following is a translation of Ibn Ṭūlūn's poem,[13] somewhat freely adapted, and followed by the original Arabic text:

O ye who seek success, in fervent hope
Of attaining your full measure of safety and tranquility
Turn to the slope of the Red Hill[14] and stay there a while
If you desire to be perfect
Lower your gaze in veneration
And comport yourself with respect and good manners.
Here rules a man who is perfection itself,
Whom the merciful God chose to be a shelter for all.
This is the Prophet Moses, who spoke with God, a man of all merits,
The holy books brought down from heaven speak about him to this day.
Moses is a prophet who performed many a wonderful and stunning miracle,
Clear miracles to all who are able to discern among all mankind.

11 See, for instance, Kāmil J. ʿAsalī, in note 1, above.

12 Sadan, "Le tombeau," 87.

13 MS Leiden Or. 2512, fol. 12r ff.

14 See above, note 10. One may add to this H. Spoer, "Das Nabī Mūsā Fest," *Z.D.P.V.* 32 (1909): 207–221.

Among the miracles, pulling out the white hand,[15] shining and illuminating
And also Moses's staff that performed great deeds.[16]
Moses also did this: He split the sea into two, the greatest miracle,
And the people (the Children of Israel) walked in it on a smooth way.
The miracle of drawing water out of a rock, a small clump of stone,
Which Moses struck, smote it with his staff and water flowed out.
Moses had the unique miracle of speech (with God),[17] as a manifest fact
And he was given the tablets as a firm and sublime act of grace.
He gave us a religious rule that determined the prayers,
Which were imposed as a more convenient commandment, their number having been reduced from fifty.
When, on Moses's advice, our Prophet Muḥammad once again asked and beseeched
The high and lofty God, as Moses had instructed him.[18]
It was on the night in which was revealed the Prophet Muḥammad's superiority
Over all the other noble prophets[19]
And he (the Prophet Muḥammad), the best of men, to whom all honor and respect are due,
None is like him. And when he was sent (by God) he sealed the entire list of prophets.
May both (Muḥammad and Moses) and all
Be blessed by God and may God's prayers constantly be with them.
O prophet who spoke to God, how great is your reverence!
To those who visit (your tomb) you are always like fresh and delectable water to a thirsty man.
O you who deserves lofty honor!
He is an impregnable fortress for all those who seek his protection.
...

15 Qur'an, 7:108; 20:22; 26:33; 27:12, and of course the commentaries and the religious-literary genre *Qiṣaṣ as al-anbiyā'* ("Stories of the Prophets") enrich these verses with more interesting details.

16 Moses's staff is mentioned several times in the Qur'an (for instance, 7:160: Moses strikes the rock and water comes out of it and 26:63: the splitting of the sea) and the religious and literary sources mentioned above, note 5. The biblical parallels are known to most of us.

17 Therefore, the Muslims call Moses *Kalīm*, the *Kalīm of God*—the Prophet who spoke with God.

18 The Prophet Muḥammad is presented as a follower and disciple of former prophets, but at the same time, as their superior.

19 See above, note 18.

We have come to you to ask for the best of gifts,
We turned to you and fortune smiled upon us.
Be an advocate for us all before God's honor, and
Ask that every grace and favor last and persevere.
…
May God's prayer be on you;
May He forever shine his face toward you.
May God's prayers be on our chosen Prophet (Muḥammad), the best of mankind
And on your father (Abraham) al-Khalīl (God's Friend), who was revealed to humankind,
And on all the other prophets the veneration of whom is
Indeed a veritable commandment, for their reverence is lofty and exalted.

Arabic Appendix*

يا طالبا نجح الفلاح مؤملا ☆ دركا تنال به الأمان مكملا
عرّج على سفح الكثيب وعج به ☆ إن كنت تبغي أن تكون محصِّلا
واغضض هناك الطرف منك تخشعا ☆ والزم به الأدب الأتمّ الأكمل
فهناك يولي بالسيادة كاملٌ ☆ من صفوة الرحمن أضحى موئلا
موسى كليم الله ذو الفضل الذي ☆ ما زال يتلى في الكتّاب منزّلا
ذو المعجزات الباهرات تعدّدا ☆ الواضحات لذي البصائر في الملا
منها اليد البيضاء يلمع ضوءها ☆ وكذا العصا تُسْعي [أو تسعَى] شجاعا هولا [أو هائلا]
وله انفلاق البحر أعجز آية ☆ تمشي الأنام به طريقا أسهلا
والماء من حجر صغير تابع ☆ من ضربه بعصا يجري منهلا
من خُص بالتكليم حقا بيِّنا ☆ وكذلك الألواح حكما فضلا [أفضلا]
وله علينا فقه في رد الصلوات ☆ من خمسين فرضا سهلا
ونبيّنا من أجلها متردّد ☆ بإشارة منه إلى رب العلا
في ليلة كان النبي محمد ☆ فيها على الرسل الكرام مفضلا

* Our book, Joseph Sadan, Ghālib ʿAnābsa, and Nādir Maṣārwa, *Arbaʿ rasāʾil* (Four treatises on questions concerning sanctity), to be published (see note 2 above), will contain an enriched edition of Ibn Ṭūlūn's text, with possible variants edited by Nādir Maṣārwa, whereas the following selected passages are copied from the manuscript, as authentic historical evidence, and nearly without changes.

خير الأنام ومن له الفضل الذي ☆ ما مثله وختامهم إذ أُرسلا
فعليهما وعلى الجميع تحية ☆ من ربنا وصلاته لن تعطّلا
ها يا كليم الله يا من فضله ☆ ما زال للوُرّاد عذبا سلسلا
يا من له الجاه الرفيع وما به ☆ للآذنين به حمى لا يختلا
...
جئناك نطلب منك أكمل نائل ☆ قصداً إليك وسعْدنا قد أقبلا
فاشفع إلى الله الكريم لجمعنا ☆ في كل إحسان يدوم تطولا
...
صلى عليك الله ثمّ سلامتُه ☆ أبدا تدوم إلى جنابك مقبلا
وعلى النبي المصطفى خير الورى ☆ وأبيكما فهو الخليل المُجتلى
وعلى جميع الأنبياء وحبهم ☆ فرض وقدرهم رفيع في العلا

Bibliography

ʿAsalī, Kāmil J. *Mawsim al-Nabī Mūsā fī Filasṭīn*. Amman: Dār al-karmil, 1990.

Elad, Amikam. "Some Aspects of the Islamic Traditions Regarding the Site of the Grave of Moses," *JSAI* 11 (1988): 1–15.

Ibn Ṭūlūn, Shams al-Dīn. *Tuḥfat al-ḥabīb fīmā warada fī'l-Kathīb*. MS Leyden. Or. 2512.

Marino, Brigitte. *Le Faubourg du Mīdān à Damas à l'époque ottomane*. Damascus: Institut Français de Damas, 1997.

Sadan, Joseph. "The Holy Site (Maqām) of Nabī Mūsā, between Jericho and Damascus: A History of a Competition between Sacred Places," *Hamizrah Hehadash* 27/1–2 (1979): 22–38 [in Hebrew].

Sadan, Joseph. "Le tombeau de Moïse, à Jéricho et à Damas; une compétition entre deux lieux saints," *Revue des Etudes Islamiques* 49/1 (1981): 59–99.

Sadan, Joseph, Ghālib ʿAnābsa, and Nādir Maṣārwa. *Arbaʿ rasāʾil ḥawla masāʾil tataʿal-laqu bihā abʿād muqaddasa*. Bāqa al-Gharbiyya: al-Qāsimī College (forthcoming).

Spoer, H. "Das Nabī Mūsā Fest," *Z.D.P.V.* 32 (1909): 207–221.

Tamari, Shmuel. "Maqām Nabī Mūsā," *Assaph: Studies in Art History* (Tel Aviv) section B, 1 (1980): 167–190.

An Anti-Jewish *Qaṣīda* by Sīdī Qaddūr al-ʿAlamī

Norman (Noam) A. Stillman

1 Introduction

Sīdī Qaddūr al-ʿAlamī (1741–1850) is the name by which the renowned Moroccan poet and mystic pietist of Meknes, ʿAbd al-Qādir b. Muḥammad b. Aḥmad b. Abī al-Qāsim al-Idrīsī al-ʿAlamī al-Ḥamdānī, is popularly known. Today he is considered a saint (*walī*) in Morocco.[1] Although reported to be illiterate, his oeuvre includes both the *malḥūn* (a vernacular poetic genre somewhat reminiscent of the Andalusian *zajal*) and poems in neo-classical Arabic.[2] While no collection of poetry (*dīwān*) of Sīdī Qaddūr's poetry appears to have been compiled, poems by him were preserved by rāwīs, often called in Morocco *ḥeffāḍ* (Cl. Ar. *ḥuffāẓ*), or reciters of verse.

The poem presented here is attributed to Sīdī Qaddūr al-ʿAlamī and was collected in the town of Sefrou, Morocco, by the anthropologist Hildred Geertz from a certain Faqīh ben ʿUmar. She kindly gave me two, slightly different, transcriptions (the poem was dictated, not recorded) with permission to publish it, and I gratefully acknowledge my debt to her. Both of us did fieldwork in Sefrou at different times, and I have over the years published studies of the town's very distinctive Judeo-Arabic dialect and genres of folk poetry.[3] That this poem, with its blatantly anti-Jewish theme, was recited in Sefrou is particularly interesting since the town, which had a large Jewish community comprising nearly forty percent of the total population, was dubbed "the little Jerusalem of Morocco" and was known for its mostly good Muslim-Jewish relations. Charles de Foucault, the French explorer and spy who reconnoitered Morocco in the early 1880s and generally a keen (though not always sympathetic) observer, noted that Sefrou and Demnate were the two places in that country where

1 The most extensive Arabic biography for Sīdī Qaddūr is in Ibn Zaydān ʿAbd al-Raḥmān b. Muḥammad al-Sijilmāsī, *Itḥāf aʿlām al-nās bi-jamāl akhbār ḥāḍirat Miknās* (Rabat: al-Maṭbaʿa al-Waṭaniyya, 1933), 5: 336–352. For a brief English-language biography with further bibliographical references, see M. Lakhdar, "Ḳaddūr al-ʿAlamī," *EI*² IV (1997): 372–373.

2 Concerning this Maghrebi genre, see Ch. Pellat, "Malḥūn," *EI*² VI (1991): 247–257, where Sīdī Qaddūr is also discussed.

3 See inter alia, Norman A. Stillman, *The Language and Culture of the Jews of Sefrou, Morocco: An Ethno-Linguistic Study* (Manchester: University of Manchester Press, 1988); idem and Yedida K. Stillman, "The Art of a Moroccan Folk Poetess," ZDMG CXXVIII, No. 1 (1978): 68–84 [68–89].

 | DOI:10.1163/9789004459120_006

Jews seemed happiest. The few anti-Jewish incidents, such as the looting of the Mellāḥ, or Jewish Quarter, were the work of rebellious tribes from without.[4]

The poem, which is referred to by its reciter as *Qaṣīdat al-Walī Sīdī Qaddūr al-ʿAlamī* (The Ode of the Saint Sīdī Qaddūr al-ʿAlamī), is presented here in my revised transliteration together with translation and notes.[5] The direct targets of the poet's vitriol are Muslims of Jewish ancestry, who not only share the bad traits of their Jewish ancestors, but are depicted as still faithful to their former religion. The poem is in vernacular Moroccan Arabic laced with classical words and literary allusions. It also contains Judeo-Arabic words of Hebrew derivation which indicates that Sīdī Qaddūr had some firsthand acquaintance with Jews, and familiarity with their communal vernacular and religious practices. The poem is designated a *qaṣīda*, and opens with a pensive, lamenting meditation (*nasīb*) on a place in ruins, just like the classical Arabic ode. But it is also a *malḥūn* due to its colloquial language, the lack of a consistent rhyme scheme, and the fact that it is set to a melody (*laḥn*). It also bears certain characteristics of the Andalusian strophic ode (*muwashshaḥ*) with a two-line refrain (*ḥerba*) that repeats every eight to fourteen verses.

Poems with specifically anti-Jewish themes—though not a common genre—are certainly not unknown in Islamic-Arabic tradition. Usually these are in the form of defamatory satire (*hijāʾ*), composed and circulated when a Jew or group of Jews were perceived as having egregiously transgressed the bounds of proper conduct as stipulated in the theoretical contract of protection (*amān* or *dhimma*) with the Islamic community. This would include rising too high in the government bureaucracy and not conducting themselves in an appropriately humble manner as prescribed in the Qurʾan and the Sunna. The two best known of these anti-Jewish poems, both from the eleventh century, are Abū Isḥāq al-Ilbīrī's poetic attack on the Jews of Granada at the time that Joseph ha-Nagid Ibn Naghrela was chief minister at the Zirid court, and another by an anonymous Egyptian poet railing against the power of Jews in the Fatimid Empire. Poetry with anti-Jewish themes and the inclusion of Judeo-Arabic vernacular words has continued all the way to modern times.[6]

---

4 Charles de Foucault, *Reconnaissance au Maroc* (Paris: Société d'éditions géographiques, maritimes et coloniales, 1939), 166. See also Norman A. Stillman, "Sefrou," in *EJIW* 4 (2010): 279–282.

5 For the poem, I have used a simplified version of the system developed by William Marçais and used by most students of the Moroccan vernacular. All other citations of Arabic follow the system of the *International Journal of Middle East Studies*, which is the modified version of the *Encyclopaedia of Islam* transcription system used by most English-speaking Arabists.

6 See Norman A. Stillman, *The Jews of Arab Lands: A History and Source Book* (Philadelphia: Jewish Publication Society, 1979), 51, 59, 214–216. The Arabic texts of these poems may be

Poetry aimed ostensibly at the *Bildiyyīn*[7] (Jewish converts to Islam in Morocco) is—to the best of my knowledge—even rarer than specifically anti-Jewish poetry. There were polemics and *fatwās* written against them. These were collected by Abū ʿAbd Allāh Muḥammad Mayyāra (d. 1662), a well-known *Bildī* scholar, in a work entitled *Naṣīḥat al-mughtarrīn wa-kifāyat al-muḍtarrīn fī'l-tafrīq bayna al-Muslimīn* (Advice for the deluded and sufficiency for those in need concerning discrimination between Muslims). Mayyāra's work is still in manuscript form; for all we know, it still contains further examples of anti-*Bildī* verse. One important distinction between Sīdī Qaddūr's poem and much of the anti-*Bildī* literature is that it accuses them of disloyalty to Islam and continuing Jewish observances, which is not the case in the usual polemics against them. Most of the opposition came from the *shurafāʾ* elite, who discriminated against them due to their base origins.

Several verses in the latter half of the poem seem to allude to war in the contemporary Middle East rather than to events in the historical past or an apocalyptic future. These may have been added by a reciter in the very nature of oral epic poetic performance. As Alfred Lord observed in his classic study of oral poetry: "For the oral poet the moment of composition is the performance." Furthermore, "the performance is a moment of creation for the singer."[8] The conclusion of the poem does talk about apocalyptic upheavals at the end of time, which would be consistent with the original overall theme of Sīdī Qaddūr's poem. It also refers exclusively to Jews, and no longer mentions the *Bildiyyīn*.

---

found respectively in Reinhart Dozy, *Recherches sur l'histoire et la littérature de l'Espagne pendant le Moyen Âge*, 3rd ed. (Paris and Leiden: Maisonneuve and Brill, 1881), 1: lxii–lxvii; and Ibn Muyassar, *Taʾrīkh Miṣr* [*Annales d'Égypte* (*les khalifes Fâtimides*)], edited by Henri Massé (Cairo: Imprimerie de l'Institut français d'archéologie orientale, 1919), 61–62.

7 A *Bildī* is a Muslim of Jewish origin from Sefrou's neighboring city of Fez (30 kms away). They were called this because they had no traditional mark of origin (Ar. *nisba*). See Mercedes García-Arenal, "Bildiyyīn," EJIW 1 (2010): 477–478. There are several Moroccan and Algerian proverbs which state that Jewish converts to Islam and their descendants even forty generations later were still untrustworthy Jews, cf. Norman A. Stillman, "Muslims and Jews in Morocco: Perceptions, Images, Stereotypes," in *Muslim Jewish Relations in North Africa*, proceedings of a seminar sponsored by the Institute for Advanced Study, Princeton, and the Academic Committee of the World Jewish Congress (New York, 1975): 13–27. Shmuel Moreh, to whose memory the present volume is dedicated, published an important study of such poetry in the oeuvre of an Iraqi Muslim poet. See Moreh, "Judeo-Arabic Dialect of Baghdad in Mullā ʿAbbūd al-Karkhī's Colloquial Poetry," in *The Tree and the Branch: Studies in Modern Arabic Literature and Contributions of Iraqi-Jewish Writers*, edited by Olga Bramson (Jerusalem: Magnes Press, 1997), 351–373 (in Hebrew). (I want to thank my student Jesse Weinberg for bringing this important essay to my attention.)

8 Albert B. Lord, *The Singer of Tales* (New York: Atheneum, 1965), 13 and 14, respectively.

2 An English Translation of the Poem

Praised be He Who rules and judges and 'taught man what he did not know.'[9]
After its walls had become dilapidated, it was whitewashed anew.
Today, sentimental people have fallen in love with it.
What is bitter (now), tomorrow, they will find delicious.
There is no drawn sword that has been appointed on its parade ground
And no horse is ridden, mounted by a mighty cavalier.
And no odor emanates from their long nose.
And if one changes, his face becomes dotted with aligned jewels.
My ancestral pride in a *Bildī* was irretrievably lost.
The whore's dirham I have changed into an iron coin.
(Refrain)
Foolish is he who puts trust in a relationship with the sons of Jews[10]
It is like someone who hides white scorpions in his garments.
Why does this thorn of a *Bildī* annoy us each new day?
We would be hurt (by him) even if he were tastier than a sea of sweets.[11]
Even if he were the progeny of sinfulness for having violated custom.
And if one of them were to come to offer advice with malice and lies
Do not believe in their religion of infidels for you would be infected.
Their hearts are harder than blackish steel.[12]
How many (a man) has been filed down, and not even his powdered filings remain after him,
Like the auctioneer who sells his grave for a profit.
(Refrain)

---

9 A quote from the well-known Qur'anic verse (96: 5).

10 The wording "sons of Jews" (*wlād līhūd*) would indicate that *Bildiyyīn* are being warned about here.

11 In modern Moroccan Arabic, *fnīd* means "candy." In medieval Andalusian and Maghrebi Arabic, it was both a variety of sugar and a sweetmeat. See Reinhart Dozy, *Supplément aux dictionnaires arabes*, 3rd ed. (Leiden and Paris: Brill and Maisonneuve et Larose, 1967), 2: 284, s.v. *fānīd.*

12 The word *hend* is used for steel in both medieval and modern Maghrebi Arabic, whereas to the best of my knowledge, Modern Standard Arabic only uses *muhannad* for a sword made of Indian iron. See Dozy, *Supplément aux dictionnaires arabes*, 2: 765–766; Richard S. Harrel (ed.), *A Dictionary of Moroccan Arabic: Arabic-English* (Washington, DC: Georgetown University Press, 1966), 55. Although in Maghrebi Arabic the usual word for black is *kḥel*, in poetry, the word *swīd* (diminutive of the Classical *aswad*) is frequently used, often as a hendiadys together with *kḥel.* See e.g. Stillman and Stillman, "The Art of a Moroccan Folk Poetess," 79, n. 47.

Foolish is he who puts trust in a relationship with the sons of Jews
It is like someone who hides white scorpions in his garments.
According to their religion, it is forbidden to believe an Arab.
When he comes to them, they sting him like scorpions.
I have been snared in the traps of the *Bildī*, one of the dirty tricks of dogs.
He eats your food, then betrays you, even if he is old and grey.
Even though the Barukhi[13] sees the truth,
He would argue with you and use evil tricks.
Their tongues pierce as they are sharper than lions' claws.
Their souls bear patiently humiliation and mistreatment
In the synagogue they read to one another with a renewed countenance[14]
By cheating Islam,[15] they reaffirm their faith in their religion.
Belief in the *Bildī*'s religion is reprehensible, a sin to be counted.[16]
Their ancestors found it in the Sefer Torah written in pearls.
Some of their forefathers converted to Islam with oaths and lies.
They are among the oldest sorcerers, and they will betray whoever questions the brethren.
(Refrain)
Foolish is he who puts trust in a relationship with the sons of Jews
It is like someone who hides white scorpions in his garments.
There is discord among the Arabs, while good comes to the enemies[17]
And this world and humiliation for the people of phylacteries.
The people who observe Minḥa and the time of Tishaʿ B'Av—grumpy and lowly

13 An epithet from the Hebrew, *barukh* (blessed), either meaning "the one who says prayers that begin with *barukh*" or perhaps "the one descended from a person named Barukh."

14 Sīdī Qaddūr is saying that the *Bildiyyīn* are still practicing Judaism despite their nominal conversion to Islam.

15 There are a number of Moroccan proverbs that describe Jews as seeking to cheat (*ghushsh*) Muslims, as e.g., *l-ihūdī ida ghashsh l-meslem ka-ikūn ferḥān f-dak l-yūm* (When a Jew cheats a Muslim, he is happy that day) and *l-ihūdī ida ṭḥak nel-meslem, ʿarfū nel-ghushsh yetḥazzem* (If a Jew laughs at a Muslim, know that he is girding himself for cheating). See Edward Westermarck, *Wit and Wisdom in Morocco* (London: G. Routledge, 1930), 130, Nos. 469–470.

16 Reprehensible (*makrūh*) is one of the five juridical qualifications of human actions in Islamic law (*al-aḥkām al-khamsa*). It is disapproved of, but not forbidden outright. However, Sīdī Qaddūr immediately qualifies it as being counted as *ḥarām*, the juridical qualification of a forbidden act, and hence a sin.

17 In Classical Arabic *qawm means* "people" but also has the sense of "enemies."

He[18] asked them from Jerusalem: O you who understand, tell me:
No respect, no pact,[19] no speech, only wiles!
The elders have not forgotten the sxina,[20] the egg, and delicious taste of fried meat.
They disbelieve the prophets and messengers, and they lack religion.
They do not beget anyone who is pious, mamzer,[21] or courageous men.
Crazy is he who makes a *Bildī* one of his intimate friends
It is as if he associated with vipers and scorpions in caves in the countryside
It is permissible to kill the sons of Simḥa;[22] and as for the sons of the Akku,[23] they are among the worst.
They are all cheats; they have no honest counsel, they are our enemies and the patent enemies of our prophet.
O you who are present, curse the dwellers of the Mellah.[24]
(Refrain)
Foolish is he who puts trust in a relationship with the sons of Jews
It is like someone who hides white scorpions in his garments.
I was deceived in friendship with sons of Simeon
Before I had observed the destroyers of religion.

18 It is not clear who "He" is here—God, the Prophet Muḥammad at the time of his miraculous night journey from Mecca to Jerusalem and thence to Heaven, or perhaps one of the Jewish prophets.

19 I.e. the Pact of ʿUmar which should govern the behavior of *dhimmī*s in the Islamic polity.

20 Sxīna, also called *dafīna*, is the Moroccan equivalent of Ashkenazi cholent, and like the latter, it is a translation of the Mishnaic Hebrew *ḥammin* (Shabbat 2:7), meaning "hot food." It is a savory mixture of meat, potatoes, chickpeas, cereal grains, hard-boiled eggs, and spices, cooked in a single pot from Friday afternoon until Saturday noon in the public oven (*ferrān*). It is considered one of the pièces de résistance of Jewish cuisine by Muslims. A kosher restaurant that I knew in Casablanca and which closed for Shabbat served Muslim customers cholent when it reopened on Saturday night.

21 It is not at all sure what Sīdī Qaddūr means here. He obviously had heard the word used by Jews but did not understand it. He imbues it with positive characteristics that Jews, in his view, do not possess.

22 A common name among Moroccan-Jewish women.

23 It is not at all clear who this could be. It is not a Jewish name. It might be a nickname meaning something like the Scoffer. See Dozy, *Supplément aux dictionnaires arabes*, 2:157, s.v. *ʿ-k-w*.

24 On this name for the Jewish quarter in Moroccan cities, see Emily Gottreich, "Mallāḥ," *EJIW* 3 (2010): 327.

I said: They have not learned a quarter of what they have read of [?][25]
They never reverted back, the rabbi[26] never made them infidels.
They have not eaten meʿqůda on the Feast of Unleavened Bread, hot and dry.[27]
They did not flee, and they did not attend the execution of Haman.
Were armies from the Levant[28] and Jerusalem, they would be annihilated by cruel suppression.
Their people would not tolerate effrontery in the presence of rows of witnesses.
Parks, homes, irrigation canals, and citadels are full
The infidels came down between the Jordan and the quiet Nile,
And Islam came out to the quiet (Nile) paying the ransom of revenge.[29]
When the white complete news is revealed, the rivers would dry up,
The treasures would disappear from the lack of rains and the bothersome beasts.
And the strife; and prices rising, and the five (daily prayers) coming back unsuccessful.
The fortuneteller came. If the dwellings came to be owned by those who became infidels.
And the Jews have rebelled in the palace of that person.
And with the losses in battles of carnage, he rides hurling insults
Dignity comes from the sword of him who slaughters the one who did not obey. Righteous will
be found, and the upright people will appear.
Then the Muslim faith rises shining.

---

25 This line, if correctly transcribed, makes little sense.

26 *Ḥezzān* is used by Muslims and Jewish women in Morocco to mean "rabbi" or "scholar," not a "cantor" as in Hebrew. See Brunot and Malka, *Glossaire judéo-arabe de Fès*, 32, for notes on this word.

27 *Meʿaqůda* (*mʿöda* in the Judeo-Arabic of Fez and Sefrou), also called *magina*, is a thick frittata of potato and egg, sometimes with pieces of carrot and peas or meat inside. *Rqāq* (sing. *rqāqa*) is the Moroccan-Arabic word for matzah used by both Muslims and Jews. Jews also use the Hebrew *maṣṣa*. If transcribed correctly, the word *sḥūn* is problematic. It could be a Hebrew term that Sīdī Qaddūr had misheard. I have translated it hot and dry from the Mishnaic Hebrew *shaḥūn*, but this is doubtful.

28 Literally, Syrians (pl. of *shāmī*), but the meaning is from the Levantine countries.

29 It is difficult to believe that this verse is from Sīdī Qaddūr's time. It seems to reflect the modern era and the Arab-Israeli conflict. As noted in the introduction to this essay, it is perfectly consistent with the nature of oral poetry for a reciter/singer to introduce his own elements while remaining faithful to the overall poetic theme and structure. Oral poetry is by its very nature composed in performance. See Lord, *The Singer of Tales*, 13–29 et passim.

(Refrain)
Foolish is he who puts trust in a relationship with the sons of Jews
It is like someone who hides white scorpions in his garments.
We have heard from the tongues of our masters the wisemen
All that will happen at the end of time—namely, chaos and wars.
The son of Canaan, Damshiqi, will descend upon them, upon Israel.
In vanquishing, he names them the "sons of putrid corpses,"[30] the cursed bloated skins.
O reciter of poetry, take this *qaṣīda* from the pure and righteous one.
And he who declares its importance has the pride of him who guards a precious object.
I have unsheathed my sword for the battle in the name of him who composes poetry.
So says ʿAbd al- Qādir al-ʿAlamī ben Mshīsh al-Halāl.[31]
(Afterword)
This is the Simeonite[32] *Qaṣīda* on the Jews.[33]

3 The Moroccan-Arabic Text

Sebḥāna men qaḍa u-ḥkem wa-ʿallama l-insāna ma lem yʿalem.
Fteḥt fī ṣůṛ mheshshem bāb kān meshdūd
Bʿad rshat ḥīṭů mbeyyeḍ ždīd
Metwelleʿ bih l-yūm bin lužūd
Likun mraru ghedda ižīhum ldīd
Ma tqelldet f-midānu b-sīf mežbūd[34]
U-la rkebt žuwād mrebbih fares shdīd
U-la nsheqet minhum nesma b-anf mengūd
U-la nbeddel muret wežhu bežůher nḍīd

30 The epithet "banū žīfa" (sons of putrid corpses) has a long tradition in Morocco and is associated with a popular *ḥadīth* that after a war with the Jews (banū Isrāʾīl), the widows of the slain Jews complained to the Prophet that they no longer had husbands. He then invited them to sleep with their dead spouses. See *Le Dictionnaire Colin d'arabe dialectal marocain*, 2: 272, s.v. *žīfa* and the literature cited there.

31 The ancestral names Ben Mshīsh al-Hilāl are not given in the sources on Sīdī Qaddūr noted in n. 1 above.

32 The poet relates in the poem that he "was deceived in friendship with sons of Simeon," and thus the name is applied to the group excoriated throughout the work.

33 This afterword may have been added later by one of the reciters.

34 For the post-Classical idiom *taqallada bi-sayf*, see Dozy, *Supplément aux dictionnaires arabes*, 2: 394, and for *majbūdh* (colloquial mežbūd), see ibid., 1: 170, s.v. *j-b-dh*.

Daʿ li selfī fel-Bildī b-ghīr meṛdūd
Derhem l-fežra beddeltu b-fils l-ḥdīd
(l-Ḥerba[35])
Hbil men yamen fil-ʿoshra di wlād lihūd
Kīf men xāzen f-tyābu ʿaqāreb l-bīḍ
Mali ʿenni shukt l-Bildī mṣelṭa ʿalīna kulla yūm ždīd
Ka-ntadaw ila mdāq men bḥar fnīd[36]
Wela ikūn nsel li-shūr men xerq l-ʾʿāda
Wela yižī ḥed menhum yenṣḥed be-shqārīn u-kdūb
La tʾamen f-dīnhum el-kuffār ila tetʿāda
Qlūbhum qṣeḥ men hend swīdī
Kemm men mebṛeḍ u-bṛīḍu ma tshīṭ men murah brūḍa
Kīf dellāl baʿ qebru b-ziyāda
(l-Ḥerba)
Ḥrām fi mellethum yiṣadqu l-ʿarab
Melli yžī l-ʿandhum yilesʿūh ki l-ʿeqāreb
Ḥṣelt ḥeṣlat fi l-beldī men xṣāyel l-klāb
Yakul ṭʿāmek w-gheḍrek wa-luw yekūn shayeb
L-ikūn l-Baruxī ʿal l-ḥeqq reggab
ižaḥdek w-ixeddem lek l-ḥyāl le-xzāyeb
Lsūnhum iṭeʿnu be-mḍa men ḍfār l-usūd
Nfūshum iṣebru leddel u-ttmermīd
Fi l-knīsa yitqaraw be-wažhů rdūd
ʿEn gheshsh l-Islām f-dīnhum ttuwkīd
Ṣṣedq f-mellt l-Bildī mekrūh ḥrām meʿdūd
Weždūh slafhum fes-sīfer[37] fel-žůher mektūb
Beʿḍ l-ždūd le-qdām yselmu be-ʿwāhed u-kdūb

---

35 For this meaning of the word, see *Le Dictionnaire Colin d'arabe dialectal marocain* (Sous la direction de Zakia Iraqui Sinaceur; Rabat: Editions Al Manahil & Ministère des Affaire Culturelles, 1994), 2: 295, s.v. *ḥărba*. This word is perhaps connected to the musical mode known as *ḥarūba*.

36 One version of the text has bḥar en-nīl (the Nile River), which a native assistant objects to as not making sense, arguing that today people say *wad nīl*. However, in medieval literary Arabic, the Nile was indeed referred to as *baḥr* and was noted for its marvelous properties as a river emanating from Paradise. Thus, this classicism might be possible, although *fnīd* works better with the rhyme scheme. See J.H. Kramers, "al-Nīl," *EI*² VIII (1995): 37–43.

37 The Hebrew word *sefer*. The word is used in Judeo-Arabic for a Torah scroll (Heb. *sefer Torah*), and never for just a book. See Louis Brunot and Elie Malka, *Glossaire judéo-arabe de Fès* (Rabat: École du Livre, 1940), 62, and Stillman, *The Language and Culture of the Jews of Sefrou*, 75. It was probably heard by Sīdī Qaddūr in Meknes with its large Jewish population.

Men qdām le-kwāhen[38] ixūnu men suwwel le-xwān
(l-Ḥerba)
Fitna b-l-ʿarab, l-xīr ža fel-qwām
U-dunya, u-della[39] f-hel tefillīm[40]
Ṣḥāb menḥa[41] u-weqt shʿabāb[42] le-mqat le-rdal
Salhum men bit l-quds, ya fahmīn, qūl-lī
La ḥya, la ʿahed, la qūl, ghīr le-ḥyāl
Ma nsaw l-kebbār be-sxīna ul-bēṭa u-leddat l-meqelli
Mkeddebin le-nbyā ur-rsūl w-naqṣīn le-dyān
Ma yweldu men huwa tāqī mamzīr[43] ržūl ṣenḍīḍu
Mahbūl lli ydīr beldī men le-ḥbāb
Kīf men ʿasher hiyyat w-ʿeqāreb f-ghīrān l-barr
Ḥell l-qtāl f-wlād Semḥa wa-amma weld li'l-ʿAkku mel l-qbāḥ
Gheshshāshīn bel-žmīʿ, ma fīhum neṣḥa, ʿadāna w-ʿadā nbīna be-ttwedḥa
Neʿlū, yā ḥadrīn, sekkān l-mellāḥ
(l-Ḥerba)
Kunt gherri f-ṣeḥba di wlād Shemʿūn
Qbel ma nergeb ʿala xerrābīn l-dyān
Qult ma ḥefḍū ṛebʿa ma graw latūn
Ma tesreddu ma kefferhum di-ḥezzān
Ma klaw meʿqūda f-ʿīd r-rqāq
Ma žfaw[44] wa la ḥeḍrů ʿen qtīl Hamān
Lů žāt žyūsh men shwāma ul-quds tefna be-dwahek shrūr

38 The word is the plural of both *kāhin* (sorcerer) and Kohen, a member of the Jewish priestly caste. A number of famous *Bildiyyīn* bear the family name *al-Kūhīn*, including Abderrahmane El Kouhen, a former Moroccan Minister of Tourism. While Sīdī Qaddūr probably intends the meaning of a pagan sorcerer or soothsayer, he also want to conjure up the image of people named Kohen which fits the tone of this anti-*Bildī* and anti-Jewish diatribe.

39 This is the Moroccan vernacular form of *dhulla* (baseness or shame) and clearly an allusion to the Qur'anic statement that the Jews "were struck with humiliation and wretchedness" (2: 61).

40 The Hebrew word *tefillin* (phylacteries).

41 Hebrew *minḥa*—afternoon prayer.

42 Hebrew Tish'a B'Av (the Ninth of Av), the day of fasting and mourning for the destruction of the two Temples.

43 The Hebrew word *mamzer* (offspring of a forbidden sexual relation) is used frequently in the Judeo-Arabic expletive *ḥrāmī-mamzīr*, a hendiadys of Arabic and Hebrew synonyms for bastard. See Norman A. Stillman, "Verbal Darts: Name-Calling, Cursing, and Gibing in Moroccan Judeo-Arabic," in *Sha'arei Lashon: Studies in Hebrew, Aramaic, and Jewish Languages Presented to Moshe Bar-Asher* (Jerusalem: Bialik Institute, 2007), 3: 145.

44 For this verb, see *Le Dictionnaire Colin d'arabe dialectal marocain*, 2: 241, s.v. *žfa*.

Ma qeblu nāsha ḍṣāra be-shwāhed ṣṭůr
U=mnāzeh u-dyār, u-sqayel u-brūj ʿamra
Tenzel l-kuffār bin el-urdun u-bḥer nil le-ṣqeṛ
W-yxeržu l-islām l-leṣqeṛ ka-yefdiw t-taṛu
Wi ban xbār ;-bīḍa l-ʿamra ttwekkeḥ le-nhār
Teghba le-knūz be-qellet mṭer u-ftān l-hushāt
W-laʿḍer w-yṭelʿů le-sʿār ul-xems wqāt tʿůd xasra
Ža bu le-žfār ila ʿādet sekna lemmen kfer
Wi-be-rzu le-ḥrůb le-mežazra yerkeb meʿyar
Yati le-hmam f-sīf le-men gzer men la taʿ lḥeq yenežber w-ibānu le-brar
W-tedḥa mellet l-islām nayra
(l-Ḥerba)
Stameʿna men lsůn sadati ahl l-ʿilm
Kul ma iwqaʿ fī axīr zamān men fetna u-ḥrūb
Aṣelha sbābha ali yeʿqūb
U-nzel ʿalihum ben kunʿān damshīqi ʿala isrāʾīl
Bel-qahūr u-sammahum banů žīfa le-ʿkāk[45] nʿil
A ḥāfeḍ le-sʿār xud qṣīda men l-xāleṣ tberr
W-ʿel dāʿī ṣultu fxer ḥžert le-ʿyār
Žerrt ṣemṣamī li'l-msaqra asm yedkeru
Iqūl ʿAbdelqāder l-ʿAlamī ben Mshīsh le-Hlāl
(Hādī qaṣīdat shemʿūniyya ʿel yahūd)

Bibliography

Brunot, Louis and Elie Malka. *Glossaire judéo-arabe de Fès*. Rabat: École du Livre, 1940.

Dozy, Reinhart. *Recherches sur l'histoire et la littérature de l'Espagne pendant le Moyen Âge*. 3rd ed. Paris and Leiden: Maisonneuve and Brill, 1881. 2 vols.

Dozy, Reinhart. *Supplément aux dictionnaires arabes*. 3rd ed. Leiden and Paris: Brill and Maisonneuve et Larose, 1967. 2 vols.

Ferré, Daniel. *Lexique marocain-français*. Fédala: Editions Nejma, n.d.

Foucault, Charles de. *Reconnaissance au Maroc*. Paris: Société d'éditions géographiques, maritimes et coloniales, 1939.

García-Arenal, Mercedes. "Bildiyyīn," *EJIW* 1 (2010): 477–478.

Gottreich, Emily. "Mallāḥ," *EJIW* 3 (2010): 327.

45 For this uncommon word, see Daniel Ferré, *Lexique marocain-français* (Fédala: Editions Nejma, n.d.), 302, s.v. *ʿokka* (pl. *ʿkek*).

Harrel, Richard S. (ed.). *A Dictionary of Moroccan Arabic: Arabic-English.* Washington, DC: Georgetown University Press, 1966.

Ibn Muyassar, *Ta'rīkh Miṣr* [*Annales d'Égypte* (*les khalifes Fâtimides*)], edited by Henri Massé. Cairo: Imprimerie de l'Institut français d'archéologie orientale, 1919.

Kramers, H. "al-Nīl," *EI*^{2} VIII (1995): 3743.

Lakhdar, M. "Ḳaddūr al-ʿAlamī," *EI*^{2} IV (1997): 372–373.

Le Dictionnaire Colin d'arabe dialectal marocain. Sous la direction de Zakia Iraqui Sinaceur. Rabat: Editions Al Manahil & Ministère des Affaire Culturelles, 1994. 8 vols.

Lord, Albert B. *The Singer of Tales.* New York: Atheneum, 1965.

Moreh, Shmuel. "Judeo-Arabic Dialect of Baghdad in Mullā ʿAbbūd al-Karkhī's Colloquial Poetry," in *The Tree and the Branch: Studies in Modern Arabic Literature and Contributions of Iraqi-Jewish Writers*, edited by Olga Bramson. Jerusalem: Magnes Press, 1997 [in Hebrew].

Pellat, Ch. "Malḥūn," *EI*^{2} VI (1991): 247–257.

Al-Sijilmāsī, Ibn Zaydān ʿAbd al-Raḥmān b. Muḥammad. *Itḥāf aʿlām al-nās bi-jamāl akhbār ḥāḍirat Miknās.* Rabat: al-Maṭbaʿa al-Waṭaniyya, 1933. 5 vols.

Stillman, Norman A. "Muslims and Jews in Morocco: Perceptions, Images, Stereotypes," in *Muslim Jewish Relations in North Africa.* Proceedings of a seminar sponsored by the Institute for Advanced Study, Princeton, and the Academic Committee of the World Jewish Congress. New York: World Jewish Congress, 1975, 13–27.

Stillman, Norman A. *The Jews of Arab Lands: A History and Source Book.* Philadelphia: Jewish Publication Society, 1979.

Stillman, Norman A. *The Language and Culture of the Jews of Sefrou, Morocco: An Ethno-Linguistic Study.* Manchester: University of Manchester Press, 1988.

Stillman, Norman A. "Verbal Darts: Name-Calling, Cursing, and Gibing in Moroccan Judeo-Arabic," in *Shaʿarei Lashon: Studies in Hebrew, Aramaic and Jewish Languages Presented to Moshe Bar-Asher.* Jerusalem: Bialik Institute, 2007, 3: 141–156.

Stillman, Norman A. "Sefrou," *EJIW* 4 (2010): 279–282.

Stillman, Norman A. and Yedida K. Stillman. "The Art of a Moroccan Folk Poetess," *ZDMG* 1 (1978): 68–89.

Westermarck, Edward. *Wit and Wisdom in Morocco.* London: G. Routledge, 1930.

"To Choose Your Own Sky": Rootedness and Dislocation in the Poetry of Saʿdī Yūsuf

Yair Huri-Horesh

Saʿdī Yūsuf has long been acknowledged as Iraq's foremost living poet and the progenitor of "the exilic poem" in modern Arabic literature. This article discusses the poetics of exile in Yūsuf's poetry from the 1960s to the present day. Applying the theoretical framework developed by Claudio Guillén, it demonstrates how Yūsuf's exilic writings reveal a gradual shift from a "narrative of exile," which is underpinned by a distinct elegiac mode, to a "narrative of counter-exile," which is characterized by a tendency toward integration, increasingly broad vistas, or even universalism.

> Between a home that immures me and a wide sky,
> how will I choose my home?
> Between my silence and my song,
> how will I choose my whisper?
>
> Saʿdī Yūsuf, "A Poem"[1]

> The interchangeability of home and exile, here and there, memory and forgetting points to the fact that all concepts of origin and belonging—whether real or invented—that one venerates are mere fictions that one can construct as well as deconstruct.
>
> Mustapha Hamil, "Exile and its Discontents"[2]

> The exiles
> will wake up one morning
> only to find that they are exiled
> even from the meaning of exile.
>
> Saʿdī Yūsuf, "One Morning"[3]

---

1 Saʿdī Yūsuf, *al-Aʿmāl al-kāmila* (Damascus: Dār al-Madā, 1995), 2: 43.

2 Mustapha Hamil, "Exile and Its Discontents," *Research in African Literatures* 35/1 (Spring, 2004), 57.

3 Yūsuf, *al-Aʿmāl al-kāmila*, 3: 95.

 DOI:10.1163/9789004459120_007

1 Exile and Literary Creativity: Some General Comments

The experience of exile has been an essential generative force for artists and writers throughout the twentieth century and arguably long before. Whether the exile is forced or voluntary, the convergence of expatriation with the experience of creativity has been an ongoing force in artistic and literary vanguardism. Exiled artists and writers throughout history have refigured and reimagined both aesthetic and geographic boundaries, and their work has often been radical, shaping changes beyond the aesthetic or formal. In this sense, by relocating themselves to different cultures, exiles inevitably give birth to more universal ideas, the result of the integration of the local mind with the universal cognitive map. Poets and writers, displaced by force or choice, have produced the type of work that shatters boundaries, perhaps mirroring the ruptures evident in their changed geographies, allowing them what Julia Kristeva has called "exquisite distance." Kristeva's account of the foreigner's "perverse pleasure" in self-alienation profoundly contributes to an understanding of exilic creativity. Her concept of the "foreigner" and the experience of being a "stranger" shows how these experiences might overlap and intersect. She writes:

> Living with the other, with the foreigner, confronts us with the possibility or not of being an other [...] this means to imagine and make oneself other for oneself. Rimbaud's *Je est un autre* ["I is an other"] was not only the acknowledgement of the psychotic ghost that haunts poetry. The word foreshadowed the exile, the possibility or necessity to be foreign and to live in a foreign country, thus heralding the art of living of a modern era, the cosmopolitanism of those who have been flayed. Being alienated from myself, as painful as that may be, provides me with that exquisite distance within which perverse pleasure begins, as well as the possibility of my imagining and thinking, the impetus of my culture.[4]

In his 1986 study, Michael Seidel maintains that "so many writers, whatever their personal or political traumas, have gained imaginative sustenance from exile [...] that experiences native to the life of the exile seem almost activated in the life of the artist: separation as desire, perspective as witness, alienation as new beginning," and concludes that "the imagination not only compensates for exilic lost but registers that loss as aesthetic gain."[5] Separation from

---

4 Julia Kristeva, *Strangers to Ourselves* (New York: Columbia University Press, 1991), 13–14.

5 Michael Seidel, *Exile and the Narrative Imagination* (New Haven and London: Yale University Press, 1986), x.

family and history therefore involve an interesting thematic ambivalence. The prime consequence of losing social institutions is to remove external definitions of the self, but its secondary effect can be the creation or discovery of a new personality.

The experience of displacement produces a unique artistic personality, one between two different topographies: home and exile. This duality has an incredible effect on the expatriate and provides a way to a global consciousness that incorporates both home and exile. At the end, as critic Abdel Malek Sayad maintains, he or she will never be the same as when forced into exile.[6] Polish-American poet Czesław Miłosz indicates that exile is not "just a physical phenomenon of crossing of borders," since for those who are involved in any exile, the question becomes the search for truth.[7] The loss of homeland in its geographical meaning creates the emergence of a new homeland. Although the reverse may happen in some cases, the intellectual enrichment and cognitive alienation put the poet in a better position to understand the homeland's realities in a wider context. In two different places, while tackling the issue of exile and creativity, writer and critic Salman Rushdie insightfully notes that:

> the word "translation" comes, etymologically, from the Latin for 'bearing [*sic* carried] across.' Having been borne across the world, we are translated men. It is normally supposed that something always gets lost in translation. I cling, obstinately, to the notion that something can also be gained.[8]
>
> Migration [...] offers us one of the richest metaphors of our age. The very word metaphor, with its roots in the Greek word for 'bearing across,' describes a sort of migration, the migration of ideas into images. Migrants—borne-across-humans—are metaphorical beings in their very essence.[9]

The experience of exile thus offers profound insights into not only marginality in its many forms, but creativity itself. There is, as Irit Rogoff observes, an important link between the lived art, the experience of being creative, and the desire to refigure geography, the sense of temporality and the boundaries of the self:

---

6 Abdel Malek Sayad, "A Land of No Return," *The UNESCO Courier* 17 (1996): 10.

7 Czesław Miłosz, "On Exile." *Parabola* 18/2 (1993): 25.

8 Salman Rushdie, *Imaginary Homelands: Essays and Criticism 1981–1991* (London: Granta Books, 1991), 17.

9 Ibid., 278.

> While the art world cannot claim for itself a fixed and concrete location, a mapped terrain with distinct boundaries, it is nevertheless a world unto itself, with a distinct cultural and linguistic tradition and a vehement sense of territoriality […] Any critical examination of the relationship between geographical materialities and the representation of coherent identities reveals that, contrary to expectations, these neither complement nor construct one another in a direct or causal manner. The mere appearance of […] recognized national entities within identifiable boundary lines […] or the representation of specific linguistic practices, do not necessarily signify a set of shared homogeneous values operating from within one shared collective identity […] the disruption of such traditions through geographical and cultural exile and dislocation, opens up possibilities for the incorporation of alternative and plural perspectival vantage points and pictoral references which forge new cultural conjunctions.[10]

2 Saʿdī Yūsuf: A Short Biography

One cannot fail to observe the astuteness of Saʿdī Yūsuf's insights as well as the poetic power in his mapping of the stages of an exile's transformation in and adaptation to exile. Although many Arab poets and writers have been exiled or have chosen expatriation or emigration, no other poet has so deeply engaged with exile as a subject and explored so obsessively the role of dispersion and fragmentation in his poetic works as Yūsuf did.

Yūsuf was born in 1934 in Ḥamdān, a small village in the district of Abū al-Khaṣīb, south of Basra. He published his earliest poetry in Baghdadi newspapers when he was still in high school, though at this stage he did not yet consider poetry writing as a career. The change occurred only when he graduated from high school and enrolled in the renowned Higher Teachers' Training Institute (*Dār al-Muʿallimīn al-ʿĀliya*) in Baghdad, where he received his BA degree in Arabic with a teacher's certificate. In the early 1950s, Yūsuf, following in the footsteps of the most highly acclaimed Iraqi poets, joined the Iraqi Communist Party (founded in 1934, the year he was born), which gathered under its wings all the intellectuals who overtly displayed their social sympathies. Yūsuf's first experience with exile took place in 1957, after an unauthorized journey to a

10 Irit Rogoff, "In the Empire of the Object," in *Outsider Art: Contesting Boundaries in Contemporary Culture*, eds. L. Zolberg and Joni Maya Cherbo (Cambridge: Cambridge University Press, 1997), 159–160.

Communist youth festival in Moscow. Facing imprisonment by the monarchic regime, he was forced to roam between Cairo and Damascus and finally settled in Kuwait, where he worked as a schoolteacher. He returned to Iraq only in 1958, the year General ʿAbd al-Karīm Qāsim overthrew the king, assumed total power, and formed a left-wing government. Qāsim's regime, which was supported by the majority of Communists in Iraq, lasted approximately five years, during which Yūsuf and other leftist intellectuals were able to express their Marxist views publicly, in nearly complete freedom.

The fall of Qāsim's regime in February 1963 was a significant turning point in Yūsuf's life. The new nationalist regime of ʿAbd al-Salām ʿĀrif conducted a sweeping political purge, in which thousands of Communists were tortured, executed, and massacred. Yūsuf himself was incarcerated for short periods of time in prisons in Basra, Nuqrat Salmān (near Samāwa on the Saudi-Iraqi border), and Baʿqūba. In 1964 he was released only to be put on trial again, this time to face a death sentence. He managed to leave Iraq and decided to settle in the recently independent Algeria and then, for a short while, in Libya. Algeria's newborn socialist regime provided Yūsuf with a relatively tolerant environment in which he could express his views freely.

Yūsuf returned to Iraq in 1972, after a new Baʿathist regime had assumed power and legalized the Iraqi Communist Party. He was appointed director of the Iraqi Ministry of Culture and editor of the literary and folkloric review *al-Turāth al-Shaʿbī*, positions which he held until 1979, when this very last Iraqi "phase" in Yūsuf's life came to an end. A few weeks after Saddam Hussein took absolute political power, Yūsuf—like most prominent Iraqi intellectuals, teachers, writers, and poets—realized that he must abscond from his homeland and return to a life in exile.

Yūsuf decided to settle in Beirut, which at the end of the 1970s was still an important literary center of the Arab world. He wrote for several Palestinian journals that were published in the Lebanese capital. In the years 1981 and 1982, he was editor-in-chief of the literary journal *al-Mawqif al-Adabī*. Following the Israeli invasion of Lebanon in June 1982, Yūsuf joined the PLO forces. He insisted on remaining in the city and became an active participant in fighting the Israeli army during the long siege of Beirut. After the Palestinian forces and other Arab volunteer fighters were driven out of Lebanon at the end of the siege, Yūsuf managed to escape Beirut under an assumed name and embarked on a ship that was headed for Tartous, Syria.

After a short stay in Syria, Yūsuf settled in Yemen, which at the time was the only Marxist country in the Arab world. In Aden—a city that he hoped would prove to be a true haven—Yūsuf worked as a cultural consultant, founded a publishing house (Dār al-Hamadhānī li'l-Nashr), and published both the country's first children's magazine and its first weekly magazine. The ghastly civil war between South and North Yemen that broke out in January 1986 found Yūsuf hiding, together with other refugees, in a school that became a target of insurgent artillery. He survived the massacre that occurred later on and managed to flee the country. Between 1986 and 1990, Yūsuf was frequently forced to flee from one country to another. He worked as a reporter in Nicosia, in Belgrade, and finally in Tunis, where he settled during the first Gulf War. Yūsuf testifies that even when he resided in a comparatively liberal Arab country he felt constantly threatened, a feeling which ultimately drove him to immigrate to Paris. Yūsuf's radically antiestablishment personality, his fiercely independent opinions, and his determination to swim upstream against the powerful currents of politics led to yet another inevitable clash, this time with the French authorities.

Yūsuf now wandered between Moscow, Cairo, Leningrad, Cyprus, Addis Ababa, and Amman, where he received the ʿArār Prize of the "Union of the Jordanian Writers" in 1986. He ultimately resided for several years in Damascus, where he was editor-in-chief of several literary journals, most notably *Majallat al-Madā al-Adabiyya* and *Majallat al-Hadaf al-Siyāsiyya*. However, in 1997 Yūsuf realized that in order to achieve absolute artistic freedom, he must reside in a non-Arab country. Yūsuf chose London, where he was recognized as a political refugee.

3 Theoretical Framework

In his seminal essay "The Writer in Exile or the Literature of Exile and Counter-Exile," literary critic Claudio Guillén distinguishes between two types of exile narratives. In the first, "exile becomes its own subject matter," and it often belongs to the elegiac mode. This kind of writing reveals a tendency towards "a direct expression of sorrow" and it is usually submerged by the hardships of displacement. In the second, "exile is the condition but not the visible cause of an imaginative response often characterized by a tendency toward integration, increasingly broad vistas or universalism."[11] He calls the latter a literature of "counter-exile," in which authors "incorporate the separation from place, class, language, or native community, insofar as they triumph over

11 Claudio Guillén, "The Writer in Exile or the Literature of Exile and Counter-Exile," in *Books Abroad* 50 (1976): 272.

the separation and thus offer wide dimensions of meanings and transcend the earlier attachment to place or native origin."[12] In this kind of narrative, Guillén claims, the writer tries to put the expulsion into perspective in a balanced and meaningful way and attempts to overcome—but not forget—the tragedy of exile. The "literature of exile," according to Guillén, is linked to "modern feelings of nationalism," whereas in the "literature of counter-exile," so Guillén argues, "no great writer can remain a merely local mind, unwilling to question the relevance of the particular place from which he writes."[13] Indeed, in a counter-exile narrative, exile is almost stripped of its "tragic edge" and becomes an elixir of freedom from the suffocating grip of national identity.

I contend that whereas Yūsuf's exilic writings until 1982 clearly belong to the first kind, those dating after his departure from Yemen belong, by and large, to the second. Yūsuf's later exilic writings do not address exile itself, but rather exemplify a type of narrative written in exile. His poems evince the exilic sensibility even though, on the whole, the poet shuns the *clear and direct* thematization of exile. The theme of exile thus becomes an undercurrent in Yūsuf's later poetry, and only occasionally surfaces in an expansive singular image. In an existentialist mode, Yūsuf iterates the poet's quest for self-identity within a vastly changing cultural configuration. Past and present historical moments interweave, unveiling persistent themes of displacement, cultural syncretism, and the search for identity. What one finds in Yūsuf's later poems is a persistent preoccupation with the themes of crossing over borders and adapting to new cultural contexts.

As a whole, Yūsuf's poems are sensitive and penetrating notations of his changing attitudes toward displacement; poems that persistently negotiate the dialectical push-and-pull of a lost homeland, a negotiation that often evokes nostalgia and continued attachment to the homeland but also a willingness to open up to the uncharted possibilities of new surroundings. As a poet who reached his poetic maturity as an exile, Yūsuf expresses in his poems a subtle interior exploration of himself in the context of the exilic condition. Exile has become for Yūsuf the crucible in which he is able to examine questions of deracination, cultural dislocation, homesickness for an elusive home, the pain of loss or dispossession, and, ultimately, the reconfiguration of his identity, and his reintegration.

---

12 Ibid.
13 Ibid., 275, 280.

4 1964–1972: Early Poetry of Exile

In his early exile poems, Yūsuf gives evidence of the sort of poetic imagination—"nomadic, decentred, contrapuntal"—which Edward Said and others have identified as characteristic of the exile. Perched precariously between his memory of his homeland and an uncharted destination, Yūsuf dexterously charges the notions of alienation and dissociation with subtle and multifaceted connotations that are interrelated and interdependent. Mythology, history, world literature, and the visual arts all provide impetus for his poetry, as does the physical world itself in both its human and non-human aspects. From a temporal point of view, Yūsuf writes two types of exile poetry: instantaneous chronicles, an interiorized history of what he has most recently seen and experienced; and retrospective poetry, looking at events from the perspective of years. In each type, however, the thematics of home, homeland, refuge, and "knowing one's place" play a central role.

Like almost all narratives of exile, Yūsuf's are, perhaps by necessity, essentially autobiographical: the experience of exile is, in this stage, so overwhelming that writing about it becomes the only way to resist the void created by the state of displacement. The literary critic Trinh Minh-ha maintains that third-world writers "are condemned to write only autobiographical works,"[14] and in the case of Yūsuf's early exilic narratives, the predominant theme is indeed almost exclusively the poet's fragmented, displaced self. Through poems underpinned by associative memory, Yūsuf's early exilic narrative foregrounds the fragmentation and sense of discontinuity experienced by the immigrant in his daily life as it uncovers the varied facets of exile and the role of memory in easing the pain and turning the trauma of exilic loss into aesthetic gain.

"An intimate relation exists between exile and the role of memory in constructing an exilic identity," asserts Philip Schlesinger and, indeed, memory plays a decisive and crucial role in Yūsuf's early poetics of exile.[15] Many of his early exile poems can be seen as instances of the pressure of memory on poetic imagination under the influence of extraordinary psychic intensity. In his poem *Kalimāt shibh Khāṣṣa* (Quasi-private words), which he dedicates to his close contemporary, the exiled Iraqi poet and intellectual ʿAbd al-Majīd al-Rāḍī, he says:

---

14 Trinh T. Minh-ha, "Other than Myself/My Other Self," in *Travellers' Tales: Narratives of Home and Displacement*, eds. George Robertson et al (London and New York: Routledge, 1994), 10.

15 Philip Schlesinger, "W.G. Sebald and the Condition of Exile," *Theory, Culture & Society* 21/2 (2004): 46.

قد يقع الإنسان
في قبضة السجّان، أو في قبضة الأزهار
...
لكنني أريد أن أخبرك الليلة
وأنت لا تجهلني—
كنّا معا في ذلك البستان—
أريد أن أخبرك الليلة
بأنني في قبضة الذكرى:
سجين دونما سجّان

> One might fall
> into the hands of the jailor, or into the hands of the flowers
> ...
> But tonight I want to tell you,
> you, who knows me—
> we were together in that garden—
> tonight I want to tell you
> that I fell into the hands of memory:
> a prisoner without a jailor.[16]

For Yūsuf, nostalgia conveys historical change metaphorically and emotionally by signaling that something or someone is gone. It registers the past as past through a special form—a kind of second order or level—of remembrance. "Home," Seidel notes, "is locus, custom, memory, familiarity, ease, security, sanctuary. And centuries of tradition do not alter the power of home as an image."[17] Here, the poem centers on the power of memory to recover past states of existence, isolated and framed and glowing with their own life as well as with the emotion that has recalled them—something in the present moment that is shared with a past state.

Yūsuf's speaker implicitly states that psychological life is largely a matter of accumulating a sense of oneself over the years, against which we balance a sense of the present state of our awareness and the flashes of memory that recall to us who and where we have been in the past. When we are cut off from

16 Yūsuf, *al-Aʿmāl al-kāmila*, 1: 331.
17 Seidel, *Exile*, 10.

our accumulated self and its “vast structure of recollection,” to use Proust’s words, the resulting depression may be an acute sense of psychic disorder, where the distress comes from a momentary disordering of the relation of present and past. For Yūsuf, however, this depression will prove to be healthy and useful, exposing him to his own vulnerability so that he can reorient himself in sheer self-defense.

What is created in Yūsuf’s exile is not only a new space to exercise his being but a medium through which to reimagine his beginnings. His homeland’s landscapes, therefore, do not just exist; they are experienced via their construction in the imagination. Yūsuf is not unique in this sense, for, as Andrew Gurr observes, most exiled writers concentrate on reconstructing the homes they left behind.[18] This is given expression in Yūsuf’s poem *Marthiya* (An Elegy), which was written in Algeria shortly after the death of Badr Shākir al-Sayyāb, Iraq’s leading poet at the time. In it he dwells wistfully and reflectively upon his separation from his homeland, while reconstructing, iconographically, the idea and image of Jaykūr:

جيكور مطفأة كان الليل عانق ساكنيها
لا التوت في الأنهار يهبط، لا السماء تشفّ فيها

…

أيوب، في جيكور، ألقى عند قنطرة عصاه
وللحظتين تماوجت في عمق عينيه المياه
والخضرة البيضاء، والصفصاف …
يا عالمَ المتوحشين ذوي البنادق
حيث الحديث عن الورود سدى …
يا عالما يَهَبُ الحياةَ لموته
يهبُ المماتَ لصوته …
من يشتري جلد المسيح؟
إنّا سلخناهُ، فيا دنيا استريحي.

*

يا بيت جدي في دجى جيكور

18 Andrew Gurr, *Writers in Exile: The Identity of Home in Modern Literature* (Brighton: Harvester, 1981), 9.

يا نخل العراق
قبري وراء التل يستبق القيامة
في وحشة المنفى الأخير، وتستظل به حمامة.
والبرد يُرجفني:
عراق... عراق... ليس سوى العراق.

Jaykūr is turned off as if the night has embraced its dwellers
Neither the mulberries fall into the rivers nor is the sky reflected in them
…
Job, in Jaykūr, has thrown his cane near an arch
and for a minute, the water flared in the depth of his eyes
so did the white plants and the poplar trees …
O world of savages with guns
where every talk about roses is worthless
O world that offers life to its death
who offers death to its voice …
Who would buy the skin of Christ?
We have skinned him. O world, rest assured, then.
…
O grandfather's house in the darkness of Jaykūr
O, palm trees of Iraq
My grave behind the hill competes with doomsday
in the solitude of last exile, and under it, a dove seeks shade …
The cold makes me tremble:
Iraq … Iraq … nothing but Iraq.[19]

Gaston Bachelard's analysis of intimate space, *La poétique de l'espace*, posits home as the crucial site of one's intimate life, the refuge where memory and imagination serve to integrate life's experiences.[20] Yūsuf's portrait of his land of birth is searing in its honesty and seems to encapsulate better than anything else the pain of alienation from the nurturing comforts and bonds of home. The arrested, blocked sadness of his lines makes his readers share a death—the death not only of a person, but of an era. The poem is technically accomplished and verbally dexterous, but its primary impact is emotional. The

19 Yūsuf, *al-Aʿmāl al-kāmila*, 1: 436–438.
20 Gaston Bachelard, *La poétique de l'espace* (Paris: Quadrige, 1994), 5.

elegy, with its fitful alternation between tranquility and violence, violence and tranquility, bids for sentiment through its virtuosity. Despite the close relationship between Yūsuf and al-Sayyāb, the former does not allow his elegy to become maudlin.

By the time the poem was written, the poet was in exile, yet the main trappings of the scene depicted are drawn from his early poetry. The poet's memories revisit experiences of his childhood in Iraq while simultaneously exhibiting an emotional interaction between the writing self and the self recalled. The tutelary spirit behind the poem is surely al-Sayyāb. Jaykūr becomes for Yūsuf, as it was for al-Sayyāb, the center of a tangled skein of associations with disparate and intertwining strands. The above lines consist of direct intertextual references to several poems written by al-Sayyāb himself, mostly in his exile years, which depict the last harsh years in the life of this preeminent Iraqi poet: *Dār jaddī* (My grandfather's house), *Sifr Ayyūb* (The book of Job), *al-Masīḥ ba'da al-ṣalb* (Christ after crucifixion), *Madīnat Sindibād* (City of Sindbad), *Unshūdat al-maṭar* (Hymn to rain), and especially his celebrated poem *Gharīb 'alā al-Khalīj* (A stranger by the Gulf), which Yūsuf uses for his poem's closure. This is how al-Sayyāb expresses both his despair and his yearning for his homeland:

الريح تصرخ بي: عراق
والموج يعول بي: عراق، عراق، ليس سوى عراق ...
بين القرى المتهيبات خطاي والمدن الغريبه
غنيت تربتك الحبيبه،
وحملتها فأنا المسيح يجر في المنفى صليبه ...

The wind cries to me: Iraq.
The wave howls at me: Iraq. Iraq. Nothing but Iraq ...
Between villages timid of my footsteps and strange cities,
I sang your beloved soil
and I carried it—for I am Christ in exile dragging his cross.[21]

Yūsuf here intends to give a mirror-like description of his native soil—an unadorned, straightforward picture. Seidel contends that an "imaginative solution to the exile's anguish is to export just enough of the homeland to the outland to

21 Badr Shākir al-Sayyāb, *Dīwān Badr Shākir al-Sayyāb* (Beirut: Dār al-'Awda, 1971), 320–323.

metonymically purify it."[22] The complex relationship between "home-haunting" and "home-hunting" as expressed in Yūsuf's poem is connected to the politics of belonging that is negotiated in the liminal spaces of cultural passages. In this regard, re-homing means keeping cultural continuity elsewhere and engaging in a continuous effort to write home out of the dislocation of life. What we witness is a mixture of contradictory trends: on the one hand, the concept of home has been diluted in the modern world; but on the other, the desire for a home has been intensified more than ever. Exilic consciousness is hence predicated on an integrated process of home-haunting and home-hunting, in which the exiled poet may experience a radical discontinuity, but at the same time develop a desire for cultural reconnection—a kind of nostalgia for retrieving a home that has been lost in the past. Therefore, although absent from the cultural specificity of "this" moment, home is often retrieved or performed in the ambiguous mirror-space of recollection/reflection.

The poet's memory also responds to the exilic setting by eliciting acrid images from the past. Some of Yūsuf's exilic poems delineate not the past as past but as a living presence and the mutability of that present, its fluidity and flux. In the prefatory poem *Baʿīdan ʿan al-samāʾ al-ūla* (Distant from the first sky), Yūsuf draws upon the material imagery of rural southern Iraq and describes Jazīrat al-Ṣaqr, a small island in Shatt al-Arab, near his childhood home:

جزيرة الصقر!
أرى أكواخك الشهباء في المنفى
منخورة الأعواد، يلهو فوقهن الريح والماء
والشمس— كالتنور—حمراء
...
غابت، وأبقت بعدها للناس ما شاؤوا
الخبز والعتمة والداء

Jazīrat al-Ṣaqr!
I see your gray huts in exile,
their canes gnawed, wind and water play above them
and the sun—like a furnace—is red
...

22 Seidel, *Exile*, 10.

> It has gone down and left for the people what they want:
> bread, darkness and disease.[23]

The poet is aware that nostalgia always emerges from something that once possessed detail, time and place, out of localness; but the effects of nostalgia tend to dematerialize the original object or event, mythifying and enveloping it in an aura. In short, when desire and nostalgia overmaster vision, poetry risks sentimentality. Being aware of this pitfall, Yūsuf does not strive to beautify the past but rather to present it in all its unsightliness and cruelty. The poem obliquely addresses the issue of the *anamnesis* of history. In *anamnesis*, according to Plato in *Meno*, we have something which modernism articulated much later as a Proustian *souvenir involontaire*. In this, there is not so much a moment of knowledge of the past, but rather an actual recreation of the past, now fully present: it is, as it were, the actualization of the virtual.[24]

It is this process of "actualization" which is central to Yūsuf's poem. The speaker travels back in time "mixing memory and desire," to use T.S. Eliot's phrase. Yūsuf is fundamentally concerned with forging a history, with remembering, as a therapeutic—and political—act which aims to "suture" the wounds of exile. The poem is structured in such a way that only in the last lines does the sinister aspect of the village come clearly to the fore. It implicitly demands that the reader not view home as static. Traveling between two spaces may suggest a paradoxical re-homing process between two cultural locations, whereas the home left behind can be found and founded again before us. Therefore, the process of traveling itself, as Sara Ahmed notes, "involves a reliving of the home," for movement is "the very way in which the migrant subject inhabits the space of home."[25] The protagonist's feeling is conveyed without threadbare sentimentality or pathos. There is no nostalgia for the innocence of childhood, no mere sentimental recollection. As with other exiled Iraqi poets, Yūsuf's "passion of the past"—to use a term coined by Tennyson to describe his lost, Edenic childhood—is neither blind nor naïve.[26] The then and the now serve not to promote misty-eyed reminiscence, but to foster a quiet contemplation of what it means to live in exile in general and by what events the poet's life has been determined in particular. This is how Michael Seidel expounds this notion:

---

23 Yūsuf, *al-Aʿmāl al-kāmila*, 1: 329.

24 Jacob Klein, *A Commentary on Plato's* Meno (Chicago: University of Chicago Press, 1989), 111; George Poulet, *Proustian Space* (Baltimore: Johns Hopkins University Press, 1977).

25 Sara Ahmed, "Home and Away: Narratives of Migration and Estrangement," *International Journal of Cultural Studies* 2 (1999): 344.

26 Saadi Simawe, "Fawzi Karim: 15 Poems," *Banipal* 19 (2004): 79.

> Exile inaugurates, the long way around, the redemption of individual souls [...] Often in the exilic fable the home place is destroyed, rendered illegitimate, contaminated, or taken over by conquerors or rival claimants. Without a native place recognized as secure, home territory itself is invalidated for those forced to remain behind in it. Thus, those in exile are saving remnants; they imagine in new surroundings the conditions that existed before the trauma that necessitated their displacement.[27]

5 The Later Exile Poetry

What constitutes the true originality in Yūsuf's later output is the combined sensation of strangeness and at-homeness which the poems create. In his later output, it is clear that Yūsuf favors the pole of "counter-exile," where poetic language acquires a sufficient level of allegory and metaphor and the local is transcended. Talking about his situation as an artist in extended exile, Yūsuf formulates the core of his creativity:

> [In exile, the poet] either shows fidelity to his heritage and his native land or, when time goes by, takes his material from the "other land" he lives in. That is, he is no longer dependent upon remembrance and longing.[28]
>
> I think of myself now as a poet who is a resident of the world. I don't feel exiled. Being outside my country has become my ordinary life. I am used to it. I feel at home wherever I am [...] I have to establish real contact with the country I am in, with the people and with the environment. I have to grasp daily life in its details and minutiae. That is how I write poetry. The details and minutiae are my raw material. I am not conditioning myself to do that; it is direct, honest contact with people, culture, with nature. It is a kind of open receptivity to the world, to the universe.[29]

Writing about his mental accommodation to exile in the later period, Yūsuf resolutely states that:

> In exile, the poet should become a local citizen. He should establish a relationship with his surroundings, with the natural sights, the people, and the language. He should establish a new spiritual balance or else he

27 Seidel, *Exile*, 8.

28 Saʿdī Yūsuf, "Interview with Saʿdī Yūsuf," *al-Waṭan* (August 21, 2003): 14.

29 Saʿdī Yūsuf, "I Have Trained Myself Hard to be Free," *Banipal* 20 (2004): 8–9.

> will lose the opportunity to go on living on the face of the earth and fall into madness, become deathly ill or commit suicide.[30]

Indeed, the later Yūsuf suggests in his poems a resident rather than a traveler or visitor. He seems to absorb more, to have been "there"—wherever "there" may be—a long time. He stands guard against the encroaching, overwhelming power of exile and from this eventuates some of the most piercing, unexpected, and vital poetry he has written. What is striking, and satisfying, about reading the later works is how well Yūsuf holds his own, and how firmly he transforms the topic he masters—how his best poems maintain themselves in passion without lacking a strict informing intelligence. What is also important to note about Yūsuf's later poems is that the poet is artistically extending his range and manipulating his material with greater skill and sophistication.

The literature of counter-exile described by Guillén relates to Deleuze and Guattari's concept of deterritorialization: if a text has transcended connections to place or native origin, then it has become deterritorialized. According to their view, deterritorialized texts are characterized by a repression of desire through the taming and confining of its productive energies.[31] The finding of the self through place becomes in Yūsuf's later poetry one of his most characteristic inventions. When asked about the way he benefited from his exilic experience, Yūsuf replied:

> I've benefited from exile in the sense that it has helped me resist my longing for my homeland [...]. The element of longing was very obvious in my works, but later I found out that the element of longing was turning into a pathological phenomenon. Since an artist must be balanced—mentally, psychologically, and cognitively—he should overcome anything that impedes this balance. I had to overpower my longing or my nostalgia, and I believe that I somehow managed to do so. Then there is a second reason why one should overpower one's longing: the text that I write is based on place. Place, therefore, is present in everything that I write. It is the foundation, whereas longing deprives you of the place, takes you to an imaginary place, which means that you will never be able to make yourself an inhabitant of the place you are in. So even if I am a peripatetic person, the text does not wander: it needs a tangible and discernible ground. For me, this is the morality of the text, its relationship with the place.[32]

---

30 Saʿdī Yūsuf, *Khaṭawāt al-Kanghar* (Damascus: Dār al-Madā, 1997), 120.

31 Gilles Deleuze and Felix Guattari, *Anti-Oedipus*, trans. Mark Hurley, Mark Seem, and Helen R. Lane (New York: Viking Press, 1977).

32 Saʿdī Yūsuf, "Muqābala maʿa Saʿdī Yūsuf," *al-Quds* (March 30, 2005): 10.

Yūsuf's later exile poetry does in fact start from a radical openness to the outer world, an openness which carries its own special danger. The poet is aware that refusing to incur that peril is tantamount to succumbing to mediocre versifying, since lyrical expression requires the hard-won and easily lost determination that Paul Tillich called "the courage to be." The later poems are rich with geographical and literary texture, which supports and gives body to the meditation that forms the main strand of the poem. These poems allow him to negotiate between his often idiosyncratic local observations, autobiographical moments, and putatively universal philosophical claims.

Clearly Yūsuf's approach undermines claims by other exiled artists to a natural connection between strong cultural identity and geographic location. His later approach deconstructs the semantic identity place unit and asserts that writers can also be "at home" when living in different, changing physical surroundings. In this context, the theoretical distinction made between place and space is helpful.[33] Place has been defined as the actual locality where people live or, in other words, the material surroundings through which they physically move during their daily routine. Space, by contrast, is "the general idea people have of where things should be in physical and cultural relation to each other."[34] In other words, space is a mental picture instead of a particular locality. Anthony Giddens also claims that in late modernity, writers' self-perception is no longer limited by identity-place discourses. He argues that

> while the milieu in which people live quite often remains the source of local attachment, place does not form the parameter of experience, and it does not offer the security of the ever-familiar which traditional locales characteristically display.[35]

Reading Yūsuf's later poetry, there can be no doubt that the poet is developing rapidly, seeking out new attitudes, mastering new subtleties of technique, responding to experience with that adaptability both as man and as poet which distinguishes the genuine artist from the talented pedant.

Yūsuf's joining Palestinian forces in Beirut and his active participation in the combat against the Israeli army marks the beginning of this new chapter in his life, personally and poetically. With the dread of war, in the poet's eyes, there coexisted a compelling attraction—the exhilaration of a new sort

33 Akhil Gupta and James Ferguson, "Beyond 'Culture': Space, Identity and the Politics of Difference," in *Cultural Anthropology* 7/1 (1992): 6–23; Anthony Giddens, *Modernity and Self-Identity* (Cambridge: Polity Press, 1991).

34 Donnan Hastings and Thomas Wilson, *Borders: Frontiers of Identity, Nation and State* (Oxford and New York: Berg Publishers, 1999), 9.

35 Giddens, *Modernity*, 146–147.

of self-knowledge, a transformation into the changelessness of a "final," permanent self. Paradoxically, it is the act of fighting alongside the Palestinian forces in a foreign land that initiated the shift in Yūsuf's poetics of exile, which proved indeed to have been the starting point for the actuation of the "counter-exile" poetics and a crucial turning point in the poet's exilic consciousness.[36] From the start, Yūsuf devoted himself to the objective reality around him. Hence, his war poems have the freshness and authenticity of personal reactions. War poems, as a principle, insist on an intimacy with often appalling personal experience, and confront readers with what the critic Paul Fussel has termed "actual and terrible moral changes."[37]

During the 1982 war, Yūsuf indeed felt compelled to grapple more openly with the fierce subject of war's brutalities. To plunge into the eye of the storm—the fighting itself—required the use of strong and new imaginative devices. The lyric poet's unflinching look at the horror that he sees around him opens up a new kind of poetry for him: instead of seeing the war as accidental, Yūsuf views it as part of the vast tragic pattern of life. As in the best tradition of war poetry, Yūsuf uses the situation of war and its attendant horrors to branch out to new poetic existential vistas.

Yūsuf speaks of imagination as the most intensive province of pleasure and pain and defines it as a creative power of the mind, representing the images of things in the order and manner in which they were received by the senses or combining them in a new manner and according to a different order. In his poem *Ilā Hāshim Shafīq* (To Hāshim Shafīq), dedicated to the exiled Iraqi poet, Yūsuf reasserts his confidence in the poetic act and in the rehabilitating power of the mind against the encroaching nature of exile:

ستكون "بلد"
يوماً، عاصمة الدنيا ...
وستبني أنتَ
—أنت الذاهل في مدن الغيتو
ساحاتٍ
وبساتينَ
وأكواخاً من سعف وجذوعٍ

36 Yāsīn al-Naṣīr, "Udabā' 'Irāqiyyūn: Sa'dī Yūsuf," *al-Nahrayn* 30 (2002): 17.

37 Paul Fussel, "War Poetry: The Great War to Vietnam," *Anglia Polytechnic University Bulletin* (14 May 1966): 2.

وستسكنها
لتكونَ، ولو نبتتْ في أوراق الدفتر،
عاصمة الدنيا.
...
من يبني عاصمةً للشاعر
غير الشاعر

You will be "a city"
one day, the capital of the world ...
you will build
—you, the befuddled who wanders in the cities of ghettos—
squares,
gardens
and huts made out of palm fronds and trunks.
You will inhabit it
and become, if only inside the leaves of a notebook,
the capital of the world.
...
Who builds a capital for the poet
if not the poet himself?[38]

Indeed, "writing," as Theodor Adorno notes in his much celebrated *Minima Moralia*, eventually "becomes a place to live." Artistic writing becomes the poet's new homeland and displacement—an important factor in his aesthetic make-up.[39] That is almost exactly what Seamus Heaney means by "redress" when he discusses the purpose of poetry: it is "the imagination pressing back against the pressure of reality."[40]

> In the activity of poetry too, there is a tendency to place counter-reality on the scales—a reality which may be only imagined but which nevertheless has weight because it is imagined within the gravitational pull of the actual and can therefore hold its own and balance out against the

---

38 Yūsuf, *al-Aʿmāl al-kāmila*, 1: 83–84.

39 Theodor Adorno, *Minima Moralia: Reflections on a Damaged Life*, trans. E.F.N. Jephcott (London: Verso, 1974), 87.

40 Seamus Heaney, *The Redress of Poetry* (London: Faber and Faber, 1995), 1.

> historical situation. This redressing effect of poetry comes from its being a glimpsed alternative, a revelation of potential that is denied or threatened by circumstances [...] The creative spirit remains positively recalcitrant in face of the negative evidence, reminding the indicative mood of history that it has been written in by force and written in over the good optative mood of human potential.[41]

In this spirit, Yūsuf's later exilic verse strives to emphasize the freedom won in the act of writing in the face of the onslaughts of time. This is how he chooses to open his poem *al-Ḥurriyya* (Freedom):

وحدك، أنت الحر
تختار سماء فتسميها
وسماء تسكن فيها
وسماء ترفضها...

Alone, you are free
You choose a sky and name it,
a sky to dwell in,
and a sky to reject.[42]

Yūsuf seems to hold out the possibility that the act of writing itself provides a kind of asylum for the displaced artist, and indeed there is something alleviating, something of a solacing and assuaging power, visible in Yūsuf's exilic writings. Writing, in Yūsuf's eyes, is an act which commits the poet to the moral responsibility of ordering the harsh absurdity of existence and replacing it with the text of resistance and its condition of exile. By pitting human resources against the recalcitrant and the inhuman, by setting the positive effort of the mind against the desolations of historical violence, and by synthesizing his perception and expression, a truly creative writer can transfigure his surroundings. Yūsuf's exile poems, with their vivid images of fractured life, of fortitude in the face of hopeless odds, do possess the authentic touch of poetry. They produce a "story" which stands firmly in its own right and yet is rich in universal significance.

41 Ibid., 3, 24.
42 Yūsuf, *al-Aʿmāl al-kāmila*, 3: 462.

Bibliography

Adorno, Theodor. *Minima Moralia: Reflections from Damaged Life*. Trans. E.F.N. Jephcott. London: Verso, 1974.

Ahmed, Sara. "Home and Away: Narratives of Migration and Estrangement," *International Journal of Cultural Studies* 2 (1999): 329–47.

Bachelard, Gaston. *La poétique de l'espace*. Paris: Quadrige, 1994.

Deleuze, Gilles and Felix Guattari. *Anti-Oedipus*. Trans. Mark Hurley, Mark Seem, and Helen R. Lane. New York: Viking Press, 1977.

Fussel, Paul. "War Poetry: The Great War to Vietnam," *Anglia Polytechnic University Bulletin*, May 14, 1966: 2–15.

Giddens, Anthony. *Modernity and Self Identity*. Cambridge: Polity Press, 1991.

Guillén, Claudio. "The Writer in Exile or the Literature of Exile and Counter-Exile," *Books Abroad* 50 (1976): 271–80.

Gupta, Akhil and James Ferguson. "Beyond 'Culture': Space, Identity and the Politics of Difference," *Cultural Anthropology* 7/1 (1992): 6–23.

Gurr, Andrew. *Writers in Exile: The Identity of Home in Modern Literature*. Brighton: Harvester, 1981.

Hamil, Mustapha. "Exile and its Discontents," *Research in African Literatures* 35/1 (Spring, 2004), 52–65.

Hastings, Donnan and Thomas Wilson. *Borders: Frontiers of Identity, Nation and State*. Oxford and New York: Berg Publishers, 1999.

Heaney, Seamus. *The Redress of Poetry*. London: Faber & Faber, 1995.

Klein, Jacob. *A Commentary on Plato's Meno*. Chicago: University of Chicago Press, 1989.

Kristeva, Julia. *Strangers to Ourselves*. New York: Columbia University Press, 1991.

Miłosz, Czesław. "On Exile," *Parabola* 18/2 (1993): 25–30.

Minh-ha, Trinh T. "Other than Myself/My Other Self," in *Travellers' Tales: Narratives of Home and Displacement*, edited by George Robertson et al. London and New York: Routledge, 1994, 9–26.

Al-Naṣīr, Yāsīn. "Udabā' 'Irāqiyyūn: Sa'dī Yūsuf," *al-Nahrayn* 30 (2002): 15–20.

Poulet, George. *Proustian Space*. Baltimore: Johns Hopkins University Press, 1977.

Rogoff, Irit. "In the Empire of the Object," in *Outsider Art: Contesting Boundaries in Contemporary Culture*, edited by Vera L. Zolberg and Joni Maya Cherbo. Cambridge: Cambridge University Press, 1997, 159–171.

Rushdie, Salman. *Imaginary Homelands: Essays and Criticism 1981–1991*. London: Granta Books, 1991.

Sayad, Abdel Malek. "A Land of No Return." *The UNESCO Courier* 17 (1996): 10–11.

Al-Sayyāb, Badr Shākir. *Dīwān Badr Shākir al-Sayyāb*. Beirut: Dār al-'Awda, 1971.

Schlesinger, Philip. "W.G. Sebald and the Condition of Exile," *Theory, Culture & Society* 21/2 (2004): 43–76.

Seidel, Michael. *Exile and the Narrative Imagination*. New Haven and London: Yale University Press, 1986.
Simawe, Saadi. "Fawzi Karim: 15 Poems," *Banipal* 19 (2004): 79–88.
Yūsuf, Saʿdī. *al-Aʿmāl al-kāmila*. Damascus: Dār al-Madā, 1995. 6 vols.
Yūsuf, Saʿdī. *Khaṭawāt al-Kanghar*. Damascus: Dār al-Madā, 1997.
Yūsuf, Saʿdī. "Interview with Saʿdī Yūsuf," in *al-Waṭan* (August 21, 2003): 13–18.
Yūsuf, Saʿdī. "I Have Trained Myself Hard to Be Free," *Banipal* 20 (2004): 2–14.
Yūsuf, Saʿdī. "Muqābala maʿa Saʿdī Yūsuf," *al-Quds* (March 30, 2005): 10–14.

Intertextuality in Samīḥ al-Qāsim's Poetry: A Philosophy of Blending

Ibrahim Taha

1 Introduction

Samīḥ al-Qāsim (1939–2014) published more than seventy books in various literary genres between 1958 and 2014, including over fifty poetry collections. The major political, ideological, intellectual, and cultural themes addressed by al-Qāsim in his poetry can be classified into five main clusters. These are: (1) the individual/personal core: Samīḥ al-Qāsim's political affiliation, his activity in the communist party, jail, house arrest, dismissal from work, death threats, and the like; (2) the Palestinian minority core: the Palestinian minority's suffering in Israel at the hands of an oppressive, hostile regime; land confiscation; and various racist policies; (3) the Palestinian core in general: the impact of the 1967 War on the beginning of the Palestinian people's transition from the idea of Arab to Palestinian nationalism; (4) the Arab core: the proliferation of Arab nationalism in the 1960s and the impact of the 1973 War; (5) the global core: the universal orientation, world liberation movements, and the "cold" clash between imperialism and socialism.

All of these interacted in shaping the overall creative experience of Samīḥ al-Qāsim's poetry for more than half a century. As they were particularly noticeable in the three parts comprising his trilogy *al-Ḥamāsa* (Sensation), I deem it a model of *qaṣīdat al-maqām*, which might be freely translated as "the context poem." This is a more general and comprehensive term than the familiar expression *shiʿr al-munāsaba* ("occasional poetry"), with its negative connotations. This does not mean that literature can never escape its historical or cultural context. However, what we are referring to here in particular is the impact of the specific context and its marked dominance at all levels of the writing process, including stylistic and aesthetic devices. While al-Qāsim was preoccupied with historical and political circumstances in the 1960s and 1970s, in the following three decades he gradually tried to emancipate himself from the powerful control of history by viewing the context from his self-experience. At this stage, al-Qāsim was preoccupied with all senses and aspects of history: politics, culture, and society, many of which were connected to the question of national identity and hence to his own identity.

 | DOI:10.1163/9789004459120_008

We can in fact reduce the above-mentioned five themes to a more compact three-cluster classification, as reflected in his latest collections of poems: (1) the individual; (2) the nation (the Palestinian people and the Arab world); and (3) humanity. These three clusters mix and interact through four specific tools: trustee, collage, intertextuality, and reincarnation/transmigration. In his later collections, Al-Qāsim combined individual and universal concerns into one distinctive mixture. He strongly believed that "there is room for all people in the universe":

في الكون متّسع لكلّ الناس .لا تسأل بما بدأ الجوابْ!
في الكون متّسع لكلّ الناس .والأشياء .والأسماء.

There is room for all people in the universe. Do not ask how the answer started!
There is room for all people, things and names in the universe.[1]

His "individual concerns," namely a deep awareness of the critical state of his health three years before his death in 2014, dominate the overall themes as they appear in two latter collections, increasing his frequent use of a trustee to include his people, not only his own relatives. In many poems in these more recent collections, trusteeship is not confined only to his sons and grandsons and is not associated with a mournful attitude. Here, at this very point, the self is tightly connected to the other, children with parents, past with future, "here" with "there." In the following paragraph, al-Qāsim literally urged his people to become an integral part of all other peoples:

وردتي نجمة في الظلام
حجري وردة للسلام
وكلامي مصير الكلام
فاحفظوا سرّ زيتونتي
واحرسوا سرّ سنبلتي
واكرزوا في جميع الأنام

1 Samīḥ al-Qāsim, *Hīrmāfrūdītūs wa-qaṣā'id ukhrā* (Amman: Wizārat al-Thaqāfa, 2012), 45.

My rose is a star in the darkness
My stone is a rose for peace
And my words are the fate of words;
So, keep the secret of my olive-tree,
Guard the secret of my spike,
And preach to the whole of mankind.[2]

Collage, which became the collective title of Samīḥ al-Qāsim's three collections, confirms the technical cohesion achieved by the trustee. Originally, *Collage* was an act of "cut and paste" that produced a rich mosaic mesh. Al-Qāsim was supposedly the first writer to transfer this technique of fine arts, which Picasso also used in his drawings and paintings, to Arabic poetry. By using the technique of collage, al-Qāsim sought to link different styles, classic and modern, to connect ideas and emphasize cohesion and extension.[3]

Intertextuality and allusion are techniques frequently used by al-Qāsim in his poetry, most specifically in his latest collections. There is no need to mention modern poetry's reliance on these techniques. Al-Qāsim made intensive and comprehensive use of historical events and universal figures. While it is true that Islamic-Arab culture dominated his intertextualities, he also made intensive use of elements found in other civilizations. He viewed modernism as a technique to help achieve some sort of universal cohesion and comprehensive unity throughout the world. We understand modernism in al-Qāsim's poetry in this sense, namely as a set of signs based on absorption and re-drafting and reached through various devices of intertextuality. If not so, then what is the purpose of intertextuality? Is it not to create a situation of "mosaic," or shall we say "a spider's web?" Intertextuality in al-Qāsim's poetry was used not to enrich meanings, but to confirm the cohesion of civilizations, generations, peoples, times, and places. In this sense, al-Qāsim did not use figures or icons from worldwide culture as neutral masks, but became fully identified with them, adapting them and turning them into meaningful components of his own identity. Therefore, his are not poems of masks, but of reincarnation, and are much more profound and more accurate than the traditional type of mask poetry. When al-Qāsim used the skull mentioned by the pre-Islamic poet al-Shanfarā (d. 525), he in fact aimed at recalling the famous *Lāmiyya* poem and its aesthetic values and cultural norms. Incidentally, al-Shanfarā's *Lāmiyya* is also called "The Desert's Poem." Desert and al-Shanfarā are recurring motifs in al-Qāsim's poetry:

2 Samīḥ al-Qāsim, *Kūlāj 3* (Beirut: al-Mu'assasa al-ʿArabiyya li'l-Dirāsāt wa'l-Nashr, 2012), 84.
3 See specifically his collection *Kūlāj 3* (*Collage 3*).

تلك جمجمتي
تلك جمجمة الشنفرى
تشتهي بعدُ أن تثأرا
من عبيدٍ وسادوا
وعبيدٍ عبيدْ.

That is my skull,
That is al-Shanfarā's skull,
It still desires to take revenge
On slaves who reigned
And slaves who remained slaves.[4]

Through this sophisticated intertextuality, al-Qāsim sought to adopt al-Shanfarā's skull to enhance his own poetry and enrich it. The story of al-Shanfarā was based on three central values espoused by al-Qāsim: the fight against injustice, especially if perpetrated by one's relatives; challenge and resistance, that is, the individual's courage to face the collective; and the fight against displacement in its political meaning, based on a deep belief in higher values. As is probably known, al-Shanfarā's skull was an eminent symbol of the right of people—even dead people—to live. Another type of mask in al-Qāsim's poetry is what we call the partial mask. Moving from al-Shanfarā to Hamlet, al-Qāsim's saying, "I am the Arab Hamlet," in fact indicated his wish to use Hamlet as a partial mask, in the same manner he had previously used al-Shanfarā:

هاملت العربيُّ أنا..
تلك جمجمتي
في أكفِّ العبادْ
وعلى كلِّ فمْ
غيمة من حليب ودمْ
في سؤالي المعادْ
هملت العربيُّ أنا

4 Samīḥ al-Qāsim, *Khadhalatnī al-ṣaḥārā* (Nazareth: Manshūrāt Iḍā'āt, 1998), 24–25.

غائبٌ في حضوري هنا
حاضرٌ في غيابي هُنا

I am the Arab Hamlet
That is my skull
In the palms of people,
And on every mouth
A cloud of milk and blood
In my repeated question
I am the Arab Hamlet,
Absent in my presence here
And present in my absence here![5]

Al-Qāsim thus blended various iconic figures from a variety of cultures to draw our attention to some similarity between al-Shanfarā and Hamlet. Both were aggrieved by their relatives, so that their stories are centered on a similar perspective. The use of different icons from different cultures, such as al-Shanfarā and Hamlet, for instance, confirms al-Qāsim's deep belief in interconnectivity and interaction between civilizations.

According to al-Qāsim's Druze faith, reincarnation/transmigration allowed this kind of mobility, and al-Qāsim used this concept to tear down walls and reopen borders. It is through such passages that generations become intertwined and grandsons ultimately become grandfathers:

يا أيها الجدُّ المجدَّدُ والمخلَّدُ
في الولدْ
غدكَ الحياةُ إلى الحياةِ
إلى الحياةِ
إلى الأبدْ..

O recreated forefather,
The immortalized one in his son,
Your tomorrow is life into life
Into life
Forever![6]

5 Ibid., 52–53.
6 Samīḥ al-Qāsim, *Muqaddimat Ibn Muḥammad li-ru'ā NūstrāSamīḥdāmūs: 111 ru'yā fī 111 thulāthiyya* (Nazareth: al-Ḥakīm, 2006), 22.

The idea of reincarnation/transmigration/adaptation was what made al-Qāsim, especially in his later collections, an ephemeral creature, unsettled, open, changeable, and movable. It is like a game of appearance and disappearance that eventually ends with a new quest:

ظهرت وغبت
وعدت ظهرت وغبت
وعدت ظهرت لأصرخ حبًا وخوفًا وحزنًا.

I appeared and disappeared,
And reappeared and disappeared,
And reappeared to cry out love, fear and sadness.[7]

In this sense, the major themes addressed in his poetry, as specified above, became one entity, the individual blending with the national and the universal. Through the merging of these three circles, al-Qāsim introduced his modified version of modernism, formulating a holistic, dynamic vision.

In this study I shall focus on the most prominent element in this process of blending, namely intertextuality, through which al-Qāsim reached a sort of reincarnation/transmigration, especially in his collection *Muqaddimat Ibn Muḥammad li-ruʾā NūstrāSamīḥdāmūs: 111 ruʾyā fī 111 thulāthiyya* (An Introduction of Ibn Muḥammad to NostraSamīḥdamus' visions: 111 visions in 111 trios). Good literature aims to transcend the constraints of standard language and to challenge it as its main source of meaning. Unlike the traditional use of figurative language in classical Arabic poetry, including its figurative and rhetoric implications, modern poetic language itself is no longer the only player in the process of semiotizing poetry.

2 The Intertextual System

Broadly speaking, through its massive use of allusions, references, citations, and cultural icons, al-Qāsim's collection operates as a hypertext. The intertextual system, which the entire collection is based on, has two communication activities: major interactive references to the well-known prophecies of the French physician and astrological consultant Nostradamus (1503–1566); and

7 Samīḥ al-Qāsim, *Hawājis li-ṭuqūs al-aḥfād* (Beirut: al-Muʾassasa al-ʿArabiyya li'l-Dirāsāt wa'l-Nashr, 2012), 50.

minor interactive references, specifically to the Qur'an and to universal culture in general. At the time that al-Qāsim produced this collection, the cumulative interdependence between modern and postmodern Arabic poetry and global culture had become commonplace and primarily aimed to attain two major objectives, as al-Qāsim did as well: namely to show the inability of contemporary cultural achievements, with all their creative abundance, to follow up on the rapid flow of reality; and to enrich the present and link it with both the past and the future. To al-Qāsim, this seemed precisely the best way to reconcile civilizations based on a humanitarian approach and to induce them to create a new, cohesive culture. He strongly believed that the traditional divisions between East and West, South and North, black and white, and the like ensured a clash of cultures.

The objective of a widespread use of an Arab, Islamic, global legacy through various intertextual activities was not to document history, but to express the concerns of the moment. Intertextuality was meant to make global history an individual concern. Throughout his collection, Al-Qāsim attempted to blend his own consciousness with that attributed to Nostradamus. In this sense, Nostradamus's forecasts served as a transparent mask that indeed, did not conceal the poet's face. On the contrary, it made it highly visible. It was a widespread belief that the significance of objects principally lay in their ability to do the jobs they were originally meant to do. So in poetry, masks are aesthetically created to disguise the real poet and offer her/him an alternative identity, commonly termed a persona.

Al-Qāsim, however, did not use Nostradamus's mask to achieve this mission; on the contrary, he viewed this iconic mask as a tool he could use to clarify his arguments. As is plainly evident from the title of the collection, al-Qāsim evenly split the name "Nostradamus" into two parts, "Nostra" and "Damus," and inserted his own first name in between. The way al-Qāsim interposed his first name within Nostradamus's surname evidently displayed his need to capitalize on someone else, so that he would be able to boldly expose his own views. In this collection, he seemed to have started from the very end of mask-making. Again, he defined both identities, his own and that of the iconic mask, so that the reader could pursue a compound study of comparisons and interviews.

It is generally believed that modernism in poetry essentially stemmed from two parallel powers: deconstruction and reconstruction. If the aesthetic value of a literary work is frequently measured by the extent of its ability to violate ordinary aesthetic conventions, the collection under discussion quite clearly "destroys" two constant familiar laws. In this collection, al-Qāsim consciously—or unconsciously—demolished two conventions until recently considered a major part of any modern poem. First, the poet's quest to hide her/his real identity, name, feelings, and views behind a neutral spokesperson, that is, some type of mask or persona; and second, her or his quest to take great advantage of an external mask, icon, or figure to represent her/him in some particular way.

Violating the first convention, i.e. involving his real first name in the very title of the collection and throughout the poems, al-Qāsim seemed intent on *not* hiding behind an artificial mask, but rather exposing his true identity and articulating his own views. Thus, he interlinked reality and art in a way that confirmed the interdependence of successive times, historical events, and the interconnectedness of humanity. In the second instance of rule breaking, al-Qāsim did not veil the identity of the external mask, namely Nostradamus. On the contrary, he patently exposed him, tightly merging their real names. Dropping all possible partitions between their real names, timem and space meant that past, present, and future were closely intertwined. In so doing, al-Qāsim reaffirmed that history seemingly moves in a circular path. In this sense he did his best to escape from the image of the narrow ideological poet. In fact, he made every endeavor to demonstrate his universal concern for all human beings. He commented on the interconnectivity of time, so that the past became part of the present and the future. In this sense, Nostradamus was not merely a historical figure or icon: he clearly meant to say something about our present conduct as human beings.

A brief comparison of al-Qāsim's collection of poetry with Nostradamus's book has produced substantial differences. The most important ones are the following:

Samīḥ al-Qāsim	Nostradamus
Visions	Prophecies
Trios	Fourfold paragraphs
111 visions	100 prophecies (forecasts)

Samīḥ al-Qāsim preferred to employ the term "vision," which he associated with Islamic legacy and thought, not because he had suddenly become religious, but because vision sounded much more poetic than prophecy. Attached to meanings of intuition is the ability to "maneuver" his vision, which is much more open and indirect than prophecies. "Prophecies" sounds less poetic, immediate, direct, or stable. However, visions in al-Qāsim's collection were based on both past and present facts, and as such they could perhaps produce personal predictions about a possible future. Thus, visions are tools for blending past, present, and future. Prophecies, on the other hand, bring up the future on the basis of personal conjecture, speculation, and charlatanism.

Visions, like dreams, are attached to some sort of conscious and deliberate act of planning. In this sense, visions—widely used in this collection—reflect reality, which enabled al-Qāsim to expand and deepen his ideological thinking.

Trisecting his collection in a way that curtailed irrelevant verbosity, al-Qāsim in fact used a minimum of language to express his intellectual messages. Traditionally, trisecting has many religious associations. In this collection, al-Qāsim "communicated" with Nostradamus's mask in a way that substantially changed Nostradamus's forecasts. The number 111 in the collection's title was the outcome of a dialogue between the Qur'an and Nostradamus's book. All sections in the latter were divided into units of one hundred years (centuries). Al-Qāsim mixed one hundred years with the prostrating eleven planets mentioned in the well-known vision of the prophet Yūsuf, introduced in the Qur'an, so that we get a total of 111, as evinced in the title. These three major changes exposed the poet's wish to challenge the intertextualized mask of Nostradamus and to introduce a modified version in which he sounded more reasonable, at least in his own eyes.

3 Philosophy of Blending

Samīḥ al-Qāsim took advantage of the books of the medieval clairvoyant to illustrate his distrust of people's tendency to use denial and anger as defense mechanisms against everyday realities. The starting point of al-Qāsim's visions was his fury towards people and their fear, despair, and total dependence on Nostradamus's fake forecasts. In his passion, al-Qāsim fervently unified reality and poetry, and perhaps established some sort of unanimity between himself, as a cultural entity, and history. However, unlike in the second part of his collection, where al-Qāsim made use of various devices of direct vocabulary and linguistic expressions, in the first section, he patently used indirect allusions and symbolic statements. Granting poetic language the power and authority to convey "the whole truth and nothing but the truth" may burden the general infrastructure of a text, in which language constitutes only one cornerstone of poetry's mechanisms.

Through his use of word and deed, language and formal structure, al-Qāsim expressed many of his beliefs as he made reference to a universal heritage. In this collection, he illustrated that poetics greatly depended on formal and structural components rather than on direct vocabulary, so that its message rested on much guesswork. On this basis of this assumption, he seemed to divide his writings into two major sections: the introduction of Ibn Muḥammad, and Nostradamus's forecasts. In the latter, al-Qāsim's mission is to uncover and clarify Nostradamus's forecasts—an enterprise which al-Qāsim obviously rejected. As clarified earlier, the name "Samīḥ," or "Ibn Muḥammad" as it appears in the title of the collection, links "Nostra" and "Damus." This unique form of interconnection between two figures evidently meant to extend times, places, and cultures, to reopen borders and try to blend cultures, as clearly expressed in vision 75:

في المشهد الأخيرِ،
من رواية الزمانْ
تختلط الأعراق والألوانْ
وبعدُ
لا يُسأل عن أسلافه إنسانْ.

In the last scene
Of the Time-tale,
Races and colors intermix,
And afterwards,
No man is asked about his ancestors.[8]

This extension did not necessarily signify a state of harmony and naïve agreement. The philosophy of blending, on the basis of five essential forms, functions as an intellectual mediator between poet and audience. These forms of mixing include:

1. Names: Samīḥ and Nostradamus (at the level of verbal overlap between names), as exemplified in the title of the collection and in vision 111:

رؤيا رؤى نوستراسميحداموس،
على متاهة الزمان والمكان
ينتصر الله على الشيطان
ويبعث الإنسان في الإنسان
ويولد الإنسان للإنسان
ويفرح الإنسان بالإنسان.

8 Al-Qāsim, *Muqaddimat Ibn Muḥammad*, 117.

NostraSamīḥdamus's vision of visions
About the labyrinth of Time and Space;
God overcomes Satan,
Man is resurrected in Man
And Man is born for Man
And Man rejoices with Man.[9]

2. Figures and functions: Between the real poet al-Qāsim and his persona, and between al-Qāsim and his "mask," namely Nostradamus, and eventually between reality and poetry. To illustrate such forms of mixing, the poet referred to himself as "Ibn Muḥammad":

فاهدأ .وخذ حمّامك الليليّ في أضواءِ نجمتك الوديعهْ
واهنأ بما تهب الطبيعهْ
ستعود من هذا الزبدْ
ستعود يا ابن محمّدٍ رؤيا لآلئك البديعهْ

Relax, and take your night shower in the lights of your meek star,
Enjoy what Nature bestows on you,
They will return from this foam,
O Muḥammad's Son, the vision of your marvelous pearls will return![10]

In some places, al-Qāsim explicitly invoked his first real name, "Samīḥ":

أقرأ في الوديانِ والسهولِ،
والتلال والجبالِ
من عالمنا الفسيحْ:
عاش هنا لبرهةٍ مسيحْ
مات هنا لبرهةٍ سميحْ..

I read in the valleys and the plains,
On the hills and the mountains
Of our vast universe:

9 Ibid., 153.
10 Ibid., 22.

Jesus lived here for a short while
Samīh died here for a short while.[11]

3. Texts (both Islamic and Christian):

في جيد الطغاة الغُبر والجبناءِ والسفهاءِ
حبلاً من مَسَدْ

Around the neck of the filthy tyrant, the coward and the impertinent,
There is a rope of twisted iron.[12]

فلتكتملْ بمشيئة الله الصلاةُ على المصلّي
ليكون مجدًا لله مكتمل العلى ويكونَ في الأرض
السلام تكونَ في الناسِ المسرّةُ..والرضا.

Following God's will, let the prayer be complete,
Let glory to God in the Heaven be complete, and on Earth,
Let people have peace, delight and fulfillment.[13]

4. Time (past, present and expected future) and space (East and West):

ستولد في أثينا طفلةٌ شاعره
يغنّي أناشيدها الساحره
تلاميذُ ديترويت وطوكيو
ولاهاي والناصره..

A baby poet will be born in Athens,
Her magical songs will be sung
By the pupils of Detroit and Tokyo,
The Hague and Nazareth …[14]

11 Ibid., 152.
12 Ibid., 21–22.
13 Ibid., 26.
14 Ibid., 105.

5. Civilizations (Western and Eastern):

فاعبر على تموز في عجَلٍ ولا تمكث طويلاً عند جلجامش
ولا تعبأ بلعبةِ فاوستً أنت الآن بين رؤاكَ
بين رؤاكَ أنت الآن..
تختصر الدهور ..بثانيهْ..

Pass by Tammuz quickly; don't linger at Gilgamesh for long,
Do not care for Faust's game; now you are among your visions;
Among your visions you are now,
Summarizing ages in one second.[15]

These very mechanisms of mixture and interdependence constitute textual meaning and help the reader formulate her/his own interpretation. In this sense, the five forms—like all structural forms in poetry—challenge the power of language, be it standard or figurative, and go beyond vocal sounds to the visual form.

4 Conciliation of Opposites

The overall structure of this collection gives rise to contradictions that create high levels of tension, which stimulate the reader to interpret the text as she/he negotiates between these "rival" opposites. Samīḥ al-Qāsim was fascinated by contradiction-making poetry. One of the major devices for achieving this is irony, which reunites conflicting factors in a way that supports the process of semiosis. Al-Qāsim based an entire collection, *Anā muta'assif* (*I am sorry*, 2009), in which he ironically apologizes to his rivals and enemies, on this device. A careful reading of the collection reveals some paradoxes of two conflicting sides, which might be summarized as disease and wellness, life and death, Hell and earthly paradise, sanctity and sacrilege, enemy and friend (see, for instance, visions 54, 68, and 72).[16] This inconsistency in the selected vocabulary highlights the significance of this collection in terms of two fundamental imperatives: recognition of the existence of opposites, and the need for change on the basis of conciliation and sharing. Since neighboring opposites have, at

15 Ibid., 24.
16 Samīḥ al-Qāsim, *Anā muta'assif* (Nazareth: al-Ḥakīm, 2009), 96, 110, 114, accordingly.

least in principle, the potential to impel human beings to continue searching for interactive and decent living conditions, al-Qāsim did not reject or criticize unpleasant factors, nor did he praise pleasant ones. Instead he allowed for the possibility of sharing the same space and for introducing a constructive dialogue.

Writing poetry, be it innate or acquired, can by no means produce an extraordinary poet if profound thought and reflection are lacking. In al-Qāsim's poem *ʿAyn al-ṣawāb* (The right thing to do, 2007), one notices the ease with which he introduces different points of view, in spite of the fact that politics occupy a central part of his consciousness. In this poem, al-Qāsim believes that "there is ample room for all people in the universe." He is fully aware that any state of confrontation cannot be realized without sharing a space with one's rivals.

Comparing *ʿAyn al-ṣawāb* with another poem, *Qaṣīdat al-intifāḍa* (The poem of the Intifada, 1988), one sees that the poet made careful use of a double-sided mask to illustrate the two opposites featuring the entire universe. On the one hand, in his powerful Intifada poem, al-Qāsim imbued the victim with the means to confront the fierce and bloody occupation of Palestinian territories. On the other hand, in *ʿAyn al-ṣawāb*, he acknowledged the occupier's right to exist, based on the slogan that "there is an ample room for all people in the universe." The strange thing is that the victim showed great tolerance towards her/his victimizers. Al-Qāsim believed that despite his weakness, the victim is able to demonstrate immense power when confronting her/his enemies. Any religion that issues a *fatwā* to erase the "other" and remain the sole power in the universe is deformed and basically inhuman. Al-Qāsim's vision guarantees enough room for both "enemy and friend." Contradiction in this collection, as well as in his other collections, including his well-known *Khadhalatnī al-ṣaḥārā* (The deserts disappointed me, 1998), is not limited to verbal paradoxes or normative distinctions between good and evil, just as it is not limited to confusing Nostradamus with al-Qāsim himself. Nevertheless, such contradiction goes further, to confront the significant paradox between existing and desirable reality.

5 Conclusion: Despair and Hope

The reader of modern poetry should primarily take into consideration that literary texts in general acknowledge the very need for rejection and denial. On the one hand, modern poetry defies stable laws and disobeys familiar conventions. On the other, it persistently keeps looking for alternative standards on both aesthetic and thematic levels. If Nostradamus's forecasts were fundamentally concerned with forewarning, al-Qāsim's visions in this collection go far beyond mere notification to give some measure of hope and inspiration. Al-Qāsim takes Nostradamus's forecasts a step further, reinterpreting them as optimistic visions. NostraSamīḥdamus—an unfamiliar mixture of two figures—presents a powerful image of reconciliation between two opposites: despair and hope. Al-Qāsim requires such a measure of despair, as described in Nostradamus' forecasts, to ensure the profound need for hope. In conditions of confusion and chaos, the visions of NostraSamīḥdamus give people much hope. According to these visions, God conquers Satan, thus reviving the humanity inherent in human beings.[17]

Bibliography

Al-Qāsim, Samīḥ. *Khadhalatnī al-ṣaḥārā*. Nazareth: Manshūrāt Iḍā'āt, 1998.

Al-Qāsim, Samīḥ. *Muqaddimat Ibn Muḥammad li-ru'ā NūstrāSamīḥdāmūs: 111 ru'yā fī 111 thulāthiyya*. Nazareth: al-Ḥakīm, 2006.

Al-Qāsim, Samīḥ. *Anā muta'assif*. Nazareth: al-Ḥakīm, 2009.

Al-Qāsim, Samīḥ. *Hawājis li-ṭuqūs al-aḥfād*. Beirut: al-Mu'assasa al-'Arabiyya li'l-Dirāsāt wa'l-Nashr, 2012.

Al-Qāsim, Samīḥ. *Hīrmāfrūdītūs wa-qaṣā'id ukhrā*. Amman: Wizārat al-Thaqāfa, 2012.

Al-Qāsim, Samīḥ. *Kūlāj 3*. Beirut: al-Mu'assasa al-'Arabiyya li'l-Dirāsāt wa'l-Nashr, 2012.

---

17 See, for instance, vision 109 in al-Qāsim, *Muqaddimat Ibn Muḥammad*, 151:

أسمع بين الريح والراياتْ
بشائرَ السنابلِ،
الأزاهرِ،
الصيحاتْ
تنتصرُ الحياةُ.عهد الله والإنسان،
أن تنتصرَ الحياةْ..

I hear among the wind and the flags
The good omens of spikes,
Flowers,
And shouts
Life overcomes. God and Man's pledge
Is that life should overcome.

PART 2

Prose and Drama

The Pimps' Maqāma: A Libertine Piece of Ornate Prose from a Manuscript of the Mamluk Period

Amir Lerner

1 Marginal Social Characters and Pimps in Medieval Arabic Literature*

Both the creators and the consumers of Arabic literature throughout the Middle Ages showed a literary interest in the life of the common people.[1] In this sense *Maqāmat al-muʿarraṣīn* (i.e. Pimps),[2] which is hereby presented for the first time in English, does not differ from other works of literature that deal with such captivating and lively topics, nor is it unique in its focus on marginal social elements. Stories about pimps were not new, as previous writers had occasionally adorned their compositions with stories, anecdotes, and verses about them.[3] Some writers distinguished themselves by devoting an entire

---

* This is an expanded, updated and enriched version of the author's "'Maqāmat al-muʿarrasīn' wa-ṣināʿāt al-qawwādīn: fi'l-nathr al-fannī al-hāzil al-mājin fī Miṣr ayyām al-Mamālīk," in *In the Oasis of Pens: Studies in Arab Literature and Culture in Honour of Professor Joseph Sadan*, eds. ʿAbd Allāh Shaykh-Mūsā, Nādir Maṣārwa and Ghālib ʿAnābsa (Cologne: Dār al-Hudā and Manshūrāt al-Jamal, 2011), 1: 68–78. I wish to express my gratitude to Prof. Nāṣir Baṣal from Tel Aviv University, whose support enabled the completion of this article.

1 See, for instance, the following surveys of sources in which writers focused on persons on the margins of society: Clifford Edmund Bosworth, *The Mediaeval Islamic Underworld—the Banū Sāsān in Arabic Society and Literature* (Leiden: Brill, 1976), 1: 30–47, 96–131; Joseph Sadan, "Kings and Craftsmen: A Pattern of Contrasts: On the History of a Medieval Arabic Humoristic Form" (part I), *Studia Islamica* 56 (1982): 5–49; (part II) 62 (1985): 89–120; idem, *al-Adab al-ʿArabī al-hāzil wa-nawādir al-thuqalāʾ: al-ʿāhāt wa'l-masāwiʾ al-insāniyya wa-makānatuhā fi'l-adab al-rāqī* (Köln: Manshūrāt al-Jamal, 2007), esp. 42–45, note 45; ʿAbd al-Muʿīn al-Mullūḥī, *Ashʿār al-luṣūṣ wa-akhbāruhum* (Beirut: Dār al-Ḥaḍāra al-Jadīda, 1993), 3: 297–700; Aḥmad al-Ḥusayn, *Adab al-kudya fi'l-ʿaṣr al-ʿAbbāsī: dirāsa fī adab al-shaḥḥādhīn wa'l-mutasawwilīn* (Damascus: Dār al-Ḥiṣād li'l-Nashr wa'l-Tawzīʿ, 2001), 249–260; Muḥammad Rajab al-Najjār, *Ḥikāyāt al-shuṭṭār wa'l-ʿayyārīn* (Kuwait: al-Hayʾa al-ʿĀmma li-Quṣūr al-Thaqāfa, 2002), 44–59: ʿAbd al-Hādī Ḥarb, *Mawsūʿat adab al-muḥtālīn* (Damascus: al-Takwīn, 2008).

2 Reinhart Dozy, *Supplément aux dictionnaires arabes* (Leiden: Brill, 1881), s.v.; Socrates Spiro, *An Arabic-English Vocabulary of the Colloquial Arabic of Egypt* (Cairo: al-Mokattam Printing Office, 1895), s.v.

3 See, for example ʿAbd Allāh b. Muslim b. Qutayba, *ʿUyūn al-akhbār* (Cairo: al-Muʾassasa al-Miṣriyya al-ʿĀmma li'l-Taʾlīf wal-Tarjama wa'l-Ṭibāʿa wa'l-Nashr, 1983), 4: 102–106; Ḥusayn

 | DOI:10.1163/9789004459120_009

chapter to this phenomenon, for example Ibn Falīta[4] in his *Rushd al-labīb ilā muʿāsharat al-ḥabīb* (The wise man's guide to intimacy with the beloved; chapter twelve, "On the mention of pimping and its adherents");[5] ʿAlī b. Naṣr al-Kātib (fl. in the tenth century) in his book *Jawāmiʿ al-ladhdha* (Various forms of delight; "Chapter on Pimping");[6] and Aḥmad b. Yūsuf al-Tīfāshī (d. 651/1253) in his *Nuzhat al-albāb fīmā lā yūjad fī kitāb* (Delight of the hearts regarding what is not to be found in any book; chapter two, "On the types of male and female pimps, anecdotes and verses about them").[7]

---

b. Muḥammad al-Rāghib al-Iṣbāhānī, *Muḥāḍarāt al-udabāʾ wa-muḥāwarāt al-shuʿarāʾ wa'l-bulaghāʾ* (Beirut: Manshūrāt Dār Maktabat al-Ḥayāt, 1961), 3: 257–259; Aḥmad b. Muḥammad al-Maydānī, *Majmaʿ al-amthāl* (Beirut: Manshūrāt Dār Maktabat al-Ḥayāt, 1961–1962), 2: 93; Aḥmad b. Muḥammad al-Maqqarī, *Nafḥ al-ṭīb min ghuṣn al-Andalus al-raṭīb* (Beirut: Dār Ṣādir, 1968), 4: 184. Did the no-longer-extant *Kitāb al-muqayyinīn wa'l-ghināʾ wa'l-ṣanʿa* by ʿAmr b. Baḥr al-Jāḥiẓ (see Charles Pellat, "Ǧāḥiẓiana III: Essai d'inventaire de l'œuvre ǧāḥiẓienne," *Arabica* 3 [1956]: 167; idem, "Nouvel Essai d'inventaire de l'œuvre ǧāḥiẓienne," *Arabica* 31 [1984]: 150), contain materials about pimps or similar topics? Note that al-Jāḥiẓ did devote a number of compositions to themes that were not so different, for example *Kitāb al-qiyān* (see *Rasāʾil al-Jāḥiẓ* [Beirut: Dār al-Jīl, 1991], 2: 143–182) and *Mufākharat al-jawārī wa'l-ghilmān* (ibid., 91–137).

4 There is some confusion about the identity of the author, who is on occasion called "Ibn Qulayta." Is this Aḥmad b. Muḥammad b. ʿAlī Abū al-ʿAbbās, the Yemeni writer (d. 231/845), or is it perhaps the Yemeni writer of the same name (d. 732/1331)? Both, according to various sources, composed a work with the same title, namely the one mentioned here. See for example Ḥājjī Khalīfa, *Kashf al-ẓunūn ʿan asāmī al-kutub wa-l-funūn* (Istanbul: Wikālat al-Maʿārif, 1941–1943), 1: 904; Carl Brockelmann, *Geschichte der arabischen Litteratur* (Leiden: E.J. Brill, 1937–1949), G1: 265, and S1: 415–416; apparently the author of this book is Ibn Falīta, the Yemeni writer who died in 1363, in line with Everett K. Rowson's statement in "Arabic: Middle Ages to Nineteenth Century," *Encyclopedia of Erotic Literature* (New York: Routledge, 2006), 58, 60, whom we thank for his valuable comments.

5 Ibn Falīta, *Rushd al-labīb ilā muʿāsharat al-ḥabīb* (Al-Māya: Tāla li'l-Ṭibāʿa wa'l-Nashr, 2006), 165–181. See our comment below on this source. The publisher mistakenly added the chapters of this book, including the chapter on pimping itself, to Jalāl al-Dīn al-Suyūṭī (d. 911/1505), *al-Wishāḥ fī fawāʾid al-nikāḥ*, 161–192, which Tāla published in 2006 as well (the error was made by the binding department at Tāla). This topic seems to be absent in other editions of al-Suyūṭī's book, while its association with Ibn Falīta's book is obvious.

6 ʿAlī b. Naṣr al-Kātib, *Jawāmiʿ al-ladhdha* (Cairo: Dār al-Bayān al-ʿArabī, 2002), 144–156. There appears to be some confusion concerning the author's name and identity. According to Dār al-Bayān al-ʿArabī, the author is ʿAlī b. ʿUmar al-Kātibī al-Qazwīnī (d. 675/1277), a conclusion that is in agreement with the edition published by Tāla li'l-Ṭibāʿa wa'l-Nashr, 2002 (see also p. 243). However, this is unlikely, and the author is probably as we noted; see also Rowson, "Arabic," 48–52.

7 Al-Tīfāshī, *Nuzhat al-albāb fīmā lā yūjad fī kitāb* (London and Cyprus: Riyāḍ al-Rayyis li'l-Kutub wa'l-Nashr, 1992), 63–92. See also the quote below from this book.

However, a perusal of these literary sources, in particular the books of Ibn Falīta and al-Tīfāshī, both of whom quite clearly focused more on the work of pimps than other writers had, makes it hard to ignore the similarities between the literary figure of the pimp and other figures on the margins of society that are found in *adab* literature. Pimps—just like beggars, parasites, thieves, or rogues—are depicted as skillful tricksters, presented in a humorous vein combining a sneaking admiration with a wisecrack attitude towards a group of people who are proud of their skills, as if they were possessed of chivalry and nobility (*futuwwa, murūʾa*) and not criminals. Yet, as literary heroes, these pimps manage to stand out (as did male slaves, prostitutes, and female slaves, all of whom—as shown below—have had sections and chapters devoted to them in *adab* compositions). Indeed, this literary amalgamation of the marginal and the sexual provides added value, as the reader derives greater pleasure from the text.[8]

2 *Maqāmat al-muʿarraṣīn*: Its Date, Place, and Author

The Pimps' Maqāma (the last part of which was lost) appears at the end of MS London, Br. Mus. Add. 19.411 (fols. 128a–131b), which contains various literary texts from the Mamluk period in Egypt (1250–1517), mainly from the thirteenth and fourteenth centuries.[9] The manuscript and its contents date from no later than 1036 AH (1626–1627), according to a date written down by a reader (named Muḥammad b. ʿUthmān) who put his signature on the manuscript (the earliest of four such signatures).

The Pimps' Maqāma was written no earlier than the end of the twelfth or the beginning of the thirteenth century, as proven by the fact that it mentions Qalʿat al-Jabal, one of the best-known sites in Cairo, which was built during that same period.[10] Furthermore, the text contains words and terms that were in use mainly during the Mamluk period, so that we can fix the time

8 This includes a variety of sexual themes, including pederasty, a theme that some poets and writers in Mamluk Egypt were attracted to; in fact, it was a recurrent topic in early *adab* literature and poetry. See Everett K. Rowson, "Two Homoerotic Narratives from Mamlūk Literature: al-Ṣafadī's *Lawʿat al-Shākī* and Ibn Dānyāl's *al-Mutayyam*," in *Homoeroticism in Classical Arabic Literature*, eds. J.W. Wright and E.K. Rowson (New York: Columbia University Press, 1997), 158–191, esp. 160–161.

9 See Gulielmus Cureton and Carolus Rieu, *Catalogus Codicum Manuscriptorum Orientalium qui in Museo Britannico asservantur, Pars Secunda: Codices Arabicos amplectens* (London: Impensis Curatorum Musei Britannici, 1846–1871), 2: 514–515.

10 See below, note 37.

with greater precision to somewhat after the Ayyubid period and within the Mamluk period itself.

The author mentions the pyramids in the same geographical context as the aforementioned site, a clear indication that he was quite familiar with Cairo and its geographical environs. When we add to this the fact that the manuscript contains additional Egyptian materials, and that *The Pimps' Maqāma* possesses Egyptian linguistic traits, it is a foregone conclusion that it was written in Egypt or, at least, by an Egyptian.

There is no hint in the text as to the identity of the author, who thus remains unknown. However, our examination of some of the other texts in this manuscript has revealed that the *maqāma* composed by Muḥammad b. Mawlāhum al-Khayālī (who lived in Egypt from the late-thirteenth to the early fourteenth century), and which addresses themes dealing with working women,[11] uses concepts, topics, and elements of literary style that are consistent with the environment and period in question. Despite the fact that the text does not fit the framework of "classical *maqāmas*," but merely presents professions and their practitioners, and the gatherings of boastful people on the margins of society, it shows a similarity to those in *The Pimps' Maqāma*. In addition to the term *maqāma*, it uses specific terms and expressions that are similar to those found in our *maqāma* (e.g., *maghānī* as the plural of *mughanniya*).[12] It quotes, among others, bathhouse attendants, weavers, broom sweepers, cooks, washerwomen, and bean sellers, as well as female pimps. So we should not be surprised that it was apparently Muḥammad b. Mawlāhum himself who composed *The Pimps' Maqāma*, although this still remains a conjecture.[13]

3 Non-Standard Arabic in Literary Salons, and Other Artistic Means

Even though the language of *The Pimps' Maqāma* deviates from Standard Arabic and makes use of numerous words and expressions taken from

11 Sadan, "Kings and Craftsmen," (part II): 115–117; Shmuel Moreh, *Live Theatre and Dramatic Literature in the Medieval Arab World* (Edinburgh: Edinburgh University Press, 1992), 134.

12 See below, note 33.

13 Furthermore, one should note that this *maqāma*, which depicts fifty working women, was written by Muḥammad b. Mawlāhum, whose epithet is known to be "al-Khayālī." Moreh argues that this epithet is taken from his profession or from that of one of his forefathers, i.e. a shadow-theatre performer, and that the text may therefore have been written with the intention of being performed before an audience. Moreh, *Live Theatre*, 108–110. May we then conclude that *The Pimps' Maqāma* is also a theatrical text?

spoken language, it cannot be said to be colloquial. The author makes use of non-standard elements as a literary device, especially in the pimps' utterances (though less so in other parts of the text). Pimps belong to the lower strata of society and the author clearly wishes to imitate the language of the masses, and of pimps in particular. By using the social and linguistic tension between *The Pimps' Maqāma*'s protagonists and the reader, who is presumed to belong to a higher social class, the author creates his own brand of humor. He clearly strives for stylistic beauty and makes generous use of ideas and themes found in classical literature. He contrasts these elements with the folk overtones that permeate his writing, demonstrating (in addition to other literary devices) the work's humorous dimension and a desire to arouse the reader's delight.[14]

There are any number of ways in which elements of colloquial and of Standard Arabic can be intermingled within a narrative text. Here we consider three:

a. Scattered pages with literary content, written by someone with no knowledge of Standard Arabic and with no intention of producing a book or even a notebook for anyone else to read, with the possible exception of a friend or a member of the family—for instance, a relatively uneducated person lends a helping hand to a grocer or a vendor in the market by collecting anecdotes, oral or written, and jotting them down on paper used for keeping accounts. Clearly there is a large gap between his folksy background and writing style, which he expresses with the utmost freedom, and the contents of the collected anecdotes.[15]
b. A text transcribed by a "narrator" or a collector of semi-popular stories and recreated or reformulated in a language that strives to attain a level of acceptable Standard Arabic, but unwittingly retains colloquial elements. A number of scholars have offered this explanation.[16]
c. Compositions in a language that is colloquial, or close to being colloquial, and written by authors who are well-versed in Standard Arabic and

14 Sadan, "Kings and Craftsmen" (part II): 89–101, 107.

15 Sadan, "Hārūn al-Rashīd and the Brewer: Preliminary Remarks on the *Adab* of the Elite Versus Ḥikāyāt: The Continuation of Some of the Traditional Literary Models, from the 'Classical' Arabic Heritage, up to the Emergence of Modern Forms," in *Studies in Canonical and Popular Arabic Literature*, eds. Shimon Ballas and Reuven Snir (Toronto: York Press, 1998), 1–22, esp. the table on 6; Sadan, "Conflicting Tendencies between Higher and Lower Strata of Humor: Some Genizah Fragments," in *Humor in der arabischen Kultur*, edited by Georges Tamer (Berlin: Walter de Gruyter, 2009), 137–149.

16 See, for example Hishām 'Abd al-'Azīz and 'Ādil 'Abd al-Ḥamīd, *Layālī al-ḥubb wa'l-'ishq: alf laylā wa-layla bi'l-'āmmiyya al-Miṣriyya* (Cairo: Dār al-Khayāl, 1977).

> capable of writing superior prose and poetry, but wish to use colloquial expressions, either for the sake of humor or even in a serious literary manner. For this reason we call such texts *adab ʿāmmī* (a term used by Aḥmad Ṣādiq al-Jammāl, meaning "deviating from Standard Arabic and making use of the colloquial" or *ʿāmmiyya*) rather than *adab shaʿbī* (that is, popular literature or folk literature).[17]

The Pimps' Maqāma, translated below, adopted the third approach. Its author did not merely use a literary-linguistic framework, but added a further literary dimension to it by presenting pimps as professional craftsmen. He also placed them in something akin to literary salons, where drinks and conversation flowed and each participant described and praised his vocation in rhymed prose and poetry (using a language near to the colloquial, as noted above). Significant artistic accomplishments could thus be achieved. This is especially true since our literary piece was written in the framework of a developing genre—literary depictions of craftsmen as an organic part of literary interest in the margins of society—which had evolved since the ninth century, when al-Jāḥiẓ (d. 255/869) composed his famous *Risāla fī ṣināʿāt al-quwwād* (Epistle on the crafts of the masters),[18] which became a literary "fashion" with its own esthetics, beauty, humor, and appeal.[19]

4 Is *Maqāmat al-muʿarraṣīn* a "Real" *Maqāma*?

The fact that the author defined his work as a *maqāma* certainly does not in any way imply that this is indeed a *maqāma* in the classical sense. Indeed, it does not comply with the necessary conditions which the two creators of this genre, Badīʿ al-Zamān al-Hamadhānī (d. 395/1008) and al-Qāsim b. ʿAlī al-Ḥarīrī (d. 516/1122), imposed on it. Thus, although it is written in rhymed prose and embellished with poetry, includes a narrator, and deals with people from the margins of society, it lacks the roguish beggar protagonist. Moreover, the narrative does not develop appreciably, nor does it contain a climax or a surprising plot twist; it consists of nothing more than a (fictitious) description of the pimps' craft and the jokes, anecdotes, conversations, clowning, and

---

17 Aḥmad Ṣādiq al-Jammāl, *al-Adab al-ʿāmmī fī Miṣr fi'l-ʿaṣr al-Mamlūkī* (Cairo: al-Dār al-Qawmiyya li'l-Ṭibāʿa wa'l-Nashr, 1977).

18 *Rasāʾil al-Jāḥiẓ*, 1: 379–393. See also Charles Pellat, *The Life and Works of Jāḥiẓ: Translation of Selected Texts* (London: Routledge, 1969), 114–116.

19 For an analysis of this literary trend, see Sadan, "Kings and Craftsmen" (part I): 5–49; (part II): 89–120.

boasts told at their gatherings. The term *maqāma* is thus apparently used in a very general and inflated sense, based on its historical evolution.[20]

5 An English Translation of *Maqāmat al-muʿarraṣīn*[21]

A dissolute man reported to me in the name of a wanton person of impressive cleverness, who said: In my time I was a lover of singing. It was decreed by fate that I should wander across the lands and associate with every kind of human being.

One day I was present at a gathering of depraved and sinful people. Among them were some companions of *al-Raqīm*,[22] whose occupation I did not [128b]

---

20 See, for example Jaakko Hämeen-Anttila, *Maqama: A History of a Genre* (Wiesbaden: Harrassowitz, 2002), 339–340; also Ibrahim Kh. Geries, *A Literary and Gastronomical Conceit: Mufākharat al-Ruzz wa'l-Ḥabb Rummān: The Boasting Debate between Rice and Pomegranate Seeds; or, al-Maḳāma al-Simāṭiyya* (*The Tablecloth Maḳāma*) (Wiesbaden: Harrassowitz, 2002), 9–10, 37–40.

21 For the critically edited Arabic text, see Lerner, "'Maqāmat al-muʿarraṣīn'," 68–78.

22 Here the author alludes to a story in Qur'an 18, a legend of Christian origin about a group of Christians who fled from the repression of the Roman emperor Trajanus Decius (r. 249–251 CE) and hid in a cave in Ephesus (in western Anatolia) in order to maintain their faith. God put them to sleep inside the cave and closed off its entrance until the beginning of the reign of the Byzantine emperor Flavius Theodosius II (r. 408–450 CE), a devout Christian himself, when they were able to escape and free themselves. The Qur'anic text makes it impossible to determine the number of people in this group, but it is believed that the story is based on "The Seven Sleepers of Ephesus," in Arabic *aṣḥāb al-kahf wa'l-Raqīm* (Qur'an 18: 9, "companions of the Cave and al-Raqīm"). Some commentators explain the word al-Raqīm as the name of the mountain where the cave was located; others that it was a tablet of lead, copper, or stone on which the names of the sleepers and their genealogy were inscribed; and still others that it was the name of a dog that guarded the cave's entrance the entire time the Christian fugitives were sleeping. Apparently, the author ironically speaks of "good company" or "a group of valorous men," but means the opposite, in order to provoke the reader's or listener's laughter. It is also quite possible that his use of the phrase serves an additional, humorous idea associated with sleep, which is a major theme in the original Christian legend, and to which the author of *The Pimps' Maqāma* alludes in two ways: the pimps' constant imbibing of wine (as the reader will see further on) and his subsequent intoxication, and (perhaps more in line with the author's intention) the pimp's profession, which consists of making women available for sexual intercourse (described as "sleeping together"). In accordance with this theme, the author chose the name "al-Naʿʿās" for the first pimp and "al-Nawwām" for the second, both meaning "sleepy" or "putting to sleep." In addition, the number of pimps in *The Pimps' Maqāma* is seven, like the number of sleepers in the cave according to the Christian legend.

know. The cups went round and round, from early evening to sunset.[23] When the darkness of night fell and the lamps were lit, people grabbed the cups, becoming overexcited and aroused.[24]

When intoxication overpowered my own senses, I became more and more importunate and said: O people of virtue and merit, do we drink without song this night? Do you know a beautiful singer, adequate for our friends? I then showed ten genuine dirhams, so as not to appear a joker. They all glanced at me and stared at the dirhams, and each of them wished that I had spoken only to him and not to the whole group and that he could be the middleman for this merchandise. I deliberated with myself for a while and then came back to my senses, realizing that I had erred in what I had said to them and that they would not see this as a golden opportunity. So I thought that I had no choice but to deceive them with a fawning speech and agree with whatever they decided. So I said: O people, why are you silent and deep in thought? Tell me your situation and what [129a] has changed it. If I erred in what I said, O you who are present, I will stand before you and ask for your forgiveness. They said: Know you, dear friend and agreeable companion, that what each of us desires has already appeared, and each drags the fire to his loaf.[25] Each one of us demonstrated his intention to gain possession of his *ghilmāniyya*'s[26] dirhams. I then asked them: What is your craft, O brothers? They said: We are seven youths. I said: What

23 In Arabic: *min al-ʿishā li-l-ghiyāb*, so "dinner" (*ʿashāʾ*) may also be considered.

24 In Arabic: *wa-ḥamiyat*, literally meaning "became heat."

25 That is, "looks after his own interests."

26 The author uses this word once more in the text. It appears to denote the prostitute herself. The root of the word has various meanings, all associated with passion and lust, with slave girls or boys, and with the sexual associations the terms aroused. However, there is also another form of the word, derived from the same origin, namely *ghulāmiyya*, the meaning of which was taken from the lives of the Abbasid caliphs and appeared in early books of history and *adab*. The word denoted a slave girl dressed up as a slave boy, a form of look ushered in, according to historical sources, by the daughter of Jaʿfar b. al-Manṣūr, Zubayda (d. 216/831), the wife of the fifth Abbasid Caliph Hārūn al-Rashīd (r. 170–193/786–809), for her son al-Amīn, the sixth Abbasid caliph (r. 193–198/809–813), who lusted after male slaves. Such "youth-like" slave girls then became fashionable in the Abbasid period, not only at court, but also elsewhere throughout the caliphate. For a description of such slave girls, see ʿAlī b. al-Ḥusayn al-Masʿūdī, *Murūj al-dhahab wa-maʿādin al-jawhar* (Beirut: Manshūrāt al-Jāmiʿa al-Lubnāniyya, 1965–1979), 5: 213–214; Ismāʿīl b. al-Qāsim al-Qālī, *al-Amālī* (Beirut: al-Maktab al-Tijārī li'l-Ṭibāʿa wa'l-Nashr wa'l-Tawzīʿ, 1965), 1: 225–226. The author quite likely wished to use an ancient social-literary term and its semantic context as the basis for his own term but constructed his word from the plural form *ghilmān* instead of from the singular *ghulām*.

kind of youths, O friends? They said: Of all types of prostitutes. So I said: By God, O band of *akyās*,[27] are there classes and types among prostitutes?

The great shaykh then became angry. He sighed and moaned, and said: Did you not know that they are seven classes? Yet, I was familiar with them all, and I said: By God, O master of pimps, will you not inform me about these seven different classes? He raged and roared, his face lengthened and scowled, and said: O you of little virtue and honor, you remnant of the best of the ignorant, as for this disgusting utterance and vulgar question, a pimp is whoever pimps his sister or mother, or his wife [129b] and cousin. We are a group of people that takes pleasure in humankind, we acquire the money of great and small, we do not heed anyone nor give a thought about who is present or absent. We do not fear emirs nor are we intimidated by the great. We show no mercy to the poor and do not stand in awe of the authority of kings, nor pay heed to robbers. If we possess a *ghilmāniyya*, we are appeased. We control ladies as we control Nubian women. They do not engage in sexual intercourse except at our command, and do not spend the night except at our command. We gather at the center, eat a third of the meat straight from the pot and drink off the top of *jalūliyyāt*.[28] We enjoy looking at beautiful faces[29] and take pleasure in intimacy with faces like moons. We lack neither dirhams nor dinars. We have our share of everything aplenty. From lovers[30] we get tips and payment. We receive tips for clothes from the ladies, we get a piece of soap and candle wax,

---

27 The word *akyās* has two meanings: the plural of *kayyis*—"seasoned and skilled"—and the plural of *kīs*—"handbag." Here the author clearly uses humor to exploit this ambiguity.

28 The word *jalūliyyāt* (or *julūliyyāt*?) is unattested elsewhere. It apparently denotes a superior kind of old wine.

29 In Arabic *al-ḥisān*, which suits the meaning but does not fit the rhyme pattern of the surrounding lines (*al-maqāmāt, laḥmāt, jalūliyyāt, al-ḥisān, ka-l-aqmār, dīnār, muwaffar*), and is therefore probably a copyist's error. Perhaps the word which the author intended here was *al-ḥisār*, as a plural form of *al-ḥāsir* (usual plural: *ḥussar*), meaning a woman who reveals her head and arms.

30 *Al-ḥarīf* in Arabic, which denotes not only someone who practices a craft which another will use for trade, but also a client or customer (especially in some regions of North Africa). More importantly, it also means "lover" in the colloquial dialect of Egypt. See Dozy, *Supplément*, s.v., who relies on *Kitāb hazz al-quḥūf bi-sharḥ qaṣīd Abī Shādūf* by the Egyptian author Yūsuf b. Muḥammad al-Shirbīnī (d. toward the end of the seventeenth century), and on Maximilian Habicht's "Breslau edition" of the *Arabian Nights* (published between 1825 and 1843), which contains a large amount of Egyptian material, especially in its two last volumes (vols. 11 and 12, to which Dozy refers!). This is the conclusion of Duncan B. MacDonald, "Maximilian Habicht and His Recension of the Thousand and One Nights," *Journal of the Royal Asiatic Society* 41 (1909): esp. pp. 688, 696, 704.

and of the nights we have Friday night. If anything is left over from the fees or payments we take it, and if [130a] a dirham turns up we grasp it, if a garment is abandoned we take it, if a *kamarān*[31] is left unattended we steal it, if they [the clients] quarrel over a drinking cup, we drink it, if anyone causes a disturbance we throw him out, if he falls asleep drunk we have sexual intercourse with him. We have no fear and no chivalry, no sense of honor or valor, no praise. We do not pimp out our sister and mother, when we speak we lie, when we make a promise we do not keep it, when people put their trust in us, we betray that trust, we are pleased when two heads come together [i.e. a man and a woman], we do not become angry over anything serious or humorous, because of us the *salūs*[32] becomes unlucky, he among us who sleeps little becomes penniless. Pleased, he then sang the following verses:

We are a company who do people favors,
with them we ascend to every place
Good souls, who in every matter set free [their] care and grief
No foolishness takes possession of us, nor are we jealous of adulterers
We satisfy people's desires and lead men to women
[130b] We have received so many good things from pimping that even the ridiculer or the aggressive speaker will tire of describing them

---

31 The word *kamarān* in this form is not part of the Classical Arabic lexicon and is not mentioned by early lexicographers. It is similar to *kamar*, which is also from an early lexicography in Arabic (the latter is perhaps of Persian origin). See Buṭrus al-Bustānī, *Muḥīṭ al-muḥīṭ* [Beirut: n.p., 1867–1870], s.v.). The meaning of both of these rare words is a belt made of hide (*al-kamar* is made of hair, according to al-Bustānī), which can also be used to hold money. See both words in Dozy, *Supplément*, s.v. In addition to the Arabic sources on which Dozy relied for his entry *kamarān* (*al-Mawāʿiẓ wa'l-iʿtibār bi-dhikr al-khiṭaṭ wa'l-āthār* by Aḥmad b. ʿAlī al-Maqrīzī—d. 845/1442, and *Nafḥ al-ṭīb* by the above mentioned al-Maqqarī), one may find also another reference made by al-Maqrīzī in his *al-Sulūk li-maʿrifat duwal al-mulūk* (Cairo: Maṭbaʿat Lajnat al-Ta'līf wa'l-Tarjama wa'l-Nashr and Maṭbaʿat Dār al-Kutub, 1934–1973), 3/1: 342, and by Badr al-Dīn Maḥmūd b. Aḥmad al-ʿAynī (d. 855/1451) in his *ʿIqd al-jumān fī ta'rīkh ahl al-zamān* (Cairo: al-Hay'a al-Miṣriyya al-ʿĀmma li'l-Kitāb, 1987–1989), 3:486. Both indicate that the plural of this word is *kamarānāt*. From this discussion, we may conclude that this rare word was current at least in Egypt during the Mamluk period (and perhaps also somewhat later). This also leads us (in addition to other evidence that we mentioned previously and to which we shall return below) to the determination of a time frame within which *The Pimps' Maqāma* was composed. Finally, we should point out that the root *k.m.r.* and the words derived from it in early Standard Arabic have meanings revolving around the male organ, and in all likelihood also played a significant role in the author's choice.

32 This is the form of the word in the manuscript. Is the correct spelling *maslūs*, meaning "insane"? Or is it *salis* "docile, pliant," as defined in early dictionaries of Classical Arabic?

You, who censure me for my pimping, desist and listen to the words of a poet of clarity
Not at all hours is philanthropy available

If I were to continue to describe at length the virtues of pandering and pimping, you would become eager to pursue these two crafts, for the tongue is incapable of grasping pimping and doing good, and would dry up were it to attempt to describe their attributes. The best of speeches are short, so farewell. As for these seven youths, they stand for the seven types: Pimps of singers[33] to the sound of the tambourine and the flute, pimps of female Bedouin singers, pimps of *kabliyyāt*, pimps of *baytūtiyyāt*, pimps of *bayyātāt*, pimps of *waqqāfāt* and pimps of *ʿulūq*, which refer to pederasty and [other types of] depravity.[34]

33 In the manuscript: *maghānī*, the plural of *maghnā* "place of singing," similar to *al-mughannā*. See Lois Ibsen al-Faruqi, *An Annotated Glossary of Arabic Musical Terms* (Westport, Connecticut: Greenwood Press, 1981), 163, 196. However, in colloquial language, it is also the plural of *mughanniya*. Dozy, *Supplément*, s.v.

34 Such detailed classification and precise terminology, based on a variety of characteristics, for a marginal class of people is not at all exceptional in early literature. It is based on a literary style that seems almost scholarly, in form presenting a mixture of indexation and scientific taxonomy, and in content showing an interest in the lower social classes. The first author to have made prominent use of this style to enhance the humorous aspect of his output was undoubtedly al-Jāḥiẓ. For example, "Ḥadīth Khālid b. Yazīd (Khalawayhi al-Mukaddī)" in *al-Bukhalāʾ* (Cairo: Dār al-Maʿārif bi-Miṣr, 1963), 46–51 (including, among others, *Kitāb fī taṣnīf ḥiyal luṣūṣ al-nahār wa-fī tafṣīl ḥiyal luṣūṣ al-layl*, which is unfortunately no longer extant and which according to its title, deals with precisely the same type of theme in the same kind of style [see Charles Pellat, "Ǧāḥiẓiana III": 164, 177]); or al-Jāḥiẓ's exposition on the types of beggars Khālid mentioned by their specific titles, and added right after the conclusion of the *ḥadīth* (al-Jāḥiẓ, *al-Bukhalāʾ*, 51–53). Our author uses this humorous literary technique (which fits in, as we already noted above, with another kindred technique which we may call "gathering of educated fools") when he makes pimps his protagonists. This is something that had already happened before in Arabic literature. Both Ibn Falīta and al-Tīfāshī, for example, divide pimps into various types, a division which is of course not bereft of humor. Ibn Falīta enumerates more than five types of pimps (*Rushd al-labīb*, 165–181) while al-Tīfāshī counts twenty-two types of both sexes in his chapter (*Nuzhat al-albāb*, 63–92) and seven types of prostitutes in chapter four of the same book (ibid., 99–126). It would appear that these classified lists are usually based on real figures, whose skill and cunning the two authors inflated and exaggerated in their depictions, transforming them into semi-realistic literary figures whose features are close to turning into caricatures. It goes without saying, of course, that this is a familiar literary technique used for shaping and presenting marginal figures. It is thus quite likely that what the author of *The Pimps' Maqāma* did here does not differ in principle from all of the above. The pimps, like other literary figures, do not necessarily constitute an accurate reflection of reality. Instead, much of what they are is the product of the author's imagination and creative literary skills. However, the features which some of them, and some of the prostitutes, are given remain a riddle. While we have no difficulty

The seven young men [131a] were attending this place. He then turned towards them, pointed to them with his index finger and said: O you of the eloquent tongue, O lads with the beautiful whores, I ask each of you in the name of Him who has permitted sexual intercourse with a contract and a document, to recite verses of his making, praising or mocking his livelihood. Whoever is most innovative in his utterance and proud of his work, vigorous and refreshed, will be granted our attention, will take our silver, and we shall spend our night in his company.

He said: Then the pimp of the tambourine singers jumped up, stood straight, picked up his cup, extended his arm and said: My greetings to whoever heard my words and understood my prose and verse. I am al-Naʿʿās,[35] O you who are strong and mighty. I walk between two and gaze at them in an instant. I speak nicely to both sides, strike trouble both ways and take two [out of ten] dirhams. I am much adorned [131b] and my acts are unfeasible, as I take tips from both women and men. My speech is delicate and I ignite and excite the client's heart.[36]

He then charmingly recited a light verse and said:

I pimp and do not listen to whoever reproves [me]
I abandon my friend who strays from the truth
I bring pyramids from the side that
Is to the west all the way to Qalʿat al-Jabal[37]

---

in understanding what was meant with the first two pimps (*qawwād maghānī al-dufūf wa'l-shabbābāt* and *qawwād maghānī al-ʿArabiyyāt*), and the seventh pimp (*qawwād yaqūd ʿalā al-ʿulūq*, which he himself explains in the next sentence), it is not clear what he meant with the third through the sixth pimps. Since the rest of the text is lost, there is nothing by which we can clarify these terms. Do the pimps of the *kabliyyāt* (*kabl*, pl. *kubūl, akbul* means "rope") control prostitutes who engage in bondage or sadomasochism? Is a *bayyāta* a slave girl who sings in the *bayāt* or *bayātī* meter? (see al-Faruqi, *Arabic Musical Terms*, 35), or perhaps a girl who receives her male clients at home or in a brothel? In a similar vein, would a *baytūtiyya* spend the night in the client's home? (see, for example, the pimps called *al-ḥawsh, ḥawsh al-ḥawsh, al-muʿarris, al-muraḥḥil* and *al-musakkin* in al-Tīfāshī, *Nuzhat al-albāb*, 66–67, 71–75). Or would a *waqqāfa* be found on a street corner? Such questions will probably have to remain unanswered until the rest of the text is found or another text is discovered that could shed light on the meaning of these terms.

35 The name is derived from a root meaning "sleep" and has an obvious and humorous connection to the pimp's vocation, as noted above.

36 In Arabic, *anā al-muḥriq bi'l-tashrīḥ qalb al-ḥarīf.* Perhaps a play on words was intended here, since having sexual intercourse with a woman lying on her side is called *al-ḥarīqa*, while if she lies on her back it is called *al-sharḥ*. See, for example ʿAbd Allāh b. Muḥammad al-Tījānī (d. after 710/1311), *Tuḥfat al-ʿarūs wa-mutʿat al-nufūs* (London and Cyprus: Riyāḍ al-Rayyis li'l-Kutub wa'l-Nashr, 1992), 390.

37 The fortress (*qalʿa*), whose construction was begun by Saladin (d. 589/1193) and completed by al-Malik al-Kāmil Muḥammad b. Aḥmad (d. 635/1238) in 1207 is located on the slope of

He then drank his cup and sat down, having slaked his thirst. Then rose another pimp by the name al-Nawwām,[38] the likes of which have never been replaced, the pimp of Bedouin women singers. He demonstrated humility and then delight, and said: Greetings to the gentlemen who are present. Now, listen to my speech and understand what is proper. I am the pimp of Bedouin prostitutes. I do not hear the speech of one who lies, I am a skilled pimp, and rule over the lowly and the base.[39] I rule every crawler lying in wait.[40]

Jabal al-Muqaṭṭam to the south-east of the Old City of Cairo. Here the pimp boasts of his strength, which is such that he can bring the pyramids to that place from their original position to the west of the city. From this verse we learn that the *The Pimps' Maqāma* was not composed before the end of the twelfth or the beginning of the thirteenth century CE and that the author was Egyptian, or at least someone who lived in Cairo and was familiar with its sites.

38 See note 35 above, about the name of the pimp of the singer who plays the tambourine and flute.

39 *Ṭinjīr* in the Arabic expression *al-ṭinjīr wa'l-zāmir* is a copper pot, but in this case the word's meaning may be more akin to what Muḥammad Murtaḍā al-Zabīdī (who lived and composed his dictionary in Cairo in the eighteenth century, although he was not originally an Egyptian) wrote in his *Tāj al-ʿarūs min jawāhir al-Qāmūs* (Beirut: Dār al-Fikr li'l-Ṭibāʿa wa'l-Nashr wa'l-Tawzīʿ, 1994): "*al-ṭinjīr* is an epithet for a cowardly or depraved person. That is how it is used by the Bedouin in our times, as if they mean by it a sedentary person who always has his food in a copper pot and plate, in contrast to the Bedouin" (s.v. *ṭinjīr*). The plural is perhaps طناجر, as Dozy, *Supplément*, s.v. notes, quoting the *Sīrat ʿAntar* according to *Extraits du roman d'Antar: (texte arabe) a l'usage des élèves de l'École royale et spéciale des langues orientales vivantes* (Paris: Typographie de Firmin Didot Frères, 1841), 41: "You were defeated by these dogs the طناجر." The plural form may also be طناجير (this is the form that is to be preferred), mentioned in *Sīrat ʿAntara b. Shaddād* (Beirut: al-Maktaba al-Thaqāfiyya, 1979), 1:347: "You were defeated by these dogs the طناجير." The quoted sentence is taken from ʿAntara's speech to al-Mundhir, king of al-Ḥīra (son of Māʾ al-Samāʾ, al-Mundhir III, d. 554) after his people were beaten and defeated by "Persian worshippers of fire." ʿAntara himself was a man of the desert, which of course is not what al-Zabīdī had in mind; rather, he was speaking about his own days. It would thus appear that this term was to some extent quite prevalent in the spoken language of Egypt in the Mamluk period. This was also the time when the stories of *Sīrat ʿAntara* took shape and were collected in Cairo. The word زامر does not only denote someone who plays the wind instrument called *mizmar*, but may also be a distortion of زَمِر, which, similarly to *ṭinjīr*, means "unmanly." The first lexicographer to have mentioned this word was Ismāʿīl al-Jawharī (d. 393/1003), *al-Ṣiḥāḥ* (Cairo: Dār al-Kitāb al-ʿArabī, 1957), s.v., who was followed by others.

40 In Arabic, *kull man dabba*. Here the author seems to have made use of a literary theme that was in fact not very common in early *adab* literature. Still, it is no doubt a well-developed theme, referring to the *dabīb*, a semi-imaginary literary figure to whom various sexual deviations are ascribed. The *dabīb* lies in ambush, waiting for the appropriate time to attack his victim. When a victim approaches, he attacks him/her and penetrates his/her backside without the victim noticing. The target may be either a man or a woman, and not only a man, as Bothworth thought (see *The Mediaeval Islamic Underworld*, 1:30). See also the following references to the *dabīb*: *al-Maḥāsin wa'l-aḍdād* attributed to al-Jāḥiẓ

Bibliography

'Abd al-'Azīz, Hishām and 'Ādil 'Abd al-Ḥamīd. 'Ādil, *Layālī al-ḥubb wa'l-'ishq: alf layla wa-layla bi'l-'āmmiyya al-Miṣriyya*. Cairo: Dār al-Khayāl, 1977.

Al-Ābī, Manṣūr b. al-Ḥusayn. *Nathr al-durr*. Cairo: al-Hay'a al-Miṣriyya al-'Āmma li'l-Kitāb, 1980–1985.

Al-'Aynī, Badr al-Dīn Maḥmūd b. Aḥmad. *'Iqd al-jumān fī ta'rīkh ahl al-zamān*. Cairo: al-Hay'a al-Miṣriyya al-'Āmma li'l-Kitāb, 1987–1989.

Al-Azharī, Muḥammad b. Aḥmad. *Tahdhīb al-lugha*. Cairo: al-Dār al-Miṣriyya li'l-Ta'līf wa'l-Tarjama, Maktabat al-Khānijī and al-Hay'a al-Miṣriyya al-'Āmma li'l-Kitāb, 1964–1976. 17 vols.

Bosworth, Clifford Edmund. *The Mediaeval Islamic Underworld—the Banū Sāsān in Arabic Society and Literature*. Leiden: Brill, 1976.

Brockelmann, Carl. *Geschichte der arabischen Litteratur*. Leiden: Brill, 1937–1949.

Al-Bustāni, Buṭrus. *Muḥīṭ al-muḥīṭ*. Beirut: n.p., 1867–1870.

Cureton, Gulielmus and Carolus Rieu. *Catalogus Codicum Manuscriptorum Orientalium qui in Museo Britannico asservantur, Pars Secunda: Codices Arabicos amplectens*. London: Impensis Curatorum Musei Britannici, 1846–1871.

Dozy, Reinhart. *Supplément aux dictionnaires arabes*. Leiden: Brill, 1881.

Extraits du roman d'Antar: (texte arabe) a l'usage des élèves de l'École royale et spéciale des langues orientales vivantes. Paris: Typographie de Firmin Didot Frères, 1841.

Al-Faruqi, Lois Ibsen. *An Annotated Glossary of Arabic Musical Terms*. Westport: Greenwood Press, 1981.

(Cairo: Maṭba'at al-Sa'āda, 1906), 228–231; 'Alī al-Kātib, *Jawāmi' al-ladhdha* (ed. Tāla), 148–151; al-Rāghib al-Iṣbāhānī, *Muḥādarāt al-udabā'*, 3: 256–257; Manṣūr b. al-Ḥusayn al-Ābī, *Nathr al-durr* (Cairo: al-Hay'a al-Miṣriyya al-'Āmma li'l-Kitāb, 1980–1985), 4: 301; Ibn Shuhayd al-Andalusī, *Dīwān* (Cairo: Dār al-Kātib al-'Arabī li'l-Ṭibā'a wa'l-Nashr, n.d.), 120; and al-Tīfāshī, *Nuzhat al-albāb*, who dedicated an entire chapter of his book to this topic, see chapter nine, entitled "On the Literature of *al-Dabb*, Interesting Anecdotes and Witty Verses" (209–220). See also Rowson, "Arabic," 51. In addition, see Muḥammad b. Aḥmad al-Azharī (d. 370/981), *Tahdhīb al-lugha* (Cairo: al-Dār al-Miṣriya li'l-Ta'līf wa'l-Tarjama, Maktabat al-Khānijī and al-Hay'a al-Miṣriyya al-'Āmma li'l-Kitāb, 1964–1976), s.v., whose comment is also worth mentioning: "A man who is *dabūb* or *daybūb* is one who pairs men and women [i.e. a pimp or a matchmaker], so called because he creeps (*yadibbu*) among them and hides." The question remains whether this was indeed the author's intention.

Here folio 131b ends and 132a begins, with a different form and a different content. It is not a continuation of 131b or *The Pimps' Maqāma*. It seems that the manuscript's owner or the merchant who sold it added this page in order to make the text look complete. The *maqāma* thus lacks the rest of the speech by the Bedouin prostitutes' pimp, as well as that of five other pimps.

Geries, Ibrahim Kh. *A Literary and Gastronomical Conceit: Mufākharat al-Ruzz wa'l-Ḥabb Rummān: The Boasting Debate between Rice and Pomegranate Seeds; or, al-Maḳāma al-Simāṭiyya (The Tablecloth Maḳāma)*. Wiesbaden: Harrassowitz, 2002.

Ḥājjī Khalīfa, Musṭafā b. ʿAbd Allāh. *Kashf al-ẓunūn ʿan asāmī al-kutub wa'l-funūn*. Istanbul: Wikālat al-Maʿārif, 1941–1943.

Hämeen-Anttila, Jaakko. *Maqama: A History of a Genre*. Wiesbaden: Harrassowitz, 2002.

Ḥarb, ʿAbd al-Hādī. *Mawsūʿat adab al-muḥtālīn*. Damascus: al-Takwīn, 2008.

Al-Ḥusayn, Aḥmad. *Adab al-kudya fī'l-ʿaṣr al-ʿAbbāsī: Dirāsa fī adab al-shaḥḥādhīn wa'l-mutaswwilīn*. Damascus: Dār al-Ḥisad li'l-Nashr wa'l-Tawzīʿ, 2001.

Ibn Falīta. *Rushd al-labīb ilā muʿāsharat al-ḥabīb*. Al-Māya: Tāla li'l-Ṭibāʿa wa'l-Nashr, 2006.

Ibn Qutayba, ʿAbd Allāh b. Muslim. *Uyūn al-akhbār*. Cairo: al-Mu'assasa al-Miṣriyya al-ʿĀmma li'l-Ta'līf wa'l-Tarjama wa'l-Ṭibāʿa wa'l-Nashr, 1983.

Ibn Shuhayd al-Andalusī. *Diwān*. Cairo: Dār al-Kātib al-ʿArabī li'l-Ṭibāʿa wa'l-Nashr, n.d.

Al-Jāḥiẓ, ʿAmr b. Baḥr. *al-Bukhalā'*. Cairo: Dār al-Maʿārif bi-Miṣr, 1963.

[Pseudo-] Al-Jāḥiẓ, ʿAmr b. Baḥr. *al-Maḥāsin wa'l-aḍdād*. Cairo: Maṭbaʿat al-Saʿāda, 1906.

Al-Jāḥiẓ, ʿAmr b. Baḥr. *Rasā'il al-Jāḥiẓ*. Beirut: Dār al-Jīl, 1991.

Al-Jammāl, Aḥmad Ṣādiq. *al-Adab al-ʿāmmī fī Miṣr fī'l-ʿaṣr al-Mamlūkī*. Cairo: al-Dār al-Qawmiyya li'l-Ṭibāʿa wa'l-Nashr, 1977.

Al-Jawharī, Ismāʿīl. *al-Ṣiḥāḥ*. Cairo: Dār al-Kitāb al-ʿArabī, 1957.

Al-Kātib, ʿAlī b. Naṣr. *Jawāmiʿ al-ladhdha*. Cairo: Dār al-Bayān al-ʿArabī, 2002.

Al-Kātib, ʿAlī b. Naṣr. *Jawāmiʿ al-ladhdha*. Al-Māya: Tāla li'l-Ṭibāʿa wa'l-Nashr, 2002.

Lerner, Amir. "'Maqāmat al-muʿarraṣīn' wa-ṣināʿāt al-qawwādīn: fī'l-nathr al-fannī al-hāzil al-mājin fī Miṣr ayyām al-Mamālīk," in *In the Oasis of Pens: Studies in Arab Literature and Culture in Honour of Professor Joseph Sadan*, edited by ʿAbd Allāh Shaykh-Mūsā, Nādir Maṣārwa, and Ghālib ʿAnābsa. Cologne: Dār al-Hudā and Manshūrāt al-Jamal, 2011, 1: 68–78.

MacDonald, Duncan B. "Maximilian Habicht and His Recension of the Thousand and One Nights," *Journal of the Royal Asiatic Society* 41 (1909): 685–704.

Al-Mallūḥī, ʿAbd al-Muʿīn. *Ashʿār al-luṣūṣ wa-akhbāruhum*. Beirut: Dār al-Ḥaḍāra al-Jadīda, 1993.

Al-Maqqarī, Aḥmad b. Muḥammad. *Nafḥ al-ṭīb min ghuṣn al-Andalus al-raṭīb*. Beirut: Dār Ṣādir, 1968.

Al-Maqrīzī, Aḥmad b. ʿAlī. *al-Sulūk li-maʿrifat duwal al-mulūk*. Cairo: Maṭbaʿat Lajnat al-Ta'līf wa'l-Tarjama wa'l-Nashr and Maṭbaʿat Dār al-Kutub, 1934–1973.

Al-Masʿūdī, ʿAlī b. al-Ḥusayn. *Murūj al-dhahab wa-maʿādin al-Jawhar*. Beirut: Manshūrāt al-Jāmiʿa al-Lubnāniyya, 1965–1979.

Al-Maydānī, Aḥmad b. Muḥammad. *Majmaʿ al-amthal*. Beirut: Manshūrāt Dār Maktabat al-Ḥayāt, 1961–1962.
Moreh, Shmuel. *Live Theatre and Dramatic Literature in the Medieval Arab World*. Edinburgh: Edinburgh University Press, 1992.
Al-Najjār, Muḥammad Rajab. *Ḥikāyāt al-shuṭṭār wa'l-ʿayyārīn*. Kuwait: al-Hay'a al-ʿĀmma li-Quṣūr al-Thaqāfa, 2002.
Pellat, Charles. "Ǧāḥiẓiana III: Essai d'inventaire de l'œuvre ǧāḥiẓienne," *Arabica* 3 (1956): 147–180.
Pellat, Charles. *The Life and Works of Jāḥiẓ: Translation of Selected Texts*. London: Routledge, 1969.
Pellat, Charles. "Nouvel Essai d'inventaire de l'œuvre ǧāḥiẓienne," *Arabica* 31 (1984): 117–164.
Al-Qālī, Ismāʿīl b. al-Qāsim. *al-Amālī*. Beirut: al-Maktab al-Tijārī li'l-Ṭibāʿa wa'l-Nashr wa'l-Tawzīʿ, 1965.
Al-Rāghib al-Iṣbāhānī, Ḥusayn b. Muḥammad. *Muḥāḍarāt al-udabā' wa-muḥāwarāt al-shuʿarā' wa'l-bulaghā'*. Beirut: Manshūrāt Dār Maktabat al-Ḥayāt, 1961.
Rowson, Everett K. "Two Homoerotic Narratives from Mamlūk Literature: al-Ṣafadī's Lawʿat al-Shākī and b. Dānyāl's al-Mutayyam," in *Homoeroticism in Classical Arabic Literature*, edited by J.W. Wright and Everett K. Rowson. New York: Columbia University Press, 1997, 158–191.
Rowson, Everett K. "Arabic: Middle Ages to Nineteenth Century," *Encyclopedia of Erotic Literature*. New York: Routledge, 2006, 1: 43–61.
Sadan, Joseph. "Kings and Craftsmen: A Pattern of Contrasts: On the History of a Medieval Arabic Humoristic Form" (part I), *Studia Islamica* 56 (1982): 5–49; (part II) 62 (1985): 89–120.
Sadan, Joseph. "Hārūn al-Rashīd and the Brewer: Preliminary Remarks on the Adab of the Elite Versus Ḥikāyāt: The Continuation of Some of the Traditional Literary Models, from the 'Classical' Arabic Heritage, up to the Emergence of Modern Forms," in *Studies in Canonical and Popular Arabic Literature*, edited by Shimon Ballas and Reuven Snir. Toronto: York Press, 1998, 1–22.
Sadan, Joseph. "Conflicting Tendencies between Higher and Lower Strata of Humor: Some Genizah Fragments," in *Humor in der arabischen Kultur*, edited by Georges Tamer. Berlin: Walter de Gruyter, 2009, 137–149.
Sadān, Yūsuf. *al-Adab al-ʿArabī al-hāzil wa-nawādir al-thuqalā': al-ʿĀhāt wa'l-masāwi' al-insāniyya wa-makānatuhā fi'l-adab al-rāqī*. Köln: Manshūrāt al-Jamal, 2007.
Sirat ʿAntara b. Shaddād. Beirut: al-Maktaba al-Thaqāfiyya, 1979.
Spiro, Socrates. *An Arabic-English Vocabulary of the Colloquial Arabic of Egypt*. Cairo: al-Mokattam Printing Office, 1895.
Al-Suyuṭī, Jalāl al-Dīn. *al-Wishāḥ fī fawā'id al-nikāḥ*. Al-Māya: Tāla li'l-Ṭibāʿa wa'l-Nashr, 2006.

Al-Tīfāshī, Aḥmad b. Yūsuf. *Nuzhat al-albāb fīmā lā yūjad fī kitāb*. London and Cyprus: Riyāḍ al-Rayyis li'l-Kutub wa'l-Nashr, 1992.

Al-Tijānī, ʿAbd Allāh b. Muḥammad. *Tuḥfat al-ʿarūs wa-mutʿat al-nufūs*. London and Cyprus: Riyāḍ al-Rayyis li'l-Kutub wa'l-Nashr, 1992.

Al-Zabīdī, Muḥammad Murtaḍā. *Tāj al-ʿarūs min jawāhir al-qāmūs*. Beirut: Dār al-Fikr li'l-Ṭibāʿa wa'l-Nashr wa'l-Tawzīʿ, 1994.

Where Is the Holy Land? A Reading of Two Seventeenth-Century Arabic Manuscripts of *Virtues of the Holy Land* Literature

Ghaleb Anabseh

1 Introduction

As is well known, the Holy Land was the subject of numerous compositions within the genre of "virtues literature" (*adab al-faḍā'il*),[1] which dealt with its status and sanctity from the earliest days of Islam until the end of the Ottoman period. These works dealt with holy Muslim cities (Mecca, Medina, Jerusalem) as well as Damascus, which attracted the attention of numerous scholars and orientalists, such as Meir J. Kister, Joseph Sadan, and many others.

In the present study we focus on later works that described Palestine and Syria in the Mamluk and Ottoman periods, in particular the cities of Jerusalem and Damascus. Works of this type, known as the literature of "the virtues of al-Sham" (*faḍā'il al-Shām*), is a religious, literary, geographical, or local patriotic genre.

1 In early Arabic literature one encounters a number of nearly synonymous terms, such as *manāqib*, *maḥāsin* and *shamā'il*. Fuat Sezgin claims that the use of such terms goes back to pre-Islamic times, when poets sang the praises of their tribes or their own exploits, or expressed love of their homeland. Among the earliest works in which Muslim holy cities are discussed are al-Azraqī's *Faḍā'il Makka* and Ibn Shādhān al-Wāsiṭī's *Akhbār al-Madīna*, which relate to cities in Hijaz. The status of the cities of al-Sham in the broad sense was already discussed before the eleventh century CE, but none of these works are extant. They are mentioned by Kāmil al-ʿAsalī in the table of contents of *Makhṭūṭāt faḍā'il Bayt al-Maqdis*. The earliest works we possess today are from the eleventh century, including al-Rabʿī's *Faḍā'il al-Shām wa-Dimashq* and Ibn al-Murajjā's *Faḍā'il Bayt al-Maqdis wa'l-Khalīl* and *Faḍā'il al-Shām*. These works were motivated by religious considerations having to do with the centrality of holy cities in Islam, especially Mecca, Medina, and Jerusalem; with the importance which the Umayyad rulers attached to Palestine and Syria; with the struggle against the Crusaders; and, last but not least, the rivalry between Jerusalem and Damascus concerning the location of Moses's tomb, as noted by Sadan in his paper (see footnote below).

 | DOI:10.1163/9789004459120_010

The region of al-Sham[2] (and especially Jerusalem) was the subject of many books composed before the fifth century AH/eleventh century CE[3] and which dealt with its religious, historical, and spiritual importance.[4] However, no such works are extant, although several are mentioned in Kāmil Jamīl al-ʿAsalī's *Makhṭūṭāt faḍāʾil Bayt al-Maqdis* (Manuscripts of the virtues of Jerusalem).[5] In contrast, beginning in the eleventh century CE, independent compositions began to appear on al-Sham in both the broad and the restricted sense. Of these we may mention, for example, *Faḍāʾil Bayt al-Maqdis waʾl-Khalīl wa-faḍāʾil al-Shām* (Virtues of Jerusalem and Hebron and virtues of al-Sham) by Ibn al-Murajjā (d. 738/1337), edited by Ofer Livne-Kafri, and *Faḍāʾil al-Shām wa-Dimashq* (Virtues of al-Sham and Damascus) by Abū al-Ḥasan ʿAlī b. Muḥammad al-Rabʿī (d. 444/1052), edited by Ṣalāḥ al-Dīn al-Munajjid.[6] It

2 In medieval historical and geographical sources, the word al-Sham may refer broadly to Palestine and Syria or, in a more restricted sense, to Syria or only the city of Damascus.

3 Books that were written about the merits of Jerusalem before the eleventh century CE apparently remained in unpublished manuscripts or were lost. Hence for example, *Kitāb futūh bayt almaqdis* (by Isḥāq b. Bishr al-Bukhārī, d. 821).

4 Emmanuel Sivan, "Le caractère sacré de Jérusalem aux XIIe–XIIIe siècles," *Studia Islamica* 22 (1967): 149–150. In this article there are numerous sources, p. 50. E.W. Ashtor; Z. Caskel; Ch. Hirschberg; A. Matthews; N. Poliak, G. Vajda; Heribert Busse, "Der Islam und die biblischen Kultstätten," *Der Islam* 42 (1966): 113–147; idem, "The Sanctity of Jerusalem in Islam," *Judaism* 17 (1968): 441–468; idem, "Jerusalem and Mecca: The Temple and the Kaaba," in *The Holy-Land in History and Thought*, edited by Moshe Sharon (Leiden: University Press, 1968), 236–246; Meir J. Kister, "You Shall Only Set Out for Three Mosques," *Le Muséon* 82 (1969): 173–196; Emmanuel Sivan, "The Beginnings of the Faḍāʾil al-Quds Literature," *Der Islam* 48 (1971): 100–110; Shmuel Dov Goitein, "The Sanctity of Jerusalem and Palestine in Early Islam," in idem, *Studies in Islamic History and Institutions* (Leiden: Brill, 1965), 135–148; Hava Lazarus-Yafeh, "The Sanctity of Jerusalem in Islam," in *Jerusalem*, eds. John. M. Oesterreicher and Anne Sinai (New York: John Day: 1974), 211–225; Joseph Sadan, "A Legal Opinion of a Muslim Jurist Regarding the Sanctity of Jerusalem," *Israel Oriental Studies* 13 (1993): 231–245; Meir J. Kister, "Sanctity Joint and Divided," *JSAI* 20 (1996): 18–65; Ofer Livne-Kafri, "A Note on Some Traditions of Faḍāʾil al-Quds," *JSAI* 14 (1991): 71–83; Ibrāhīm Maḥmūd, *Faḍāʾil Bayt al-Maqdis fi makhṭūṭāt ʿarabiyya qadīma* (Kuwait: Maʿhad al-Makhṭūṭāt al-ʿArabiyya, 1985); cf. Meir J. Kister, "A Note on the Antiquity of Traditions on the Praises of Jerusalem," *Topics in the History of the Land of Israel under Muslim Rule*, edited by Moshe Sharon (Jerusalem: Ben-Zvi Institute, 1976), 69–71 (in Hebrew); Joseph Sadan, "Three New Sources from the Praises of the Holy Land Literature in Arabic in the 16th–17th centuries," *Cathedra* 11 (1979): 186–206 (in Hebrew).

5 Kāmil Jamīl al-ʿAsalī, *Makhṭūṭāt faḍāʾil Bayt al-Maqdis* (Amman: Dār al-Bashīr, 1984), Introduction.

6 See al-Musharraf b. al-Murajjā, *Faḍāʾil Bayt al-Maqdis waʾl-Khalīl wa-faḍāʾil al-Shām* (Shafāʿamr: Dār al-Mashriq liʾl-Tarjama waʾl-Tibāʿa waʾl-Nashr, 1995); Alī al-Rabʿī, *Faḍāʾil al-Shām wa-Dimashq* (Damascus: Maṭbūʿāt al-Majmaʿ al-ʿIlmī al-ʿArabī bi-Dimashq, 1950).

appears to us that the Ottoman period, specifically the sixteenth and seventeenth centuries, was rich in works on the sanctity of al-Sham in both the broad and the restricted sense, as we have shown in the footnote above.

Our aim here is not to determine the nature of the concept of the Holy Land,[7] but rather to show the role which traditions relating to al-Sham, including local traditions, played in defining the Holy Land in works of the genre in question.

In this study we base ourselves on Jospeh Sadan's work (published in French in 1981) on the rivalry between the centers in Jerusalem and Damascus concerning the location of Moses's tomb.[8] Sadan mentions dozens of printed and manuscript texts composed in the Mamluk and Ottoman periods which discuss this issue. He showed that writers geographically associated with the Jerusalem center located the shrine near Jericho, while those who were geographically aligned with the Damascus center identified it near the al-Qadam Mosque (also known as al-Aqdām or al-Kathīb al-Aḥmar) south of Damascus.[9] For us this means that the writers on both sides championed their own respective regions and naturally espoused the cause of the shrine located

7 The Qur'an contains quite a number of verses in which the Holy Land is mentioned. See Qur'an 21:17, 81; 17:1; 5:24, and more. These refer to "the land which God blessed," the land of al-Sham, Palestine, Damascus, and part of Jordan, or al-Ramla, Jordan and Palestine, or Jericho, or parts of Jericho, Palestine, and Syria, or parts of Jerusalem.

8 Joseph Sadan, "Le tombeau de Moïse à Jéricho et à Damas: Une compétition entre deux lieux saints principalement à l'époque ottomane," *Revue des études Islamiques* 49/1 (1981): 60–99.

9 Joseph Sadan, "A Legal Opinion of a Muslim Jurist Regarding the Sanctity of Jerusalem," 231–245. However, according to standard Muslim tradition, its location is not known. Still, in the "virtues literature" there are numerous reports on its purported site, which is variously identified as Midyan, Tayh Bani Isra'il, Lydda, Damascus, Bosra near Damascus, al-Balqā' and Jericho, not far from Jerusalem. See Shams al-Dīn Muḥammad al-Khalīlī, *Ta'rīkh al-Quds wa'l-Khalīl 'alayhi al-salām* (London: Mu'assasat al-Furqān li'l-Turāth al-Islāmī, 2004), 10–87. The manuscript was edited by Muḥammad 'Adnān al-Bakhīt and Nawfān Rajā al-Sawāriya. As far as I could tell, the author of the manuscript (MS clark 33: Oxford) is not mentioned. See also Shams al-Dīn b. Ṭūlūn, *Tuḥfat al-ḥabīb fīmā warada fi'l-Kathīb* (MS Leyden Or. 2512), fol. 1 v., 2 r., in which the shrine is located next to al-Kathīb al-Aḥmar since, according to Muslim tradition, the Prophet saw Moses there during his night journey: 5v. Although this tradition would seem to place Moses's shrine near Jericho, while the tradition placing the shrine in al-Sham in the broad sense would seem to be in favor of Damascus, there is in fact no difficulty in considering al-Kathīb al-Aḥmar as being located near Jericho. Cf. Shihāb al-Dīn al-Maqdisī, *Muthīr al-gharām ilā ziyārat al-Quds wa'l-Shām* (Beirut: Dār al-Jīl, 1994), 273, where it is said with respect to Moses: "In the past the rock was the direction in which he prayed. The Prophet and his Companions prayed to it for sixteen or seventeen months, then turned to the Ka'ba. The Prophet saw him on the night of the midnight journey (*al-isrā'*) as he was praying at his tomb at al-Kathīb al-Aḥmar." Al-Maqdisī does not mention the shrine but does say that it is in Palestine.

nearby.[10] However, this is not always the case. Thus, for example, ʿAbd al-Ghanī al-Nābulusī (d. 1731), who belonged to the Damascus center, states that Moses's shrine is the one located near Jericho.[11]

We mention the rivalry between these two centers not for purposes of comparison. In fact, there is no comparing the two, since Jerusalem is considered the third holiest city of Islam, after Mecca and Medina.[12] However, Damascus, too, enjoyed considerable religious, administrative, historical, and economic importance.

2 Traditions in Keeping with Islamic Thought and Local Traditions

A perusal of compositions in the "virtues of the Holy Land" genre reveals that they contain traditions going back to early Islam, which mention the Holy Land as part of an exegesis of the Qur'an, or belong to official Ḥadīth literature. On the other hand, we also encounter traditions that are not consistent with Islamic thought and do not occur in official Ḥadīth collections. In the present study, which is limited to the seventeenth century and to two manuscripts from that time which were made available to us by Sadan in the course of our studies at Tel Aviv University, we shall for brevity's sake limit ourselves to mentioning the sources used by the two authors in question: Ṣāliḥ b. Aḥmad al-Tamartāshī (d. 1645) and Muḥammad b. Ḥabīb (d. 1649). The sources they used in compiling the materials for their compositions include the Qur'an, commentaries on the Qur'an, Ḥadīth literature, *adab* literature, works on geography and history, and previous works in the "virtues" genre. At the same time, we see that they also used local traditions of doubtful validity that contradict Islamic thought, and traditions that can be interpreted as referring to more than one geographical region. This fact has been noted by a number of investigators of the genre, among them the historian Ṣalāḥ al-Dīn al-Munajjid, who, in his edition of al-Rabʿī's *Faḍāʾil al-Shām wa-Dimashq*, divided the traditions mentioned in that work into three parts: the so-called "Israelite" ḥadīths (*Isrāʾīliyyāt*), fabricated ḥadīths, and valid ḥadīths.[13] For the purposes of his edition, he sought the opinions of clerics such as Nāṣir al-Dīn al-Arnāʾūṭ and

10 Joseph Sadan, "Le Tombeau de Moïse à Jéricho et à Damas," 60–99. Heribert Busse, "Der Islam und die biblischen Kultstätten," 137–140; "The Sanctity of Jerusalem in Islam," 441–468.

11 ʿAbd al-Ghanī al-Nābulusi, *Riḥlati ilā al-Quds* (My journey to Jerusalem) (Cairo: Maktabat al-Qāhira, 1902), 46.

12 Kister, "You Shall Only Set Out for Three Mosques," 173–196.

13 See al-Rabʿī, *Faḍāʾil al-Shām wa-Dimashq*, 89.

Nāṣir al-Dīn al-Albānī regarding the validity and acceptability of the traditions upheld in the book as an act of religious purism and out of a desire to please the clerics and Muslim society in general.

3 The Rivalry between Jerusalem and Damascus

It is a well-known fact that the rivalry between the centers in Jerusalem and Damascus began with a dispute regarding the nature of the Holy Land and, to judge by the manuscripts and other texts that we examined, later spread to additional issues, such as the location of Moses's tomb. The rivalry was limited to a specific geographical region, as shown by Sadan (see above), and not one that concerned the Muslim world as a whole, as dealt with by Kister and Sourdel-Thomine.[14]

In our perusal of the two seventeenth-century manuscripts, we found that the rivalry in question concerned the definition of the concept of the Holy Land.[15] This raises the following questions: Can we find traditions of a local character used as elements of this rivalry? Can we find traditions that can be interpreted in more than one way? For example, among the ways the term "al-Sham" can be understood, should we adopt the more restricted sense (that is, the city of Damascus), as demanded by the ruler of that city, who insisted that the city was the Holy Land? We wish to point out that our task in the present study is not to discuss the traditions commonly accepted as valid since the inception of Islam. Important as they are, they do not pertain to the subject under discussion here. Such traditions, which go back to the times of the Prophet, or were ascribed to him at a later date, are irrelevant here, despite their intrinsic importance, except perhaps with respect to what we can learn about the way such traditions appeared in different times and places.

In the seventeenth century, two oral debates took place on whether or not Damascus was the Holy Land, as shown by the two aforementioned manuscripts.

14 Kister, "You Shall Only Set Out for Three Mosques," 173–196; and "Sanctity Joint and Divided," 18–65; Janine Sourdel-Thomine, "Une image de Jérusalem au début du XIIIe siècle," in *Jerusalem, Rome, Constantinople*, in the series *Cultures et civilizations médiévales*, edited by Daniel Poirion (Paris: Sorbonne, 1986), 217–233.

15 The concept of the Holy Land, as we shall see, is not well-defined. Ibn Ḥabīb understands the term al-Sham in the narrow sense, that is, the city of Damascus. See Qur'an, 5: 21. There are a number of different definitions in Islam of the concept of the Holy Land, for example "the land which God blessed," the land of al-Sham, Palestine, Damascus, and part of Jordan, or al-Ramla, Jordan, and Palestine, or Jericho, or parts of Jericho, Palestine and Syria, or parts of Jerusalem. Qur'an, 21: 71,81; 17: 1; 5: 24; 1: 93; 7: 133; 24: 36; 21: 105; 5: 41.

In order to clarify the matter, we chose a passage from the manuscript composed by Ṣāliḥ b. Aḥmad al-Tamartāshī, a resident of the city of Gaza, entitled *al-Khabar al-tāmm fī dhikr ḥudūd al-arḍ al-muqaddasa wa-Filasṭīn wa'l-Shām* (Complete report mentioning the boundaries of the Holy Land, Palestine, and Syria).[16] It should be noted that al-Tamartāshī wrote his book in the wake of an oral debate on whether or not Damascus was the Holy Land, a debate that took place in Egypt in the presence of clerics and men of government. The passage reads as follows:

> I traveled away from my family and homeland, said farewell to my children and brothers, and set out for Cairo, may God guard it and the lands of the Muslims forever from the evils of injustice and aggression. In Cairo I heard, as I did also in my country, that His Excellency [...] the representative of the Ottoman State [...] the Vizier ʿAlī Pasha, now in Cairo, may God protect him [...] loves scholars and honors the pious and the wise. His Excellency held a meeting, which I too attended, with Khalīl Efendi al-Rūmī, a teacher at the al-Shaykhūniyya school and other Cairene dignitaries.[17]

The manuscript then goes on to explain the reason that the epistle was written, by way of an oral dispute that took place at the gathering of the aforementioned vizier:

> During the gathering at His Excellency ʿAlī Pasha's, a question was raised about Damascus al-Sham—whether it is a holy land or not. I asked God for guidance and composed this epistle, which contains a mention of the lands of al-Sham, its boundaries and why it was named as it was. It also mentions the land of Palestine and why it was named thus, as well as the holy lands, their boundaries and why they were called that.[18]

What is interesting here is how the author uses the word *al-Shām*, which may be understood in the general sense, that is Palestine and Syria, or in the more restricted sense, of Syria alone, which contradicts the epistle's purpose, or perhaps it refers just to the city of Damascus, which would make it consistent with

---

16 Based on the Istanbul MS, Asʿad Efendi, MS. No. 2212/2, composed by Ṣāliḥ b. Aḥmad al-Tamartāshī al-Ghazzī. See his biography in Khayr al-Dīn al-Zirkilī, *al-Aʿlām* (Beirut: Dār al-ʿIlm li'l-Malāyīn, 2002), 3:195.

17 Al-Tamartāshī, MS *al-Khabar al-tāmm*, 6v–7r.

18 Ibid., 6v–7v.

the epistle's stated purpose. Thus, for example, he says elsewhere: "Scholars are agreed that al-Sham is the best of sites after Mecca and Medina."[19]

Another example is provided by traditions taken from *Taʾrīkh madinat Dimashq* (History of Damascus), by Ibn ʿAsākir (d. 499/1176), regarding the prompting of the people of al-Sham, as in the following passage:

> As narrated by ʿAbd Allāh b. Ḥawwāla al-Asadī: The Messenger of God said: "You shall conscript armies, an army in al-Sham, an army in Iraq and an army in Yemen." Then Ibn Ḥawwāla said to him: "Choose for me, oh Messenger of God." He replied: "Take al-Sham, and whoever refuses let him adhere to the south and let him conscript whoever betrayed him. Indeed, God has guaranteed to me al-Sham and its people."[20]

Then another tradition is quoted, an Israelite tradition transmitted by Abū al-Ḥasan al-Rabʿī in his *Faḍāʾil al-Shām wa-Dimashq*: "[...] Kaʿb narrated: It was said: 'God blessed al-Sham from al-ʿArīsh to the Euphrates.'"[21]

Here, too, the report may be interpreted as referring to al-Sham in either the broad or the restricted sense. Al-Tamartāshī collected the materials for his manuscript from various other religious, historical, and geographical sources, in order to impress a local venerable with his erudition in matters of history and religion, and hopefully to obtain a good position with him. To judge by the manuscript's contents, he speaks about the geographical boundaries of al-Sham, as well as about Palestine and its virtues, but uses the opportunity to also discuss the virtues of Gaza, the city of his birth. By focusing on a town that was small, at least relative to the large Muslim cities that are usually the subject of works on the "virtues of al-Sham," he was displaying a measure of local patriotism.[22] The status of Jerusalem is somewhat obscured, however. Only at the end of the manuscript does he note the fact that "Jerusalem is the center of the earth." This is what he writes:

19 Ibid., 9v.

20 Ibid., 10r, 9v. Nāṣir al-Dīn al-Albānī treats this ḥadīth as very reliable: Nāṣir al-Dīn al-Albānī, *Takhrīj aḥādīth faḍāʾil al-Shām wa-Dimashq li'l-Rabʿī* (Damascus: al-Maktab al-Islāmī, 1960), 13.

21 Al-Tamartāshī, op.cit., 12r.

22 Ibid., 14v, 17v. According to this MS, "It is one of the most beautiful towns in the neighborhood of Jerusalem. In it Sulaymān, son of Dāwūd, peace be upon them both, was born [...] The *imām* Muḥammad b. Idrīs al-Shāfiʿī, may God be pleased with him, was born in it before that; the place of his birth is known and is a pilgrimage destination."

> The al-Aqṣā (literally: "the furthest one") Mosque was called so because it is the middle of the world [...]. It was related in the name of ʿAlī b. Abī Ṭālib, may God be pleased with him, who said: "The middle of the two earths is the Temple in Jerusalem (*bayt al-maqdis*), and the highest of the two earths towards the heavens is the Temple in Jerusalem."[23]

He ends his composition with a delineation of the Holy Land:

> As for the boundaries of the Holy Land, (they are) in the direction of prayer the Land of Hijaz [...] in the east beyond Dūmat al-Jandal, the desert of al-Samāwa, which is large and extends to Iraq [...] in the north the Euphrates river [...] and from the west the Byzantine Sea, which is the Salt Sea, and in the south the Egyptian desert.[24]

In this context the word "boundaries" (*ḥudūd*) is used as a definition referring to a geographical area rather than an abstract concept. The reason why this interpretation is clearly preferred is because various writers who used the term "boundaries of the Holy Land" or "boundaries of al-Sham" do not in fact provide complete borders, but only enough to define a geographical region. Furthermore, the division to which they refer is one that reflects a geographical reality in antiquity and does not express the historical situation at the time the texts were written.

As for the name Holy Land, the reason for it appears in a commentary on the verse "My people, go into the Holy Land":[25] "It was called this because it was the abode of the prophets and the residence of the believers. Some say that it is Mt. Sinai (*al-Ṭūr*) and its surroundings, others that it is Damascus, Palestine and parts of Jordan, and still others that it is al-Sham only."[26]

However, what is of interest to us here is the word al-Sham and its reference to the city of Damascus, which appears in the sources from which our writer borrowed. The term al-Sham is used in various traditions that speak of its sanctity, but these may be interpreted as referring either to the general sense of the term, that is Palestine and Syria, or just Syria, or even just the city of Damascus. In other words, they do not make it possible to claim with certainty that the

---

23 See MS *al-Khabar al-tāmm*, 18v.

24 Ibid., 17v.

25 Qur'an, 5: 21.

26 MS *al-Khabar al-tāmm*, 17r. The work in question is the commentary of Abū al-Suʿūd al-ʿImādī (d. 982/1574), *Irshād al-ʿaql al-salīm ilā mazāyā al-Qur'ān al-karīm* (Guidance of the healthy mind towards the merits of the noble Qur'an).

city of Damascus is the Holy Land.[27] In addition, the fact that the writer treats a variety of topics shows that he realized the uncertainty surrounding the concept of the Holy Land, and that addressing this was the main reason for composing this work.

A more certain conclusion concerning the possible interpretation "the Holy Land" as referring to the city of Damascus can be arrived at from a perusal of another manuscript, also composed in the seventeenth century. This work, entitled *Durr al-niẓām fī maḥāsin al-Shām* (Arrangement of pearls on the beauties of Syria), was written by Muḥammad b. Ḥabīb,[28] a resident of the city of Nablus. The manuscript is of interest because the author himself is not clear about his own definition of the Holy Land. He occasionally uses the word al-Sham in its restricted sense (Damascus) and occasionally in the more extensive sense (that is, as referring to Syria and Palestine).[29] This stands in contradiction to the stated reasons for the book's composition, as we shall show below.

According to the manuscript itself, it was composed in the wake of a disputation that took place in the presence of the governor of Damascus and the local governor of Nablus. The ruler of Damascus had a text read out aloud in his presence to the effect that the Holy Land was al-Sham in the narrow sense, that is, the city of Damascus. The quoted tradition was a local one, which he promulgated despite the opposition expressed by the scholars and clerics who attended the debate. This shows the extent to which the official religious establishment rejected this kind of ḥadīth. In order to win the approval of the ruler of Damascus, the governor of Nablus, upon his return to his city, asked a moderately cultured local man to compose a work that would prove the aforesaid tradition's validity.

The tradition pronounced by the ruler of Damascus, the validity of which the governor of Nablus wished to prove, is quoted in Ibn Ḥabīb's text, as follows:

> I was at a gathering of the Prince of Princes […], the Honorable Sulaymān Pasha, the prince of the district of Nablus […], and the above-mentioned vizier noted that he had been at a gathering of […] the king Yūsuf

---

27 See MS *al-Khabar al-tāmm*, 7v–8v.

28 MS Princeton Yehuda Collection Els. 1862. We have not been able to locate any biography of this writer.

29 See MS *Durr al-niẓām fī maḥāsin al-Shām*, in which the author quotes well-known traditions on the status of Palestine and the sanctity of Jerusalem. On folio 6r he says: "Ibn ʿAbbās said: Bayt al-Maqdis is holy because there one is purified of one's sins." On folio 7v there is an interesting tradition where Jerusalem is compared with Damascus: "It has been said that Damascus is the best region of al-Sham except Bayt al-Maqdis." Folio 13v.

> al-Zamān Sinān Katkhuda and the victorious army at the time in the city of Damascus al-Sham […]. Yūsuf al-Zamān mentioned al-Sham and its virtues, and Damascus and its beauties, and what was said in praise of its inhabitants, that it was the Holy Land par excellence in whose praise God, may He be glorified, said in the holy ḥadīths: "I am Allah, Lord of al-Sham." But how could he pronounce such an utterance, when God is Lord of the heavens and the two earths, without any specified place? Does this mean that his lordship extends to al-Sham but not elsewhere? Furthermore, the chain of transmission of this tradition is weak, with great error and sin […]. Some teachers of his country were present at the gathering […] and they spoke at length in this vein, and I had no choice but to listen patiently before rebutting their claims and proving the ḥadīth's validity to them.[30]

It would thus appear that the governor of Nablus wished to demonstrate the truth of this tradition at the gathering itself, in order to ingratiate himself with the ruler of Damascus. The manuscript then goes on:

> I then arose and quoted the Almighty's words as proof of the validity of this holy ḥadīth: "If you help God, He will help you."[31] I wanted to clarify this noble ḥadīth with a good chain of transmission and said: "Yes, this is a true ḥadīth […] for this exalted ḥadīth is holy and noble, glorified in the place of revelation, saying: 'I am Allah Lord of al-Sham, I shall not tolerate injustice by the unjust in it.'"[32]

Ibn Ḥabīb mentioned the sanctity of al-Sham in the broad sense in accordance with various traditions, as well as in the narrow sense of Damascus, since this was the reason why he had composed his epistle. He took his materials from a variety of sources, including commentaries on Qur'anic verses that include words variously taken to refer to Damascus and Jerusalem.[33] He also cited the verse about the Prophet's midnight journey, which he used indirectly to say something at least about the sanctity of Jerusalem, although this might also be perceived as contradicting his aim in writing the book. He did this by

---

30 MS *al-Khabar al-tāmm*, 1v, 2r.

31 Qur'an, 47: 7.

32 Ibn Ḥabīb, MS *Durr al-niẓām fī maḥāsin al-Shām*, folio 2r, 2v. It is possible that Ibn Ḥabīb hoped to obtain a position in Nablus from that city's governor.

33 Ibid., folio 3v. For example, Qur'an, 95: 1–3, where the figs symbolize the mosque of Damascus and the olive trees that of Jerusalem.

combining traditions dealing with the sanctity of Syria and Damascus with those that deal with the sanctity of Jerusalem.

Let us see, for example, how the author manages to bring Jerusalem into the discussion despite the fact that he is supposedly writing about the status of Damascus: "It has been said that Damascus is the best region of al-Sham, with the exception of Jerusalem."[34] In his epistle Ibn Ḥabīb does not refrain from quoting the local traditional text noted above that was recited at the gathering in the presence of the ruler of Damascus ("I am Allah the Lord of al-Sham") in which, although the word "al-Sham" could be interpreted in the more extensive sense, the author clearly intends it in the sense of the city of Damascus, since this was, after all, the purpose for which the epistle was written.

Elsewhere in the manuscript Ibn Ḥabīb refers to the boundaries of al-Sham:

> The First al-Sham is Gaza [...], Jerusalem and its large city Palestine.[35] The Second al-Sham is Jordan [...] and its large city Tiberias. The Third al-Sham is al-Ghūṭa [...] and its large city Damascus. The Fourth al-Sham is Qartab, Homs and Hama [...] and its large city Homs. The Fifth al-Sham is al-ʿAwāṣim [...] and its large city Antioch.[36]

In this passage, Ibn Ḥabīb describes a geographical division of al-Sham that does not reflect the situation in the Ottoman period, but that of an earlier time. Like al-Tamartāshī in the manuscript described previously, he uses the opportunity to display his local patriotism and discuss the virtues of his own town, Nablus.[37]

---

34 Ibid., folio 7v. This tradition is quoted by ʿIzz al-Dīn b. ʿAbd al-Salam al-Sulamī, *Targhīb ahl al-Islām fī suknā al-Shām* (Jerusalem: no publisher, 1940), 22.

35 Notably, Palestine is not a city, but a geographical area, according to geographical references. See Muhammad b. Ahmad al-Maqdisī, *Ahsan al-taqāsīm fī maʿrifat al-aqālīm* (Beirut: al-Muʾassasa al-ʿArabiyya li'l-Dirasat wa'l-Nashr, 2003), p. 158.

36 MS *Durr al-niẓām*, folio 5r.

37 Here is a passage from the manuscript, folio 12r:
In his document, al-Musharraf reported in Kaʿb's name, who said: The country God loves most is al-Sham and the part of al-Sham that God likes best is Jerusalem, and the part of Jerusalem God likes best is Mount Nablus [...] Many scholars, venerable and pious men, have come out of it. It is filled with springs, trees, and fruit. The most common trees in its surroundings are olives. It has been said that our Lord Joseph, peace be upon him, has his tomb near the city of Nablus between the village of Balāṭ and ʿAskar. It has also been said that this is Joseph, the friend who provided for Mary.

See: Ghaleb Anabseh, "Selection of Traditions on the Virtues of Nablus in Arabic Virtues of Palestine (*Faḍāʾil*) Literature," *Cathedra* 124 (2007): 21–30 (in Hebrew).

4 The Use of Deviant Local Traditions

In our perusal of the manuscript texts of "the virtues of al-Sham" in the extensive as well as the restricted sense, we found that both authors collected materials from a variety of different sources (e.g. religious, geographical, historical). Since it is our aim here to show the role played by local traditions that were not accepted by the official religious establishment, especially with respect to holy places, we have pointed out that several writers in the genre of "virtues literature" have quoted traditions that were quite suspect, especially when they divided tradition into three types: traditions that supposedly go back to the Prophet's time and are ascribed to him; traditions that are ascribed to the Prophet's Companions; and the *isra'īliyyāt*. To these types we add another, namely traditions stemming from a later period—that is, local traditions that had been suspended for a while and then reappeared at a later time.

Among the local traditions found in works on "the virtues of al-Sham" we find, for example, the tradition about "the cities of Paradise," which is quoted in some of these works, and where the term al-Sham was used in both the extended and the more restrictive sense. Thus, in the Mamluk period, Shihāb al-Dīn al-Maqdisī (d. 765/1363) in his *Muthīr al-gharām ilā ziyārat al-Quds wa'l-Shām* (Arouser of a love for pilgrimages to Jerusalem and al-Sham) quotes:

> Narrated by Abū Hurayra, may God be pleased with him: The Messenger of God, may God bless him and give him peace, said: "Four are the cities of Paradise: Mecca, Medina, Damascus, and Jerusalem, and four are the cities of Fire: Constantinople, Tyana, Antioch, and Sana'a."

Elsewhere he quotes a tradition in which Jerusalem appears before Damascus.[38] As for the Ottoman period, the ḥadīth quoted by Ibn Habib is as follows:

> Narrated Abū Hurayra, quoting the Prophet, may God bless him and give him peace, who said: "There are four cities of Paradise: Mecca, Medina, Damascus, and Jerusalem."[39]

---

38 See al-Maqdisī, *Muthīr*, first ḥadīth, p. 124; second ḥadīth, p. 259.

39 Ibn Ḥabīb, MS *Durr al-niẓām*, folio 13r. The tradition is quoted in folio 13r. The tradition *Faḍā'il al-Shām* (Damascus: Dār al-Thaqāfa al-ʿArabiyya, 1992), where Jerusalem is mentioned before Damascus: ḥadīth no. 19. The same is true of the version quoted in al-Rabʿī, *Faḍā'il al-Shām wa-Dimashq*, ḥadīth no. 53, 54, and also in Ibn al-Murajjā who, however, also quotes another tradition in Kaʿb's name:

No doubt that Ibn Ḥabīb intentionally put Damascus before Jerusalem, since that was the entire purpose of writing his composition, despite the fact that this ḥadīth may well have belonged to local traditions that are relatively plentiful in the literature of the virtues of al-Sham in both the broad and the restricted sense.

The tradition about the "four cities of Paradise" is also quoted in al-Rabʿī's *Faḍāʾil al-Shām wa-Dimashq*, but there Jerusalem appears before Damascus (the order being: Mecca, Medina, Jerusalem, Damascus). In his explanation of the ḥadīths, Ṣalāḥ al-Dīn al-Munajjid in his aforementioned work relies on the work of Nāṣir al-Dīn al-Albānī, who states: "I recorded an unattested ḥadīth."[40] Such traditions represent local traditions, not accepted in canonical Islam.

Actually, traditions in which Damascus precedes Jerusalem do not represent the official establishment in Islam. These traditions are rare and do not often appear in collections. The order Mecca, Medina, Jerusalem, Damascus fits in with what is considered acceptable in Islamic thought, irrespective of a particular tradition's validity or lack thereof (indeed, the tradition in question is considered to be fabricated, as noted above). Placing Damascus before Jerusalem simply contradicts the status of these cities in Islam.

We are of the opinion that the order of cities as given above reflects their relative sanctity in the authors' views. We may also compare the official order in which the holy cities are placed, according to their relative status, with the "lashing the saddle" (*shadd al-riḥāl*) ḥadīth, discussed by Kister, which represented the sanctity of Islam's holy cities by degree.[41] However, according to al-Albānī and others who wrote in the "virtues of al-Sham" genre, we have here, at the very least, an official tradition ("lashing the saddle of the holy cities of Islam") and a local one ("the cities of Paradise"), even when Jerusalem is placed before Damascus. We may compare the way the status and relative sanctity of Muslim cities appear in the "lashing the saddle" tradition, with the relative size of certificates of pilgrimage to al-Sham handed out to pilgrims in the Ayyubid periods: a large register of holy places in Mecca; a smaller one with the holy places in Medina; and an even smaller one with the holy places in Jerusalem.

"There are five cities of Paradise: Homs, Damascus, Jerusalem, Bayt Jibrin, and Zafar in Yemen, and five cities of Hell: Antioch, ʿAmmūriyya, Constantinople, Tadmur, and Sanʿa in Yemen (paragraphs 217–218)."

An anonymous MS, *Kitāb fī faḍāʾil Bayt al-Maqdis wa-fīhi kitāb fī faḍāʾil al-Shām*, Britain, MS Cambridge Qq 91.7, folio 127r, mentions Jerusalem before Damascus; cf. Aḥmad al-Baṣrī, *Tuḥfat al-anām fī faḍāʾil al-Shām* (Damascus: Dār al-Bashāʾir, 1998), 26, where Jerusalem precedes Damascus.

40 See the appendix of ḥadīths in al-Rabʿī's book, by Nāṣir al-Dīn al-Albānī, 99.

41 Kister, "You Shall Only Set Out for Three Mosques," 173–196.

The latter were studied by Dominique Sourdel and Janine Sourdel-Thomine. Although not every pilgrim received such certificates, their study provides a method for the identification of the official Islamic position by way of local works that highlight the sanctity of specific places. The problem is whether one can thereby identify the natural Islamic view.

In fact, what is important here, in addition to the rivalry between Jerusalem and Damascus, is the appearance of local traditions of other cities in a different context, such as traditions about the cities of Homs, Nablus, and Bisan, as indeed happens in the "virtues of al-Sham" genre.[42] Clearly, such traditions about Jerusalem, Damascus, or other cities constitute a local phenomenon that is not recognized by disparate sources. Perhaps we are faced with a literary and folkloristic phenomenon that is both similar and different from official ḥadīths.

5 Conclusion

In a number of traditions that mention al-Sham and appear in works in the "virtues of the Holy Land" genre, al-Sham does not always refer to Palestine and Syria in a broad sense, but has a more restricted denotation, referring to Syria only, or even just to the city of Damascus. Quite a few of these traditions aim at bolstering the status of Damascus and are therefore used in an unaccustomed manner to show that "al-Sham" (that is, Damascus) is "God's land." Such traditions could have been expected to disappear, but they remained in place and reappeared at a later time.

Al-Tamartāshī and Ibn Ḥabīb both tried to prove the sanctity of Damascus and to define the concept and boundaries of the Holy Land, although the issue remains somewhat obscure in both their compositions. In the case of al-Tamartāshī, this lack of clarity concerns the definition per se, while in the case of Ibn Ḥabīb, it has to do with his reliance on a late geographical division. Both writers mention the sanctity of Jerusalem and their own places of birth (Gaza and Nablus, respectively, both of which belonged to the Jerusalem center) as a show of local patriotism. Another important point is that one should not analyze the traditions used in the "virtues literature" according to Islamic criteria, but rather in light of cultural and literary considerations that help clarify how local traditions emerge and how, although they were not

42 Here we refer to the ḥadīth in which Homs is mentioned as one of the cities of Paradise and is listed before Jerusalem and Damascus. The second city listed is sometimes Damascus and sometimes Jerusalem.

gathered into official Ḥadīth collections, they have remained living materials with local color and used by later generations.

Bibliography

Al-Albānī, Nāṣir al-Dīn. *Takhrīj aḥādīth faḍāʾil al-Shām wa-Dimashq liʾl-Rabʿī*. Damascus: al-Maktab al-Islāmī, 1960.

Anabseh, Ghaleb. "Selection of Traditions on the Virtues of Nablus in Arabic Virtues of Palestine (Faḍāʾil) Literature," *Cathedra* 124 (2007): 21–30 [in Hebrew].

Al-ʿAsalī, Kāmil. *Makhṭūṭāt faḍāʾil Bayt al-Maqdis*. Amman: Dār al-Bashīr, 1984.

Al-Baṣrī, Aḥmad. *Tuḥfat al-anām fī faḍāʾil al-Shām*. Damascus: Dār al-Bashāʾir, 1998.

Busse, Heribert. "Der Islam und die biblischen Kultstätten," *Der Islam* 42 (1966): 113–147.

Busse, Heribert. "Jerusalem and Mecca: The Temple and the Kaaba," in *The Holy Land in History and Thought*, edited by Moshe Sharon. Leiden: Leiden University Press, 1968, 236–246.

Busse, Heribert. "The Sanctity of Jerusalem in Islam," *Judaism* 17 (1968): 441–468.

Goitein, Shmuel Dov. "The Sanctity of Jerusalem and Palestine in Early Islam," in *Studies in Islamic History and Institutions*, edited by S.D. Goitein. Leiden: Brill, 1965, 135–148.

Ibn Ḥabīb, Muḥammad. *Durr al-niẓām fī maḥāsin al-Shām*. MS Princeton Yehuda Collection. Els. 1862.

Ibn al-Murajjā, al-Musharraf. *Faḍāʾil Bayt al-Maqdis waʾl-Khalīl wa-faḍāʾil al-Shām*. Shafāʿamr: Dār al-Mashriq liʾl-Tarjama waʾl-Tibāʿa waʾl-Nashr, 1995.

Ibn Ṭūlūn. *Tuḥfat al-ḥabīb fīmā warada fīʾl-Kathīb*. MS Leyden. Or. 2512.

Al-Khalīlī, Shams al-Dīn Muḥammad. *Taʾrīkh al-Quds waʾl-Khalīl ʿalayhi al-salām*. London: Muʾassasat al-Furqān liʾl-Turāth al-Islāmī, 2004.

Kister, Meir J. "You Shall Only Set Out for Three Mosques," *Le Muséon* 82 (1969): 173–196.

Kister, Meir J. "A Note on the Antiquity of Traditions on the Praises of Jerusalem," *Topics in the History of the Land of Israel under Muslim Rule*, edited by Moshe Sharon. Jerusalem: Ben-Zvi Institute, 1976, 69–71 [in Hebrew].

Kister, Meir J. "Sanctity Joint and Divided," *JSAI* 20 (1996): 18–65.

Kitāb fī faḍāʾil Bayt al-Maqdis wa-fīhi kitāb fī faḍāʾil al-Shām. MS Cambridge. Qq 91.7.

Lazarus-Yafeh, Hava. "The Sanctity of Jerusalem in Islam," in *Jerusalem*, edited by John. M. Oesterreicher and Anne Sinai. New York: John Day, 1974, 211–225.

Livne-Kafri, Ofer. "A Note on Some Traditions of Faḍāʾil al-Quds," *JSAI* 14 (1991): 71–83.

Maḥmūd, Ibrāhīm. *Faḍāʾil Bayt al-Maqdis fi makhṭūṭāt ʿarabiyya qadīma*. Kuwait: Maʿhad al-Makhṭūṭāt al-ʿArabiyya, 1985.

Al-Maqdisī, Muhammad b. Ahmad. *Aḥsan al-taqāsīm fī maʿrifat al-aqālīm*. Beirut: al-Muʾassasa al-ʿArabiyya liʾl-Dirasat waʾl-Nashr, 2003.

Al-Maqdisī, Shihāb al-Dīn. *Muthīr al-gharām ilā ziyārat al-Quds wa'l-Shām*. Beirut: Dār al-Jīl, 1994.

Al-Nābulusi, 'Abd al-Ghanī. *Riḥlati ilā al-Quds*. Cairo: Maktabat al-Qāhira, 1902.

Al-Rabʿī, ʿAlī. *Faḍā'il al-Shām wa-Dimashq*. Damascus: Maṭbūʿāt al-Majmaʿ al-ʿIlmī al-ʿArabī bi-Dimashq, 1950.

Sadan, Joseph. "Three New Sources from the Praises of the Holy Land Literature in Arabic in the 16th–17th Centuries," *Cathedra* 11 (1979): 186–206 [in Hebrew].

Sadan, Joseph. "Le Tombeau de Moïse à Jéricho et à Damas: Une compétition entre deux lieux saints principalement à l'époque ottomane," *Revue des études Islamiques* 49/1 (1981): 60–99.

Sadan, Joseph. "A Legal Opinion of a Muslim Jurist Regarding the Sanctity of Jerusalem," *Israel Oriental Studies* 13 (1993): 231–245.

Al-Samʿānī, ʿAbd al-Karīm. *Faḍā'il al-Shām*. Damascus: Dār al-Thaqāfa al-ʿArabiyya, 1992.

Sivan, Emmanuel. "Le caractère sacré de Jérusalem aux XIIe–XIIIe siècles," *Studia Islamica* 22 (1967): 149–150.

Sivan, Emmanuel. "The Beginnings of the Faḍā'il al-Quds Literature," *Der Islam* 48 (1971): 100–110.

Sourdel-Thomine, Janine. "Une image de Jérusalem au début du XIIIe siècle," in *Jerusalem, Rome, Constantinople*, in the series *Cultures et civilizations médiévales*, edited by Daniel Poirion. Paris: Sorbonne, 1986, 217–233.

Al-Sulamī, ʿIzz al-Dīn b. ʿAbd al-Salam. *Targhīb ahl al-Islām fī suknā al-Shām*. Jerusalem: n.p., 1940.

Al-Tamartāshī, Ṣāliḥ b. Aḥmad al-Ghazzī. *al-Khabar al-tāmm fī dhikr ḥudūd al-arḍ al-muqaddasa wa-Filasṭīn wa'l-Shām*. MS Asʿad Effendi, Istanbul. Esat Ef. 2212/2. Istanbul.

Al-Zirkilī, Khayr al-Dīn. "Ṣāliḥ b. Aḥmad al-Tamartāshī al-Ghazzī," in idem, *al-Aʿlām*. Beirut: Dār al-ʿIlm li'l-Malāyīn, 2002, 3:195.

Samīr Naqqāsh: From One Universe to Another—Iraq to Israel

Geula Elimelekh

1 Introduction: From Exile to "Double Diaspora"

"By the rivers of Babylon we sat and wept when we remembered Zion." This, the opening verse of Psalm 137, reflects the anguish and the yearning of the Judean exiles to Babylon after the conquest of their homeland and the destruction of the First Temple.

This sense of expatriation is reflected in Haim Hillel Ben-Sasson's contemporary observation that "the feeling of exile does not necessarily accompany the condition of exile."[1] Exile is not only a physical condition, but also—and perhaps mainly—a psychological reaction.

The concept of exile is a pivotal theme in the Jewish religion and consciousness and also the ethos motivating the Zionist Movement. In his article "Invisible Exile: Iraqi Jews in Israel," Zvi Ben-Dor notes that the myth of the Jewish exile helped "create a justification for—an understanding of the necessity of—the Jewish return to Zion," and adds that the negation of exile is an important principle of Zionism.[2]

However, for many Jews who immigrated to Israel and became new citizens of the Jewish homeland, the immigration experience was not a homecoming, but rather an act of leaving home behind and arriving in an alien land. The unique condition of being a citizen of Israel yet feeling like a foreigner or refugee there exposes the unbridgeable discrepancy between the mythos of the Jews' return to Israel, as expressed in Zionist ideology, and the feeling of alienation that many new immigrants felt. Ironically, the land that epitomizes the exilic concept in Western culture—Iraq (Babylon)—was the homeland of many people who experienced this paradox most acutely.[3] Referring to Iraqi Jews who came to Israel between 1950 and 1952, Nancy Berg writes that their immigration was part of realizing the Zionist vision, yet for many of them,

1 Haim Hillel Ben-Sasson, "Galut," *Encyclopaedia Judaica* 7 (1971): 275–297.

2 Zvi Ben-Dor, "Invisible Exile: Iraqi Jews in Israel," *Journal of the Interdisciplinary Crossroads* 31 (April 2006): 142; also Israel Yuval, "The Myth of the Jewish Exile from the Land of Israel: A Demonstration of Irenic Scholarship," *Common Knowledge* 12/1 (2006): 33.

3 Ben-Dor, "Invisible Exile," 142.

 | DOI:10.1163/9789004459120_011

leaving their birthplace resulted not in a sense of homecoming but rather in a hopeless state of uprootedness and dislocation. Berg argues that leaving one place for another, emigrating from one country to settle elsewhere, has unique connotations and an absolute emotional value that can be associated with the exilic state, whether that state is a consequence of compulsion or choice.[4]

The Iraqi Jews' emigration can undeniably be described as forced, because already from World War II and even earlier, they had faced an increasing wave of persecution.[5] True, the Jews who emigrated did so also out of a desire to realize the 2,000-year-old dream of returning to the Jewish homeland. However, Berg contends that even people who appear to leave their birthland willingly actually often do so due to factors beyond their control. They may not wish to leave, but there are circumstances when leaving is preferable to staying. Hence, an exile is a person deprived of his or her homeland.[6] Berg's characterization is applicable to the Iraqi Jews since, were it not for the new sociopolitical and economic circumstances that emerged in Iraq in the 1940s, most of them would probably have stayed in Iraq, despite their yearnings for the Land of Israel. Osman Hajjar writes that the Jews of Iraq considered themselves an integral part of Iraqi society and the blatant activities of the Zionist Movement conflicted with their desires. Many Iraqi Jews did not wish to leave their birthplace and "return" to a homeland that existed for them only in the Torah. The end of Iraqi Jewry, says Hajjar, was tragic, because in Israel this community suffered cultural and linguistic alienation.[7]

---

4 Nancy Berg, *Exile from Exile: Israeli Writers from Iraq* (New York: SUNY Press, 1996), xiii, 3.

5 Esther-Meir Glitzenstein writes in her book *Zionism in an Arab Country*: "Only the unforeseen reactions by Iraqi society to the Denaturalization Law and the resultant changes in economic, social and security conditions convinced the Iraqi Jews that they had no chance of security and stability in Iraq and prompted the masses to register. Most people registered voluntarily, on the assumption that their future in Israel, despite all the difficulties, would be better than the future that awaited them in Iraq. But due to the circumstances described above, they arrived in Israel as persecuted, destitute deportees." Glitzenstein, *Zionism in an Arab Country: Jews in Iraq in the 1940s* (London and New York: Routledge, 2004), 209.

6 Berg, *Exile from Exile*, 4.

7 Osman Hajjar, "Exile at Home: Samir Naqqash—Prophesy as Poetics," in *Arab Literature: Postmodern Perspectives*, eds. Angelika Neuwirth, Andreas Pflitsch, and Barbara Winckler (London: Saqi Books, 2010), 274, 279. We should also mention that "transit camp literature," which Iraqi-born writers have compiled in Hebrew, is generally characterized by the stark contrast between the expectations of the new immigrants and the fact that the veteran residents did not welcome them. This literature describes the grim physical conditions of the transition process, in contrast to the lifestyle enjoyed in Iraq, and the culture clashes that occurred between the new immigrants and the established residents. See Berg, *Exile from Exile*, 67.

In fact, many Iraqi Jews found themselves in a state of "double diaspora," as S.T. Schwartz calls it.

> Double diaspora [...] is the sense of being caught between sets of discrepancies between homeland and hostland that contradict each other; a double-diasporic person is caught between two contradictory relationships of belonging.[8]

For a Jew to experience double diaspora, or "a second Babylonian exile,"[9] in the State of Israel is no simple matter, for how can Israel, the Jewish State that is supposed to be the Jews' place of redemption, be a place of exile for them?[10] It nevertheless transpires that Israel, which was founded on the principle of "ending the Diaspora," and which aspired to transform the Jews' mythical-religious bond with their ancient homeland into an actual relationship within a modern state, managed to create a double diaspora for some of its new citizens, as well as the Palestinians.[11]

Exile, even when it is not "double," is associated with concepts of instability, anxiety, alienation, and wandering. In their study of nationalism, Gilles Deleuze and Felix Guattari suggest that since humanity is in constant flux, with people moving from place to place, individuals do not really have a fixed and finite homeland that belongs to them. This puts into question the idea that nations are stable entities associated with a particular territory and that nationalism means identifying with one single state.[12]

2 Samīr Naqqāsh in Linguistic and Cultural Crisis

Among the wrenching experiences suffered by Baghdadi Jews as described in Jewish narratives, one is especially pervasive and common, namely, leaving the city behind. How, then, does one reconstruct a lost world, a lost life? For most,

---

8 S.T. Schwartz, "The Concept of Double Diaspora in Sami Michael's *Refuge* and Naim Kattan's *Farewell, Babylon*," *Comparative Studies of South Asia, Africa and the Middle East* 30/1 (2010): 93.

9 Shimon Ballas, *HaMa'abarah* (Tel Aviv: Am Oved, 1964) (in Hebrew), 51; see also fn. 34 below.

10 Ben-Dor, "Invisible Exile," 138.

11 Schwartz, "The Concept of Double Diaspora," 94.

12 Gilles Deleuze and Felix Guattari, *What Is Philosophy*? Hugh Tomilson and Graham Burchell, trans. (New York: Colombia University Press, 1994), 21.

memory is capricious and unreal. However, Samīr Naqqāsh defied the forces of history to insist on an almost preternatural remembering in the face of physical and temporal distance.[13]

Naqqāsh (1938–2004) was born into a wealthy Jewish family in Baghdad which, like many families, was forced to leave in the early 1950s. He never felt at home in Israel and continued to write in Arabic. To him, the great wave of emigration to Israel was a forced expulsion from the paradise of his childhood in Baghdad. He tried several times to leave Israel, going to Turkey, Iran, Lebanon, Egypt, India, and finally to the United Kingdom, but he was always disappointed and returned to Israel. In his novels, Naqqāsh represented the collective conscience of the Jews of Iraq, depicting their sudden uprooting from their natural milieu to a new home that was not prepared to receive them in a respectable or respectful way. He considered himself an Iraqi exiled writer, whether he lived in Israel or abroad.

Naqqāsh was not alone in his life-long traumatic identity crisis resulting from his forced emigration. Reuven Snir in his recently released book *Who Needs Arab-Jewish Identity?* presents "six [Iraqi literary] personalities whom even scholars have referred to as having one identity" but goes on to write:

> However, it can easily be seen that what has united these individuals has been their tendency towards inessential solidarities, that is, a community of intellectuals presented as monolithic proved to be nothing other than singularities. Take the film *Forget Baghdad*, for example,[14] with its five participating personalities: Sami Michael, Shimon Ballas, Musa Huri (1924–2010), Samir Naqqash (1938–2004), and Ella Shohat (b. 1959). Apart from their common ethnic origins, they hardly have anything in common. The differences between those joint layers of identity that all of them share, such as Iraqiness and Arabness, are more significant than the differences between the layers of identity such as Israeliness and Hebrewness that they share with non-Arabized Jews.[15]

13 Lital Levy, "Self and the City: Literary Representations of Jewish Baghdad," *Prooftexts* 26/1–2 (Winter/Spring 2006): 190.

14 Samir, *Forget Baghdad: Jews and Arabs—The Iraqi Connection*. Documentary Film (Seattle: 2002). The mononymous Samīr is an Iraqi who was born into a Shi'i Muslim family in Baghdad in 1955 but has been living in Switzerland since 1961.

15 Reuven Snir, *Who Needs Arab-Jewish Identity? Interpellation, Exclusion, and Inessential Solidarities* (Leiden: Brill, 2015), 174.

3 Naqqāsh's Works of Jewish-Iraqi Nostalgia

We have seen that exile is the loss of or separation from one's homeland, to be disconnected from a particular geographic environment, from society and family, in other words, to be in exile means to lose the physicality of one's heritage though not necessarily a sense of heritage that can be borne in the mind, language, and culture. Exile in Naqqāsh's works carries not so much a geographical significance of transiting from one country to another, but rather it has the meaning of an internal mental exile.

Naqqāsh's affinity for the Jewish people and Jewish tradition is very evident in his works. This sense of exile, a kind of overarching second exile, which the writer carries in his heart, is a consequence of a profound sense of loss of Jewish tradition. And from his perception, it is an absurdity that Israel, the Jewish State, has detached so many of the Jewish people from their ethnic and religious roots.

This acute sense of exile is especially prevalent in the works of Samīr Naqqāsh, who came to Israel as a boy of thirteen. He often deals, directly or indirectly, with the poignant question of whether the Iraqi Jews' immigration to Israel really ended their state of exile.

In examining his works, one finds that his answer to this question is clearly negative. The Iraqi community's immigration to Israel—whose establishment was supposed to be the Jews' salvation—not only failed to save them, but in his view left them in a far worse condition. They lost the advantages they had enjoyed in Iraq and found themselves in a shocking and humiliating state of affairs that sometimes led to abject poverty and a complete loss of human dignity.

Exile, as noted at the outset, is not just a physical condition but also a psychological state, which involves an acute sense of alienation and longing for the "old country." In Berg's words, it leads to the development of "certain mental structures, ways of attempting to bridge the distance."[16] Indeed, in Naqqāsh's works, Iraq becomes an object of yearning and nostalgia. His memories of the past are far more vivid and real than his experience of the present. He tried to return to Iraq physically, by fleeing to Lebanon with his cousin at the age of 15, only two years after arriving in Israel, and also mentally, through constant nostalgic reminiscing.

In an interview with Ammiel Alcalay, he explained that he had never managed to acclimate in Israel:

16 Berg, *Exile from Exile*, 4.

> I cannot bring myself to terms with this society. I am an honest man, and society here is not straight, it's as simple as that. Everyone is at war with each other. [...] Even in Egypt [...] I feel an enormous difference. When I am there, I simply find myself. I can enter into society. [...] Israeli society is still composed of a number of societies. [...] The society hasn't crystallized completely.[17]

On another occasion Naqqāsh said,

> The move from Iraq to Israel represented not only a movement through space, but also through time. They put us back hundreds of thousands of years—a dramatic transformation from one universe to another, a dislocation far greater than covered by an airplane crossing a mere 600 kilometers from one Middle Eastern location to another.[18]

In fact, Naqqāsh did not even attempt to integrate in Israel, but rather sought to maintain his connection to Iraq by cleaving to his Baghdadi-Arabic dialect, culture, and customs, and enshrining them in his works. He also attempted to find a "third homeland," traveling to Lebanon, Iran, India, and England—but ultimately, he returned to Israel. Like many immigrants from Iraq and elsewhere, he developed a crisis of identity, which involves a sense of alienation from one's surroundings and even from oneself.

Other Iraqi-Jewish writers describe a similar sense of exile. Sami Michael described his own internal conflict: "From the moment I arrived in Israel, there was a struggle between 'the State of Sami Michael' and 'the State of Israel.'"[19] Shimon Ballas, who lived in Tel Aviv and Paris, also described exile as a pivotal element in his life.[20]

Naqqāsh indeed attempted to overcome the loss of his childhood home and motherland through his writing, which is profoundly autobiographical. Lillian Dabby-Joury writes,

---

17 Ammiel Alcalay, "Signs in the Great Disorder: An Interview with Samir Naqqash," in *Keys to the Garden*, edited by idem (San Francisco: City Light Books, 1996), 108–109.

18 Ben-Dor, "Invisible Exile," 136.

19 Samir, *Forget Baghdad*.

20 In his work *Last Winter*, Ballas describes the lives of Middle Eastern Communists living in exile in Paris. His novel *Outcast* is based on the life of a real individual, Ahmad Soussa, a Jew from Baghdad who converted to Islam in the 1930s. The "real" Soussa chose to become part of modern Iraqi society, but Ballas' Soussa spends his life in a state of double exile: a stranger in both the Jewish community he left and the new Iraq. Ben-Dor, "Invisible Exile," 136.

> The resounding oath of the Book of Books, uttered by the first exiles on the rivers of Babylon, mysteriously reverses its direction and flows [backwards], from Zion to Iraq, in the works of the last generation of the Babylonian exiles. The literary enterprise of Samir Naqqash preserves and perpetuates Iraq as an essence and a timeless experience. [It preserves] the geographical Iraq as well as the one which transcends the geographical boundaries: the exterritorial Iraq that the Jews carry in their hearts, while holding in their memory the rivers of Babylon and pledging, in the words of the ancient oath, "If I forget thee, O Iraq."[21]

As for the question of language, the writer in exile usually finds himself in a new linguistic environment, and must choose whether to continue writing in his native language or try writing in a newly acquired tongue. This is a decision of momentous significance for, as noted by Nurit Buchweitz in the introduction to the book *To Write in the Language of the Other* (Tel Aviv: Resling, 2010), language is not just a practical convention used by a certain ethnic group in speaking or writing, but is also, and perhaps mainly, a vehicle for expressing that group's culture and consciousness. Language expresses the self and cannot be separated from thought and awareness.

These observations definitely reflect the persona and work of Samīr Naqqāsh, who wrote in Arabic though he lived in the Hebrew-language environment of Israel from a relatively young age. Hajjar believes that Naqqāsh suffered from a morbidly traumatic sense of dislocation, and therefore cleaved tenaciously to his native Arabic.[22] Naqqāsh refused to forgo his native language, not only because it was difficult for him to learn and gain fluency in his new language, but because he asked, as did Milbauer, "Why [...] would a foreigner take such a painful and exhaustive endeavor as mastering a new language in order to eventually make it into a medium of his art, a means to reach an audience, an instrument of intellectual survival?"[23] He also clung to it out of a desire to hang on to the language, culture, spirit, and essence of Baghdadi Jewry, including its

---

21 Of course, the original is "O Jerusalem." Lillian Dabby-Joury, "Samir Naqqash—An Examination of His Narrative Works," in *Zion and Zionism among the Jews of Spain and the Orient*, eds. Warren Harvey et al. (Jerusalem: Misgav Yerushalayim, 2002), 579 (in Hebrew).

22 Hajjar, "Exile at Home," 275.

23 Asher Z. Milbauer, *Transcending Exile: Conrad, Nabokov, I.B. Singer* (Gainesville, FL: University Presses of Florida, 1985), xii.

branches in Persia and India and its new incarnation: the first generation of Israeli-Iraqi Jews.[24]

4 Stories of Two Competing Worlds

After immigrating to Israel, Naqqāsh, a Mizrahi Jew, was seen as the "other" in Israeli society. He chose to cling to his native tongue in order to preserve his cultural heritage, for language, as Foucault noted, reflects identity. By writing in Arabic, Naqqāsh declared himself part of the Iraqi nation and denied his Israeli identity.

In Samīr Naqqāsh's works, the feeling of exile expresses itself by creating a constant contradiction between two worlds: his childhood in Iraq, representing a world that no longer exists, in contrast to his then-present life in Israel. The author constantly wanders between Iraq and the Land of Israel, between the here and the there, and vice versa. His longing for the old world is also a longing for the Iraqi-Jewish tradition lost forever, or as his sister Samīra says, "We kept the holidays and the customs. For him tradition was associated with romanticism. He was a romantic, and for him tradition was a longing for the life he had in Baghdad before he emigrated to Israel."[25]

Stories sprinkled throughout his collections provide a fair number of examples of the conflict between his two worlds. In the anthology *Yawm ḥabilat wa-ajhaḍat al-dunyā* (The day the world conceived and miscarried), several stories deal with the lives of the Iraqi Jews and contain numerous religious and traditional motifs. The setting of *Laylat ʿaraba* (Willow night),[26] the fourth story in the collection, is in a *sukkah*, the temporary shelter built for the Sukkot festival (or the Feast of Tabernacles). It is Hoshana Raba, the last night of the seven-day holiday, which Iraqi Jews called Willow Night.[27]

---

24 Dabby-Joury, "Samir Naqqash," 578. In Ballas' novel *HaMa'abarah*, Haim-Vaad is a symbol for integration into Israeli society. He was born in Iraq, but he learned Hebrew fluently and quickly grasped the ways of Israeli bureaucracy.

25 Neri Livneh, "Samir Who?" *Ha'aretz* (August 3, 2004) (in Hebrew).

26 Samīr Naqqāsh, *Yawm ḥabilat wa-ajhaḍat al-dunyā* (Jerusalem: al-Sharq, 1980), 161–226.

27 Among the customs of this night are the wearing of white clothing and the lighting of many candles, as one does on Yom Kippur, the Day of Atonement, because according to the Kabbalah this is the day on which God finalizes His judgment of all mankind—the dead as well as the living. People stay up all night and study Torah. See Mordechai Eliahu, *Observances of Tabernacles and the Celebration of the Torah* (Jerusalem: Darkhei Hora'a le-Rabbanim, 2000), 41 (in Hebrew).

The story contrasts an Israeli Willow Night, here and now, with the way the tradition was kept in Iraq thirty years previously.[28] The opening comprises the following questions: "What is this profound silence that lies heavy on one's breathing? Why does this wandering silence not remove its ice-cold hands from us?"[29]

The Jews' detachment from their past had brought about their downfall: "Today things collapsed. They fell, broken like statues, and we were emptied, turned into ruins. Nothing was left inside us except for old age and fear of everything. The only thing that remained was the cruel silence."[30]

In the same collection, *Fī bayt al-khiraq wa'l-khawāriq* (In the house of tatters and wonders) tells the tale of two elderly sisters who immigrated to Israel. They take solace in their visits from Menashe, the old man who comes to their house every Friday to eat lunch. The unnamed narrator, a relative of the sisters, follows their inner world while also exposing the reader to the collapse of the world of his own childhood in Iraq and his descent into the Israeli inferno.[31] Thirty years have passed since the two sisters came to Israel and abandoned their safe haven in Iraq. "The tall fortress collapsed. It was the most secure of all fortresses, in which mind, axiom and human life lived in peace [...] And suddenly your new world arises, made of pure legend."[32]

In the story "Ṭanṭal," from another book *Anā wa-hā'ulā'i wa'l-fiṣām* (I, they and ambivalence), the sense of exile is amplified. In the first part of the story entitled "Baghdad 1946," an anonymous narrator shows us a wonderful lost world. Comparing the past with the present, the narrator describes the large house with much sentimentality and nostalgia, saying, "but the old was always more beautiful than the new."[33]

The longing for this house materializes in the description of the fragrance of orange peel drying on a coal oven (*manqal*); the decorated wicker fans (*marāwiḥ al-khūṣ al-munaqqash*), which were safer and quieter than the electric fans; the tea that has been heated in a steaming samovar and which was more palatable than the tea prepared on an electric stove; and the small, delicious pita breads (*al-ḥannūn*), which Umm Jamīl, the baker, brought out of his oven for the children.[34] The most impressive part of the old house was his

28 Naqqāsh, *Yawm ḥabilat wa-ajhaḍat al-dunyā*, 173.

29 Ibid., 161.

30 Ibid., 165.

31 Reuven Snir, *Arabness, Jewishness, Zionism: A Clash of Identities in the Literature of Iraqi Jews* (Jerusalem: Ben-Zvi Institute, 2005), 219 (in Hebrew).

32 Naqqāsh, *Yawm ḥabilat wa-ajhaḍat al-dunyā*, 63.

33 Samīr Naqqāsh, *Anā wa-hā'ulā'i wa'l-fiṣām* (Jerusalem: al-Sharq, 1978), 67.

34 Ibid., 68.

grandmother's room with a Qashānī rug (*sajjāda qashāniyya*), on which there was a large, adult-sized "cradle" in which the mother or grandmother could sleep and hold a baby.

In the second part of the story, entitled "Israel, at the beginning of the fifties," the narrator and his family are cast into another world, where a dark, dusty tent has replaced the big house. While his grandmother does not complain, because that has never been in her nature, "thick rust clouds up her face and wraps it in patient, silent grief."[35]

The narrator—a boy only twelve years old at the time embodies Naqqāsh, who was about the same age on arriving in Israel—sheds his childhood and instantly becomes an old man. He cannot accept the new reality of life in a transit camp. There, he and the others fall victim to floods, hunger, thirst, and a life of idleness, while the government representatives shirk off any responsibility, telling them, "You came from backward countries in which people live no differently than they did in the Middle Ages."[36] However, most of the camp's residents become accustomed to the new reality and forget their former lives, which in Naqqāsh's eyes might have made them seem at odds with his memories.

In the story's third section, "Israel, 1970," the narrator gives dramatic expression to his sense of loss and exile. Now thirty-year-old man, he returns to the transit camp "after I wasted long years abroad in search of my lost life," defining himself as being with "downtrodden head, body and soul."[37] The transit camp has been improved in the years that have passed, but nevertheless, seeing it he feels completely detached and repressed, as someone who has lost his whole world—both his Iraqi past and his Israeli past—and feels that all is vanity, all is a delusion.

The devastating effects of exile are also reflected in the collection of short stories *Nubūʾāt rajul majnūn fī madīna malʿūna* (Prophecies of a madman in a cursed city). Published in 1995, some fifteen years after "The day the world conceived and miscarried," this book also laments the loss of the old values and, in fact, echoes a deepening of Naqqāsh's pessimism. It shows the characters sinking into a later stage of exile, which is much worse than the earlier years. This because the society they now inhabit pitches them into an abyss of corruption and bondage driven by their abject instincts and desires, which ultimately lead them into total madness.

---

35 Ibid., 79.

36 Ibid., 80.

37 Ibid., 84, both quotations.

The first story in this collection, "The voice of the whip and the silence of the creator," portrays Israeli society as the complete antithesis of Iraqi-Jewish society and describes the exodus from Iraq as a terrible and fateful mistake.

> Years ago the mistake was made and it was as sharp as a sword, as decisive as fate, as obliterating as an eraser [...] For 40 years I have been careful not to fall. The tree was once tall and stood firm in the storm, and I said, "I shall not fall victim to the temptation of the [local] norm." Astonished by the number of idols and graven images, I said, "Infidels! I shall not worship what you worship," and I kept my promise.[38]

The protagonist, who lives in an alienating environment and tries his best not to be tempted by the ways of the "infidels," is subject to the rule of several authorities and is caught in a hopeless situation. "I fell into the stinking and reeking swamp of wretchedness. The stench of rot choked me and its turbid waters surrounded me from every direction."[39]

The corruption of the people around him is evident in many ways, and he lives in constant terror that the filth will contaminate him and harm his "sanity of mind." He has long since been exposed to the lies and deception that hide behind many masks. Even the emblems of beauty, such as butterflies, have disappeared and are replaced with germs, snakes, and scorpions. He therefore decides to isolate himself, mentally and spiritually, from the world, but his friends and family beseech him and do not allow it. Eventually, he capitulates and becomes enslaved to an ugly and tyrannical wife. She hits him with a whip, shouting: "Say 'I hear and obey!' Say 'I hear and obey!'"[40]

Exile is a form of bondage and, wishing to escape it, the protagonist (like Naqqāsh himself) can only return to the world of his childhood. Recalling his early years, he extols the kindness and morality that characterized the old world, presenting it as the complete opposite of corrupt Israeli society. He recalls how one day he hit a foolish girl named Badriyya, who had lice-ridden hair and was filthy. His father gently rebuked him, telling him that the girl was no different from himself and his sisters, but poverty and neediness had brought her to this state. His aunt bathed the child, combed out the lice, and dressed her in clean clothes.

---

38 Samīr Naqqāsh, *Nubūʾāt rajul majnūn fī madīna malʿūna* (Jerusalem: Association for Jewish Academics from Iraq, 1995), 75.

39 Ibid.

40 Ibid.

The protagonist's experiences are now completely different: he is surrounded by scoundrels and villains and has even lost his freedom, sinking into the depths of hell and so becoming no different than Badriyya. Now he is wretched, forced to eat peels and scraps like a dog.

Tragically, he understands that neither hallucinations, daydreams, nor memories of the past will save him from his state of exile and destroy the deadly forces to which he is enslaved. In the second part of the story, a monster appears and forces him to carry out Sisyphean tasks: "After midnight, bent under the weight of the rock, I took one last step before it repeated its endless tumble back into the abyss."[41] The allusion to the myth of Sisyphus is not accidental; it evokes the absurdity, loneliness, deception, and alienation that are the lot of modern man.[42] However, unlike Camus' Sisyphus, who is liberated through his struggle,[43] the narrator in the Naqqāsh story is unable to escape from the bondage of his inner torment.

Corruption and madness come to a head in the collection's title story, "Prophecies of a madman in a cursed city." This story is surreal in character and contains intertextual allusions to biblical characters and episodes. The narrator is instructed by God to take a woman named Gomer for a wife, though he is sterile. This is a transparent allusion to the Prophet Hosea, whose book begins, "Go, take yourself a wife of whoredom and have children of whoredom, for the land commits great whoredom by forsaking the Lord. So he went and took Gomer, the daughter of Diblaim" (Hosea 1: 2–3). Hosea prophesied at a time of great crisis for the people of Israel and foresaw the impending destruction. The command to take "a wife of whoredom" lent personal poignancy to his prophecy. Having experienced betrayal on his own flesh, he could more effectively rebuke the people of Israel for betraying their God. Naqqāsh's story likewise describes a reality in which people betray the Creator by choosing to emulate the devil instead of Him: "I created you in my image, but you disobeyed Me and refused to be cast in My image."[44]

The narrator in the story has a friend, Ezekiel, from among "the exiles of Tel Aviv." This is an allusion to Ezekiel 3: 15: "I came to the exiles who lived at Tel Aviv near the Kebar River." The reference to the cursed town of Tel Aviv is no coincidence. The last part of the story, which mentions "a city in which man

41 Ibid., 81.

42 In *Myth of Sisyphus*, Camus presents nature and the world as hostile to man, which is the source of alienation, existential absurdity, and man's inability to understand the world. Albert Camus, *The Myth of Sisyphus* trans. Justin O'Brien (New York: Knopf, 1964), 14.

43 Camus writes, "The struggle itself toward the heights is enough to fill a man's heart. One must imagine Sisyphus happy." Camus, 123.

44 Naqqāsh, *Nubū'āt*, 26.

has died and God demonstrates his tyranny,"[45] again expresses the author's despair of life in Israel.[46]

The narrator has a divine revelation in which God addresses him as "son of man"—an intertextual allusion to the vision of the dry bones in Ezekiel. However, unlike Ezekiel, what he sees is not a hopeful vision of resurrection but rather a nightmarish vision of incest, idol worship, and unbridled lust:

> What do you see in the vast wasteland around you? [the Lord asked]. I freed myself from the grip of Gomer, of my children, of the gullible old man, of my psychiatrist, and finally even of the midget-giant [...] I cast my eyes over the wasteland and was horrified at what I saw. I whispered to my Lord, hardly hearing my own dying, whispering voice; I see a wasteland, Lord, full of corpses: dead men and women, naked as on the day they were born, their shame exposed. And lo! The naked corpses arise. The men, my Lord, seek out the women and the women seek out the men. I see them lusting after flesh [...] Fathers are not ashamed to copulate with their daughters and sisters with their brothers [...] I see the heavens, your heavens, raining gold, and everyone rushes forth [to collect it] [...] Without waiting to wash themselves of the corruption [of the grave], they rush toward the showers of gold [...] A man who just copulated with his sister now sinks his claws into her to tear the gold out of her hands, and a woman who just copulated with her father now closes her fingers around his throat until he faints [...] Lord, in an eye blink the gold is formed into a calf, and now they dance around it yelling, chortling and fornicating.[47]

At the end of the story, the narrator's psychiatrist wants to hospitalize him, but he decides to flee.[48] The story ends with the narrator trapped in a state of obsessive paranoia.

---

45 Ibid., 27.

46 Snir, *Arabness*, 234.

47 Naqqāsh, *Nubū'āt*, 14–15.

48 Taking flight from the horrors of corrupt humanity living in hellish worlds is an ending that Naqqāsh deems a natural and fitting escape in his storytelling. Like the narrator in *Prophesies of a Madman*, Shaul Hillel in the title story of the collection *The Day the World Conceived and Miscarried* flees from the synagogue on the Day of Atonement after witnessing grotesque worshippers and repulsive behavior there. As he retreats from the synagogue, Shaul is moved to ask, "Is the moment of the world's destruction drawing near?" (Naqqāsh, *Nubū'āt*, 44).

Another story in the book, under the Arabic title *Dunyā al-makhālīf* (Topsy-turvy world), describes a Sodom-like city of villains. "The supreme heavenly being" decides to raze the city to the ground. Generations later another city like it appears, but this time the supreme heavenly being is absent. In this latter-day setting, an anonymous voice tells the narrator about a utopian city that once existed, where the people had glowing faces, their doors were always open to the poor and the needy, and all their deeds were charitable. From what we know of the author's inclinations, it is not difficult to identify this utopian city with Baghdad of the 1940s, which Naqqāsh adored, and the Sodom-like city with Tel Aviv, which the previously mentioned story explicitly describes as a cursed city.

In the title story of the collection, *Anā wa-hā'ulā'i wa'l-fiṣām* (I, they and ambivalence)—just like in the story "Ṭanṭal"—the narrator waxes nostalgic about his wealthy childhood home in Baghdad. He was taken to school by a private driver, his room was full of toys and he was surrounded with love. The narrator also misses the particular atmosphere of the city, the unique traditional dishes, and the family's large garden abundant in fruit trees and singing birds.

Gurjī is the protagonist's Hebrew teacher, who teaches him to read, write, and pray. Gurjī is a unique character. He is a poor old man dressed in filthy rags, and a great miser who is afraid to marry lest his wife poison him and take his money. But he is also a devoted teacher who works from dawn until dusk and walks great distances, even in the scorching summer heat and bitter winter cold, to visit the homes of the Jewish families whose children he teaches. He and the boy read from the Bible, and the boy thinks,

> I read about the Promised Land, but it is in Iraq that I live and breathe. It is here that I learn and dream and plan the future. On holidays, people shake hands and say, may you live long, God willing. Next year in Jerusalem. [...] May they announce the establishment of the State of Israel tonight.[49]

Another wretched character is Moshe, the carpenter who comes to the family home to fix a lock but only manages to break it further. Despite this, the narrator's mother feeds him and invites him to come and eat at their house every day.

The process of exile—for Naqqāsh sees the exodus from Iraq as a second exile—begins when rumors start spreading about the impending establishment

---

49 Naqqāsh, *Anā wa-hā'ulā'i wa'l-fiṣām*, 131–132.

of the State of Israel. Riots and street protests break out, and the Jews fear attacks on their homes. This is the first stage of the crisis in which Iraq's Jews found themselves in the late 1940s. The boy is deeply affected by the situation. He feels as though a violent storm is shaking the Jewish community. And indeed, armed men break into the homes of the Jews, search them frantically, and arrest men, women, and even children, who are taken to prison and tortured. Jewish civil servants are fired, first senior and then minor ones. One of the latter is Salīm, a friend of the family who works as an inspector for the telephone company. After being fired, he tries to commit suicide and eventually, starts working in his uncle's butcher shop. Even Gurjī is arrested, for teaching Hebrew. Asked by the interrogator if he does not know teaching Hebrew is forbidden, he answers, "I'm an Iraqi and the son of an Iraqi. I have been teaching Torah for as long as I can remember, and as you know, the Torah is written in Hebrew. This has been our Torah since the creation of the world. Do you expect us to pray in German?" The interrogator says, "Zionist traitor. Take him inside."[50]

The boy's family is in a better position, for his father has a Muslim business partner and many Muslim friends in high places. The family therefore continues to live peacefully, with armed soldiers guarding their home. "In our house friendly parties are held every night," the boy says.[51] In a conversation with the father and his partner, the boy's aunt nevertheless suggests that perhaps the Jews should emigrate to Palestine, but the father warns her about the poverty that prevails there, and refuses to acknowledge the persecution of Iraq's Jews. Sammy the engineer, a family friend who is aware of the persecution, advises the family to emigrate to Iran. Full of confusion, the boy asks his father where the Jews' country is, and the father replies, "We have lived and will continue to live in Iraq. This is our land, but that land [Palestine] is our land as well."[52]

After Iraq passes a law revoking the citizenship of any Jews who leave the country, the family decides to flee Baghdad. They ride in the car of the father's Muslim business partner, and manage to pass all the checkpoints. On their way, they visit the tombs of the prophets, where they all mumble: "Who knows if we will ever meet you again […] Perhaps this is the last time."[53]

Gurjī very poignantly expresses the terrible tragedy of Iraq's Jews who are forced to move to a "strange land." He weeps, and his tears mingle with those of his ancestors who sat by the river of Babylon and wept as they remembered

50 Ibid., 146.
51 Ibid., 142.
52 Ibid., 132.
53 Ibid., 159.

Zion. However, Gurjī is weeping not because he yearns for Zion but for the opposite reason, because he is being forced to return there.

> Two tears stand in his lightless eyes and then slide down his ruined face. His life's work all gone. Such a shame, all the toil and the weariness. [...] Where will we go now? We have been anchoring here for 2,000 years. Our homes, our livelihood and the tombs of our ancestors are all here. Shall we go now and live in a strange land? Shall we cast our souls into danger, like blind birds?[54]

Gurjī tells the boy's mother that he has heard there is hunger in Palestine and that the people all live in tents. He considers staying in Iraq, trusting God to provide his livelihood. Asked why he is unwilling to give up his Iraqi citizenship, he replies, "Khākhām Dāwīd (Rabbi David) said in his Sabbath sermon that it is still early. Letters arriving from Palestine tell of the hardship and hunger of the new immigrants. We must not act like a herd."[55]

The carpenter Moshe is likewise reluctant to leave for Israel. He says he plans to give up his citizenship, yet he finds excuses to delay, stating that he must finish his work first. Gurjī intervenes and supports Moshe, asking people to stop pressing him to emigrate. "Do you want him to chase after the fetid swamp? Only I have been wise and have not given up my citizenship."[56] One day, when the family is certain that Moshe has already left Iraq, the boy sees him and happily runs to tell his mother. Moshe mumbles that he was ashamed to visit the family after he had lied and said he was going to Israel. He explains that he has stayed because the Jews need him. With everybody gone, he has been asked to serve as the synagogue caretaker. For Moshe, this is an opportunity to change. Now that people need his help, his status improves, and the crudeness that previously characterized him is replaced with humanity.

The family members hang their heads and "silently live the contradiction and the mute tears that flow in secret and tell the tale of the harmony that was severed by the parting [from the homeland]."[57] Telling of the brotherhood that

54 Ibid., 160, 173.

55 Ibid., 146.

56 Ibid., 165–166.

57 Ibid., 168. The motif of tears permeates this story. The author's image evokes a perfect picture of the profound sorrow that lasted throughout the Babylonian exile and—in Naqqāsh's opinion—even after the return to the Land of Israel in 1948. Naqqāsh chose two pitiable characters, Gurjī and Moshe, whose tears mingle with their exiled forefathers' teardrops that fell like rain into the Tigris and Euphrates Rivers of Babylon 2,000 years earlier.

prevailed between the Jews and the Muslims and of the bitter and painful parting from Muslim friends, the narrator adds, "We have been left without an identity. Our roots, sunk deep into this land for thousands of years, have been torn but not severed. Baghdad, half of whose residents were Jewish, is changing. The Jews are growing few, gradually disappearing."[58] The synagogues empty of worshipers, schools empty of their Jewish pupils, and hospitals empty of their Jewish doctors and nurses. The tombs of the saints are left silent and bereft of visitors. The boy suffers an internal rift. On the one hand, he understands the Jews must leave Iraq, but on the other, he still lives and breathes his wonderful childhood that is "like a good, solid tree" with roots planted deep in the soil. This chapter of the story ends with a lament: "I mourn for you, oh halls of childhood! I mourn for the seat of joy and of cherished memories! I mourn for the fathers, the prophets and the saints [...] I mourn for you, my soul! I mourn for you, all things that have been lost!"[59]

Upon arriving in Israel, the narrator says, "The era of slaps has begun."[60] Even before the newcomers disembark from the plane, a man and a woman arrive and spray them with DDT. He says, "From the very beginning the voice of our humanity was smothered in insecticide."[61] Sha'ar Aliya immigration camp seems to him like a prison, where the process of obliterating the newcomers' human dignity is completed.

Some eighteen months after their arrival, the boy and his family, walking around Jerusalem, find Gurjī lying on the sidewalk. He has become a homeless man who sells newspapers and sleeps on the street. He has aged and is even filthier than before, and his face reflects a deep sadness. Eventually he dies. "Here in the eternal city he gave up the ghost, penniless."[62]

5 Conclusion: Escape through Memory

Naqqāsh's portrayal of Gurjī and Moshe the carpenter is compassionate and even admiring, despite their apparent crudeness and repugnant physical appearance. Through them, he challenges the false world in which we live, a world that worships material wealth and physical beauty. For him, these two wretches embody all that is genuine and true: inner beauty, simplicity, and

58 Ibid., 169.
59 Ibid., 160.
60 Ibid., 182.
61 Ibid.
62 Ibid., 190.

wisdom free of pretense or deception. They represent the old world, the first Babylonian exile that is lost and is replaced with the infinitely more bitter exile in Israel.

When a man like Samīr Naqqāsh is exiled from his homeland, he loses not just a home but the very civilization, the ancient and rich world that gave him a sense of identity and belonging, and indeed made him the person he was. The Jewish community in Iraq, whose families could trace their heritage back to the Babylonian exile, lived and cherished their unique religious observances, customs, and traditions. So when circumstances wrenched the whole community out of one orbit and into another, the loss was physical as well as mental, emotional, and spiritual. As shown in this article, Naqqāsh and other like-minded Iraqis apply memory to their fiction in an attempt to restore and preserve their old world.

Bibliography

Alcalay, Ammiel. "Signs in the Great Disorder: An Interview with Samir Naqqash," in *Keys to the Garden*, edited by Ammiel Alcalay. San Francisco: City Light Books, 1996, 100–132.

Ballas, Shimon. *HaMa'abarah*. Tel Aviv: Am Oved, 1964 [in Hebrew].

Ben-Dor, Zvi. "Invisible Exile: Iraqi Jews in Israel," *Journal of the Interdisciplinary Crossroads* 31 (April 2006): 135–162.

Ben-Sasson, Haim Hillel. "Galut," *Encyclopaedia Judaica* 7 (1971): 275–297.

Berg, Nancy. *Exile from Exile: Israeli Writers from Iraq*. New York: SUNY Press, 1996.

Camus, Albert. *The Myth of Sisyphus*. Trans. Justin O'Brien. New York: Knopf, 1964.

Dabby-Joury, Lillian. "Samir Naqqash—An Examination of His Narrative Works," in *Zion and Zionism among the Jews of Spain and the Orient*, edited by Warren Harvey et al. Jerusalem: Misgav Yerushalayim, 2002, 575–599 [in Hebrew].

Deleuze, Gilles and Felix Guattari. *What Is Philosophy?* Trans. Hugh Tomilson and Graham Burchell. New York: Colombia University Press, 1994.

Eliahu, Mordechai. *Observances of Tabernacles and the Celebration of the Torah* (Jerusalem: Darkhei Hora'a le-Rabbanim, 2000) [in Hebrew].

Glitzenstein, Esther-Meir. *Zionism in an Arab Country: Jews in Iraq in the 1940s*. London and New York: Routledge, 2004.

Hajjar, Osman. "Exile at Home: Samir Naqqash—Prophesy as Poetics," In *Arab Literature: Postmodern Perspectives*, edited by Angelika Neuwirth, Andreas Pflitsch, and Barbara Winckler. London: Saqi Books, 2010, 272–286.

Levy, Lital. "Self and the City: Literary Representations of Jewish Baghdad." *Prooftexts* 26/1–2 (Winter–Spring 2006): 163–211.

Livneh, Neri. "Samir Who?" *Ha'aretz*. August 3, 2004 [in Hebrew].

Milbauer, Asher Z. *Transcending Exile: Conrad, Nabokov, I.B. Singer*. Gainesville, FL: University Presses of Florida, 1985.

Naqqāsh, Samīr. *Anā wa-hā'ulā'i wa'l-fiṣām*. Jerusalem: al-Sharq, 1978.

Naqqāsh, Samīr. *Yawm ḥabilat wa-ajhaḍat al-dunyā*. Jerusalem: al-Sharq, 1980.

Naqqāsh, Samīr. *Nubū'āt rajul majnūn fī madīna mal'ūna*. Jerusalem: Association for Jewish Academics from Iraq, 1995.

Samir. *Forget Baghdad: Jews and Arabs—The Iraqi Connection*. Documentary film. Seattle, 2002.

Schwartz, S.T. "The Concept of Double Diaspora in Sami Michael's Refuge and Naim Kattan's Farewell, Babylon," *Comparative Studies of South Asia, Africa and the Middle East* 30/1 (2010): 92–100.

Snir, Reuven. *Arabness, Jewishness, Zionism: A Clash of Identities in the Literature of Iraqi Jews*. Jerusalem: Ben-Zvi Institute, 2005 [in Hebrew].

Snir, Reuven. *Who Needs Arab-Jewish Identity? Interpellation, Exclusion, and Inessential Solidarities*. Leiden: Brill, 2015.

Yuval, Israel. "The Myth of the Jewish Exile from the Land of Israel: A Demonstration of Irenic Scholarship," *Common Knowledge* 12/1 (2006): 16–33.

Representations of Women in the Literary Works of Egyptian Writer Jamāl al-Ghīṭānī

Yona Sheffer

Jamāl al-Ghīṭānī (1945–2015), one of the most talented writers of the "generation of the 1960s" in Egypt, writes:

> A woman's appearance shall quench my thirst; the liquor from a female's [lips] shall alleviate my gloomy days; a woman's presence shall rejuvenate my inner self and it is a woman that shall cause me insomnia.[1]

With these words he expresses man's ambivalent attitude toward women as beings who arouse both joy and suffering.

Al-Ghīṭānī lived in a patriarchal society that endeavored to keep pace with the West, albeit not always successfully. It is, therefore, interesting to examine how he dealt with this dichotomy: how he depicted women, whether the women in his work shared any common traits, and whether he made any discernible moral judgment regarding certain types of women. This study discusses the characters of mother, wife, unwed careerist, and unattainable beloved in al-Ghīṭānī's writing.

1 Introduction

While most Egyptian novels of the 1950s focused on patriotic themes, the late 1950s marked a new stage in the development of Egyptian literature, a stage that arose out of—among other things—the need to express disillusionment with the 1952 revolution's failure to fulfill its promises, and the corruption and oppression exerted by the regime against its dissidents.[2]

Side by side with Najīb Maḥfūẓ (1911–2006), the most prominent novelist of the 1960s, a new generation of young writers emerged. Like Maḥfūẓ, those

1 Jamāl al-Ghīṭānī, *Kitāb al-tajalliyāt, al-asfār al-thalātha*, 3rd ed. (Cairo: Dār al-Shurūq, 2007), 530.

2 Sabri Hafez, "The Egyptian Novel in the Sixties," *JAL* 7 (1976): 70; Hilary Kilpatrick, "The Egyptian Novel from Zaynab to 1980," in *Modern Arabic Literature*, edited by Muhammad M. Badawi (Cambridge: Cambridge University Press, 1992), 253–254.

 | DOI:10.1163/9789004459120_012

writers were influenced by Western literary techniques. In the changing sociopolitical reality in Egypt during the 1960s, these Western influences contributed to the adaptation of literary works depicting alienation, disillusionment, oppression, and lack of freedom. The young writers challenged literary conventions, making extensive use of myth, folklore, and the Arabic literary heritage.[3]

These changes fulfilled the need for a new sensibility that suited the new social, political, and cultural climate. It appeared in various forms in the Egyptian novels of the 1960s, most of which belonged to the realistic stream that managed to assimilate and express the new sensibility of the 1960s. During the first part of the decade, the main achievements belonged to the elder generation including—among others—Najīb Maḥfūẓ, Yūsuf Idrīs (1927–1991), and Fatḥī Ghānim (1924–1999).[4]

It was, however, only after the 1967 military defeat, which exposed the failures of the revolution, that a new generation gathered around the literature and culture periodical "Gallery 68" and its editor, Idwār al-Kharrāṭ, voicing their rebellion against the establishment in all its forms and expressing their own values and style. Those writers became known as "the young authors" or "the authors of the 1960s."[5] Jamāl al-Ghīṭānī belonged to this group, many of whose members became leading figures among short story writers and novelists from the 1970s onward.[6]

2 A Short Biography of al-Ghīṭānī

Al-Ghīṭānī was born in 1945 in the village of Juhayna in Upper Egypt and grew up in Cairo. He studied carpet design and worked as a designer from 1962 until 1968. In 1963, he published his first two short stories. Between 1969 and 1974, he served as a military correspondent on the Egyptian front with Israel. He established the weekly *Akhbār al-Adab* (Literature News) in 1993, and served as its editor until 2011.[7] He has published over 30 novels, short story collections, and

3 Kilpatrick, "The Egyptian Novel," 258; Hafez, "The Egyptian Novel," 71–72; Muhammad M. Badawi, *A Short History of Modern Arabic Literature* (Oxford: Clarendon Press/Oxford University Press: 1993), 158.

4 Hafez, "The Egyptian Novel," 71–72.

5 Céza Kassem Draz, "In Quest of New Narrative Forms: Irony in the Works of Four Egyptian Writers: Jamāl al-Ghīṭanī, Yaḥyā al-Ṭāhir ʿAbdallah, Majīd Ṭubyā, Ṣunʿallah Ibrāhīm (1967–1979)," *JAL* 12 (1981): 137.

6 Kilpatrick, "The Egyptian Novel," 266–267.

7 Jamāl al-Ghīṭānī, "Jadaliyyat al-tanāṣṣ," *Alif* 4 (1984): 72; idem, *Yawmiyyātī al-muʿlana* (Cairo: Dār Suʿād al-Ṣabāḥ, 1992), 373–374; Samia Mehrez, *Egyptian Writers between History and*

historical and literary researches, and has been awarded many prizes for his works, both in Egypt and abroad.

Al-Ghīṭānī was a literary autodidact. As a youth, he became acquainted with Arabic translations of European works and with classical Arabic literature, especially Sufi literature and the Arabic sources of the history of Islamic Egypt. One of the novels that exercised a tremendous influence on him was George Orwell's *Nineteen Eighty-Four* (1949), an influence that is clearly visible in some of his own works. Although al-Ghīṭānī said that he had read few works by modern Arab authors, two of those writers—Najīb Maḥfūẓ and the Palestinian Emile Ḥabībī (1922–1996)—influenced him profoundly. In addition to belles-lettres, he read books from other disciplines, such as psychology and philosophy, and was interested in the spiritual heritage of various religions, among others, Buddhism. Al-Ghīṭānī attested that he had always aspired to be innovative in the field of style and in efforts to link the Arabic-Islamic heritage to the Western novel.[8] According to Paul Starkey, reliance on the literary and the historiographical heritage of the classical period is more evident in al-Ghīṭānī's works than in those of his contemporaries.[9]

3 Works under Discussion

1. *Al-Zaynī Barakāt* (1974): al-Ghīṭānī wrote this novel between 1970 and 1971, immediately after Jamāl ʿAbd al-Nāṣir's death, but because of Egyptian censorship restrictions, it was published first in Damascus in 1971 and appeared in Egypt only in 1974. This novel is considered to be one of the most significant literary texts of the Arab world from the 1970s[10] and, in Samia Mehrez's words, "the jewel that crowns Jamāl al-Ghīṭānī's long list of literary works."[11]

The plot takes place in early sixteenth-century Cairo, shortly before the decisive defeat that the Mamlukes suffered at the hands of the Ottomans in 1516 and the subsequent Ottoman occupation. The novel is named after al-Zaynī Barakāt b. Mūsā, an historical figure who, at the height of his career

Fiction (Cairo: The American University in Cairo Press, 1994), 97; Paul Starkey, "al-Ghīṭānī, Jamāl," *Encyclopedia of Arabic Literature* (1998), 1: 253; idem, "Egyptian History in the Modern Egyptian Novel," in *The Historiography of Islamic Egypt* (*c. 950–1800*), edited by Hugh Kennedy (Leiden: Brill, 2001), 258.

8 Al-Ghīṭānī, *Jadaliyyat*, 73–77.

9 Starkey, *Egyptian History*, 258.

10 Ibid., 259.

11 Mehrez, *Egyptian Writers*, 96.

under the Mamlukes, was the acting ruler of Egypt.[12] At the outset, al-Zaynī seems to direct his attention to the restoration of justice and security, but, as the plot proceeds, it becomes clear that he is as cruel as his predecessor and seeks to gain control over every aspect of people's lives. Al-Zaynī is a clear metaphor for 'Abd al-Nāṣir, whose remaining in power after the defeat in the 1967 War parallels al-Zaynī's remaining in power after the 1516 defeat and the ensuing Ottoman occupation.[13] Al-Zaynī Barakāt is absent/present in the novel. He appears mainly through the consciousness of other characters. He is nowhere, yet at the same time he is everywhere (like Orwell's Big Brother).

Another central character in the novel is Saʿīd al-Juhaynī, a student at al-Azhar University, who dares to challenge al-Zaynī and, as a result, is imprisoned and tortured until he is broken. One form of torture is forcing him to watch his beloved making love with her husband.[14]

The main source for this novel was the chronicle of Egyptian historian Ibn Iyās (d. 930/1524), whose text served as a model for al-Ghīṭānī. In this novel, al-Ghīṭānī endeavored to depict events in his own time—under 'Abd al-Nāṣir's rule—without referring directly to it, thus evading censorship for criticizing the regime.[15]

2. *Waqāʾiʿ ḥārat al-Zaʿfarānī* (The chronicles of the Zaʿfarānī neighborhood, 1976): This novel also deals with themes of power and oppression, this time in a lower-class Cairene neighborhood in the 1970s. The mysterious Shaykh ʿAṭiyya casts a spell on the al-Zaʿfarānī neighborhood—in the form of a contagious impotence that befalls all men—thus establishing his rule and imposing a legal system that will create equality and abolish all classes, i.e. establish

12 About the historical figure of al-Zaynī Barakāt, see Muḥammad b. Aḥmad b. Iyās, *Badāʾiʿ al-zuhūr fī waqāʾiʿ al-duhūr*, edited by Muḥammad Muṣṭafā (Cairo: al-Hayʾa al-Miṣriyya al-ʿĀmma li'l-Kitāb, 1984), 4: 50–55: 214.

13 Starkey, *Egyptian History*; Mehrez, *Egyptian Writers*, 100. In contrast to Starkey and Mehrez, al-Ghīṭānī denied that al-Zaynī is a metaphor for 'Abd al-Nāṣir. According to him, the novel comes out against oppression in general and tells the story of an opportunistic character (al-Ghīṭānī in *al-Sharq al-Awsaṭ*, March 7, 2007, http://www.aawsat.com/details.asp?section=19&issueno=10326&article=409423&feature=1 [accessed September 19, 2007]).

14 Saʿīd's character can be seen as representing al-Ghīṭānī's generation—those Egyptians who were raised on 'Abd al-Nāṣir's ideology, but were disillusioned and ultimately broken by the regime (Starkey, *Egyptian History*, 259; Mehrez, *Egyptian Writers*, 101–102). His character can also be seen as representing al-Ghīṭānī himself, who was arrested in 1966 because of his political views; that experience infiltrated this novel as well as the trilogy *Kitāb al-tajalliyāt* (The book of epiphanies) (Mehrez, *Egyptian Writers*, 98; Ma'mūn 'Abd al-Qādir al-Ṣimādī, *Jamāl al-Ghīṭānī wa'l-turāth: dirāsa fī aʿmālihi al-riwāʾiyya* (Cairo: Maktabat Madbūlī, 1992), 6; al-Ghīṭānī, *Tajalliyat*, 111–113, 247, 522, 572–576, 592, 595–597).

15 Draz, "In Quest of New Narrative Forms," 140–143; al-Ghīṭānī, *Jadaliyyat*, 79.

an ideal world. ʿAṭiyya's initiative takes shape when it appears that moral degeneration has become so widespread that it poses a far-reaching danger to the whole of society. The neighborhood is a microcosm of Egypt and the surrounding world, so that the spell spreads from Egypt to encompass the entire world. Since reality cannot be fixed by rational means, irrationality is imposed.[16] In choosing impotence as the axis around which the plot turns, al-Ghīṭānī showed much courage because he chose a subject that was—and still is—taboo in Arab society.[17]

3. *Khiṭaṭ al-Ghīṭānī* (al-Ghīṭānī's quarters, 1980): This novel was even more influenced by Orwell's *Nineteen Eighty-Four* than *al-Zaynī Barakāt*. The events take place in a country named al-Khiṭaṭ (lit. "Quarters," plural of *khiṭṭa*), in a nameless city, where the most important building is that of *al-Anbāʾ* (The News) newspaper, the center of national power and authority. The name of the newspaper's chief editor is unknown, apart from his epithet, the Master (*al-ustādh*). Although the time period of the novel is not specified, various signs scattered throughout the book hint that al-Khiṭaṭ symbolizes Egypt in the period after the 1952 Revolution. The newspaper symbolizes the centralist regime, and the Master represents ʿAbd al-Nāṣir.[18] As the plot progresses, the state deteriorates. The Master disappears following a military defeat and is replaced by corrupt successors, who take measures that turn the citizens into strangers in their own land and sign a humiliating peace treaty with the sworn enemies of the state (i.e. Israel).

In this novel, as in *al-Zaynī Barakāt*, al-Ghīṭānī turned to the Egyptian historiographical tradition of the Middle Ages. This time, he chose the historiographical genre of *Khiṭaṭ*. Writing history in the form of *Khiṭaṭ* is an encyclopedic project dealing with a specific place. Two such works that influenced al-Ghīṭānī stylistically are *al-Mawāʿiẓ wa'l-iʿtibār fi dhikr al-khiṭaṭ wa'l-āthār* (Lessons and morals concerning the quarters and antiquities) by al-Maqrīzī (d. 845/1441) and *al-Khiṭaṭ al-jadīda al-Tawfiqiyya* (The new quarters of [Khedive] Tawfīq) by ʿAlī Pasha Mubarāk (d. 1893).[19]

4. The trilogy *Kitāb al-tajalliyāt* (The Book of epiphanies, published 1983–1987): this semi-autobiographical novel was inspired mainly by *al-Futūḥāt al-Makkiyya* (The Meccan revelations) by the Sufi scholar Muḥyī al-Dīn b. ʿArabī (d. 638/1240), to whom al-Ghīṭānī turned after a psychological crisis

16 Al-Ṣimādī, 128.

17 Badawi, *A Short History of Modern Arabic Literature*, 171.

18 Mehrez, *Egyptian Writers*, 64–65; Starkey, *Egyptian History*, 261. For further analysis of the novel, see: Yona Sheffer, *The Individual and the Authority Figure in Egyptian Prose Literature* (New York: Routledge, 2018), 9–10.

19 Starkey, *Egyptian History*; Mehrez, *Egyptian Writers*, 65.

following his father's death while he himself was abroad. The Sufi influence, mainly that of Ibn ʿArabī, is evident throughout the trilogy.[20] The narrator/al-Ghīṭānī sets out on a mystical journey during which he meets historical figures and friends from the past. The trilogy interweaves personal, autobiographical, and mystical elements with social and political criticism against al-Sādāt's domestic policy and his signing the peace treaty with Israel. Unlike al-Sādāt, ʿAbd al-Nāṣir is enveloped in an aura of holiness that seems surprising given the fact that al-Ghīṭānī had been held in custody for six months because of his views on ʿAbd al-Nāṣir's regime. A possible explanation, however, for his changed attitude could be that ʿAbd al-Nāṣir's rise to power had guaranteed the livelihood of the lower classes in general and the livelihood of al-Ghīṭānī's father in particular.[21]

These literary works contain several women characters, some of which are main characters, while others are ostensibly marginal though they still play a key role in the plot, shedding light on the protagonists' inner selves. The study, as stated above, discusses four types of female characters: the mother, the wife, the unwed careerist, and the unattainable beloved.

4 The Mother

In the second part of *Kitāb al-tajalliyāt*, the narrator/al-Ghīṭānī reaches a station in his mystical journey where he sees himself in an "alternative creation" (*khalq badīl*),[22] i.e. as he could be in another life. In his "original" life, the narrator/al-Ghīṭānī's working-class parents are from Upper Egypt, and he has

---

20 Al-Ghīṭānī, *Jadaliyyat*, 78–82; Issa J. Boullata, "New Directions in the Arabic Novel: An Interview with Jamal al-Ghīṭānī," *Mundus Arabicus* 5 (1992): 4; Alexander Knysh, "Sufi Motifs in Contemporary Arabic Literature: The Case of Ibn ʿArabi," *The Muslim World* 86/1 (1996): 41.

21 Knysh, "Sufi Motifs," 41; Starkey, *Egyptian History*, 261; al-Ghīṭānī, *al-Tajaliyyāt*, 482. It may be worth noting that in the above-mentioned novels the political criticism is implicit, albeit clear, while in this trilogy it is explicit. As to whether the trilogy can be considered an autobiography, and what type of autobiography it is, see e.g. ʿAbd al-Salām al-Kiklī, *Al-Zaman al-riwāʾī, jadaliyyat al-māḍī wa'l-ḥāḍir ʿinda Jamāl al-Ghīṭānī, min khilāl al-Zaynī Barakāt wa-kitāb al-tajaliyyāt* (Cairo: Maktabat Madbūlī, 1992), 104–120.

22 The term is coined by Ibn ʿArabī, the narrator's guide during this part of the journey (al-Ghīṭānī, *al-Tajaliyyāt*, 293). Unlike the narrator/al-Ghīṭānī, his "other self" is a young person, not yet in his 20s, who differs from him in physique (ibid., 293, 344, 354). Since the "alternate self" is in fact himself, sometimes the narrator/al-Ghīṭānī uses the first person to tell about the relationship between him and his parents or his sweetheart. The "alternate self" does not know that he has another existence (ibid., 293).

three siblings (two brothers and a sister). The "alternate self," in contrast, is an only child whose parents are from Cairo; the family lives in a European city because the father was persecuted in Egypt for his political views (specifically, his opposition to the peace treaty with Israel). The father is a famous, albeit frustrated, poet, and the mother works at two jobs to support the family. While the "original" parents' names are Bakhīta and Aḥmad (the exact same names as those of al-Ghīṭānī's own parents), and the "original self's" name is Jamāl, the narrator/al-Ghīṭānī does not name the "alternate" parents, nor does he name the "alternate self."[23] The "original" and "alternate" mothers are the main motherly characters in al-Ghīṭānī's works. Other motherly characters are depicted in lesser detail, but they share certain characteristics that mainly recall the "original" mother.

The "original" mother respects the father's efforts to support her and meet her needs. Sometimes she is submissive and even dependent, but at other times she is assertive and imposes her will on the "original" father. At home, there is a distinct division of roles between the parents—the father works to support the family, while the mother runs the household and takes care of the children's education.[24]

The "alternate" mother does not trust her husband to be a reliable wage earner because of his unstable temperament and mental instability and in fact, she considers herself to be the family's main breadwinner. She is the anchor sustaining the family, mainly the future of her son. Indeed, unlike the "original" mother, she is hardly at home and does not run the household, due to the fact that she works from dawn to dusk.[25]

Al-Ghīṭānī uses some of the "original" mother's beliefs, customs, and traits to depict other motherly characters and tasks in his works. Thus, for example, the mother attempts to protect her sons by performing superstitious rituals, such as introducing the newborn as a baby girl, and voodoo-like rituals against the evil eye.[26] In a similar manner, in *Waqāʾiʿ ḥārat al-Zaʿfarānī*, the mother of al-Takarlī (al-Takarlī is one of the neighborhood's dignitaries) dresses him in girls' clothes and even gives him a girl's name.[27] In *Khiṭaṭ al-Ghīṭānī*,

23 Al-Ghīṭānī, *al-Tajaliyyāt*, 321–326, 394, 428, 430. When the narrator/al-Ghīṭānī gives details about his life, he relates to himself as "my origin" (*aṣlī*), Jamāl, and even as "my friend," in order to keep distance from the "original existence" (see ibid.: 619–621, 627, 633). However, when the "original" mother dies, the narrator/al-Ghīṭānī reunites with his origin (ibid., 794).

24 Ibid., 420, 422–424, 428, 565, 585–586.

25 Ibid., 328–329, 352, 417, 424–426.

26 Ibid., 53, 156, 543–545, 653; idem, *Yawmiyyātī*, 361.

27 Jamāl al-Ghīṭānī, *Waqāʾiʿ ḥārat al-Zaʿfarānī*, 2nd ed. (Cairo: Maktabat Madbūlī, 1985), 98.

Bakhīta—the mother of Khālid, a leading figure in the resistance movement against the regime—conducts a voodoo-like ritual to protect her sick son.[28] In this case, the close affinity to al-Ghīṭānī's biography is evident, first and foremost in the mother's name—Bakhīta—the same name as the "original" mother, but also in the name Khālid, which, as he writes in *Kitāb al-tajalliyāt*,[29] is one of the names al-Ghīṭānī chose for himself in his novels.

As to the relationship between mother and children, it is apparent that the "original" mother is a prototypical character, whose beliefs and traits appear in motherly characters in other works by al-Ghīṭānī. In fact, the mother in *Khiṭaṭ al-Ghīṭānī* is a clear reflection of the "original" mother. It is interesting that the same beliefs and traits usually appear in characters that are more traditional, and from the lower classes with origins in Upper Egypt. The "alternate" mother, the modern Cairene, middle-class woman, is not ruled by superstition.

In *Kitāb al-tajalliyāt*, al-Ghīṭānī depicts two types of mother: a rural, traditional mother, for whom the father is the pillar of the family's existence; and a modern mother upon whom the family's existence depends. Nevertheless, the special circumstances in which the "alternate" mother lives should not be ignored. She lives and acts in a foreign environment, with a declining husband who cheats on her and neglects their son, and she does not know how long he will stay before leaving them altogether.[30]

Those two family cells are interesting in terms of the "balance of power" between husband and wife. In the "original" family, there is harmony between the parents, who make a concerted effort to attend to their children's education. Although the mother has become dependent on the father ever since her arrival in Cairo (as illustrated by her habit of waiting for hours until he returns from work), she has the power to make him do as she wills (as when she convinces him to sell her jewelry for the sake of the children's future).[31]

In the "other" family, the family unit is unstable, even though the mother spares no effort to keep the family united. For this, she is willing to tolerate her husband's adulteries, even as he ceases to fulfill his duties to her as a husband and wage earner. Nor does she hesitate to confront him about his conduct when he tries to blame her for his misfortunes.[32] Al-Ghīṭānī depicts her as a positive character who takes care of the family, in contrast to the father, who breaks down and stops functioning.

---

28 Jamāl al-Ghīṭānī, *Khiṭaṭ al-Ghīṭānī*, 2nd ed. (Cairo: Maktabat Madbūlī, 1991), 166.

29 Al-Ghīṭānī, *al-Tajaliyyāt*, 520. As for other details that indicate the affinity between Khālid and al-Ghīṭānī, see idem, *Khiṭaṭ*, 81.

30 Al-Ghīṭānī, *al-Tajaliyyāt*, 328–329, 352, 417, 423.

31 Ibid., 397–398, 407–412, 428, 554, 565–566.

32 Ibid., 328–329, 421–426.

The descriptions of the motherly characters in al-Ghīṭānī's works suggest that the mother is responsible for the children's wellbeing and for easing her husband's worries so that he will be able to continue his work. In al-Ghīṭānī's eyes, "motherhood is tenderness, and tenderness is affection."[33] In light of this sentiment, it is easy to understand why the character of the mother in his writing is generally a positive one.

5 The Wife

In al-Ghīṭānī's works, the character of the wife can be classified as one of three subtypes: the "good" wife (the pillar of the household who sustains the family in difficult economic circumstances or takes care of the children's education); the assertive or unfaithful wife; and the betrayed wife.

Waqāʾiʿ ḥārat al-Zaʿfarānī abounds with female characters, particularly assertive wives, some of whom are violent and use abusive language. A short while after Shaykh ʿAṭiyya casts his spell of impotence on the men, Buthayna—the wife of ʿAbduh Murād, a public transport driver—exclaims: "O women of the neighborhood, O neighborhood of women."[34] What she means is that after the spell is cast, men are no longer men; one could also argue, however, that these words hint at the dominance of women over men, especially after the spell has been cast. Buthayna's assertion, uttered in anger during a quarrel with other wives in the community, that nothing will ever be good in the neighborhood "as long as hearts are ungrateful, and women and those [females] who resemble scorpions are nesting in it," reflects the way most of the wives in the neighborhood are depicted in this novel.[35]

The neighborhood residents continuously expect quarrels to erupt among women or between women and other people. These are "the best shows in the neighborhood," mainly because of their rich, yet foul, language, curses, similes, and a variety of gestures, including at times even violence.[36] Following the spell, the women attempt to guess the identity of the only man who has remained unharmed by it, and flirt with potential "candidates." As a result, the quarrels between them escalate. As to the women's attitude towards Shaykh ʿAṭiyya, the ongoing spell disconcerts them, so that they blame the men for sitting back and doing nothing to counter his actions. One woman even

33 Ibid., 554.
34 Al-Ghīṭānī, *Waqāʾiʿ*, 102.
35 Ibid., 101.
36 Ibid., 141.

threatens to break into "this damned Shaykh's room, and let him do to her whatever he will; she is not afraid at all."[37] Buthayna's attitude towards him is ambivalent: on the one hand, she praises him when she sees one of her rivals complaining about the spell while, on the other hand, she curses him as her physical and mental state deteriorates (mainly because no one can satisfy her sexual urges).[38]

Since the cases of the positive, treacherous, or materialistic wives are obvious, I would like to highlight the predicament of a betrayed wife. This is the case of Īthār (in *Khiṭaṭ al-Ghīṭānī*), the wife of Majdī Ramzī, a senior official who, bit by bit, becomes the most powerful man in the country. The relationship between the two is characterized by Īthār's subjugation to Majdī and his total disregard for her. Īthār has been in love with Majdī since their schooldays, when she predicted a brilliant future for him, imagining herself standing by his side at the Nobel Prize award ceremony when he is recognized for his discoveries in alchemy, answering journalists' questions, and becoming a celebrity in her own right as "the little wife." Her love for him, as well as the desire to make her dream come true, encourages her to follow him abroad (where he goes to study) and even live with him for a year and a half before they get married. She works as a teacher and gives him her salary, while he leaves her a miserly spending allowance. She sits for hours without moving, while Majdī's eyes wander aimlessly through an empty space, lest she disturb his thinking and keep him from the innovations that would eventually lead him to the longed-for prize. Majdī, for his part, brings girlfriends into their home before the wedding and even after it, and sleeps with them in front of her, explaining that this helps him recharge his batteries on the road to a scientific breakthrough. He never approaches her. Īthār submissively accepts his attitude, but only for the sake of the prize and for the public attention she will eventually get.[39]

Nevertheless, Majdī's disregard for her feelings affects her badly. When they return to the al-Khiṭaṭ, it is evident that she has lost weight and her joie de vivre. In front of her worried mother and friends, she dissembles, claiming that she is a full partner in Majdī's research efforts. Gradually, Īthār begins to understand that Majdī's political role in the country does not fit with his studies and his excuses for discontinuing his research do not satisfy her. As a result, she decides to carry out a plan she conceived while they were abroad—to cheat on Majdī. In the past, after Majdī's departure abroad when she was left alone, she would find refuge with Khālid, who had been in love with her; now she returns

37 Ibid., 268.

38 Ibid., 101–102, 143, 195.

39 Al-Ghīṭānī, *Khiṭaṭ*, 275–277, 311–316.

to him. However, just as Majdī has treated her, she now treats Khālid, imitating Majdī's words and gestures, and hurting Khālid's feelings as Majdī had hurt hers. She does not love Khālid but insists on meeting him.

But when she tells Majdī that she has betrayed him with Khālid in their apartment, Majdī does not seem to care. As a result, she resolves to divorce him once he has been awarded the Nobel Prize and their photo has been brought to public notice. Implausible as it may sound, she still hopes that he will reciprocate her love and fulfill her dreams. As far as she is concerned, the most important thing about the prize would be her photograph beside Majdī and interviews in the media, in which she would talk about their life together and explain what he has done for his country, things much more significant than "merely" transforming cheap metals into gold. Īthār considers herself a saint, since she plans to keep out of the spotlight, and publish her memoirs without harming Majdī.[40]

Īthār's dream shatters when the spotlight shines on Majdī at the welcoming ceremony for the enemy's army as it enters the country. Majdī refuses to take her to the ceremony despite her begging, and he locks her up in their home after reproaching her and beating her. At the end of the novel, when the country plunges into chaos, Īthār expresses a wish to return to the past, even if for a moment, to stand by Majdī's side.[41]

Īthār's betrayal seems trivial in light of her husband's actions, to such an extent that she is not even able to stir up his jealousy when she tells him that she is cheating on him with Khālid, who serves as a vehicle for the release of her frustrations in her relationship with Majdī. On the other hand, hurting Khālid's feelings can be held against her, especially because Khālid is al-Ghīṭānī's alter ego in this novel.

6 The Unwed Careerist

One of the most interesting female characters in al-Ghīṭānī's works is Rawnaq, the Master's multifaceted right hand in *Khiṭaṭ al-Ghīṭānī*. Rawnaq, daughter of a former ambassador, has studied in England, traveled the world, and mastered several languages, including that of their enemy (i.e. Hebrew). The Master agrees to employ her, but on condition that he himself will deflower her—a condition her father accepts. When he appoints her as his private secretary, he informs her that she will know everything about the newspaper and

40 Ibid., 275, 311–316.

41 Ibid., 421–422, 429, 434.

its employees, except for the information he will withhold from her. Rawnaq eventually replaces the treasurer of *al-Anbāʾ* when the latter suffers a heart attack.[42]

Indeed, Rawnaq comes to know everything about everyone. All the newspaper's workers, both veterans and newcomers, pour out their hearts to her as she listens willingly, expressing solidarity with them through her reactions. Even al-ʿInānī—who serves as the fearsome head of the Directorate of Security after the Master's disappearance—unburdens himself to her, even though she is the one he fears most in the newspaper, and not just because of her close relations with the Master. She uses a startling range of facial expressions, from cruel, like that of an executioner, to a gentle, sympathetic, even shy bearing. Al-ʿInānī hence both fears and likes her.[43]

Rawnaq supplies the Master with young women, while remaining the only newspaper employee with whom the Master has regular sexual intercourse. Despite the close relationship between them, even the Master does not know everything about her, and he is surprised and delighted when he learns that she has been arrested in a brothel. Doing whatever comes into her head, she began to practice prostitution secretly as a way to come into contact with those who fear and desire her, as well as those who are afraid to express their feelings towards her openly.[44] Perhaps, as a result, she will be perceived to be the Master's mirror image—at least with regard to their shared wish to be covertly all-knowing. Because of her new occupation, the Master regards her as a prototype for the "new person," the robot-like person he wishes to see throughout the country after he has completely ruined it.[45]

Rawnaq fears the Master, although she does not know exactly why—whether the because she cannot fathom what he thinks and plans, or because she feels that he is both tangible and intangible at the same time. She wonders what she really wants from him. At times, she wants to abandon him and leave the country; at other times, she imagines telling him that she is afraid of him. But she cannot keep away from him precisely because she has not yet deciphered his inner self. She feels aversion towards him but is, at the same time, strongly attracted to him. She seems to be dependent upon him emotionally, just as he is dependent upon her organizationally.[46]

42 Ibid., 22–24, 125.
43 Ibid., 47–48.
44 Ibid., 62, 69–71.
45 Ibid., 110.
46 Ibid., 106.

Rawnaq is not jealous of women who are having sexual intercourse with the Master. She acknowledges his claim that he has sex with some women employees while keeping others waiting in order to tighten his control over them. She despises and hates them, feels disgusted when she imagines them pregnant or breastfeeding, and wishes to see them humiliated when they conceive. She is revolted by everything that involves childbirth and by every traditional woman's role.[47]

As for her relationships with men other than the Master and the brothel's clients, her attitude is also ambivalent. At some point, a young, 20-year-old man falls in love with her. She shows him affection, but in her heart she despises and curses him, and after forty meetings she rebuffs him (when he loses his self-control, having seen her naked during their last meeting). Though he repeatedly begs her to give him another chance, she ignores him. A possible reason is that she is in love with Barnaq, a vagrant who often loiters near the entrance of the *al-Anbāʾ* building. After the Master's disappearance, Barnaq claims that he has slept with her and that she has told him that only he is a real man, that he has no rival. When some employees of the newspaper beat him, he proclaims that she is going to marry him. He is even seen riding in the same car with Rawnaq.[48]

After the Master disappears, his heir, al-Tanūkhī, proposes that she become his personal secretary or fill any other position, since "the entire newspaper is her property."[49] She rejects his offer, saying that she has not yet decided what to do. Indeed, Rawnaq is well aware of her position in the newspaper during the Master's era and afterwards, as made plain by Barnaq's greeting "Long live her royal majesty!"[50] Eventually, Rawnaq disappears, never to be seen again.[51]

Rawnaq is one of several unwed careerist women in al-Ghīṭānī's works, all of them quite repulsive. Some are cruel to their suitors, and behave rudely towards others. Others are materialistic and greedy; among those are women who smuggle drugs in order to increase their wealth and improve their social status.[52]

---

47 Ibid.

48 Ibid., 172, 205, 209–210, 436.

49 Ibid., 201–202.

50 Ibid., 108, 165, 191.

51 The narrator does not reveal when she disappears. After the Master's disappearance, she hardly plays a role in the story, only as a distant memory of one of the main characters in the novel (ibid., 283).

52 See for example Jamāl al-Ghīṭānī, [*al-Aʿmāl al-kāmila:*] *al-Aʿmāl al-riwāʾiyya* (Cairo: al-Hayʾa al-Miṣriyya al-ʿĀmma li'l-Kitāb, 1995), 5: 118, 133–135, 267–283, 379–411.

7 The Unattainable Beloved

As we have seen, Rawnaq illuminates the Master's character in *al-Ghīṭānī's Quarters*. In a similar manner, in *al-Zaynī Barakāt*, Samāḥ throws a light on the omnipotent character of al-Zaynī. Samāḥ is the sweetheart of Saʿīd al-Juhaynī, the novel's protagonist in this novel, and indirectly helps him to discover al-Zaynī's true colors.

Saʿīd relates to most women as mere sex objects, undressing them with his eyes when he passes them in the street. An exception is Samāḥ, whose father is a protégé of the regime and one of al-Zaynī's friends. Saʿīd regards her as pure, unattainable, rather like a saint; she is more of an abstract person than a tangible one.[53]

For Saʿīd, Samāḥ is like a beam of light in the dark, "the hope to survive an era"[54] of oppression and cruelty. Once, when he leaves her father's house, he imagines himself walking with her in a city that knows no plagues and where virgins are not kidnapped, poor people are not arrested, and there are no cruel punishments for slight transgressions.[55] Thus, he associates her with a utopian world, a world in which justice prevails over injustice, and a man of his social class can marry a woman of Samāḥ's class.

Saʿīd's dreams shatter when al-Zaynī organizes her marriage with a dignitary. All the sultanate dignitaries, including al-Zaynī, are present at the wedding. On the wedding night, Saʿīd loses his self-control; it is "the night he was slaughtered, but Gabriel—peace be on him—did not redeem him."[56] In his grief, he has nothing left but to dream about a future in which he will find his way to Samāḥ. However, he imagines the gentle Samāḥ making love to her husband, who violates her body. In the past, he did enjoy similar erotic daydreams, but to imagine Samāḥ as an ordinary woman is too heavy a burden for him to bear.[57]

One day, al-Zaynī delivers a speech in the mosque. Hearing his lofty words about justice, Saʿīd recalls the sounds from Samāḥ's wedding. Even before the

---

53 Jamāl al-Ghīṭānī, *al-Zaynī Barakāt*, 3rd ed. (Cairo: Dār al-Mustaqbal al-ʿArabī, 1985), 25, 75–76, 73–74.

54 Ibid., 78–79.

55 Ibid., 27, 73, 78–79, 107.

56 Ibid., 212. This is an allusion to the story of the Binding as it appears in Qur'an, 37: 99–107 and in some exegeses (as the commentators disagree as to the identity of Abraham's bound son—Isaac or Ishmael. See, e.g.: Abū Muḥammad al-Ḥusayn b. Masʿūd al-Farāʾ al-Baghawī, *Maʿālim al-tanzīl fi'l-tafsīr wa'l-taʾwīl* (Beirut: Dār al-Maʿrifa, 1407/1987), 4: 34–35; Abū Jaʿfar Muḥammad b. Jarīr al-Ṭabarī, *Jāmiʿ al-bayān fī taʾwīl āy al-Qurʾān*, edited by Aḥmad Muḥammad Shākir (Beirut: Muʾassasat al-Risāla, 2000), 21: 72–79.

57 Al-Ghīṭānī, *al-Zaynī*, 208–209.

wedding, Saʿīd had already suspected al-Zaynī's intentions, when he appointed Zakariyya b. Rāḍī—the notorious head of the Secret Police—as his deputy. But he discovers al-Zaynī's true nature through the prism of his organizing Samāḥ's marriage, an act by which al-Zaynī harms him personally. Saʿīd therefore decides to follow the example of an old lady who once shouted at al-Zaynī, accusing him of being wicked, after which she vanished into thin air (Saʿīd assumes that al-Zaynī killed her). He shouts that al-Zaynī is lying, and more people join his loud claims.[58]

Saʿīd is imprisoned, and during his detention he is taken to a place from which he is forced to watch Samāḥ having violent sexual intercourse with her husband. As a result, his hair turns white. This is the culminating point of the psychological torture he undergoes in prison. After he is released, a broken man, Saʿīd wonders how he ever loved her, how he ever thought her to be pure. He compares Samāḥ to a fertile land turned into a desert. His love for her is dead. Nevertheless, it appears that he is not able to uproot her from his heart: when the Ottomans approach Egypt, he fears that they will conquer the village in which she has found shelter with her husband and will rape her.[59]

Al-Ghīṭānī's works contain multiple examples of unattainable loved ones, as well as unfulfilled loves or loves that, even when, they are fulfilled, end in disappointment. Thus, for example, in both *Kitāb al-tajalliyāt* and *Risāla fi'l-ṣabāba wa'l-wajd* (A letter about tender loving and the ecstasy of love, 1989), the narrator/al-Ghīṭānī follows his spiritual mentor, Ibn ʿArabī, for whom women are symbols for everything that is loved: desire is a symbol for attaining what is desirable, and sexual unity is a symbol for the Sufi unity with God.[60] In these cases, it is evident that the lover is a first-person narrator, an alter-ego of al-Ghīṭānī or even al-Ghīṭānī himself. The lover deifies his beloved, describes her as a mystic being hovering above ground, or as a cosmic body around which he himself revolves. Furthermore, he uses Sufi terms to link the act of love and unity with God. However, in each and every case, the narrator fails to fulfill his wishes.[61]

58 Ibid., 63, 212–213.

59 Ibid., 209, 252–253, 255.

60 Ma'mūn ʿAbd al-Qādir al-Ṣimādī, *Jamāl al-Ghīṭānī wa'l-turāth*, 141; Muḥyi al-Dīn Muḥammad b. ʿAli b. Muḥammad b. ʿArabi, *Fuṣūṣ al-ḥikam*, edited by ʿĀṣim Ibrāhīm al-Kayyālī al-Ḥusaynī al-Shādhilī al-Zarqāwī (Beirut: Dār al-Kutub al-ʿIlmiyya, 2003), 204–205.

61 Al-Ghīṭānī, *al-Tajaliyyāt*, 369–370; also, his *Risāla fi'l-ṣabāba wa'l-wajd* (Cairo: Dār al-Shurūq: 1989), 35, 42–44, 52, 58–60, 93–94.

8 Conclusion

Al-Ghīṭānī lived and wrote in a patriarchal society, in which the man must be obeyed implicitly; nevertheless, within the family unit, the woman (as mother or wife) is usually a strong character whom the husband cannot control. On the contrary, sometimes she controls him. The woman is the pillar around which the household revolves, while the husband is busy chasing a livelihood or his desires.

The less amiable characters, the "interesting" ones, in al-Ghīṭānī's works are depicted in much greater detail than the positive characters, the "dull" ones. As for his attitude towards female characters, it is evident that he admires the mother figure, who is completely devoted to her family and sometimes even prepared to accept—albeit reluctantly—her husband's betrayals, just to keep the family cell intact. As for the wives in the al-Zaʿfarānī neighborhood, things are often turned upside down. When the men lose their potency, most of them cease to be men inside the house as well as outside, and as a result, the women take their place, having the courage to challenge Shaykh ʿAṭiyya—a courage the men lack. Most of the unwed women in al-Ghīṭānī's works are seen as a threat to men, and they sometimes do indeed pose a threat to the men since they are depicted as men in women's clothing.

Indeed, al-Ghīṭānī does not like strong women, either as family women or as unwed women, and he depicts them as being quite repulsive. As to the wives, some play with their husbands' feelings and treat them cruelly—beating or cursing them, or imposing a sexual ban on them. Some of the wives and the unwed women are also described as materialistic and greedy. It seems that in al-Ghīṭānī's eyes, a woman can be strong as long as she knows her place and does not attempt to take that of the man.

Falling in love is doomed to failure. In a few cases, al-Ghīṭānī describes the love for a woman from a Sufi perspective, i.e. an attempt to reach full unity with God by fulfilling a man's desire for a woman. However, in his view, the beloved is a vehicle whose purpose is to allow the lover to be at peace with himself and this he is unable to achieve. The beloved is unattainable, and the lover is always to blame for the unfulfilled love—he fears, recoils, and perceives the end of the relationship from its very outset.

It appears that al-Ghīṭānī sympathizes with some types of women and on the whole, dislikes women who try to take a man's place or to humiliate him undeservedly. To a considerable extent, he also dislikes women eager to demonstrate their power to the men around them.

Bibliography

Badawi, Muhammad M. *A Short History of Modern Arabic Literature*. Oxford: Clarendon Press/Oxford University Press, 1993.

Al-Baghawī, Abū Muḥammad al-Ḥusayn b. Masʿūd al-Farāʾ. *Maʿālim al-tanzīl fiʾl-tafsīr waʾl-taʾwīl*. Beirut: Dār al-Maʿrifa, 1987. 5 vols.

Boullata, Issa J. "New Directions in the Arabic Novel: An Interview with Jamāl al-Ghīṭānī," *Mundus Arabicus* 5 (1992): 1–9.

Draz, Céza Kassem. "In Quest of New Narrative Forms: Irony in the Works of Four Egyptian Writers: Jamāl al-Ghīṭānī, Yaḥyā al-Ṭāhir ʿAbdallāh, Majīd Ṭūbyā, Ṣunʿallāh ʾIbrāhīm (1967–1979)," *JAL* 12 (1981): 137–159.

Al-Ghīṭānī, Jamāl. "Jadaliyyat al-tanāṣṣ," *Alif* 4 (1984): 71–82.

Al-Ghīṭānī, Jamāl. *Waqāʾiʿ Ḥārat al-Zaʿfarānī*. 2nd ed., Cairo: Maktabat Madbūlī, 1985.

Al-Ghīṭānī, Jamāl. *al-Zaynī Barakāt*. 3rd ed., Cairo: Dār al-Mustaqbal al-ʿArabī, 1985.

Al-Ghīṭānī, Jamāl. *Risāla fiʾl-ṣabāba waʾl-wagd*. Cairo: Dār al-Shurūq, 1989.

Al-Ghīṭānī, Jamāl. *Khiṭaṭ al-Ghīṭānī*. 2nd ed., Cairo: Maktabat Madbūlī, 1991.

Al-Ghīṭānī, Jamāl. *Yawmiyyātī al-muʿlana*. Cairo: Dār Suʿād al-Ṣabāḥ, 1992.

Al-Ghīṭānī, Jamāl. *al-Aʿmāl al-kāmila: al-aʿmāl al-riwāʾiyya*. Cairo: al-Hayʾa al-Miṣriyya al-ʿĀmma liʾl-Kitāb, 1995, 5: 6–462.

Al-Ghīṭānī, Jamāl. *Kitāb al-tajalliyāt, al-asfār al-thalātha*. 3rd ed., Cairo: Dār al-Shurūq, 2007.

Hafez, Sabri. "The Egyptian Novel in the Sixties," *JAL* 7 (1976): 68–84.

Ibn ʿArabī, Muḥyī al-Dīn Muḥammad b. ʿĀlī b. Muḥammad. *Fuṣuṣ al-ḥikam*, edited by ʿĀṣim Ibrāhīm al-Kayyālī al-Ḥusaynī al-Shādhilī al-Zarqāwī. Beirut: Dār al-Kutub al-ʿIlmiyya, 2003.

Ibn Iiās, Muḥammad b. Aḥmad. 1404/1984. *Badāʾiʿ al-zuhūr fī waqāʾiʿ al-duhūr*, edited by Muḥammad Muṣṭafā. Cairo: al-Hayʾa al-ʿĀmma al-Miṣriyya liʾl-Kitāb, 1984. 5 vols.

Al-Kiklī, ʿAbd al-Salām. *al-Zaman al-riwāʾī, jadaliyyat al-maḍī waʾl-ḥāḍir ʿinda Jamāl al-Ghīṭānī, min khilāl al-Zaynī Barakāt wa-kitāb al-tajaliyyāt*. Cairo: Maktabat Madbūlī, 1992.

Kilpatrick, Hilary. "The Egyptian Novel from Zaynab to 1980," in *Modern Arabic Literature*, edited by Muhammad M. Badawi. Cambridge: Cambridge University Press, 1992, 223–269.

Knysh, Alexander. "Sufi Motifs in Contemporary Arabic Literature: The Case of Ibn ʿArabī," *The Muslim World* 86/1 (1996): 33–49.

Mehrez, Samia. *Egyptian Writers between History and Fiction*. Cairo: The American University in Cairo Press, 1994.

Sheffer, Yona. *The Individual and the Authority Figure in Egyptian Prose Literature*. New York: Routledge, 2018.

Al-Ṣimādī, Ma'mūn 'Abd al-Qādir. *Jamāl al-Ghīṭānī wa'l-turāth: dirāsa fī a'mālihi al-riwā'iyya*. Cairo: Maktabat Madbūlī, 1992.

Starkey, Paul. "al-Ghīṭānī, Jamāl," *Encyclopedia of Arabic Literature* 1 (1998): 253–254.

Starkey, Paul. "Egyptian History in the Modern Egyptian Novel," in *The Historiography of Islamic Egypt (c. 950–1800)*, edited by Hugh Kennedy. Leiden, Boston, Köln: Brill, 2001, 253–262.

Al-Ṭabarī, Abū Ja'far Muḥammad b. Jarīr. *Jāmi' al-bayān fī ta'wīl āy al-Qur'ān*, edited by Aḥmad Muḥammad Shākir. Beirut: Mu'assasat al-Risāla, 2000, vol. 21.

Shared Passion: Imam Ḥusayn in Persian and Arabic Drama

Peter Chelkowski

1 Introduction

In his book *Live Theatre and Dramatic Literature in the Medieval Arabic World* (1992),[1] Shmuel Moreh boldly and assertively proved that the notion prevalent among Arabs and Westerners that Arabic theatre had its roots in the West was erroneous. He upended accepted theories on the history of Arabic dramatic art and opened up new paths of inquiry on this subject. Indigenous theatrical forms such as puppetry, shadow plays, improvised comedies, and traditional storytelling have not only existed, but thrived in Islam for centuries. These theatrical forms have been linked to holidays, religious festivals, and rites of passage such as weddings, births, and circumcisions. My research in the field of performing arts in Iran supports Professor Moreh's thesis: as modern Arabic theatre has its roots in Arabic culture, the roots of contemporary Persian drama are to be found in Iran, rather than in the West. *Taʿziya*, the Shiʿi passion play, is the fruit of centuries of Persian mourning rituals and is the only form of serious drama to have developed in Iran prior to the mid-nineteenth century (when Western influences began to be felt).

The origin of mourning rituals in Iran should be looked for in the tragedy of the battle of Karbala in 61/680, when the grandson of the Prophet Muḥammad, Ḥusayn, was brutally killed along with (according to tradition) 72 of his male children, brothers, cousins, and companions as he contested his right to the caliphate. His death is considered by the Shiʿis to be the greatest example of martyrdom in human history. The horrific event occurred on the tenth day of the Muslim month of Muḥarram, the ʿĀshūrāʾ day. Ḥusayn was journeying to visit his supporters in Kufa (in modern-day Iraq) and was intercepted by the forces of the Caliph Yazīd, who surrounded the travelers on the arid desert plain. For ten days, Ḥusayn and his party were cut off from water and subjected to intense physical and psychological suffering under the scorching sun as they refused to give in to Yazīd's soldiers. Historical sources tell us that the enemy forces finally attacked the camp in the early afternoon on ʿĀshūrāʾ and

1 Shmuel Moreh, *Live Theatre and Dramatic Literature in the Medieval Arab World* (Edinburgh: Edinburgh University Press, 1992).

 DOI:10.1163/9789004459120_013

slaughtered Ḥusayn and all the males; the females were shackled and taken to Damascus, the capital of the Umayyad Caliphate (661–750). Epic tradition relates that the outcome of the battle depended on single combat between warriors from the two sides.

2 Shiʿi Commemoration of Ḥusayn's Passion

The commemoration and rituals of Imam Ḥusayn's passion and death that developed and continue to evolve are charged with unusual emotions in Shiʿi communities around the world. Although they may differ in form, enthusiastic devotion is universal. The belief that participating in the annual observance of Ḥusayn's sacrifice will be an aid to salvation on the Day of Judgment gives an additional impetus for devout Shiʿis to take part in mourning rituals. As Elias Canetti observed, participation in these rituals

> became the very core of the Shiʿi faith [...] a religion of lament more concentrated and more extreme than any to be found elsewhere [...]. No faith has ever laid greater emphasis on lament. It is the highest religious duty, and many times more meritorious than any other good work.[2]

So it is not surprising that over the centuries, the historical truth surrounding the death of Ḥusayn has been embellished, from both a popular and emotional standpoint, by the epic tradition which is so strong in Iran. The national epic, the *Shzāh-nāma* by Firdawsī, is still cherished by thousands of people who listen to it daily as it is related by storytellers in local coffee houses.

Thanks to this epic tradition, many plays—known as *majlis*—have been devoted to Ḥusayn and members of his camp, including his elder son ʿAlī Akbar, his baby son ʿAlī Asghar, his half-brother ʿAbbās, his nephew Qāsim, and his sister Zaynab. Historical facts are interwoven with legendary heroic deeds to create a rich body of works. In this fashion, the *taʿziya* repertory for the first to the tenth days of the month of Muḥarram is devoted each day to a different member of Ḥusayn's family. One of the *majlis* is also devoted to a member of Yazīd's forces named Ḥurr, who switched sides knowing that he would die as a result of his defection to Ḥusayn's camp.

2 Elias Canetti, *Crowds and Power* (New York: Seabury Press, 1973), 146.

FIGURE 12.1 *Ta'ziya* of "The Martyrdom of 'Abbās"
Note: 'Abbās, the standard-bearer and half-brother of Ḥusayn, had a reputation as a valiant fighter. His story is particularly popular with Iranian women, who often organize female-only gatherings at which he is celebrated. In this scene, the enemy forces have chopped off both of his hands and are preparing to kill him. Ḥusayniya Mushīr, Shiraz Art Festival, 1976. Image taken by the author.

FIGURE 12.2 The arch-villain, Shimr, on horseback in a processional *taʿziya*
Note: Mehriz, 1976. Image taken by K. Bayegan.

The martyrdom of Ḥusayn is always performed on ʿĀshūrāʾ, while several other *majlis*es are performed after ʿĀshūrāʾ, such as the one depicting the plight of the women taken to Yazīd's prison in Damascus. The 20th day of the following month of Ṣafar, known as *arbaʿīn*, falls 40 days after ʿĀshūrāʾ, and the martyrdom of Ḥusayn is performed again. Some *majlis*es are not connected directly with the tragedy at Karbala, but it is always referred to through the technique of *gurīz*, which might take the form of a direct verbal reference to Ḥusayn's martyrdom, or a brief scene depicting some aspect of his tragedy, or both. Through the *gurīz*, all *taʿziya* drama expands beyond spatial and temporal constraints to merge past and present into one unifying moment of intensity, thus allowing the spectator to be simultaneously in the performance space and at Karbala:

> Karbala becomes the focal point of human history, all the past leading up to it and all the future—until the Day of Judgement—flowing out of it, a fiery moment in which the beginning of time and the end of time coalesce [...] Karbala has thus become a compendium containing signs and intimations of Man's predicament, his journey through this vale of suffering and tears, his social and spiritual values, his destiny and final redemption.[3]

3 Karrar Husain, "The Social and Spiritual Significance of Urdu Marthiya," *Alserat* (1986): 267.

There are hundreds of *majlis*es—the Vatican Library alone holds the 1,055 *ta'ziya* manuscripts the Italian ambassador Enrico Cerulli collected while traveling in Iran in the 1950s. There are also collections of *ta'ziya*s in France and in Iran itself. Most of these plays are versions of the same stories with the addition of local color. I estimate that there are probably 150–200 different *ta'ziya* plays. One difficulty in ascertaining the exact number of *ta'ziya*s is that until recently, there were no *majlis*es in libretto form. That is to say, written scripts for a *ta'ziya* as a whole did not exist: actors used to read their lines from little folded scripts which they held in the palms of their hands and which only contained the words for their particular role. Despite the fact that *ta'ziya* texts are in verse—and some of these are very moving and powerful—it is debatable whether *ta'ziya* can be considered as a literary form since the lines are written down only for acting and not for reading.[4]

Ta'ziya as we know it today is a result of centuries of commemoration of the tragedy at Karbala. It is the outcome of a fusion of ambulatory and stationary rites. The ambulatory ritual is called *dasta*, a procession or parade. *Dasta* takes place in the streets and public squares, and in the countryside. It can be a simple march or an elaborate pageant with performers dressed in colorful costumes, walking or riding camels and horses. In addition, live tableaux/floats carrying very graphic representations of various aspects of the bloody battle of Karbala as well as musicians playing and singing dirges. These floats are interspersed with marchers flagellating themselves. The flagellants often synchronize their movements: some beat their chests with their hands (*sīnazanī*), others beat their backs with chains (*zanjīrzanī*). Another group of mourners beat their heads with swords and knives until blood runs down their faces and chests; they are called *shamshīrzanī*. These forceful demonstrations express the participants' grief for the wounds the martyrs suffered at Karbala. There is no doubt that the Ḥusayn *dasta* were influenced by the earlier ritual parades commemorating the unjust and sudden deaths of such heroes as Siyāvush and Adonis/Tammuz. The Muḥarram/Ṣafar procession grew from a simple parade during the Buyid period in tenth-century Baghdad to a very elaborate procession with great numbers of costumed characters marching and riding horses and camels in the Safavid period (1501–1722).

The most famous stationary ritual is known as *rauḍa-khᵛānī*, a ritual chanting of elegies about Ḥusayn and the other Karbala martyrs. All classes of society participate in *rauḍa-khᵛānī*, which can take place in a public square, a courtyard, a mosque, or special buildings called *Ḥusayniya* or *takiya*. *Rauḍa*, as it is colloquially known, usually begins with a laudatory invocation to the Prophet

4 Peter J. Chelkowski, "Dramatic and Literary Aspects of *Ta'ziya-khani*—the Iranian Passion Play," *Review of National Literatures* (Spring 1971), 2: 121–138.

and the saints that alternates between recitation and singing in slow cadences. A performer called a *rauḍa-khᵛān* manipulates the emotions of the assembled audience, using his creative skills in storytelling, body language, voice tonality, and, above all, the art of oration.

Performances may take several hours to an entire day, and even go well into the night, with alternate *rauḍa-khᵛān*s taking turn to chant. As with the *dasta*, participants may engage in weeping, breast-beating, and flagellation. Depending on which events they choose to relate and how they modulate their voices, the *rauḍa-khᵛān*s control the emotional atmosphere of the gathering. They may furthermore make digressions and comparisons with contemporary political, moral, and social situations that could motivate the audience to take action in different spheres of modern society:

> [The *rawzeh-khan*'s] rapid chanting in a high-pitched voice is interrupted by sobbing and crying. Towards the end of the performance, when the audience has been aroused to intense emotion, the *rawzeh-khani* ends with congregational singing of dirges called *nawha*.[5]

The term *rauḍa-khᵛānī* comes from the title of the book, *Rauḍat al-shuhadā* (The garden of the martyrs), written by Ḥusayn Vāʿiẓ Kāshifī in the year 1501, at a time when the Safavid shahs were imposing Twelver Shiʿism as the state religion of Persia.

Rauḍa-khᵛānī means "recitation or reading from *The Garden* [*of the Martyrs*]," which was written in Persian but titled in Arabic. I surmise that Kāshifī desired to link his work to the Arabic genre of literature known as *maqātil* (*maqtal* or "the act of killing") since his story depicted the killing of the grandson of the Prophet. This Arabic genre began in the second Muslim century and endures until today. The oldest and most important *maqātil* are those attributed to Abū Mikhnaf Lūṭ b. Yaḥyā. Soon after *Rawḍat al-shuhadā*ʾ appeared, it became customary to read or recite one chapter from *rauḍa* during the first ten days of Muḥarram. Over time, "The Garden" began to be recited throughout the months of Muḥarram and Ṣafar, and now it is performed year round.

Gradually the *dasta* and the *rauḍa-khᵛānī* came together to produce the dramatic theatre form of *taʿziya*. *Dasta* gave *taʿziya* movement and costumes while *rauḍa* contributed text. There is some debate over when this fusion finally occurred: some scholars claim that it took place in the late Safavid period at the end of the seventeenth and beginning of the eighteenth centuries. Another

5 Peter J. Chelkowski, "Popular Shiʿi Mourning Rituals," *Alserat* (1986), 215.

view holds that the union happened in the second half of the eighteenth century. However, it is unanimously agreed that the *taʿziya* reached its zenith during the Qajar era (1796–1925).

A further contributing factor to the development of *taʿziya* was a revival of classical Persian literature during the Safavid period that included poetry devoted to the Shiʿi saints. From this period, the most important poet extolling the virtues of Ḥusayn and his fellow martyrs was Muḥtasham Kāshānī (1500–1580). His *haft-bands* are simple and direct and can move the reader to tears. *The Elegy on the Death of Imam Ḥusayn* by Qāʾānī (d. 1853) reads more like a dramatic script. Two voices alternate in asking and answering questions about Ḥusayn's sacrifice:

> What rains down? Blood! Who? The Eye! How? Day and Night! Why?
> From grief! What grief? The grief of the Monarch of Karbalā!
> What was his name? Ḥusayn! Of whose race? ʿAlī's!
> Who was his mother? Fāṭima! Who was his grandsire? Muṣṭafā!
> How was it with him? He fell a martyr! Where? In the Plain of Māriya!
> When? On the tenth of Muḥarram! Secretly? No, in public!
> Was he slain by night? No, by day! At what time? At noontide!
> Was his neck severed from the throat? No, from the nape of the neck!
> Was he slain unthirsting? No! Did none give him to drink? They did!
> Who? Shimr! From what source? From the source of Death!
> Was he an innocent martyr? Yes! Had he committed any fault? No!
> What was his work? Guidance! Who was his friend? God!
> Who wrought this wrong? Yazīd! Who is this Yazīd?[6]

This passage shows a shift in Persian literature from the descriptive to the dramatic that coincides with the peak of the development of *taʿziya*.

Taʿziya can be performed anywhere—in the open air or within the walls of *Ḥusayniya* or *takiya*. Throughout the nineteenth century, *takiya*s were built all over Iran. They do not share a common architectural style: from the outside it is not possible to identify a *takiya* by sight. However, a round (very occasionally rectangular), curtainless center stage, raised about three feet above ground level, is found in almost all *takiya*s. Sometimes there are auxiliary stages on the periphery of the main stage. A sand-covered path encircles the main stage and is the place for battles and skirmishes relating to the drama and is also used by

---

6 E.G. Brown, *A Literary History of Persia* (London and New York: Cambridge University Press 1969), 4: 180 (with slight modernization of the diacritics).

the performers to indicate passage through space and time. Scene changes are indicated by the actors jumping off the stage and circumnavigating it. Thus, the *takiya* is a progression of expanding spaces: the main stage surrounded by the sandy path, enclosed by optional auxiliary stages, and the whole embraced by the audience.

The most magnificent *takiya* was the famous Takiya Daulat built in Tehran in the 1870s by Naṣr al-Dīn Shāh. According to some foreign observers, its splendor overshadowed many of Europe's greatest opera houses. One of the best descriptions of the Takiya Daulat comes from Samuel Greene Wheeler Benjamin, the first American envoy to Iran:

> On looking over the vast arena a sight met my gaze, which was indeed extraordinary. The interior of the building is nearly two hundred feet in diameter and some eighty feet high. A domed frame of timbers, firmly spliced and braced with iron, springs from the walls, giving support to the awning that protects the interior from the sunlight and rain [...]. A more oriental form of illuminating the building was seen in the prodigious number of lusters and candlesticks, all of glass and protected from the air by glass shades open on the top and variously colored; they were concentrated against the wall in immense glittering clusters. Estimating from those attached on one box, I judged that there were upwards of five thousand candles in these lusters [...]. In the center of the arena was a circular stage of masonry, raised three feet and approached by two stairways. On one side of the building a pulpit of white marble was attached to the wall. The entire arena with the exception of a narrow passage around the stage was absolutely packed with women, thousands on thousands. At a rough estimate it seemed to me that quite four thousand women were seated there cross-legged on the earthen floor, which was made slightly sloping in order to enable those in the rear to see over the heads of those before them.[7]

The theatre-in-the-round aspect of the *taʿziya* has always fascinated Western visitors to Iran. Since the majority of popular Shiʿi rituals are conducted in public, from the seventeenth century onward, many observers—diplomats, missionaries, and merchants—were able to provide extensive written accounts of what they saw. In 1789, Sir Lewis Pelly noted:

7 Samuel Greene Wheeler Benjamin, *Persia and the Persians* (London: John Murray, 1887), 382–388.

FIGURE 12.3 The interior of the famous Takiya Daulat in Tehran, after Kamāl al-Mulk's painting
Note: Many believe that Naṣr al-Dīn Shāh, who commissioned the Takiya Daulat, was inspired by the Albert Hall, which he saw on a visit to London. Kamāl al-Mulk, *Takiya Daulat*, 1892, Royal Court of Persia (Qajar Dynasty), Tehran, Iran, https://qajar.files.wordpress.com/2010/10/tekiyehdowlat.jpg?w=472&h=622 (accessed October 21, 2019).

> If the success of a drama is to be measured by the effects which it produces upon the people for whom it is composed, or upon the audience before whom it is represented, no play has ever surpassed the tragedy known in the Mussulman world as that of Hasan and Husain.[8]

And theatre director Peter Brook observed exactly one hundred years later:

> I saw in a remote Iranian village one of the strongest things I have ever seen in theatre: a group of 400 villagers, the entire population of the place, sitting under a tree and passing from roars of laughter to outright sobbing—although they knew perfectly well the end of the story—as they saw Ḥusayn in danger of being killed, and then fooling his enemies, and then being martyred. And when he was martyred, the theatre form became a truth.[9]

This dynamic interaction between the actors and the audience was one of the major attractions for Western theatre directors of the 1960s and the 1970s, who were trying to move beyond the traditional box theatre with its strong demarcation between actor and spectators. This close working relationship between actors and the audience has been missing in Western theatre for some 200 years.

Since there is no stage décor and props are rudimentary and symbolic, *taʿziya* requires an active imagination on the part of the audience. For example, a basin of water represents the Euphrates River and a little tree branch symbolizes a grove of palms. It is a musical drama in which vocal and instrumental performances are of great importance. Singers are accompanied by trumpets, cymbals, and flutes and sing *a capella* in classical Persian modes. Good characters sing their parts and predominantly wear green (the color of Paradise and the family of the Prophet), while bad characters recite their lines and mainly wear red. Women's roles are played by men veiled in black from head to toe. In the past, actors were chosen for their appearance and vocal ability; for example, Ḥusayn was always played by a tall, well-built man with a black beard. Today there is more leeway in casting. *Taʿziya* performers are not well paid and, as in the past, often come from families in which acting in the Shiʿi passion play is a long-held tradition.

---

8 Sir Lewis Pelly, *The Miracle Play of Hasan and Husain* (London: H. Allen Co., 1879), 2 vols.

9 Peter Brook, "Leaning on the Moment: A Conversation with Peter Brook," *Parabola* 5 (1979), 2: 47–59.

FIGURE 12.4 *Taʿziya* of "The Martyrdom of Ḥusayn"
Note: Ḥusayn's white shroud, worn over his green garments, indicates that he is ready to die as a martyr. Ḥusayniya Mushīr, Shiraz Art Festival, 1976. Image taken by the author.

Many Shiʿi rituals were exported from Iran to other Shiʿi communities, such as those in South Lebanon and on the Indian subcontinent, and even some in the Caribbean basin. *Taʿziya*, however, did not make inroads in Shiʿi communities outside of Iran. There were some attempts in Iraq and south Lebanon to introduce it, but these efforts more closely resembled the separate rituals of *dasta* and of *rauḍa* as they existed at the end of the eighteenth century before they fused to form *taʿziya*. It is surprising that in India, which has such a great tradition of theatre, these Shiʿi popular rituals were not converted to theatrical mode. There, Muḥarram is a great affair with thousands marching and riding on camels, elephants, and horses. Participants wave banners and carry interpretive representations of Ḥusayn's tomb.

This enthusiastic observance of Muḥarram rituals was carried to the Caribbean by Indian indentured servants beginning in the mid-nineteenth century. Today, the population in Trinidad is roughly divided into two groups: fifty percent of African origin and fifty percent of Indian descent. Among those who are Indian, only seven percent are Muslim, and only about two percent of these are Shiʿis. Nevertheless, the ʿĀshūrāʾ celebrations have become the

FIGURE 12.5 Takiya Muʿāvin al-Mulk in Kermanshah
Note: The battle of Karbala is reenacted before a large audience of women in chadors. Kermanshah, 1990. Image taken by the author.

biggest yearly event on the island for people of all backgrounds. It is astonishing that the annual celebration of pan-Indian unity is a Shiʿi Muslim mourning ritual.

Political and social changes in Iran during the twentieth century eroded financial support for the *taʿziya* and forced acting troops to operate on a commercial basis. The situation changed again after the Iranian Revolution in 1979. Ayatollah Khomeini, who consciously used the Ḥusayn paradigm on the ʿĀshūrāʾ day itself to further his cause from the very beginning of his push for revolution in 1963,[10] continued to use this paradigm to strengthen spirit and military preparedness in the war against Iraq in 1980–1988. *Taʿziya* now enjoys the patronage of the Ministry of Islamic Guidance. Today, professional *taʿziya* companies in Iran usually stay in one place for a ten-day to two-week period, putting on a different play every day and occasionally giving performances both in the afternoon and the evening.

10 Peter J. Chelkowski, "Iran: Mourning Becomes Revolution," *Asia* (May/June 1980): 30–45; Peter J. Chelkowski and Hamid Dabashi, *Staging a Revolution: The Art of Persuasion in the Islamic Republic of Iran* (London: Booth Clibborn Editions, 1990), 45–137.

3 The Ḥusayn Paradigm in Arab Dramas

Ḥusayn's story and character are admired not only by Shiʿis, but also by Sunnis. Modern Arabic dramas about Ḥusayn are not markedly different from the *taʿziya*, however by and large—in contrast to *taʿziya*—they are meant to be read rather than staged. The Ḥusayn paradigm is applied to current events and political situations as they impact Arabs (this was particularly true after the 1967 Arab-Israeli War). Notable Arab dramatists employing this paradigm include the Egyptian playwright ʿAbd al-Raḥmān al-Sharqāwī, the Iraqi writer Muḥammad ʿAlī al-Khafājī, and the Tunisian dramatist Muḥammad ʿAzīza.

Al-Sharqāwī's play, *Thaʾr Allāh*, (God's vengeance) is considered by many to be the best utilization of Ḥusayn as the exemplar of revolutionary spirit in the contemporary Islamic world. It opens in Medina in an atmosphere of corruption and injustice, with Ḥusayn being pressured to pledge allegiance to Yazīd. The parallels between the time of the Yazīd caliphate and the period in Egypt just prior to and after the 1967 war are obvious. Ḥusayn is presented as the ideal of Arab manhood and the conscience of Muslims for all time. He is seen as a martyr who fights and dies for the Islamic ideal of social and political justice and sacrifices his life for the poor, the oppressed, and the voiceless. The first part of the play, called *al-Ḥusayn thāʾiran* (Ḥusayn, a rebel), is akin to a modern passion play. The second half, entitled *al-Ḥusayn shāhidan* (Ḥusayn, a martyr), highlights the universal and timeless qualities of Ḥusayn's sacrifice. His death is portrayed not as a tragic waste, but as a turning point in the history of mankind. Towards the end of the play, Ḥusayn's spirit addresses the audience in a revolutionary manifesto:

> Remember me by rescuing truth from the tyranny of falsehood, by struggling on the path, so that justice may prevail. […] Remember me when virtues become homeless and vices alone become the favourite beloved. […] If you acquiesce to deception, if man accepts humiliation, I will be massacred anew, I will be killed every day a thousand times […] and a new Yazīd will rule over you.[11]

Muḥammad ʿAlī al-Khafājī's drama *Thāniyatan yajīʾu al-Ḥusayn* (Ḥusayn will come one more time) also underlines the parallels between Ḥusayn's death and the Arab defeat in the 1967 war. However, the religious dimension of

11 ʿAbd al-Raḥmān al-Sharqāwī, *Thaʾr Allāh* (Cairo: Dār al-kātib al-ʿArabī li'l-Ṭibāʿa wa'l-Nashr, 1969), 2 vols. The first volume consists of the poetic play *al-Ḥusayn thāʾiran*. The second volume consists of the poetic play *al-Ḥusayn shāhidan*.

Ḥusayn's sacrifice, and particularly the difference between Shiʿis and Sunnis, is downplayed. Instead, al-Khafājī emphasizes how moral decline and corruption among the political and social elite leads to conflicts, power struggles, and inequality. Ḥusayn is presented as a revolutionary figure fighting for freedom, justice, and equality.

Ālām al-Ḥusayn (The suffering of Ḥusayn) by Muḥammad ʿAzīza portrays Ḥusayn more as a classic Arab hero than as a revolutionary. ʿAzīza based his drama on actual *taʿziya*s included in manuscripts collected by the nineteenth-century diplomat Alexander Chodzko.[12] The play opens with Ḥusayn learning of the murder of his envoy, Muslim, by the citizens of Kufa. Naturally a peace-loving man, Ḥusayn becomes a "lion" for the cause of justice. The long soliloquies about parting and farewells are very similar to speeches found in the *taʿziya*, both in content and in the cathartic effect they have on the audience or readers.

Both Persian and Arab theatre have roots in their respective cultures, but they can be said to be bridged by a mode of dramaturgy based on the saga of Ḥusayn. Whether acted by *taʿziya* performers or written by Arab playwrights, aspects of Ḥusayn's character and sacrifice are used to motivate audiences religiously, socially, politically, and emotionally. His life and example hence resonate with a broad spectrum of Muslim society.

Bibliography

Benjamin, Samuel G. Wheeler. *Persia and the Persians*. London: John Murray, 1887.

Brook, Peter. "Leaning on the Moment: A Conversation with Peter Brook," *Parabola* 5 (1979), 2: 47–59.

Brown, E.G. *A Literary History of Persia*. London and New York: Cambridge University Press, 1969.

Canetti, Elias. *Crowds and Power*. New York: Seabury Press, 1973.

12 Alexander Chodzko (1804–1891), a scholar, diplomat, and author of books on Persian poetry, grammar, and customs, was greatly impressed with the *taʿziya* during his travels in Iran in the 1830s. He bought a manuscript of thirty-three plays from the director of the court theatre. This manuscript was later deposited by Chodzko in the Bibliothèque Nationale de France. Chodzko edited and published two of the plays under the title *Djungi Chehadat* in Paris in 1852. In 1878, he published *Le Théâtre persan: choix de tazie*. Muḥammad ʿAzīza mentions the influence of this collection in an unpublished article entitled, "Le Tazie aujourd'hui." This article was shown to me in Paris in 1976 by Dr. Farokh Ghaffari, the director of Shiraz-Persepolis Festival.

Chelkowski, Peter J. *Ta'ziya: Ritual and Drama in Iran.* New York: New York University Press, 1979.

Chelkowski, Peter J. "Iran: Mourning Becomes Revolution," *Asia* (May/June 1980): 30–45.

Chelkowski, Peter J. "Popular Shi'i Mourning Rituals," *Alserat* 12 (1986): 209–226.

Chelkowski, Peter J. "From Karbala to New York: *Ta'ziya* on the Move," *The Drama Review* 49 (Winter 2005): 12–14.

Chelkowski, Peter J. and Hamid Dabashi. *Staging a Revolution: The Art of Persuasion in the Islamic Republic of Iran.* London: Booth Clibborn Editions, 1999.

Husain, Karrar. "The Social and Spiritual Significance of Urdu Marthiya," *Alserat* 12 (1986): 265–274.

Moreh, Shmuel. *Live Theatre and Dramatic Literature in the Medieval Arab World.* Edinburgh: Edinburgh University Press, 1992.

Al-Mulk, Kamāl. *Takiya Daulat*, 1892. Royal Court of Persia (Qajar Dynasty), Tehran, Iran. https://qajar.files.wordpress.com/2010/10/tekiyehdowlat.jpg?w=472&h=622 (accessed October 21, 2019).

Pelly, Lewis. *The Miracle Play of Hasan and Husain.* London: Wm. H. Allen and Company, 1879. 2 vols.

Al-Sharqāwī, 'Abd al-Raḥmān. *Tha'r Allāh.* Cairo: Dār al-Kātib al-'Arabī li'l-Ṭibā'a wa'l-Nashr, 1969. 2 vols.

Fūl, Egypt's National Food: A Key Component of Egyptian Identity and Its Reflections in Modern Egyptian Literature

Gabriel M. Rosenbaum

1 Introduction*

Fūl (scientific name: *Vicia faba* L., commonly called fava/faba beans or broad beans; also field beans, bell beans, tic beans) is a protein-rich legume renowned as Egypt's national food. Hassan-Wassef defines it as "the most popular and most widely consumed food" in Egypt.[1] A staple of most Egyptians' daily diet, *fūl* is an integral element of Egyptian identity. It is omnipresent in everyday life, a constant topic of conversation, regularly referenced in literary works, and the root of a multitude of Egyptian words and phrases. The aim of this cultural-linguistic-literary study is to demonstrate the dominant role of *fūl* in Egyptian society and daily life. To this end, we will identify and describe *fūl* terminology as used in Egypt today and examine examples of it—mostly contemporary—in the nation's literature.

This study is based on my personal observations during four years of living in Cairo and numerous visits to Egypt over the course of more than thirty years; on written texts, fiction and non-fiction; and on field work with informants. During my long-term lexicographic research on Egyptian Arabic, I became aware of the cultural significance of *fūl* through many conversations with Egyptians from all strata of society: young and old, males and females, Muslims, Christians, and Jews. I also came across numerous references to this

* This research was supported by THE ISRAEL SCIENCE FOUNDATION (grant No. 849/18). A preliminary version was first presented at the Institut français d'archéologie orientale (IFAO) and Polish Centre of Mediterranean Archaeology (PCMA) conference on "Studying Food and Drink in Egypt and Sudan," held in Cairo on March 21–23, 2018; a revised version was presented at the colloquium in honor of Prof. Albert Arazi on the occasion of his 80th birthday, held at the Hebrew University of Jerusalem on May 28, 2019. All photos in this article were taken by the author. I wish to thank my friend and colleague Prof. Manfred Woidich, the renowned expert on Egyptian dialects, for reading a draft of this article and for his illuminating comments and suggestions.

1 Habiba Hassan-Wassef, "Food Habits of the Egyptians: Newly Emerging Trends," *La revue de santé de la Méditerranée orientale* 10/6 (2004): 901. This article is an important source on Egyptian dietary habits.

 | DOI:10.1163/9789004459120_014

comestible in modern Egyptian literature (prose, drama, and, to a lesser extent, poetry).[2] While other foods receive little attention in Egyptian literature, *fūl* is a recurring topic, sometimes discussed at length. The examples quoted below are typical of the references that abound in Egyptian literature, mostly since the mid-twentieth century.[3]

Before concluding this study, I worked with a primary group of informants that comprised eight native Egyptians, men and women, all middle-class or lower-middle class Cairenes. I also occasionally consulted with other Cairenes for this article. Most of the information below concerning *fūl* was rechecked with these informants, generally in long discussions. At a later stage, I

2 It should be noted that there are also many reports and comments about *fūl* in Egypt on Arabic-language websites.

3 Of course, references to *fūl* also appear in earlier literary and non-fiction works from Egypt and elsewhere in the Arabic-speaking world. A well-known example is al-Shirbīnī's *Kitāb hazz al-quḥūf*, written in Egypt in the seventeenth century (see Yūsuf al-Shirbīnī, *Kitāb hazz al-quḥūf fī sharḥ qaṣīd Abī Shādūf* (Cairo: al-Maṭba'a al-'Āmira al-Sharafiyya, 1904), 172–176); on this book, see, e.g. al-Shirbīnī, *Kitāb hazz al-quḥūf bi-Sharḥ qaṣīd Abī Shādūf* ("Brains confounded by the ode of Abū Shādūf expounded"), edited by Humphrey T. Davies (Dudley, MA: Peeters, 2004). Taymūr, in his lexicon on colloquial Egyptian Arabic, discusses *fūl* terminology and quotes earlier works, including some from the Middle Ages. (Aḥmad Taymūr, *Mu'jam Taymūr al-kabīr* (Cairo: Dār al-Kutub wa'l-Wathā'iq al-Qawmiyya/Markaz Taḥqīq al-Turāth, 2002), 3: 285–286). On preparing and eating *fūl midammis* in the first half of the nineteenth century see Edward William Lane, *An Account of the Manners and Customs of the Modern Egyptians* (Cairo and New York: The American University in Cairo Press, 2003), 134. On consuming *fūl* in Medieval Cairo see Paulina B. Lewicka, *Food and Foodways of Medieval Cairenes: Aspects of Life in an Islamic Metropolis of the Eastern Mediterranean* (Leiden and Boston: Brill, 2011). On several types and terminology of *fūl* dishes see Cérès Wissa Wassef, *Pratiques rituelles et alimentaires des coptes* (Le Caire: Institut français d'archéologie orientale du Caire, 1971), 345–348. Many other sources published on the internet contain information about *fūl*; some of these have been consulted, too. Brief references to *fūl* appear in Shukrī's guide for field-work on eating habits and table manners in Egypt ('Alyā' Shukrī, *Dalīl al-'amal al-maydānī li-jāmi'ī al-turāth al-sha'bī: al-dirāsa al-'ilmiyya li-'ādāt al-ṭa'ām wa-ādāb al-mā'ida* (Alexandria: Dār al-Ma'rifa al-Jāmi'iyya, 1993), 4: 85–86); some expressions containing the word *fūl* appear in Aḥmad Amīn, *Qāmūs al-'ādāt wa'l-taqālīd wa'l-ta'ābīr al-miṣriyya* (Cairo: Matba'at Lajnat al-Ta'līf wa'l-Tarjama wa'l-Nashr, 1953), 312–313, and in Majīd Ṭūbyā, "Mā yaf'aluhu al-fūl fi'l-'uqūl," in *al-Ta'rīkh al-'arīq li'l-ḥamīr wa'btisāmāt ukhrā* (Cairo: al-Dār al-Miṣriyya al-Lubnānīyya, 1996), 59–63. A list of such expressions, with audio explanations, appears on an AUC site: aucegypt.edu, "Beans: Proverbs—*amthāl sha'biyya 'an al-fūl*," in https://academic.aucegypt.edu/omeka/exhibits/show/foul/proverbs. This site also contains links to the following: "Egyptian Beans—*al-fūl al-miṣrī*," in https://academic.aucegypt.edu/omeka/exhibits/show/foul; "Bean Recipes—*waṣfāt al-fūl*," in https://academic.aucegypt.edu/omeka/exhibits/show/foul/recipes; "Beans: Interviews and Stories—*al-fūl: ḥakāwī wa-liqā'āt*," in https://academic.aucegypt.edu/omeka/exhibits/show/foul/interviews; idem, "About Beans—*'an al-fūl*," in https://academic.aucegypt.edu/omeka/exhibits/show/foul/aboutbeans.

distributed a questionnaire to another group of eight middle-class Cairenes in order to confirm my previous findings. Thus the findings here largely reflect what Cairenes think and know about *fūl*. Since many of them have relatives in other provinces, however, and frequently visit them, or meet with non-Cairene Egyptians, they are sometimes aware of different alimentary traditions outside of Cairo (except for a brief mention, such differences are not discussed here).

2 *Fūl* and Favism in Egypt and Elsewhere

Fūl has been known in the Middle East for thousands of years, both as a type of bean and as a cooked dish. It is mentioned in the Bible (Ezekiel 4: 9 and 2 Samuel 17: 28, together with other staples.) Meletis and Konstantopoulos write that "fava beans are mentioned several times by Homer," and report that "fava beans intake originated in the Near East in late Neolithic times; they were afterwards cultivated in ancient Egypt, Greece and Rome."[4] Shillingburg declares that fava beans are "nearly as old as sin and twice as nutritious," and reports that:

> Fava beans were developed as an agricultural crop from wild ancestors in the Mediterranean Basin and North Africa more than nine thousand years ago. They are one of the plants cultivated in early gardens and fields along with peas, lentils and garbanzo beans and have been found in kitchen middens [def. dump of domestic waste] from prehistoric Swiss lake sites in Europe.[5]

The seeds of *fūl* (*ḥabb, ḥubūb*), like those of other kinds of beans, grow in a pod (*arn*, pl. *urūn*). Fresh *fūl* beans are called *fūl ḥirāti*; because they are green, they are also known as *fūl akhḍar* (green *fūl*).

Dried *fūl* beans are brown and yield a similarly brown dish named *fūl midammis* (see Types of *Fūl* below) or for short, *fūl*—far and away the most common Egyptian way of consuming the food. *Biṣāra* (also: *buṣāra, bisāra, busāra*) is another version, in which the shelled beans are cooked with spices and herbs.[6] Most Egyptians' dish of choice, however, is *fūl midammis*.

---

4 John Meletis and *Kostas* Konstantopoulos, "From the Avoid Fava Beans of Pythagoras to the Present," *HAEMA* 7/1 (2004): 17.

5 Darrol Shillingburg, "Veggies: A to Z—Fava Beans (*Vicia faba L.*)," *Master Gardener Newsletter* (November 2010): 15.

6 Cf. Wassef, *Pratiques rituelles*, 347.

Since locally grown Egyptian *fūl* (called *baladi*) is insufficient to meet the country's demand, imported varieties [known generically as *mustawrad* (imported)] are available. According to Shillingburg, "the Mediterranean Basin was the center of [fava bean] production until the 1950s when China began out-producing that region and exporting to the world."[7] The imports are usually smaller and cheaper than the *baladi* beans. Though Egyptians usually prefer the latter, which they believe taste better, they often buy the less expensive beans.

Favism is a genetic enzyme deficiency [often called in Egypt *anemya il-fūl*, (*fūl* anemia)] that causes a severe reaction in people eating *fūl*.[8] Except for a few individuals, most Egyptians are not among those who suffer from this deficiency.[9] On the contrary: *fūl* is mentioned in very old prescriptions found in documents from the Cairo Genizah, and in traditional medical volumes on the treatment of certain diseases.[10]

3 Types of *Fūl* and Cooking Methods

Though fresh green *fūl* can be cooked in various ways, it is used only sparingly in the Egyptian kitchen and thus plays a limited role in daily life. The most prevalent cooked *fūl* dish, as noted above, is *fūl midammis*, *fūl* beans simmered for hours over low heat. The verb *dammis* (the gerund form is *tadmīs*) in modern Egyptian Arabic means "to cook (e.g. broad beans, lentils, or tripe) in a stoppered container over a slow fire, or buried in hot ashes."[11] Some people soak the beans in water for hours before cooking them; others prefer to cook

7 Ibid.

8 The following is a concise definition of this enzyme deficiency: "A condition characterized by hemolytic anemia (breakup of red blood cells) after eating fava beans (*Vicia fava*) or being exposed to the pollen of the fava plant. This dangerous reaction occurs exclusively in people with a deficiency of the enzyme glucose-6-phosphate dehydrogenase (G6PD.)" (MedicineNet.com, "Medical Definition of Favism," in https://www.medicinenet.com/script/main/art.asp?articlekey=3397 ([accessed May 13, 2016]).

9 Dr. (Med.) Abdullatif, Personal Communication; I wish to thank Dr. (Med.) Abdullatif from Syria for his illuminating explanations of favism in general and favism in Egypt in particular.

10 Efraim Lev and Zohar Amar, *Practical Materia Medica of the Medieval Eastern Mediterranean According to the Cairo Genizah* (Leiden: Brill, 2008), 110–111.

11 El-Said Badawi and Martin Hinds, *A Dictionary of Egyptian Arabic: Arabic English* (Beirut: Librairie du Liban, 1986), 302.

them without soaking.[12] The common term *fūl tadmīs* means "*fūl* beans for cooking over a slow fire."

Taymūr explains that *fūl midammis* derives its name from the *dims* in which it is buried.[13] Woidich reports that *dims* in Upper Egypt means sweepings in the house that contain organic rubbish (straw, little pieces of wood, dried animal droppings, etc.) and is a bit moist, so that it does not burn, but only smolders; he also reports that this term is used in Barīs and al-Khārija in the al-Wādī al-Jadīd Province in the meaning of "a smoldering fire".[14] The term *dims* is not used in Cairo; one Cairene informant told me that she knew the word *wiʾīd* (from the root WQD), with a meaning similar to *dims*; this word, *wiʾīd*, is mentioned by Taymūr as a term used in the countryside.[15]

Fūl may be prepared in a *dammāsa*, a pot with a tight-fitting lid, or in a big urn-shaped vessel, *ʾidrit il-fūl* (lit. *fūl* vessel), usually shortened to *ʾidra* (vessel; in Standard Arabic: *qidra*). The *dammāsa* (which is also occasionally referred to as *ʾidra*) is usually used at home, while the much larger *ʾidra* is used in restaurants and at *fūl* carts and stands. In the past, all these vessels were made of copper (*niḥās, naḥās, nuḥās*); today they are usually produced from aluminum (*alamonya*; in Standard Arabic: *aluminyum*). There are also contemporary *fūl* pots made of stainless steel (*stanlis, stallis, sallis* or *istanlis*, from the English "stainless"), some of them lined with teflon (*tifāl*, from the French brand name Tefal, an amalgam of teflon and aluminum). When the *fūl* is completely cooked, it is stirred in the *ʾidra* and then scooped with a *kabsha* (ladle) onto a plate or into a bowl. In the countryside the term *ʾidrit il-fūl* may refer to earthenware pottery; Woidich reports that the term *ʾidrit* (also: *gidrit*) *il-fūl* is common in rural dialects, in which they denote earthenware pottery.[16] The term *fawwāla* (singular and plural) sometimes serves as a synonym of *dammāsa*;[17] it is not common in the spoken language, but appears on the Internet. The term *fawwāl*

12 Various *fūl* recipes appear in cookbooks; see e.g. Samia Abdennour, *Egyptian Cooking: A Practical Guide* (Cairo: The American University in Cairo Press, 2000); Najlāʾ Muḥyī al-Dīn, *Dalīl al-maʾkūlāt al-shaʿbiyya* (Cairo: al-Dār al-Dawliyya li'l-Nashr wa'l-Tawzīʿ, 1994). Many other recipes appear on the Internet.

13 Taymūr, *Muʿjam*, 3: 285. Taymūr also quotes several other sources that refer to vocabulary derived from the root DMS (285–286).

14 Prof. Manfred Woidich, Personal Communication. On burying the *fūl* in smoldering fire, cf. below the term *mustawqad/mustawʾad*).

15 Taymūr, *Muʿjam*, 3: 286.

16 Prof. Manfred Woidich, Personal Communication. For examples of such earthenware *fūl* potterry from al-Fayyūm, al-Dākhila and Qinā, see the images in Nessim Henry Henein, *Poteries et proverbes d'Égypte* (Le Caire: Institut français d'archéologie orientale, 1992), 75.

17 Badawi and Hinds, *Dictionary*, 678.

FIGURE 13.1 *Fūl tadmīs*, for cooking over a slow fire (Sayyida Zēnab market)

FIGURE 13.2 *Fūl madshūsh*, the main ingredient of falafel (Sayyida Zēnab market)

FIGURE 13.3
Aluminum *dammāsa*

FIGURE 13.4
ʾIdra with a *kabsha* in it (in a popular *fūl* restaurant)

(singular masculine) denotes a seller of dry beans (*fūl tadmīs*) while the term *bitāʿ il-fūl* denotes a seller of cooked *fūl* (*fūl midammis*).

Fūl beans can be soaked in water until they sprout, when they are given the name *fūl nābit*. *Ṣhurbit fūl nābit* (sprouted *fūl* soup) is considered a beneficial food for the ill.

In previous centuries, it was common to bring big vessels of *fūl* to a *mustaw'ad* (in Standard Arabic: *mustawqad*), i.e. a furnace fueled by burning trash: the heat and embers of the furnace slow-cooked the *fūl* overnight. Though these furnaces gradually closed down and have now mostly disappeared, they can still be seen, vessels of *fūl* simmering inside them, here and there in Cairo. Some restaurants and owners of *fūl* carts still take their *fūl* to be cooked in the traditional way in a furnace, but nowadays the heat comes from propane gas in cylinders rather than burning garbage.[18]

4 Place and Time: Where and When *Fūl* Is Cooked and Eaten

Egyptians cook and eat *fūl* on a daily basis—at home, on the street, and in restaurants. Two or three generations ago, many families would prepare *fūl* at home. Today, even those who would prefer to eat their *fūl* at home generally purchase it elsewhere, either from a *fūl* cart or stand on the street or from a local restaurant, thereby avoiding the labor-intensive, time-consuming culinary demands of making it themselves.

It is usually women who cook *fūl* at home although men occasionally help with the preparation of the beans. Many women—and particularly those who work outside the home—would rather not spend long hours cooking *fūl* on a daily basis. During the week, therefore, working people customarily buy their *fūl* ready-made, and in some families *fūl* is cooked in the household only on weekends.

Families in search of *fūl* outside their homes often head to their favorite restaurant. In Cairo, one of the most famous is *al-Jaḥsh*, in the Sayyida Zēnab quarter; its popularity is confirmed by the many times its name crops up in Egyptian literature.

On Fridays, before or after the noon prayer, *fūl midammis*—whether home-made or from a restaurant—is usually the main attraction of a family meal, especially among the lower and middle classes (though it has no connection to any religious ceremony).

---

18 Regarding the furnaces, see the following interviews with furnace owners: https://www.youtube.com/watch?v=XrFEvN3Pc_Q; https://www.youtube.com/watch?v=HaGiuY8ogn8.

FIGURE 13.5 *Fūl* stand

The slow cooking, as reported by my Cairene informants, usually takes place at night, from about 10 PM to 5 AM. In the month of Ramadan, the *fūl* is put on the fire at about 8:00 PM so that it will be ready for the *suḥūr*, the prefast meal that must be consumed before the new fast day begins. According to popular Egyptian lore, *fūl* takes a long time to digest, helping people endure their long hours of fasting. During Ramadan, therefore, it is common to see peddlers wandering with their pushcarts around less prosperous neighborhoods, selling *fūl* and sometimes *bilīla*, a dish of cooked wheat with milk and sugar. At this time of year, one also sees whole families going out at dawn to eat *fūl* for the *suḥūr*; alternatively, they may spend the whole night out, waiting for the start of the prefast repast. Still others spend the night cooking *fūl* at home. Wherever it is eaten, however, *fūl* is the featured item at the *suḥūr*.

Like Muslims, Egyptian Christians (most of whom are Copts) depend on *fūl* for sustenance. *Fūl* actually plays an important role in Copts' lives because

FIGURE 13.6 *Fūl* cart

of the many annual religious fast days they observe, when they are prohibited from eating meat, fish, eggs, or any product that comes from animals. At such times, they eat a vegan diet comprised of foods called *ṣiyāmi* (permitted during the fasting period). Thus, *fūl* as well as falafel often appear as the main course on fast-day menus. Furthermore, on Good Friday (variously known as *il-gumʿa il-ḥazīna* [Sad Friday], *il-gumʿa il-ʿaẓīma* [Great Friday], and *il-gumʿa il-kibīra* [Big Friday], among other terms), Copts traditionally consume *fūl nābit* (sprouted *fūl*) and *ṭaʿmiyya* (falafel), which is also made of *fūl* (see below).[19]

19 Cf. Wassef, *Pratiques rituelles*, 347. On eating *fūl nābit* on Good Friday see Lane, *Account*, 488–489; Lane also gives a definition of *fūl nābit* (489, footnote 1).

FIGURE 13.7
Raw bread dough for *ʿēsh baladi*, sitting on a layer of *radda*

5 Accompaniments to *Fūl*

5.1 *Bread* (ʿēsh)

Fūl comes to the table in a bowl or on a plate. All Egyptians agree that there is no point in eating it without *ʿēsh* (bread), a generic name for flat, round Egyptian bread (which looks similar to pita but differs in texture, color, and taste). "You must chew the *fūl* together with bread," all my informants agreed, when asked about this, "otherwise you don't get the real desired taste of *fūl*." Thus the bean dish is typically accompanied by what in Cairo is called *ʿēsh baladi*, local Egyptian bread baked with whole wheat and a layer of bran (*radda*, also pronounced *raḍḍa*)[20] on the lower side that colors it a dark brown. Restaurants may serve their *fūl* with *ʿēsh shāmi* (lit. Syrian bread), a white-flour pita bread baked without bran and usually thinner and softer than *ʿēsh baladi*. Egyptian bread is usually produced in bakeries although rural housewives may bake it at home, in which case it goes by the name of *ʿēsh bēti* (homemade bread). Virtually the only Egyptians who enjoy their *fūl* without bread are small children and sometimes the elderly, who may eat it with a spoon or fork rather than bread.

20 There is also an Egyptian bread made only of bran flour (*ʿēsh sinn*), eaten mainly for health reasons.

FIGURE 13.8
Baked *ʿēsh baladi*

Egyptian bread and *fūl* are eaten together in either of two ways. In the first, the diner dips a slice of bread into the bowl or plate, scooping some *fūl* onto it. The verb for dipping the bread into the cooked beans is *ghammis*; *ghumūs* refers to *fūl* eaten with bread (and also to any kind of dip eaten in the same way), or to the act of eating it thus.

At street carts (*ʿarabiyyit il-fūl* or *ʿarabīt il-fūl*; in Standard Arabic: *ʿarabat al-fūl*) and in popular restaurants, *fūl* is most commonly spooned into a pocket of Egyptian bread. The bread is usually precut into two halves, across the diameter. Each half is called *sandawitsh* (from English: sandwich), or *shaʾʾa* (piece, chunk, half of something). The term *sandawitsh* may refer to both *ʿēsh baladi* and *ʿēsh shāmi*, while the term *shaʾʾa* refers only to *ʿēsh baladi*. The word *nuṣṣ* (lit. half) may also be used for half a bread filled with *fūl*; in this context, *nuṣṣēn* means "two halves of bread with *fūl*." One meal often consists of two halves of Egyptian bread with *fūl* (*shaʾʾitēn*, *sandawitshēn*, or *nuṣṣēn*), though of course there are those who limit themselves to a single half—and those who put away more than two halves at a time.

5.2 *Oil* (zēt)

Fūl is usually eaten with oil (*zēt*) drizzled on top. The oil most typically identified with *fūl* is *zēt ḥār*, the common nickname for *zēt bizrit il-kittān* (linseed oil). Those Egyptians who do not like its taste may prefer to pour on other kinds of oil: *zēt zatūn* (olive oil) or *zēt ḥilw* (lit. sweet oil), a general name for ordinary, less expensive types of oil produced, for instance, from *dura* (corn) or *ʿabbād ish-shams* (sunflower seeds). On occasion, *fūl* is topped with *zibda* (butter) or *samn/samna* (clarified butter).

5.3 Fūl *Seasonings*

After the raw beans have been cooked, they are called *fūl sāda* (plain *fūl*, i.e. with nothing extra). The addition of spices and other ingredients is referred to by the verb *ḥawwig* (to add spices or other ingredients to food); its passive participle, *miḥawwig*, yields the term *fūl miḥawwig* (seasoned *fūl*). Among the most common condiments are oil, lemon, salt, cumin, and tahini.

Vegetables may be added to the *fūl* too. At the top of the list are *baṣal akhḍar* (green onions) and *baʾdūnis* (parsley). The dish may be further garnished with ingredients like chopped hardboiled eggs or *basṭirma* (pastrami, spicy smoked slices of meat).

Fūl ʾiskandarāni (lit. Alexandrian *fūl*) is a *fūl* dish with added vegetables and seasoning. Cairenes do not agree about its precise ingredients (apparently because there are many possible versions; many more recipes can be found on the Internet).

More complex versions of *fūl*, with various and unusual additions, are created inside and outside the home. Like chefs everywhere, domestic cooks and restaurant owners alike may invent their own names for *fūl* dishes that they serve. *Fūl biʾl-omlēt* (*fūl* with omelet), for instance, appeared on the menu hanging on the wall of a popular Cairene restaurant, but even my more knowledgeable informants, who recognized the word *omlēt*, were not familiar with this new incarnation of *fūl*.

5.4 Fūl *and falafel*

When I asked my informants what they considered the most popular and typically Egyptian fare, the unanimous answer was "*fūl*." Many of them indicated both *fūl* and *ṭaʿmiyya* (*fūl* and falafel). In this case, *fūl* was always mentioned first, then *ṭaʿmiyya*. (It should be noted that the word *ṭaʿmiyya* is used in Cairo, while the same food is called *falāfil* in Alexandria as well as in other countries in the region outside of Egypt, whence the well-known term "falafel" that has made its way throughout the West).

Egyptian falafel is made of *fūl madshūsh*, the peeled halves of dry *fūl* beans that have been soaked and ground with green herbs and spices. Rolled (often by hand) into balls and then flattened, they are deep fried in oil. Crispy brown on the outside, they are green inside due to the plentiful herbs used in the mix—unlike non-Egyptian "falafel," which is usually ball-shaped and made of *ḥummus* (chickpeas), retaining a brownish color outside and within.

In Egyptian Arabic the word *ʾurṣ* (lit.: "disc"; pl. *ʾiʾrāṣ*) is often used to refer to or to count objects that have a round shape (for example: pills). Thus, it may be used when referring to any number of falafel patties, for example *ʾurṣēn ṭaʿmiyya* (two or several falafel patties); *ʿāwiz ḫamas tiʾraṣ ṭaʿmiyya* (I want five falafel patties).

Although both *fūl midammis* and *ṭaʿmiyya* are made from *fūl* beans, Egyptians often eat them together, with the soft texture of the former complemented by the crunch of the latter.[21]

6 *Fūl* in Popular Discourse

The dominant role of *fūl* in Egyptian society is expressed in a multitude of terms, which can be seen in the following examples from daily discourse.

6.1 Fūl *versus Meat*

Rich in protein, *fūl* is relatively cheap. On the opposite side of the Egyptian food scale is *laḥma* (meat)—also protein-rich but very expensive and unaffordable for many Egyptians. In the summer of 2018, for instance, a kilo of buffalo or cow meat could cost 85 Egyptian *ginēh* (Egyptian pound) at Cairo's government-sponsored supermarket, or 150 to 180 *ginēh* at the butcher's shop; a kilo of raw *fūl* could be purchased for 15 to 25 *ginēh*. A kilo of meat would provide dinner for 6 to 12 people (depending on how it was prepared); a kilo of *fūl* could feed 15 to 25. The price of one *fūl* "sandwich" would range between 3 and 6 *ginēh* (depending on the venue, the kind of bread, and the additional ingredients).

Hence meat and *fūl* are commonly referred to as rich people's versus poor people's fare, respectively (which does not negate the fact that the rich love *fūl* as much as everyone else). *Fūl* is nicknamed *akl il-ghalāba* or *aklit il-ghalāba* (food of the poor), or, ironically, *laḥmit il-ghalāba* (poor folks' meat), while

21 Two other "most Egyptian" repasts often listed after *fūl* were *kushari* and *shurbit ʿads*. *Kushari* is a dish of noodles, lentils, and sometimes also rice, finished off with fried sliced onion and tomato sauce on top and an optional splash of lemon juice and hot sauce. Hot *shurbit ʿads* (lentil soup) is eaten mainly in winter while *kushari*, like *fūl* and *ṭaʿmiyya*, is eaten year-round.

ṭaʿmiyya/falāfil is called *kabāb il-ghalāba* (the poor man's shish kebab [skewers of grilled meat]).

6.2 Fūl's *Effect on the Human Body*

All Egyptians know that *fūl* can be felt in the stomach and stays there for a long time, staving off hunger for many hours. Not surprisingly, a number of graphic expressions have been coined in the country to describe these effects:

Kharasān il-miʿda (concrete of the stomach)
Gibs il-miʿda (plaster of the stomach)
Asmant il-miʿda (cement of the stomach)
Musmār il-baṭn or *musmār il-miʿda* (nail of the belly or nail of the stomach)
Zayy-iz-zalaṭ wir-ramla (like gravel and sand)
Ana kabisha fūl (I am stuffed with *fūl*)
Ana mifawwil (I am completely loaded)

Though the word *mifawwil* may be said of any food, in this case it can be regarded as a pun based on the verb *fawwil* (refuel, which refers to a car's gas tank and is apparently taken from the English "full tank") and the root FWL, from which the word *fūl* is derived:[22] *Ana mifawwil ful tank* (lit. I am a fully refueled tank, i.e. I am fully loaded and cannot eat any more). This expression, like the previous one, may refer to any food, and both may be accompanied by a satisfied pat on the belly with the palm of the hand. Here, there is a play on the root FWL and the word full.

6.3 Fūl's *Effects on the Human Mind*

Egyptians often say, sometimes in jest but sometimes with utmost seriousness, that *fūl* has a deleterious effect on the human mind. They claim that it slows the brain, causing people to look stupid and feel heavy or even groggy. Thus the following expressions are often heard in the home and particularly in the classroom:

Il-Fūl bikhalli -n-nās mashya mitayyisa (*Fūl* makes people groggy)
Shaklu bāyin ʾinnu wākil fūl (He has obviously eaten *fūl*)

---

22 Though the word *fūl* may come from ancient Egyptian, it is also a Semitic word (Aramaic: POLA; Hebrew: POL [modern pronunciation is influenced by the Arabic one]); its root in modern Arabic is FWL.

Il-Mudarris: Inta mi'affil lēh kida? (The teacher: why do you look so dumb?) *Kullukum mi'affilīn lēh kida? Kullukum waklīn fūl 'a-ṣ-ṣubh?!* (Why do you all look so thickheaded? Did you all eat *fūl* this morning?!).

7 *Fūl* in Egyptian Proverbs and Idioms

As a dominant element in Egyptian daily life, *fūl* also serves as the basis of several Egyptian proverbs and idioms, such as those below:

فولة واتقسمت نصين:

Fūla wit'asamit nuṣṣēn (lit. a *fūl* bean that has been split into two halves), said of two people who look or act like twins;

ما تتبلّش/يتبلّش في بقه فولة:

Ma titballish/yitballish fi bu''u fūla (lit. a *fūl* bean never gets wet in his mouth), describing someone who cannot keep a secret (since he never keeps his mouth shut, a *fūl* bean held in it has no chance of getting wet);

الفول فى الصبح أكل الامير والضهر أكل الفقير وبالليل أكل الحمير:

Il-Fūl fi -ṣ-ṣubḥ 'akl-i -l-'amīr wiḍ-ḍuhr 'akl-i -l-fa'īr wubil-lēl 'akl-i -l-ḥimīr (lit. *fūl* in the morning is food for the prince, at noon it is food for the poor, and at night it is food for the donkeys), i.e. *fūl* is good fare for everyone and for all strata of society the rich and poor, and animals, too;

أكل فوله ورجع لأصوله:

Akal fūlu wirigi' li'uṣūlu (lit. he ate his *fūl* and returned to his origins), referring to people who reverted to their old habits;

الفول يربّي العجول:

Il-Fūl yirabbi -l-ugūl (lit. *fūl* can nurture calves), that is, *fūl* is good for you, you should eat *fūl* (said to encourage people, especially children, to eat *fūl*—which is good for both human beings and domesticated animals—because it is healthy and will help one to grow and be strong);

على قد فوله قدّفوا له:

ʿAla ʾadd-i fūlu ʾaddiffū-lu (lit. according to his *fūl* row for him),[23] in other words, serve him according to what he has paid.[24] This proverb, based on a pun (*ʾadd-i fūlu*, according to his *fūl*, sounds like *ʾaddiffū-lu*, row for him) is the refrain of the song *ʿAla ʾadd-i fūlu* (According to his *fūl*) performed by Ḥasan ʿAbd al-Majīd in 1991;

كل فولة ولها كيّال:

Kull-i fūla wiliha kayyāl (lit. every *fūl* bean has its measurer), meaning there is a suitable match for everyone; and similarly:

كل فولة مسوسة ولها كيّال أعور:

Kull-i fūla misawwisa wiliha kayyāl ʾaʿwar (lit. every weevily *fūl* bean has its blind measurer), also suggesting that there is a suitable match for everyone;[25]

أردب فول ولا أردب شعير:

ʾArdabb-i fūl wala ʾardabb-i shiʿīr (lit. [it's better to have an] ardeb of *fūl* and not an ardeb of barley),[26] in other words, *fūl* is better and more satiating than barley;

يا أهل القبور كلوا ترمس وفول:

Ya ʾahl-i -l-ʾubūr kulu tirmis wufūl (lit. You people of the cemeteries, eat *fūl* and lupine beans), i.e. people who live in the cemetery are so poor they should be satisfied with the simplest of foods;

---

23 The literal translation is meaningless, but Egyptians enjoy the play on words.

24 See also Aḥmad Taymūr, *al-Amthāl al-ʿāmmiyya* (Cairo: al-Ahrām, 1986), 327.

25 This is the full, original version of the previous proverb, with the same meaning. See Taymūr, *Amthāl*, 402. Today few are familiar with the original.

26 Ardeb (*ʾardabb*) is a "dry measure of 198 litres" (Badawi and Hinds, *Dictionary*, 14.)

اللى يشوف الفول ولا ياكلش يحب ولا يطولش:

Illi yishūf il-fūl wala yakulsh-i yiḥibb-i wala yiṭūlsh-i (lit. He who sees *fūl* and does not eat it is like one who is in love and does not attain his beloved), which is to say that seeing *fūl* and not eating it is extremely painful;

فهم الفولة:

Fihim il-fūla (lit. understood the *fūl* bean), i.e. understood the matter or grasped the idea;

لقط الفولة:

La'aṭ il-fūla (lit. grasped the *fūl* bean) means the same as *fihim il-fūla*, above;

يعرف الفولة ومين زرعها:

Yaʿraf il-fūla wumīn zaraʿha (lit. He knows the *fūl* bean and who sowed it), i.e. he knows everything or he knows every little detail;

إن خلص الفول أنا مش/غير مسئول:

In khiliṣ il-fūl 'ana mish/ghēr mas'ūl (lit. If the *fūl* is all gone, I am not responsible), an inscription that often appears on *fūl* carts and stands and is iterated by *fūl* vendors, cheerfully encouraging their customers to hurry and buy *fūl* before it is sold out—thus laying the blame on their customers when they run out of it;

اللوز! الفول!:

Il-Lōz! il-fūl! (lit. Almonds! *fūl*! [*Fūl* as good and tasty as almonds!]), a cry of *fūl*-bean peddlers in praise of their merchandise.

8 References to *Fūl* in Egyptian Literature

Since the bean is so ubiquitous in Egyptian daily life, it is hardly surprising that *fūl* and *fūl*-related terminology appear frequently in the country's literature. Writers feel no need to explain them, assuming that their Egyptian readership is familiar with *fūl* and the terms associated with it. In some literary works, both fiction and non-fiction, these in fact become a recurring theme which is sometimes discussed at length within the work itself. The following examples, which emphasize the connection between *fūl*, Egyptians, and Egyptian identity, are typical.

8.1 *References to* fūl *and* fūl-*Related Terminology*

Fūl terminology is the main theme in the first part of the short story *al-Ḥāwī khaṭaf al-ṭabaq* (The magician has snatched the plate) by Najīb Maḥfūẓ. The plot: A mother sends her young son, for the first time in his life, to buy *fūl* for the amount of one piaster (*qirsh*; this price indicates that the story took place decades ago). Unfamiliar with *fūl* terminology, the poor boy runs into trouble.

When he gets to the *fūl* seller and naïvely asks for *fūl*, the vendor asks whether he wants *fūl* that is plain, with oil, or with clarified butter. The boy does not understand the terms, and returns home empty-handed. His angry mother exclaims: You good-for-nothing! What do you eat every morning? When the boy says he does not know, she rebukes him and directs him to ask for *fūl* with oil. The boy goes back and requests *fūl* with oil, but the same scene repeats itself, this time with the terminology for oil: Does the boy want linseed oil, regular oil, or olive oil? Again he goes home empty-handed, and his angry mother sends him back to the *fūl* seller to buy *fūl* with linseed oil.[27] The following examples come from contemporary Egyptian literature:

A perfect breakfast served by a perfect wife:

شايلة له فطار إنما إيه؟.. فول بالزبدة وبيضة وكوباية شاي بحليب.

> She was carrying an amazing breakfast for him: *fūl* with butter, an egg, and a glass of tea with milk.[28]

The classic combination of *fūl* and falafel:

طيب حاروح اجيب فطار.. شوية سندوتشات فول وطعمية من عندعم سيد.

> Well, I'll go and bring breakfast, some *fūl* and falafel "sandwiches" from "Uncle" Sayyid.[29]

27 Najīb Maḥfūẓ, "al-Ḥāwī khaṭaf al-ṭabaq," in *Taḥt al-miẓalla* (Cairo: Maktabat Miṣr, n.d.), 55–65.

28 Samīr ʿAbd al-Bāqī, "Mōt is-Sayyid afandi," in *Ākhir ḥudūd iz-zagal* (Cairo: Dār Qubāʾ, 1999), 395.

29 Sāmiḥ Faraj, *Banhof ishtrāsse: ḥikāyat al-usṭā al-kahrabāʾī* (Cairo: al-Markaz al-Miṣrī al-ʿArabī, 1999), 15.

Fūl as repetitive daily fare:

يشرب ويتكرع ويحمد ربنا عالفول والبصل والعيش.هيه نفس الأكلة ف صباحه وف مساه.

He drinks and burps and thanks the Lord for the *fūl*, the onions, and the bread. This is the same food he has in the morning and the evening.[30]

Fūl as the daily meal:

طبعا حا لاقيها محضرة لي نفس الغدا بتاع كل يوم لي أنا والأولاد.. طبق الفول.

Of course, I would find that she had prepared the same dinner as every other day for me and the children: a plate of ful.[31]

Fūl as a dish for working people:

إلى جوارنا كانت جماعة الحمالين الذين يعملون في مكتب النقل المجاور يأكلون وأمامهم مجموعة من أطباق الفول وأرغفة العيش وحزم البصل الأخضر.

Next to us a group of porters who worked in the nearby transport office were eating, while before them were selections of *fūl* dishes, bread loaves, and bunches of green onion.[32]

A reference to al-Jaḥsh, the famous *fūl* restaurant:

ما تخافش.. حانتعشى فول عند الجحش في السيدة زينب.

Don't worry, we will eat *fūl* for supper at al-Jaḥsh in Sayyida Zēnab [quarter].[33]

Fūl versus bread:

أبوك ياكل الكفتة والكباب ويتركها تاكل الفول والعيش.

30 Yūsuf al-Qaʿīd, *Laban il-ʿaṣfūr* (Cairo: Dār al-Hilāl, 1994), 95.
31 Yūsuf ʿAwf, *Kursi fi'l-kulubb: ʿagāyib* (Cairo: al-Dār al-Miṣriyya al-Lubnāniyya, 2005), 103.
32 Ibrāhīm Aṣlān, *Wardiyyat layl* (Cairo: Dār Sharqiyyāt, 1992), 35.
33 ʿAlī Sālim, *Ma tīgu niḍḥak il-lēla di* (Cairo: Madbūlī al-Ṣaghīr, 2001), 64.

> Your father eats *kufta* [minced meat in the shape of balls or fingers, prepared with a variety of vegetables and seasoning] and shish kebab, and lets her [your mother] eat *fūl* and bread.[34]

Fūl versus meat:

> ياما نفسي آكل أكل زي البني آدمين.. لحمة مش شعير وفول.
>
> How I wish to eat food like human beings. Meat, not barley and *fūl*.[35]

The combination of *fūl midammis* and linseed oil:

> يغادر الغرفة وينهمك في إعداد طبق من الفول المدمس بالزيت الحار.
>
> He [my father] leaves the room and begins to get busy preparing a plate of *fūl midammis* with linseed oil.[36]

Buying *fūl* on the street during Ramadan:

> أخرج مرة أخرى قبل المغرب لشراء فول مدمس للسحور. البائع خلف قدرته في مدخل الحارة. حوله زحام من الأطفال والبنات. أيديهم ممدودة بالأطباق والحلل. يتصايحون كي يلفتوا انتباهه. نتابع في لهفة خروج يده اليمنى من القدرة بكبشة الفول. أشاركهم الصياح مادًا يدي اليمنى بالطبق واليسرى بالنقود.
>
> I go out again before sunset to buy *fūl midammis* for the *suḥūr*. The vendor behind his *fūl* vessel (*ʾidra*) is at the entrance to the quarter. He is surrounded by a crowd of boys and girls. Their hands are outstretched with plates and cooking pots. They are shouting to get his attention. We yearningly follow his right hand as it emerges from the *fūl* vessel with the ladle of *fūl*. I shout along with them while stretching my right hand out with the plate, and the left one with the money.[37]

---

34 Muḥammad al-Fakhrānī, *Fāṣil li'l-dahsha* (Cairo: al-Dār, 2007), 21.

35 Al-Sayyid Ḥāfiẓ, *Khaṭafūni wilād il-ēh!!* (Cairo: al-Hay'a al-Miṣriyya al-ʿĀmma li'l-Kitāb, 2004), 50.

36 Ṣunʿ Allāh Ibrāhīm, *al-Talaṣṣuṣ* (Cairo: Dār al-Mustaqbal al-ʿArabī, 2007), 33.

37 Ibid., 192.

Fūl cart and the *fūl* dish as a luxurious dinner:

ثم يعودان برجل يجر امامه عربة فول مدمس كاملة.. ومع كل واحد منهما كميات من العيش البلدي والبصل والفجل.. ويحولوا محتويات العربة إلى سفرة القصر.. قدرة الفول كاملة بالزيت الحار والشطة وسلطة الطماطم بالفلفل الاحمر والبصل.

Then both of them return with a man who is pushing a *fūl* cart complete [with all the ingredients] in front of him. And each one of them has loads of *ʿēsh baladi*, onions and radishes with him. They turn the contents of the *fūl* cart into a dining table fit for a palace: the *fūl* vessel, complete with linseed oil, chili, and tomato salad with red pepper and onions.[38]

A description of a complete meal of *fūl* in a popular restaurant:

ملأ له "سلامة" طبقه فولا، ثم رش عليه بعض الزيت من إحدى الزجاجات الموضوعة بجواره، وغرف له فوق الفول بعضا من "سلطة القوطة" ووضع له نصف ليمونة ثم سلمه الطبق فعاد به إلى منضدته بعد أن تناول رغيفا وجلس يأكل.

Salāma filled the plate for him [the client] with *fūl*, then sprayed on it some oil from one of the bottles placed next to him, added some tomato salad on top of the *fūl*, gave him half a lemon, and then handed him the plate. After taking bread he went back with the plate to his table and sat down to eat.[39]

Mind-stopping effect of *fūl*:

سامعين يا مشايخ والا الفول كابس على نافوخكم.

Have you heard, shaykhs, or has the *fūl* blocked your heads?[40]

---

38 Isʿād Yūnis, *al-Mutasawwilūn* (Cairo: Dār al-hudā, 1995), 77.

39 Yūsuf al-Sibāʿī, *Is-Saʾʾa māt* (Cairo: Muʾassasat al-Khānjī, 1975 [1952]), 23–24.

40 Muṣṭafā Musharrafa, *Qanṭara alladhī kafara* (Cairo: Markaz Kutub al-Sharq al-Awsaṭ, 1965), 37.

Expressions that mention *fūl* (*ma titballish fi bu’’u fūla*):

هوه عارف أن لسانها فالت، ما تتبلش ف بقها فولة.

He knows that she is loose-tongued and that she cannot keep a secret (lit. a *fūl* bean never gets wet in her mouth).[41]

Expressions that mention *fūl* (*fihim il-fūla*):

حس من كلامها أنها فهمت الفولة.

Based on what she said, he felt that she had understood the matter (lit. understood the *fūl* bean).[42]

8.2 Fūl *as a Marker of Egyptian Identity*

In both Egyptian fiction and non-fiction, writers who want to reflect or emphasize the connection between *fūl* and Egyptian identity employ metalinguistic and metacultural references in which the narrator or other characters are fully aware of *fūl*'s dominant role in everyday Egyptian life and as a marker of Egyptian identity.

For instance, in the play *Ahlan ya bakawāt* (Welcome, Sirs) by Lenīn al-Ramlī, the two protagonists, Burhān and Nādir, find themselves in an unfamiliar warehouse due to an explosion. (They later realize that they have gone back in time to Mamluk Egypt.) They have no idea where they are and start searching the place. When they find a sack and look inside, they immediately and joyfully conclude that they are in Egypt since the sack contains *fūl*:

برهان: (ينظر في جوال) نادر إحنا في مصر..
نادر: إيش عرفك؟
برهان: بص الركيبة دي فيها إيه؟
نادر: فول. الحمد لله.. نبقى في مصر!

Burhān (Looking into a sack) Nādir, we are in Egypt.
Nādir How do you know?

41 Al-Qaʿīd, *Laban*, 108.
42 Musharrafa, *Qanṭara*, 81.

Burhān Look what is inside this sack.
Nādir *Fūl*. Thank God, we are in Egypt![43]

When I attended a performance of this play in the early 1990s, at the National Theatre in Cairo, the audience reacted with laughter and applause to the last line of this dialogue, clearly identifying with the message it conveyed. Another example: At the outset of Nihād Jād's play *Maḥaṭṭit ʾutubīs* (Bus station) one of the protagonists, Bilya, a street vendor of haberdashery, arrives at a bus station but sees no one there. Surprised, he assumes that there is a strike and starts a monologue on the subject, declaring that any strike is possible in Egypt—except a strike against *fūl*:

الناس اللي بتركب الأتوبيس دي كلها عاملة اضراب على طول.. اضراب عن اللحمة.. اضراب عن السمك.. والفراخ والجواز.. والشقق اللي بتتبني ما حدش قادر يسكنها.. اضراب عن كله..مش عاملين معاهدة صلح الا مع حاجة واحدة مفيش غيرها.. الفول.. حاكم الفول ده تراث.. ومن ساب قديمه تاه.

> The people riding the buses are on strike all the time. A strike against meat, a strike against fish, and poultry, and marriage, and apartments being built that no one can live in. A strike against everything. They make a peace agreement with only one thing and nothing else: *fūl*. Because *fūl* is heritage, and whoever abandons his old (heritage) is doomed to perish.[44]

When Egyptians are far from Egypt, they are also far from *fūl*. Though they can sometimes buy cans of preserved *fūl* beans and cook them, the result barely resembles the real thing for which they hunger.[45] Their longing for *fūl* is manifested in several literary works, as well as in non-fiction. In a novel published

43 Lenīn al-Ramlī, *Ahlan ya bakawāt* (Cairo: al-Markaz al-Miṣrī al-ʿArabī, 1989), 28.

44 Nihād Jād, "Maḥaṭṭit utubīs," in *ʿAdīla wamaḥaṭṭit ʾutubīs* (Cairo: Maktabat Gharīb, 1985), 79.

45 Bardenstein and Naguib quote Claudia Roden and Colette Rossant, cookbook authors who emigrated from Egypt and who both relate how eating *fūl midammis* outside Egypt has been a means of expressing their longing for the country. See Carol Bardenstein, "Transmissions Interrupted: Reconfiguring Food, Memory, and Gender in the Cookbook-Memoirs of Middle Eastern Exiles," in *Gender and Cultural Memory*, eds. Marianne Hirsch and Valerie Smith, Special Issue of *Signs—Journal of Women in Culture and Society* 28 (2002): 353–387; Nefissa Naguib, "The Fragile Tale of Egyptian Jewish Cuisine: Food Memoirs of Claudia Roden and Colette Rossant," *Food & Foodways* 14 (2006): 35–53.

recently by ʿAbd al-Munʿim, the narrator states that whenever he goes abroad, he misses Egypt and *fūl*:

> حتى لو كنت بباريس أو لندن أو جنيف [...] !!فإنني أشتاق إليها وإلى أهلها الطيبين وعربة الفول أبو زيت حار.
>
> Even if I am in Paris or London or Geneva!! […] I miss her [Egypt] and her good people and the cart of *fūl* with linseed oil.[46]

In his autobiographical novel *Madīnat al-ghurabāʾ: maṭāliʿ nyuyorkiyya* (The city of strangers: New York lookouts), Jamāl al-Ghīṭānī describes his stay and feelings in New York and refers to *fūl* as follows:

> كافة عناصر الحياة المفتقدة، بعيدة المنال تصبح شعرًا أو تكاد الفول المدمس الذي يعد جزءًا من حياتنا اليومية، الإفطار الخاص جدًّا بالمصريين والذي لا يفهمه بعض الأعراب فيعايروننا به مع أن تدميس الفول وإنضاجه وتقديمه جزء من عملية حضارة معقدة، هذا الفول يصبح شعرًا في ذاكرة المصريين المهاجرين، يحنون إليه ويسعون إلى اقتنائه وتقديمه إلى ضيوفهم القادمين من مصر.
>
> All elements of life that are missing and are far from being reached become poetry or almost poetry. *Fūl midammis*, which is considered a part of our daily life, the very special breakfast of the Egyptians, which some Arabs do not understand and which they therefore rebuke us for, in spite of the fact that putting the *fūl* on a slow fire, cooking it well and serving it are part of a complex act of civilization. This *fūl* becomes poetry in the memory of emigrant Egyptians. They miss it and seek to purchase it and to serve it to their guests who come from Egypt.[47]

Eating *fūl* is an act that is so obviously Egyptian that any Egyptian who does so may be defined instantly as a true, genuine Egyptian. In the following excerpt, taken from a contemporary Egyptian play dealing with some of the problems in Egyptian society (Bus station, quoted above), we see how this applies to Jamāl ʿAbd al-Nāṣir, the country's former president. Describing the president as a *fūl* eater clearly delivers the message: He is one of us.

---

46 Tāmir ʿAbd al-Munʿim, *Mudhakkirāt filūl* (Cairo: Dār Samāʾ, 2018), 53.

47 Jamāl al-Ghiṭānī, *Madīnat al-ghurabāʾ: maṭāliʿ nyuyorkiyya* (Cairo: Nahḍat Miṣr, 2011), 113.

جمال عبد الناصر هو احنا.. واحنا هو.. [...] خارج من تراب مصر.. واكل فول زينا.

> Jamāl ʿAbd al-Nāṣir is us, and we are him. [...] He came out of the soil of Egypt. He has eaten *fūl* like we do.[48]

The next selection, from a satirical short story, demonstrates that only Egyptians can really understand the importance of *fūl* and how, when one is far away from Egypt, gathering and sharing *fūl* with one's compatriots strengthens one's sense of Egyptian identity and solidarity. The story is also a testament to the fact that foreigners can neither share nor comprehend the powerful bond between *fūl* and Egyptians—an intimate relationship, imbued with strong feelings, between a people and their primary food. The author, Bahjat Faraj, speaks about two Egyptians, the protagonist and his colleague, who live in Paris where prices are very high. They cannot afford to buy enough food and gradually lose weight, until an Egyptian who is going back home gives them a gift: a *dammāsa* for cooking *fūl*. They find a place to buy *fūl* beans and start cooking all kinds of *fūl* dishes, gain weight, and feel much better. Other Egyptians start coming to their place to eat *fūl*, so it also has a beneficial effect on their social life.

Since the protagonist goes to buy large quantities of *fūl* beans at least twice a week, his relationship with the French *fūl* vendor becomes quite close. The following dialogue, however, shows the huge gap of understanding between them:

واقترب مني صاحب المحل مبتسما وقال لي إزي صحة الحصان بتاعك... وأخذني السؤال للوهلة الأولى ولكن ابتسمت وسألته كيف عرفت أنني أملك حصانا. قال هذه مهنتنا فمن نوع المشتروات نعرف انك تقتني قطا أو كلبا و حصانا وأنت تشتري الفول بانتظام وهو أكل طيب للحصان ولكن لك عندي نصيحة أن كمية الفول التي تشتريها أكثر بكثير مما يتطلبه الحصان. وقد تسبب له كثرة الفول بعض المشاكل في المعدة وأنا أرى أن يقتصر إطعامه الفول على مرتين في الأسبوع فقط وابتسمت ابتسامة باهتة وشكرت الرجل على نصيحته ولكن مرتين فول في الأسبوع لا تكفي.. وبدأت أبحث عن محل جديد يبيع الفول الناشف حتى نستكمل به باقي أيام الأسبوع.

---

48 Jād, *Maḥaṭṭa*, 100.

> The owner of the shop approached me smilingly and said to me, "How is your horse's health?" At first the question took me by surprise, but I smiled and asked him, "How did you know that I owned a horse?" He said, "This is our profession, so by the type of goods you purchase, we know whether you own a cat or a dog or a horse. You regularly buy *fūl*, which is a good food for horses, but I have a piece of advice for you: The amount of *fūl* that you buy is much more than the horse needs, and this large amount of *fūl* may cause him some stomach problems. I believe that he should be fed *fūl* only twice a week." I smiled a perplexed smile and thanked the man for his advice, but *fūl* twice a week is not enough, so I started looking for a new shop selling dry *fūl* so that we would be able to buy enough for the rest of the days of the week.[49]

It is appropriate to finish this survey with one of the most famous contemporary Egyptian poems, *Mawwāl il-fūl wil-laḥma* (The ballad about *fūl* and meat). Written by the rebel poet Aḥmad Fu'ād Nijm in 1974, it was sung and recorded by the blind singer Shaykh Imām. The background: Apparently a government official, hoping to encourage Egyptians to eat *fūl* and avoid meat, announced that the beans were much healthier than meat. The response of Nijm and Imām became one of the most famous statements in Egypt regarding these opposites—*fūl* and meat, the food of the poor and the food of the rich. Nijm mocks the government official for his declaration and concludes by suggesting that government officials should enjoy the healthy *fūl* while allowing the poor to suffer the consequences of eating meat:

إحنا سيبونا نموت باللحمة
وانتو تعيشوا وتاكلوا الفول
ما رأيك يا كابتن محسن
مش بالذمة كلام معقول.

> Leave us to die with meat,
> And let you live and eat *fūl*.
> What do you think, Mister Muḥsin,
> Isn't this really reasonable?[50]

---

49 Bahjat Faraj, "Fūl ʿalēna bukra," in *Miʿza likull muwāṭin* (Cairo: Dār Sfinkis, 1996), 136–137.

50 Aḥmad Fu'ād Nijm, "*Mawwāl il-fūl wil-laḥma*," in *al-Aʿmāl al-kāmila* (Cairo, al-Minyā: Dār al-Aḥmadī li'l-Nashr, 1998), 481.

9 Conclusion

While *fūl* is indeed staple fare and the most popular main dish for Egyptians, it is much more than mere food. Frequently mentioned and discussed both in common parlance and in literature, *fūl* plays an important role in Egyptian daily life on both a practical and an existential level. Its ubiquitous presence has contributed a rich terminology to the spoken language and is an integral component of Egyptian identity.

Fūl is so closely associated with Egypt and Egyptians that the two cannot be separated: *fūl* is part of the modern Egyptian, body and soul. Often disparagingly called "the food of the poor," it is nevertheless beloved by all Egyptians, indigent and wealthy alike. Their emotional attachment to the food is perhaps most clearly manifested when they are far from Egypt, longing to taste it and eagerly trying to find it in foreign climes.

It is no wonder, then, that *fūl* also appears regularly in Egyptian literature, as a constituent element of Egyptian daily life and a unique marker of Egyptian identity.

Bibliography

ʿAbd al-Bāqī, Samīr. "Mōt is-Sayyid afandi," in *Ākhir ḥudūd iz-zagal*. Cairo: Dār Qubāʾ, 1999, 394–399.

ʿAbd al-Majīd, Ḥasan. "ʿAla ʾadd-i fūlu," http://www.ournia.co/ar/song/على-قد-فوله, 1991.

ʿAbd al-Munʿim, Tāmir. *Mudhakkirāt filūl*. Cairo: Dār Samāʾ, 2018.

Abdennour, Samia. *Egyptian Cooking: A Practical Guide*. Cairo: The American University in Cairo Press, 2000.

Amīn, Aḥmad. *Qāmūs al-ʿādāt wa'l-taqālīd wa'l-taʿābīr al-Miṣriyya*. Cairo: Maṭbaʿat Lajnat al-Ta'līf wa'l-Tarjama wa'l-Nashr, 1953.

Aṣlān, Ibrāhīm. *Wardiyyat layl*. Cairo: Dār Sharqiyyāt, 1992.

aucegypt.edu. "About Beans—*ʿan al-fūl*," in: https://academic.aucegypt.edu/omeka/exhibits/show/foul/aboutbeans.

aucegypt.edu. "Beans: Interviews and Stories—*al-fūl: ḥakāwī wa-liqāʾāt*," in: https://academic.aucegypt.edu/omeka/exhibits/show/foul/interviews.

aucegypt.edu. "Beans: Proverbs—*amthāl shaʿbiyya ʿan al-fūl*," in: https://academic.aucegypt.edu/omeka/exhibits/show/foul/proverbs.

aucegypt.edu. "Bean Recipes—*waṣfāt al-fūl*," in: https://academic.aucegypt.edu/omeka/exhibits/show/foul/recipes.

aucegypt.edu. "Egyptian Beans—*al-fūl al-miṣrī*," in: https://academic.aucegypt.edu/omeka/exhibits/show/foul.

ʿAwf, Yūsuf. *Kursi fi'l-kulubb: ʿagāyib*. Cairo: al-Dār al-Miṣriyya al-Lubnāniyya, 2005.
Badawi, El-Said and Martin Hinds. *A Dictionary of Egyptian Arabic: Arabic English*. Beirut: Librarie du Liban, 1986.
Bardenstein, Carol. "Transmissions Interrupted: Reconfiguring Food, Memory, and Gender in the Cookbook-Memoirs of Middle Eastern Exiles," in *Gender and Cultural Memory*. Eds. Marianne Hirsch and Valerie Smith. Special Issue of *Signs—Journal of Women in Culture and Society* 28 (2002): 353–387.
Al-Fakhrānī, Muḥammad. *Fāṣil.. li'l-dahsha*. Cairo: al-Dār, 2007.
Faraj, Bahjat. "Fūl ʿalēna bukra," in *Miʿza likull muwāṭin*. Cairo: Dār Sfinkis, 1996, 136–137.
Faraj, Sāmiḥ. *Banhof ishtrāsse: ḥikāyat al-usṭa al-kahrabāʾī*. Cairo: al-Markaz al-Miṣrī al-ʿArabī, 1999.
Al-Ghīṭānī, Jamāl. *Madīnat al-ghurabāʾ: maṭāliʿ nyuyorkiyya*. Cairo: Nahḍat Miṣr, 2011.
Ḥāfiẓ, al-Sayyid. *Khaṭafūni wilād il-ʾēh!!* Cairo: al-Hay'a al-Miṣriyya al-ʿĀmma li'l-Kitāb, 2004.
Hassan-Wassef, Habiba. "Food Habits of the Egyptians: Newly Emerging Trends." *La revue de santé de la Méditerranée orientale* 10/6 (2004): 898–915.
Henein, Nessim Henry. *Poteries et proverbes d'Égypte*. Le Caire: Institut français d'archéologie orientale, 1992.
Ibrāhīm, Ṣunʿ Allāh. *al-Talaṣṣuṣ*. Cairo: Dār al-Mustaqbal al-ʿArabī, 2007.
Jād, Nihād. "Maḥaṭṭit utubīs," in *ʿAdīla wamaḥaṭṭit ʾutubīs*. Cairo: Maktabat Gharīb, 1985, 77–124.
Lane, Edward William. *An Account of the Manners and Customs of the Modern Egyptians*. Cairo and New York: The American University in Cairo Press, 2003.
Lev, Efraim and Zohar Amar. *Practical Materia Medica of the Medieval Eastern Mediterranean According to the Cairo Genizah*. Leiden, Boston: Brill, 2008.
Lewicka, Paulina B. *Food and Foodways of Medieval Cairenes: Aspects of Life in an Islamic Metropolis of the Eastern Mediterranean*. Leiden and Boston: Brill, 2011.
Maḥfūẓ, Najīb. "al-Ḥāwī khaṭaf al-ṭabaq," in *Taḥt al-miẓalla*. Cairo: Maktabat Miṣr, n.d., 55–65.
MedicineNet.com. "Medical Definition of Favism," in: https://www.medicinenet.com/script/main/art.asp?articlekey=3397 (accessed May 13, 2016).
Meletis, John and Kostas Konstantopoulos. "From the Avoid Fava Beans of Pythagoras to the Present," HAEMA 7(1) (2004): 17–21.
Muḥyī al-Dīn, Najlāʾ. *Dalīl al-maʾkūlāt al-shaʿbiyya*. Cairo: al-Dār al-Dawliyya li'l-Nashr wa'l-Tawzīʿ, 1994.
Musharrafa, Muṣṭafā. *Qanṭara alladhī kafara*. Cairo: Markaz Kutub al-Sharq al-Awsaṭ, 1965.
Naguib, Nefissa. "The Fragile Tale of Egyptian Jewish Cuisine: Food Memoirs of Claudia Roden and Colette Rossant," *Food & Foodways* 14 (2006): 35–53.

Nijm, Aḥmad Fu'ād. "Mawwāl il-fūl wil-laḥma," in *al-Aʿmāl al-kāmila*. Cairo, al-Minyā: Dār al-Aḥmadī li'l-Nashr, 1998, 479–481.

Al-Qaʿīd, Yūsuf. *Laban il-ʿaṣfūr*. Cairo: Dār al-Hilāl, 1994.

Ramlī, Lenīn. *Ahlan ya bakawāt*. [Cairo]: Printed by al-Markaz al-Miṣrī al-ʿArabī, 1989.

Sakkut, Hamdi. *The Arabic Novel: Bibliography and Critical Introduction 1865–1995*. Cairo, New York: The American University in Cairo Press, Cairo, 2000. 6 volumes.

Sālim, ʿAlī. *Ma tīgu niḍḥak il-lēla di*. Cairo: Madbūlī al-Ṣaghīr, 2001.

Shillingburg, Darrol. "Veggies: A to Z—Fava Beans (Vicia faba L.)," *Master Gardener Newsletter* (November 2010): 15.

Al-Shirbīnī, Yūsuf. *Kitāb hazz al-quḥūf fī sharḥ qaṣīd Abī Shādūf*. Cairo: al-Maṭbaʿa al-ʿĀmira al-Sharafiyya, 1904.

Al-Shirbīnī, Yūsuf. *al-Shirbīnī's Kitāb hazz al-quḥūf bi-Sharḥ qaṣīd Abī Shādūf* (Brains confounded by the ode of Abū Shādūf expounded), ed. Humphrey T. Davies. Dudley, MA: Peeters, 2004.

Shukrī, ʿAlyā'. *Dalīl al-ʿamal al-maydānī ligāmiʿī al-turāth al-shaʿbī: al-dirāsa al-ʿilmiyya liʿādāt al-ṭaʿām wa'ādāb al-mā'ida*. Alexandria: Dār al-Maʿrifa al-Jāmiʿiyya, 1993, vol. 4.

Al-Sibāʿī, Yūsuf. *Is-Sa''a māt*. Cairo: Mu'assasat al-Khānjī, 1975 [1952].

Spencer, P.F. and F. Berman. "Plant Toxins and Human Health," in *Food Safety: Contaminants and Toxins*, edited by J.P.F. D'Mello. Wallingford, UK: Cabi Publishing, 2003, 1–24.

Taymūr, Aḥmad. *al-Amthāl al-ʿāmmiyya*. Cairo: al-Ahrām, 1986.

Taymūr, Aḥmad. *Muʿjam Taymūr al-kabīr*. Cairo: Dār al-Kutub wa'l-Wathā'iq al-Qawmiyya/Markaz Taḥqīq al-Turāth, 2002, vol. 3.

Ṭūbyā, Majīd. "Mā yafʿaluhu al-fūl fī al-ʿuqūl," in *al-Ta'rīkh al-ʿarīq li'l-ḥamīr wa'btisāmāt ukhrā*. Cairo: al-Dār al-Miṣriyya al-Lubnānīyya, 1996, 59–63.

Wissa Wassef, Cérès. *Pratiques rituelles et alimentaires des coptes*. Le Caire: Institut français d'archéologie orientale du Caire, 1971.

Yūnis, Isʿād. *al-Mutasawwilūn*. Cairo: Dār al-Hudā, 1995.

Contemporary Arabic Literature and Its Obsession with the Internet

Eman Younis

1 Introduction

If the linguistic definition of "obsession" comprises all thoughts that come to mind,[1] it is possible to argue that the internet in its different manifestations represents a powerful obsession that occupies the minds of Arab writers and is reflected in both their poetry and prose. What leads us to adopt this argument is the noticeable increase since the last decade of the twentieth century in the accumulation of literary texts that have been inspired by the internet, at both the local and international levels.

The internet has become a concrete reality in our daily life due to the different kinds of services that it offers through its social communication websites, such as Facebook, Twitter, and various other chat websites. These websites have grown into a world of their own, where people meet people from different countries and cultures. These social communication websites have provided people with the opportunity to create relationships that range from family to professional associations, or among people who share practices and hobbies. In addition, many political activists, groups, and parties use electronic websites as their principal platform, thus facilitating communication among their members and the spread and popularization of their ideas. Nor do governments ignore the internet as a means of communication, creating their own sites and blogs to communicate with the public. In short, these ubiquitous websites have made people move from a real social world to a virtual one. Moreover, internet sites have brought about considerable changes in the lifestyle, social relations, and way of thinking and culture in people around the world.[2]

1 Majmaʿ al-Qāsimī li'l-Lugha al-ʿArabiyya, *Qāmūs al-majmaʿ fi'l-alfāẓ al-ʿArabiyya al-muʿāṣira wa'l-turāthiyya al-shāʾiʿa* (Kufr Qaraʿ: Dār al-hudā, 2012), 1267; "هاجس," in *Qāmūs al-Maʿānī*, www.almaany.com/ar/dict/ar-ar/هاجس/ (accessed January 2, 2015).

2 Robert Kraut et al., "Internet Paradox: A Social Technology that Reduces Social Involvement and Psychological Well-Being?," *American Psychologist* 53/9 (1998): 1017–1031; Manuel Castells, *The Rise of Network Society of the Information Age: Economy, Society and Culture* (Oxford: Blackwell, 1996).

 | DOI:10.1163/9789004459120_015

This study aims to analyze literary texts that adopted the internet's virtual world to show how literature has dealt with these changes and to describe the attitudes of Arab writers to those changes.

2 The Internet as a Virtual Reality: Between Phobia of Delusion and Pleasure of Self-Assertion

The term virtual reality (VR) is one of utmost importance in the world of information technology, especially in those aspects of it that are dominated by computers and the internet. The term refers to the computer's ability to imitate and create environments that can be emulated in the real, material world.[3] David Crystal defines virtual reality as an "imagined environments that people can enter to be involved in an imaginative social interaction that is based on a text."[4]

In her book *Narrative as Virtual Reality* (2001), Marie-Laure Ryan postulates two aspects of VR. The first is "delusion," which entertains and gives pleasure via a so-called reality that does not actually exist. Consequently, there is no danger that we should fall victims to deceptive tricks. Here, readers unconsciously realize that the VR world is fictitious, and they can return to their social reality whenever they please. The second aspect of VR is "challenge," which interprets the world according to our tendencies and desires. In virtual reality, we achieve dreams and aspirations that we most likely will not achieve in our real lives.[5]

However, a short review of the literary Arabic texts that have used the internet as a principal theme shows that Ryan's hypothesis applies only partially to Arabic literature. Many texts are intrinsically different from what Ryan postulates and even warn the reader specifically of the possibility of falling into the trap of such "delusion." However, other texts confirm the correctness of the second part of the hypothesis, which says that virtual reality creates a kind of balance in the individual by satisfying his desires and achieving ambitions that look unachievable in his social reality. Thus, despite the treatment by Arab writers of issues that are related to the internet, their preoccupation with it

---

3 *Al-Muʿjam al-shāmil li muṣṭalaḥāt al-ḥāsūb al-ālī wa'l-Intirnit* (Riyadh: Maktabat al-ʿAbikān, 2011).

4 David Crystal, *Language and the Internet* (New York: Cambridge University Press, 2005), 25; also Elizabeth Hanst et al., "Collecting User Requirements in a Virtual Population: A Case Study," *Web Net Journal: Internet Technologies, Applications & Issues* 2/4 (2000): 20–27.

5 Marie-Laure Ryan, *Narrative as Virtual Reality, Immersion and Interactivity* (London: Johns Hopkins University Press, 2001), 40–44.

shows that they are still wavering between two fundamental aspects of the Net: a phobia of the deception that the internet hides within its virtual worlds on the one hand, and the pleasure and self-satisfaction that these worlds bring them by enabling them to bridge the barriers they face in their social reality. In the following sections, I will try to pinpoint this anxious wavering through the writings of authors from different Arab countries.

3 Rajāʾ al-Ṣāniʿ: *Banāt al-Riyāḍ* (Girls of Riyadh)[6]

In her novel *Banāt al-Riyāḍ*, the Saudi writer Rajāʾ al-Ṣāniʿ reveals the hidden feelings, emotions, and ambitions of girls living in the city of Riyadh, a conservative society clinging to strict customs and traditions.

The writer turns the space of the internet into an outlet that give voice to the concerns of those girls. The screen is turned into a space to express their forbidden desires and impulsive practices. She realizes that the censorship authorities in Saudi Arabia will not allow her to publish the stories of her friends in book form. Therefore, she resorts to the internet as an escape from censorship. Similarly, the girls about whom she writes are looking for freedom and a way to avoid the oppression from which they are suffering, as we can see in the following quote:

> The telephone wires in this country spread out more than in other countries so that they were able to transmit all the stories people wanted to transfer through them; stories of lovers' undrawn sighs and moans, and kisses that could not be received or given because of religious teachings and social customs.[7]

In spite of this positive feature of the internet, the writer does not forget that it is often exploited in a negative way. The main point is that the internet raises many fears and requires careful use. This is what the writer stresses throughout the characters' dialogues. For example, Lamīs advises Qamra not to give her real name in online chat rooms as these chats are merely make-believe or a lie and cannot lead to real love and marriage:

---

6 Rajāʾ al-Ṣāniʿ, *Banāt al-Riyāḍ* (Beirut: Dār al-Sāqī, 2006).

7 Ibid.

> The most important thing, Qamra, is that you should not trust anyone or believe anyone. Remember that it is only a ploy and all these young men are swindlers and intend to deceive foolish girls.[8]

The reader concludes that the writer intends to convey some of her views about the nature of the internet and the benefits to be gained from it. For her, it is a way to feel free and relieve some pressure, even though it remains a virtual reality; at the same time, young people should not pin their hopes and aspirations on it as, after all, it remains a delusional dream.

4 Nadā al-Dānā: *Aḥādīth al-Intirnit* (Internet Chats)[9]

The search for "intimate relations through the internet" is considered to be one of the most prominent impacts the internet has had on the lives of individuals, young people in particular.

This topic has drawn the attention of psychologists and sociologists who study its causes and social and psychological effects. Their conclusion was that a high percentage of young men who got to know members of the other sex only via the internet admitted to the failure of such relations and described them as false relations.[10]

This theme has also drawn the attention of Arab writers. For example, the Syrian writer Nada al-Dana deals with this theme in the four stories that make up her collection *Aḥādīth al-Intirnit.* In these stories, al-Dānā describes how young men exploit each other's feelings and emotions in chat rooms or via e-mails. Here are some examples of al-Dānā's stories:

1. *Thalāthat ālāf* (Three thousand)

Thalāthat ālāf, the first story in al-Dānā's collection *Aḥādīth al-Intirnit*, relates the story of a girl who regularly visits a certain internet chat site. She intentionally writes the number 3,000 next to her name. When she is asked why, she gives a different answer each time. One time she says that she has 3,000 admirers, another time she says that she has destroyed the hearts of 3,000 men, and the third time she says that she has sent off 3,000 greetings. However, in the

8 Ibid.

9 Nadā al-Dānā, "Aḥādīth al-Intirnit," *Arab World Box* (2007), http://www.arabworldbooks.com/ArabicLiterature/story45.htm (accessed February 15, 2007).

10 Ḥilmī Sārī, *Thaqāfat al-Intirnit* (Amman: Dār Majdalāwī li'l-Nashr, 2005), 186.

end she tells the truth: this number refers to the third millennium. By doing so, the writer wants to reflect the world of young people in the third millennium, admitting that the internet has dominated their lives and that they have become internet and chat room addicts.

2. *Luʿbat ḥubb* (Game of love)
The second story, *Luʿbat ḥubb*, tells the story of a girl who meets a young man on the internet and calls him "my lover," but when he accesses her e-mail, he discovers that she addresses many other young men with the same words. Nonetheless, he falls in love with her and proposes marriage, but she says that she wants to continue her academic studies at the university and that for her, love is merely a game she practices on the internet. In short, al-Dānā considers the feelings that young people express on the internet as false, imaginary, and unrealistic. For many of these youngsters, love expressed through the internet is a mere game and a waste of time.

3. *Khayba* (Disappointment)
The third story, *Khayba*, talks about a young a man who meets a girl named Rāniya on the internet and falls in love with her. He arranges to meet her but when he does, he is shocked to discover that he had been talking with a young man and not a young woman. The story implies that the writer wants to shed light on another negative aspect of the internet, that is, a place to hide and conceal one's identity. Each person chooses the mask that he or she likes, thus causing dismay and disappointment when the truth is revealed.

4. *Shaghab* (Naughtiness)
The fourth story, *Shaghab*, talks about a young man who meets a girl on the internet. She describes herself as extremely beautiful. He falls in love with her and fixes a date to meet her with the intention of offering to marry her. When he meets her, he is surprised to discover that she is only ten years old. She apologizes, saying that she was only kidding.

In her short stories, al-Dānā expresses her views about the New Age. She shows the negative effects of the internet on the lives of young men and women and reveals what takes place in the chat rooms, where people meet in virtual worlds to exchange ideas about love and marriage. She stresses that they rush and follow their ambivalent feelings and decide to marry a person they have not even met. They believe the virtual feelings that they exchange on the Net and whatever they may say to each other in e-mails.

5 Fāṭima Būziyān: *Barīd iliktrūnī* (E-mail)[11]

In this story, the Moroccan writer Fāṭima Būziyān highlights a crucial social issue that reflects the negative effect of the internet on emotional relationships between married people.[12]

In the story, a man sends an e-mail to an artist whose website he used to visit frequently. He expresses his strong admiration for her art and paintings, and tells her that he has become a captive to her website and to her as well. He also admits that he has fallen in love with her and imagines her to be an extremely beautiful woman. He also confesses that he is married and happy in his marriage, but he then continues to say: "Who doesn't feel that they are missing something?" The central theme is that people may try to compensate for emotional insufficiency in their married life by turning to the virtual world of the internet in a search of a temporary satisfaction of their desires and needs.

At the end of his message, the man says: "I cannot hide my feelings and cannot go back to where I started, and you can make fun of me as much as you like." The woman replies that he has lighted the extinguished candles of her heart and returned warmth to her limbs after a long period during which she received nothing but harsh words from critics and artists, who sent their trivial and tasteless comments on her work. The woman also adds that she feels comfortable with him, as if she has known him for a long time. However, she also notes that she does not know how their story will end and closes her message with the words: "Will we remain dangling in our cages at the end of e-mail ropes, only to reside in a mere electronic net?"[13]

In the story's denouement, it turns out that the man who sends her these messages is her husband. He does so just to amuse himself in his free time. However, not anticipating that his wife will respond to this "virtual man," he expects her to acerbically reprimand her unknown correspondent. Her message takes him by surprise, arousing his anger, jealousy, and suspicions.

The man is severely conflicted and torn apart. On the one hand, he knows that the man that she responded to does not exists in reality. On the other

11 Fāṭima Būziyān, "Barīd iliktrūnī," *al-Ḥiwār al-mutamaddin*, January 31, 2006, http://www.ahewar.org/debat/show.art.asp?aid=56094 (accessed April 19, 2008).

12 A study that has been conducted to investigate this issue shows that electronic emotional relations have nearly destroyed the conjugal and family life of 29.1% of married young men and women. This is not a low percentage in conservative Arab society. Sārī, *Thaqāfat al-Intirnit*, 187.

13 Būziyān, *Barīd.*

hand, he denounces his wife's heartfelt response and is furious at her behavior. In spite of this, he tries to justify what she has done, by persuading himself that she recognized his style and manner of speaking, and simply tried to join in his lighthearted game. As a result, the man entertains various thoughts, ranging from resentment, doubt, distrust, and rage to ridicule and mockery. At one point he considers damning her, shouting at her and telling her the truth. But he then retreats and tries to find excuses for her, looking for pretexts and justifications to consider her behavior as mere amusement and fun. The story ends with the man left at the height of confusion and emotional upheaval, unable to reach a decision about what he ought to do.

Through this story, Būziyān points out how virtual reality has the potential to cause serious damage to married life. It foretells the future, especially misfortune. Ryan Laurie refers to what the Western critic, Levy Pierre, claimed when he wrote that virtual reality is not something that is not real, but something that has the power to become real.[14] It seems that Būziyān expresses the same conviction when she makes the husband fall victim to virtual reality. She says: "Virtualization creates fantasms, and fantasms create excitement, and excitement creates what you know and I know!"[15]

6 Ṭāhā ʿAdnān: *Wa-lī fīhā ʿanākib ukhrā* (And I Have Other Spiders in It)[16]

The title of this collection of poems refers to the World Wide Web through its intertextuality with the Qurʾanic verse: "It is my staff, he said, I lean on it; restrain my sheep with it; I also have other uses for it" (Qurʾan 20: 18). The "staff" is the stick or rod of Moses, which he uses in the wilderness for different purposes. It becomes an electronic tool with which the poet hunts spiders via the internet.

The collection includes five poems in which the poet deals with the internet world from different points of view, showing its positive and negative sides. In the last poem of the collection, *al-Shāsha ʿalaykum!* (May the screen be upon you!), the poet states that, despite its disadvantages, the internet also has numerous advantages. He generously praises it and expresses love for it, acknowledging its positive attributes. He says that he can no longer live outside

---

14 Ryan, *Narrative as Virtual Reality*, 26–27.

15 Būziyān, *Barīd.*

16 Ṭāhā ʿAdnān, "Wa-lī fīhā ʿanākib ukhrā," *Moḥammad Salīm Website* (2007), http://aslimnet.free.fr/ress/t_adnane/index.htm (accessed July 28, 2007).

its virtual reality, through which he achieves all that he wishes for. He leads a virtual life, which he creates and formulates as he pleases, to such an extent that he prefers virtual reality to social reality:

هنا أتنفّس العالم نقيًا ومُضاء
لا حياة خارجكِ، فضُمّيني إلى ذبذباتكِ
أيّتها الإلكترونات الرّحيمة
أنا أسيرُك المُساق برِضاي
سآتيكِ كاملاً غير منقوص
سآتيك بما أخفي وما أُعلن
وبما لم يخطر على بالي بعد
سآتيك بأحلامي وأوهامي
بأسماء دخولي كلّها
وبكلمات السر
سأحمل روحي على فأرتي
وألقي بها في مهاوي الكوكيز
لم أعد قادرًا على العيش خارجكِ
يا مدينة الكهرباء
العالم خارجك محض إشاعة
وحدهم البسطاء يصدّقونها

Here I breathe a pure and shining world
There is no life outside you, join me to your frequencies,
Oh merciful electrons,
I am your willingly driven captive
I will come to you entirely, not incomplete
I will come to you with all that I hide and all that I declare
And with everything that has not come to mind yet
I will come to you with my dreams and illusions
With all my log-in names!
With all my passwords
I will carry my soul on my mouse

And throw them into the abysses of the cookies
I can no more live outside you!
O City of Electricity!
The world outside you is merely a rumor!
Only simple people do believe them![17]

Thus, the poet admits the effect of the internet on his life. In fact, he sees that the virtual world that he lives in is much better than the real world that surrounds him. In the virtual world, he lives his life exactly as he likes—easily, comfortably and freely—and according to his own standards and personal wishes.

It seems that Ṭāhā ʿAdnān is in agreement with Muḥammad Sanājla, as reflected in *Riwāyat al-wāqiʿiyya al-raqmiyya* (The novel of digital reality, 2005), the latter's book about mankind's fate. Sanājla believes that "people will live full lives in a virtual way; they will study at virtual universities, shop in virtual markets, be treated by virtual doctors, marry virtually and have a virtual bank account."[18]

In his above-mentioned poem, ʿAdnān stresses that the virtual world possesses the ability to influence people's real lives, to such an extent that the real world becomes a virtual world, and the virtual world becomes a real one. Ḥusayn Rāshid, the president of the Arab Union of Electronic Media said in an article: "What was called 'virtual world' a short time ago has become the real world [...] and the tools of the digital world are no longer as they used to be in their virtual reality; in fact, they have changed into a reality that is inescapable, unless an end be put to the Net."[19]

This implies that virtual reality can have a more powerful effect on the individual than the lived-in world and that it can even abolish the latter and replace it. Often virtual reality affects individuals to such an extent that they will turn to it, whether willingly or unwillingly, as it upsets their values and principles regarding real things, ultimately choosing the virtual world.

---

17 ʿAdnān, *Wa-lī fīhā ʿanākib ukhrā.*

18 Muḥammad Sanājla, *Riwāyat al-wāqiʿiyya al-raqmiyya* (Amman: al-Muʾassasa al-ʿArabiyya li'l-Dirāsāt wa'l-Nashr, 2005), 36.

19 Ḥusayn Rāshid, "Wāqiʿiyyat al-ʿālam al-iftirāḍī wa-iftirāḍ a-ʿālam al-wāqiʿi," *Dunyā al-waṭan* (2008), https://pulpit.alwatanvoice.com/content/print/153650.html (accessed September 6, 2020).

7 Suhayl Kīwān: *Raḥīl munāḍil kabīr* (Death of a Great Struggler)[20]

This story is about the death of an old man who had lost his memory two years earlier. The family of the deceased gathers at his home to receive condolences from the villagers. The first day passes smoothly, but the following day, the house witnesses a strange change as large numbers of visitors from different parts of the country and abroad come to convey their condolences. Telegrams also arrive, sent by members of significant political bodies and movements who mourn the deceased man. The house no longer has any room for the steady stream of delegates. The streets are crowded with people and the police are compelled to put up barriers and block the roads. Flags are raised on electric posts; the many visitors offer the deceased glowing tributes and catchphrases, such as "great struggler" or "adamant struggler against imperialism and its consequences." A head of one of the delegations suggests organizing a commemorative ceremony for the deceased.

All this happens against the will of the family, who feel shocked and embarrassed. The old man's son explains that there must be some misunderstanding. His father was nothing but a simple peasant and had none of the traits that were attributed to him. Eventually, it becomes clear that the grandson of the old man had "promoted" his grandfather, making him out to be a great hero on his Facebook page, someone who has gained the people's love and the support of various countries in the Arab homeland. The story ends with the grandson's reply to his father's accusations and threats: "So what? Is it too much for this village to have a fighter? Ugh! What can happen? Will the world be ruined?"[21]

The story sheds light on many features of the virtual relations and worlds that are produced by social media sites, and it shows why people, especially the younger generation, are interested in these sites. In this context, the Tunisian social scientist Ḥilmī Sārī explains people's engagement in the internet in his book *Thaqāfat al-Intirnit* (Culture of the internet, 2005):

> Virtual communication gives individuals the opportunity to introduce themselves to others freely and without any limits [...]. Virtual communication is mostly characterized by ambiguity, which makes the individual feel anonymous. This means that he feels he is nearly unknown to the other person and this motivates him to make up details about himself

20 Suhayl Kīwān, "Raḥīl munāḍil kabīr," *al-Quds al-ʿArabī* (March 3, 2008), http://www.alquds.co.uk/index.asp?fname=data\2008\03\03-20\18m12.htm (accessed March 6, 2003).

21 Ibid.

> that are not real and that idealize him. Virtual communication also gives the individual the opportunity to expand the net of his relations with others at the local, regional, and international levels, irrespective of their political, racial, and social backgrounds, allowing him to cross the geographical borders that divide him from others.[22]

It is quite clear that Suhayl Kīwān is familiar with all these features. He tries to point them out in the story, presenting the reaction of the large crowds visiting the grieving family as evidence of the virtual world's ability to polarize public opinion and satisfy individual aspirations that cannot be satisfied in reality.

However, all this does not prevent the writer from seeing the negative facets of virtual reality. He realizes that it deceives people who have become "victims of virtual realities." The grandson seeks to create a heroic imaginary character in order to achieve his dream that "this village can produce a struggler!" He gives a misleading account of his grandfather's personality, covering it with a mask that hides its real features, and introducing it to the public in a way that arouses admiration and satisfies his own, personal aspirations.[23]

This particular feature of virtual reality, which allows the individual to conceal his own character and to introduce another, imaginary one is a double-edged sword. On the one hand, it enables the individual to realize dreams that he cannot realize in reality, giving him a temporary feeling of self-fulfillment. On the other hand, however, it misleads others and exposes them to a false representation of the facts. It is at this point that conflict arises between the two characters.

However, the end of the story hints at the writer's tendency to tip the scales in favor of the real world. Despite the many positive attributes of the virtual world, he looks at the internet with suspicion because he realizes that the public has become a victim of fake facts and misrepresentations spread by electronic websites.

---

22 Sārī, *Thaqāfat al-Intirnit*, 29–30.

23 See also Ibrāhīm Farghalī, "Thaqāfa iliktrūniyya, tawābiʿ al-fisbuk," *Majallat al-ʿArabī* (December 1, 2012), http://www.alarabimag.com/arabi/common/showhilight.asp (accessed December 8, 2012).

8 ʿĀyda Naṣr Allāh: *al-Baṭala al-iftirāḍiyya* (The Virtual Heroine)[24]

In her story *al-Baṭala al-iftirāḍiyya*, ʿAyda Naṣr Allāh deals with the issue of gender in Arab society and decides to wage war against conservative backward masculinity, which recognizes only the physical dimension of women—that is, woman as a body. The heroine of the story is a female writer who has not received the respect and appreciation that she deserves from writers and critics. She decides to get it by force, by exploiting the weak points of those males and by using another self, or alter ego, on the internet. She says: "I will prove to them that their horizons are narrow, those who do not see me. I am the owner of the text!"[25]

This heroine intentionally attaches a false photo to all the texts she publishes electronically on various websites. She chooses a photo of a beautiful woman with Middle Eastern features, a light brown skin tone, and honey-colored eyes. Immediately after she uploads her first text with the picture, comments start pouring in expressing admiration for her texts. The writer wants to point out that Arab women are well aware of the mentality of Middle Eastern men and their way of thinking, and of the unfair treatment she is subjected to as a result of this mentality.[26]

The virtual heroine receives not only appreciative comments, but also a love poem from nearly every male reader. She feels she has received more than enough critical approval of her texts. When the critics finally admit their admiration for her photo, she decides to reveal the truth: "They acknowledged the value of your texts. They said things they had not said about any other woman before. You won the websites and the poems. You proved to them their lightheadedness and the fact that their education is centered between their legs!"[27]

The writer then sends her real-life photo to those men, proclaiming her rebellion against their disgraceful outlook on gender and loudly voicing her resentment to it. She knows she deserves to be appreciated for her literary competence and not for her body or an attractive photo: "No one can amuse himself on my account after today!"

Through this story, Naṣr Allāh confronts us with an important issue that deserves thought and consideration. It shows us that the virtual world does not differ from the real world regarding the issue of gender. Virtual communication

24 ʿĀyda Naṣr Allāh, "al-Baṭala al-iftirāḍiyya," *al-Ḥiwār al-Mutamaddin* (February 12, 2006), http://www.ahewar.org/debat/show.art.asp?aid=57088 (accessed December 2, 2010).

25 Ibid.

26 Ibid.

27 Ibid.

between males and females is based on preconceived ideas and beliefs that are related to biology and gender, though it is mistakenly presumed that virtual reality would abolish such thoughts and would deal with the issue of gender without bias.

Psychologist John Suler, author of *Psychology of Cyberspace* (2013), introduces a hypothesis regarding the nature of virtual relations and their forms. The main characteristic of such relations is the absence of gender differences. Suler supposes that virtual communication makes people equal. They are evaluated according to one criterion: the "text" that they write without any regard to any other considerations. He explains his idea as follows:

> In the case of frontal communication, people are evaluated by each other according to the interactive result that is produced by that communication, especially when this connection is between a male and a female. However, this effect does not exist in virtual communication, and therefore evaluation is based on the text and any thoughts and ideas that it includes, which the other one accepts or refuses.[28]

It seems that Suler's hypothesis is merely a hypothesis because reality shows the opposite. People approach virtual reality from within a specific culture that determines the features of their relationships in the here and now. Such relations are not different from their equivalents in the real world, as confirmed by the author of *al-Baṭala al-iftirāḍiyya*.

9 ʿAbd al-Nūr Idrīs: *ʿAshīqa rqmiyya* (A Digital Mistress)[29]

The poem *ʿAshīqa rqmiyya* is part of the collection *Tamazzuqāt ʿishq raqmī* (Lacerations of digital love), written by the Moroccan poet ʿAbd al-Nūr Idrīs. The stories are grouped under three main headings: *Tamazzuqāt ʿishq raqmī*; *Tamazzuqāt nittiyya* (Internet lacerations); and *Ṣahīl al-hadhayān al-raqmī* (The neigh of digital delirium). The connection between the three headings is quite clear as they share the element of laceration. Everything that is digital refers to a tearing apart that is both metaphorical and psychological. The poet describes his beloved digital mistress as follows:

28 John Suler, *The Psychology of Cyberspace* (New Jersey: Rider University, 2013).

29 ʿAbd al-Nūr Idrīs, "ʿAshīqa raqmiyya," *al-Ḥiwār al-Mutamaddin* (May 29, 2011), http://www.ahewar.org/debat/show.art.asp?aid=261037 (accessed January 3, 2015).

وكنتِ لي مدينة الظل
تمزق جسدها كلّما ذراني غبار النت في انفعالات الغمام
وكنت أنتِ امرأة تستحضرها ابتهالات فأرتي المرقّطة
وكنتِ خدعة بصرية
وكنتِ لي معبودة من سيليكون

And you were the city of shadow for me,
Whose body was torn whenever the dust of the net scattered me in the emotions of clouds
And you were a woman invocated by my spotted mouse
And you were a visual illusion,
And you were for me an idol of silicon![30]

The section above shows how the image of the female body is formulated in the poet's imagination through his involvement with the luminous tracks of the internet. By clicking his mouse, visual illusions are created, and out of them, the poet produces a silicon photo of a woman he could like and crave.

The poet invokes a new virtual Shahrazād by the use of words and terms that are drawn from the internet lexicon and help him in his invocation, such as: silver screen, nylon lights, internet dust, supplications of my mouse, visual illusions, and digits. Thus, the speaker/poet expresses his love for his sweetheart through "internet" language.

Passionate love (*ʿishq*) directs us to a new type of love poetry (*ghazal*), addressed to a virtual woman invoked by the poet whenever he feels he is disintegrating, like dust, in the space of the internet. The poet generates this woman as he wants, using computer programs like photoshop, for instance. Idrīs's woman is a digital woman but her emotional effect is so powerful and inordinate that she becomes both mistress and ideal. Again, this emotional description of the poet's love shows the profound effect of the virtual world and its virtual characters, not only on our emotions, but also on our behavior, which may even reach addiction levels.

30 Ibid.

10 Muqbil Aḥmad al-ʿUmarī: *Karihtu al-nit* (I Hate the Net)[31]

In his poem *Karihtu al-nit*, the Yemenite poet Muqbil Aḥmad al-ʿUmarī deals with the disadvantages of the internet and his reasons for hating it and keeping away from it. The poet mentions several problems—including fraud, cheating, and deception—related to the world of the internet:

كرهت النت حتى ضقت نتا / واسبابي لهذا الكره شتى
فمن هفواته اني ألاقي / به قوما من الحسنات بهتا
لهم اخلاق نت سيئات / وقد صنعوا لهم منها بيوتا
تخالطهم على شرف وصدق / وهم يبغونها عوجا وامتا

I hate the Net so much so that I cannot bear it
And I have numerous reasons for this hatred
One of its misdeeds is that I meet
Untruthful, beautiful ladies
They have bad Net manners
And they have made the Net their home
You mix with them with honesty and truth
But they are inclined to dishonesty and deception.[32]

11 Muḥammad Sanājla: *Shāt* (Chat)[33]

This novel, written by Jordanian writer Muḥammad Sanājla and published on the website of *The Arab Association of Arab Writers* in 2007, is an interactive digital novel. From the thematic point of view, the novel belongs to the realistic digital novel, which uses the new forms produced by the digital age, specifically the techniques of connected texts and multimedia effects. It expresses the metamorphosis that man undergoes from real human being to virtual

31 Muqbil Aḥmad al-ʿUmarī, "Karihtu al-nit," *al-Majlis al-Yamanī* (August 1, 2008), https://www.ye1.org/forum/threads/272148/ (accessed January 3, 2015).

32 Ibid.

33 Muḥammad Sanājla, "Shāt," *Ittiḥād kuttāb al-Intirnit al-ʿArab* (2007), http://www.arab-ewriters.com/chat (accessed January 6, 2011).

human being.[34] *Shāt* reflects this transformation in a precise way, making use of multimedia tools of writing and expression.

The novel starts with a visual digital cover that shows the changed position of two digits, zero (0) and one (1), from the top to the bottom of the screen. These two numbers express the equations used in computer language numbering; this differs from the printed novel, which does not use such a formula. Then the title *Shāt* appears, flashing onto the screen to suggest the digital nature of the novel and its literary genre and shedding light on the tools of the novel and its elements. It also draws the reader's attention to the fact that he is dealing with a novelistic work whose original content tackles new issues and concerns that have come to light in the wake the internet's entrance into our lives.

The first chapter, *al-ʿAdam al-ramlī* (Sand nothingness), opens with the appearance of a desert photo on the screen and the sound of wind in the background. The movement of sand dunes against the background of the wind provides a full scenic visual of the entire chapter, including the overwhelming loneliness and boredom in the real life of the hero, Muḥammad.

The author uses a stream of consciousness technique to clarify the hero's contradictory emotions and feelings. He remembers his beloved, from whom he had fled to this desert, his place of exile, where he experiences a killing routine and dreary loneliness. The same situation applies to anyone who lives in that region. He says: "People here are bodies without souls; they move mechanically, there is no life in this place […] just work and desert, death and sleep!"[35] Then he dreams of the life that he will live after two years, when he has saved a considerable sum of money. While he is immersed in his thoughts, dreams, and contemplations, an SMS reaches him, and changes the direction of his life.

The events of the novel can be divided into two parts: Part one describes the events that happen in Muḥammad's real world while he is working as an environmental engineer for a multinational company in the Sultanate of Oman. Part two describes the hero's life in his virtual reality, starting with his experience of entering a chat room on his mobile phone, using a pseudonym.

In the chat room, Muḥammad happens to meet a girl called Manāl through an SMS he has left on his mobile by mistake. This girl asks him to talk to her on Messenger. Here he admits that he had never had any interest in the internet before because he considered it a trivial thing. Nevertheless, he decides

---

34 ʿAbd al-Nūr Idrīs, "al-Nashr al-iliktrunī wa'l-adab al-tafāʿulī min khilāl riwāyat Shāt," *Durūb* (March 10, 2006), http://www.doroob.com/?p=6075 (accessed March 27, 2006).

35 Ibid.

to accept her offer. He goes to an internet café, the only one in town. Day by day, he begins to feel that he is increasingly attracted to the screen, which he calls the Blue Cyberspace. Manāl introduces him to new friends—Guevara, Ṣaddām, Bin Lādin, Lamīs, Fṭīma, and al-Muhandis, among others—that he meets in different chat rooms, especially the Politics Room on the *Maktūb* website.

The journey of transformations in Muḥammad's life starts here. Having lived in an endless desert in *al-ʿAdam al-ramlī*, he is now living in a small room in front of a blue computer screen. Here, he meets characters from many backgrounds who discuss various issues ranging from communism to socialism to religion, love, sex, and alcohol, expressing their opinions in complete freedom.

Discussions between chatters sometimes become immoral. They attack one another, using negative nicknames and offensive words. After choosing a fake name—Nizār—the hero, Muḥammad, decides to leave the room and set up a new room called Kingdom of Lovers. He crowns himself its king and appoints a queen and a minister. However, after a while, quarrels and disagreements erupt between the friends. Some of them demand the kingdom be turned into a democratic republic and adhere to the principle of freedom that the king preaches.

Elections between supporters and opponents of the republic end with the victory of Nizār and his monarchy. Some, while accusing him of cheating and manipulating the elections, wage an immoral war against him. He is forced to abolish the digital kingdom and leave. He fades digitally soon after he switches off his computer and, having reassumed his natural identity, decides to abolish his digital homeland and withdraw from it completely as he is now sure that his homeland is a mere illusion, existing only on optic fibers. However, after his return to the real world, he soon discovers the great emptiness of that world and its ugliness. He ultimately decides to return to the digital world with a new name, Lorca. He builds a new room and a new homeland and calls it The Homeland of Poets, believing that the virtual world, despite its disadvantages, is more beautiful and has the power to help him fulfill his personal destiny, unlike the tedious real world.

In this novel, Sanājla examines the world of young adults who rely on chat rooms for their emotional well-being. Young men and young women gather to express their concerns and relieve their feelings of oppressed freedom in the real world via a virtual world. They hide behind fake names to discuss their political, social, emotional, and sexual issues. Through these debates, Sanājla tries to show, as he did in his book *Riwāyat al-wāqiʿiyya al-raqmiyya* (The novel of digital reality, 2005), that a virtual world is not completely "good," but rather is a society that comprises all the "good" and all the "evil" that the real world does.[36]

Nabīl ʿAlī maintains that the virtual world broadens our knowledge of ourselves and of others since we can live in it without fear or shame. The hidden things in our subconscious come to the surface when they are relieved from the shackles of our bodies and from social pressures.[37] This is also reflected in the novel as Nizār clearly expresses his sexual desire for his sweetheart. This desire is reciprocated as they have full sexual intercourse. Strangely, he describes the smallest details of the sexual act freely and daringly through the e-mails that they exchange. Sanājla maintains that "the virtual human being will be solitary, secluded, and self-satisfied, with only a minimal need for others. The self of such a human being will be his own basic concern, which is why he will return to his basic nature of seclusion and isolation."[38] This probably explains the writer's disinterest in the fate of his characters: Nizār does not care for anyone or anything except himself and his personal issues. He focuses on himself and takes his decisions by himself without consulting anyone or caring about anyone else's affairs. This is where the play ends.

At the same time, Sanājla realizes the drawbacks of this virtual world and its effect on people's lives. The hero of the novel has become addicted to this reality, so that he is often late for work. As a result, his is fired from the company. Nonetheless, the writer thinks that virtual reality is better than reality per se, as it allows us to express ourselves and find fulfillment.

12 Conclusion

The need to communicate with other people is an inborn human trait. Though virtual reality provides the opportunity for everyone to communicate in unprecedented ways, Arabic literature does not consider this topic to be simple. From my analysis of a number of texts, it becomes clear that most Arab writers look at the issue of virtual reality and the nature of the relations that it develops from two different points of view.

The first point of view appears in their negative approach to this reality and their fear of the tremendous damage it could inflict on visitors to a virtual

36 Sanājla, *Shāt*.

37 Nabīl ʿAlī, *al-Thaqāfa al-ʿArabiyya wa-ʿaṣr al-maʿlumāt: ruʾyā li-mustaqbal al-khiṭāb al-thaqāfī al-ʿArabī* (Kuwait: ʿĀlam al-Maʿrifa, 2001).

38 Sanājla, *Riwāyat*, 44.

world. On the one hand, the writers realize the importance of virtual reality in allowing people to cross barriers of time and place; overcome obstacles of religion, race, and ethnicity; and create of different kinds of acquaintances and friendships—not to mention the entertainment and enjoyment they benefit from. On the other hand, it can falsify facts and conceal them, and enable the same person to appear wearing several masks, all of which are far removed from his real identity. For other people, it is a waste of time, a window to corruption, abundant dangers, and social and moral dilemmas. In addition, it is a place where weak and deviant people visit to hunt for their victims, mostly adolescent boys and girls.

The second point of view expressed by Arab writers is a positive attitude towards the virtual world since it enables people to achieve their dreams, wishes, and hopes, which would be unachievable in reality, especially in a strict conservative society attached to specific customs and traditions that cannot be foresworn. The appearance of the internet seems to them like an eagerly awaited savior. The door is opened wide to young men and women who suffer from oppression in their societies, allowing them to achieve fulfillment in a number of ways. It also opens channels of communication; enables them to break taboos about sex, religion, and politics; and engages them in daring debates. In addition, it also enables them to achieve victories and perform heroic national deeds that they aspired to in the shadow of suppressive tyrannical systems. It enables girls, specifically, to declare their rebellion against various forms of social discrimination in a masculine society.

Bibliography

ʿAdnān, Ṭāhā. "Wa-lī fīhā ʿanākib ukhrā," in: http://aslimnet.free.fr/ress/t_adnane/index.htm (accessed July 28, 2007).

ʿAlī, Nabīl. *al-Thaqāfa al-ʿArabiyya wa-ʿaṣr al-maʿlumāt: ruʾyā li-mustaqbal al-khiṭāb al-thaqāfī al-ʿArabī*. Kuwait: ʿĀlam al-Maʿrifa, 2001.

Būziyān, Fāṭima. "Barīd iliktrūnī," *al-Ḥiwār al-mutamaddin*, in: http://www.ahewar.org/debat/show.art.asp?aid=56094 (January 31, 2006) (accessed April 19, 2008).

Castells, Manuel. *The Rise of Network Society* (*The Information Age: Economy, Society and Culture, Volume 1*). Oxford: Blackwell, 1996.

Crystal, David. *Language and the Internet*. New York: Cambridge University Press, 2005.

Al-Dānā, Nadā. "Aḥādīth al-Intirnit," in: http://www.arabworldbooks.com/ArabicLiterature/story45.htm (accessed February 15, 2007).

Farghalī, Ibrāhīm. "Thaqāfa iliktruniyya, tawābiʿ al-fisbuk," in: http://www.alarabimag.com/arabi/common/showhilight.asp (accessed December 8, 2012).

Hanst, Elizabeth et al. "Collecting User Requirements in a Virtual Population: A Case Study," *Web Net Journal: Internet Technologies, Applications & Issues* 2/4 (2000): 20–27.

Idrīs, ʿAbd al-Nūr. "al-Nashr al-iliktrunī wa'l-adab al-tafāʿulī min khilāl riwāyat Shāt," in: http://www.doroob.com/?p=6075 (accessed March 27, 2006).

Idrīs, ʿAbd al-Nūr. "ʿAshīqa raqmiyya," in: http://www.ahewar.org/debat/show.art.asp?aid=261037 (May 29, 2011) (accessed January 3, 2015).

Kīwān, Suhayl. "Raḥīl munāḍil kabīr," in: http://www.alquds.co.uk/index.asp?fname=data\2008\03\03-20\18m12.htm (March 3, 2008) (accessed March 6, 2003).

Kraut, Robert et al. "Internet Paradox: A Social Technology that Reduces Social Involvement and Psychological Well-Being?," *American Psychologist* 53/9 (1998): 1017–1031.

Majmaʿ al-Qāsimī li'l-Lugha al-ʿArabiyya. *Qāmūs al-majmaʿ fī'l-alfāẓ al-ʿArabiyya al-muʿāṣira wa'l-turāthiyya al-shāʾiʿa*. Kufr Qaraʿ: Dār al-Hudā, 2012.

Al-Muʿjam al-shāmil li muṣṭalaḥāt al-ḥāsūb al-ʾālī wa'l-Intirnit. Riyadh: Maktabat al-ʿAbikān, 2011.

Naṣr Allāh, ʿĀyda. "Al-Baṭala al-iftirāḍiyya," in: http://www.ahewar.org/debat/show.art.asp?aid=57088 (February 12, 2006) (accessed December 2, 2010).

Rāshid, Ḥusayn. "Wāqiʿiyyat al-ʿālam al-iftirāḍī wa-iftirāḍ a-ʿālam al-wāqiʿi," in: https://pulpit.alwatanvoice.com/content/print/153650.html (accessed September 6, 2020).

Ryan, Marie-Laure. *Narrative as Virtual Reality, Immersion and Interactivity*. London: Johns Hopkins University Press, 2001.

Sanājla, Muḥammad. *Riwāyat al-wāqiʿiyya al-raqmiyya*. Amman: al-Mu'assasa al-ʿArabiyya li'l-Dirāsāt wa'l-Nashr, 2005.

Sanājla, Muḥammad. "Shāt," in: http://www.arab-ewriters.com/chat (accessed January 6, 2007).

Al Ṣāniʿ, Rajāʾ. *Banāt al-Riyāḍ*. Beirut: Dār al-Sāqī, 2006.

Sārī, Ḥilmī. *Thaqāfat al-Intirnit*. Amman: Dār Majdalāwī li'l-Nashr, 2005.

Suler, John. *The Psychology of Cyberspace*. New Jersey: Rider University, 2013.

Al-ʿUmarī, Muqbil Aḥmad. "Karihtu al-nit," in: https://www.ye1.org/forum/threads/272148/ (August 1, 2008) (accessed January 3, 2015).

PART 3

Historiography

An Unknown Chronicle of Ottoman Egypt and Its Historiographical Implications

Jane Hathaway

1 Introduction

This contribution concerns an historical chronicle known as *Akhbār al-nuwwāb fī dawlat Āl ʿUthmān min ḥīn istawalā ʿalayhā al-sulṭān Salīm Khān* (History of the representatives of the Ottoman State from the time when Sultan Selim [I] took control of it), which is housed in the Topkapı Palace Library in Istanbul, part of the library's Hazīne manuscript collection. When the palace was transformed into a museum in the 1920s, following Mustafa Kemal Atatürk's abolition of the Ottoman Sultanate in 1922 and the caliphate in 1924, this work, along with hundreds of others, was found in the palace treasury (*hazīne* in Turkish).[1]

2 The Question of the Author's Identity

The author of this chronicle is not specified in the manuscript. His work, which consists of ninety-four folios, is composed in a more-or-less straightforward Arabic that is free of colloquialisms and Ottoman Turkish loanwords. It also lacks the oral performance prompts that one sees in the chronicles of the so-called Damurdāshī group,[2] and in Aḥmad Shalabī b. ʿAbd al-Ghanī's *Awḍaḥ al-ishārāt fī man tawallā Miṣr al-Qāhira min al-wuzarāʾ waʾl-bāshāt* (The clearest signs regarding ministers and pashas who governed Egypt).[3]

The Topkapı manuscript of *Akhbār al-nuwwāb* is written in a fairly typical hand, with the horizontal orientation characteristic of Arabophone scribes, in black ink with chapter headings in red and no illustrations. In the margins

1 See N.M. Penzer, *The Harem: An Account of the Institution as It Existed in the Palace of the Turkish Sultans, with a History of the Grand Seraglio from Its Foundations to Modern Times* (Philadelphia: J.B. Lippincott, 1936; 2nd ed., London: Spring Books, 1965; reprint New York: Dover Press, 1993), 242–244.

2 On these, see P.M. Holt, "al-Jabartī's Introduction to the History of Ottoman Egypt," *BSOAS* 25/1 (1962): 42–45.

3 Aḥmad Shalabī b. ʿAbd al-Ghanī, *Awḍaḥ al-ishārāt fī man tawallā Miṣr al-Qāhira min al-wuzarāʾ waʾl-bāshāt*, edited by A.A. ʿAbd al-Raḥīm (Cairo: Maktabat al-Khānjī, 1978).

 | DOI:10.1163/9789004459120_016

of the first several folios, however, are brief summaries—three in Ottoman Turkish, one in Arabic—all written in a hand different from that of the copyist, of what the chronicle reports; with one exception, these all concern the *qāḍīs*, or judges, who arrived in Egypt in the years immediately following the Ottoman conquest. This could conceivably indicate that a later owner of the manuscript was himself a *qāḍī*, perhaps even one of the chief judges (singular, *qāḍī ʿaskar* or *qāḍī al-quḍāt*) appointed to Cairo from Istanbul; these figures were Turkish speakers and exponents of the official Ḥanafī legal rite. It is even conceivable that the author of the work was himself such a chief judge. This might explain why the manuscript uses Ottoman Turkish orthography, in preference to Arabic orthography, in its rendering of certain names, notably Frenk Aḥmad, instead of Ifranj Aḥmad, in the excerpt quoted below.

Nonetheless, there are indications that the author was a native, or near-native, speaker of Arabic. Indeed, his text contains little or none of the occasional diglossia that appears in the Damurdāshī chronicles or in Muḥammad b. Yūsuf al-Ḥallāq's *Tārīkh-i Mıṣr-ı Ḳāhire* (History of Cairo), a Turkish chronicle covering the years from the Ottoman conquest through 1127/1715.[4] Instead of a chief judge, then, the author probably was a so-called *nāʾib*, or deputy, one of the "native" judges who assisted the chief judge and presided over Cairene courts that adhered to the non-Ḥanafī legal rites.[5] In that case, the preference for Turkish orthography may have resulted from the fact that the manuscript was copied by a Turcophone scribe.

3 The Chronicle's Content and Structure

So far as its content is concerned, *Akhbār al-nuwwāb* is a straightforward example of what the late P.M. Holt termed the "sultan-pasha chronicle."[6] That is

4 Muḥammad b. Yūsuf al-Ḥallāq, *Tārīkh-i Mıṣr-ı Ḳāhire*, Istanbul University Library, T.Y. 628. On diglossia in this work, see Jane Hathaway, "Sultans, Pashas, *Taqwīms*, and *Mühimmes*: A Reconsideration of Chronicle-Writing in Eighteenth-Century Ottoman Egypt," in *Eighteenth-Century Egypt: The Arabic Manuscript Sources*, edited by Daniel Crecelius (Claremont, CA: Regina Books, 1990), 55. For an example of diglossia in the Damurdāshī chronicles, see Aḥmad Katkhudā ʿAzabān al-Damurdāshī, *al-Durra al-muṣāna fī akhbār al-Kināna*, British Library, MS Or. 2073, 11, line 8, where the Turkish *böylece* ("thus," "like that") is abruptly inserted into an Arabic sentence.

5 Jane Hathaway, *The Arab Lands under Ottoman Rule, 1500–1800*, with contributions by Karl K. Barbir (Harlow, Essex: Pearson/Longman, 2008), 116–117; Galal H. El-Nahal, *The Judicial Administration of Ottoman Egypt in the Seventeenth Century* (Minneapolis and Chicago: Bibliotheca Islamica, 1979), 14–17.

6 Holt, "al-Jabartī's Introduction to the History of Ottoman Egypt," 39.

to say, it begins with Selim I's conquest of Egypt from the Mamluk Sultanate in 1517 and is organized according to the reigns of the succeeding Ottoman sultans and the tenures of the governors whom they appointed to administer Egypt. The work's title indicates as much. In the physical manuscript, a governor's name functions as a literal rubric, rendered in red ink so that it stands out from the rest of the text, and framed within a border as a *de facto* chapter heading. The "chapter" formed by a governor's tenure inevitably begins with the start and end dates of the governor's service in Egypt and a calculation of the total number of years (if applicable), months, and days. In exceptional cases, a few details may be added, usually to do with a peculiar nickname ("known as al-Ṣūfī," for example), with major charitable works that the governor commissioned in Egypt, or with extraordinary events during the governor's term, such as a rebellion or his own murder or execution. Even the sultan's reign seems somewhat secondary to the governor's tenure; the chronicler informs us that a new sultan has taken the throne on a particular date and that a particular governor is the first *wālī* of Egypt under his reign, but the sultan receives no additional attention.

Within a particular governor's tenure, narrations of events, known in the Arabic plural as *akhbār*, are arranged chronologically by date, following the Muslim calendar (*taqwīm* in Arabic). This manner of laying out a chronicle goes back to the famous universal history *Taʾrīkh al-rusūl wa'l-mulūk* (History of the prophets and kings) of the Abbasid-era chronicler Muḥammad b. Jarīr al-Ṭabarī (d. 310/923) and is a prominent feature of the major chronicles of the Mamluk Sultanate, notably those of Taqī al-Dīn Aḥmad al-Maqrīzī (d. 845/1442), Abū al-Maḥāsin Yūsuf b. Taghrī Birdī (d. 874/1470), and Muḥammad b. Aḥmad b. Iyās (d. 930/1524), with which the author of *Akhbār al-nuwwāb* would presumably have been familiar. Ottoman court chronicles share this *taqwīm*-based arrangement, although the chronological litany is occasionally interrupted by digressions on momentous events—such as the deposition or murder of a government official, or a military rebellion—placed under topical subheadings. Ottoman-era chronicles of Egypt tend to follow both schemes, varying according to the language in which they are composed. Thus, Arabophone chroniclers usually adhere strictly to the calendar, avoiding topical digressions, while Turcophone chroniclers occasionally employ these digressions (a prominent example is al-Ḥallāq's chronicle, which repeatedly deploys the storytelling prompt *Ez-īn cānib*, literally "From this side," to announce sometimes quite lengthy digressions.)

Akhbār al-nuwwāb appears to be roughly contemporary with the chronicles of Aḥmad Shalabī, al-Ḥallāq, and the Damurdāshī authors, referenced above. All these works are much longer than *Akhbār al-nuwwāb*, with Aḥmad Shalabī's chronicle running to over 600 pages in print, the longest of the Damurdāshī chronicles to 488 pages, and al-Ḥallāq's chronicle to 328 folios, or 656 pages. All the same, their chronological scope is similar. Both *Awḍaḥ al-ishārāt* and *Tārīkh-i Mıṣr-ı Ḳāhire* begin with Selim I's conquest of Egypt and the governorate of Khayrbāy, the former Mamluk governor of Aleppo who defected to Selim during the latter's confrontation with the Mamluk Sultan Qānṣawh al-Ghawrī at Marj Dābiq in northern Syria. While al-Ḥallāq's chronicle ends in 1126/1715, Aḥmad Shalabī's runs to 1150/1737. The Damurdāshī chronicles, in contrast, begin with the deposition of Sultan Meḥmed IV (r. 1648–1687) and end in, variously, 1152/1739, 1168/1754–1755, and 1169/1756. Moreover, the Damurdāshī chronicles are not organized according to the terms of governors, nor do they strictly follow a *taqwīm*, albeit they do proceed chronologically. *Akhbār al-nuwwāb* more closely resembles *Awḍaḥ al-ishārāt* and *Tārīkh-i Mıṣr-ı Ḳāhire*, and could almost be considered an Arabic abridgement of the latter.

Akhbār al-nuwwāb opens with typical paeans to God, followed by the briefest of explanations of the work's purpose, from which the title is drawn: "This is the book comprising the reports of the representatives of the Ottoman state from the time when Sultan Selim took control of it until the present time, including the achievements,[7] exploits, faults … and what occurred during his days, and exactly what is related about him of oppression and justice."[8] The text then proceeds to Khayrbāy's governorate.

4 How *Akhbār al-Nuwwāb* Compares to Contemporary Chronicles in Its Coverage of Egypt's 1711 "Revolution"

Shortly before 1125/1714, the last year covered in *Akhbār al-nuwwāb*, Egypt was convulsed by a "revolution" among the provincial military forces. The episode can be summarized as follows: Ifranj Aḥmad, a lower-ranking officer (*başodabaşı*, chief of the barracks heads) in the provincial Janissary (Mustaḥfiẓān) regiment, an infantry corps assigned to the Ottoman governor's council, or *divan*, in Cairo's citadel, had come to hold sway over the entire regiment, alienating a number of higher officers who fled to the rival ʿAzab

7 *Maʾāthir*. This word usually connotes pious foundations and/or edifices that the governor left behind in Egypt.

8 *Akhbār al-nuwwāb*, fol. 1b:

"Fa-hādhā kitāb yashtamilu ʿalā akhbār al-nuwwāb fī dawlat Āl ʿUthmān min ḥīn istawalā ʿalayhā al-sulṭān Salīm Khān wa-ilā hādhā al-awān, ḍammantuhu [?] mā li-kull wāḥid minhum min al-maʾāthir waʾl-mafākhir waʾl-maʿāyib waʾl-maṭālib wa-mā waqaʿa fī muddat ayyāmihi wa-mā yunqalu ʿanhu min al-jawr waʾl-ʿadl fī aḥkāmihi."

regiment and proceeded to attack Ifranj Aḥmad and the Janissaries. The conflict escalated and came to include Egypt's sanjak beys, who did not belong to the regiments, but instead held the tax farms (Arabic singular, *iltizām*) of Egypt's subprovinces, as well as the critical administrative offices of pilgrimage commander (*amīr al-ḥajj*) and chief financial officer (*defterdār*). The beys of Egypt's Faqārī faction allied with Ifranj Aḥmad and the Janissaries against the beys of the Qāsimī faction, who sided with the ʿAzabs and the Janissary officers who had taken refuge with them. Ultimately, the Qāsimī/ʿAzab combination emerged victorious.[9] The convoluted events connected with this conflict are described in detail in *Akhbār al-nuwwāb*, as they are in all the other chronicles mentioned above. They have been analyzed in a number of studies, including my own, and I do not propose to repeat them here.[10] However, the narrative of certain of these events demonstrates how *Akhbār al-nuwwāb* compares to these better-known chronicles, in terms of both presentation of events and chronology. I shall therefore compare a relatively succinct passage in *Akhbār al-nuwwāb* with its corresponding passages in al-Ḥallāq's *Tārīkh-i Mıṣr-ı Ḳāhire* and Aḥmad Shalabī's *Awḍaḥ al-ishārāt* with this perspective in mind. But first of all, I shall compare this passage to its counterpart in ʿAbd al-Raḥmān al-Jabartī's *ʿAjāʾib al-āthār fīʾl-tarājim waʾl-akhbār* (The marvelous chronicles: biographies and events) to demonstrate how this famous work, until recently considered a unique anomaly,[11] participates in the *taqwīm*-based "sultan-pasha" genre.

The passage in question marks the beginning of the Hijri year 1123, the year when the "revolution" erupted, corresponding roughly to 1711 of the Gregorian calendar. In *Akhbār al-nuwwāb*, it begins this way:

---

9 On the origins of the Faqārī and Qāsimī factions, see Jane Hathaway, *A Tale of Two Factions: Myth, Memory, and Identity in Ottoman Egypt and Yemen* (Albany: State University of New York Press, 2003).

10 See André Raymond, "Une 'Révolution' au Caire sous les Mamelukes: La crise de 1123/1711," *Annales Islamologiques* 6 (1966): 95–120; P.M. Holt, *Egypt and the Fertile Crescent: A Political History, 1516–1922* (Ithaca: Cornell University Press, 1966), 88–90; Jane Hathaway, *The Politics of Households in Ottoman Egypt: The Rise of the Qazdağlıs* (Cambridge: Cambridge University Press, 1997), 71–74.

11 This is the view expressed by David Ayalon, "The Historian al-Jabartī and His Background," *BSOAS* 23 (1960): 217–249. For revisionist views, see the articles in Crecelius (ed.), *Eighteenth-Century Egypt: The Arabic Manuscript Sources*; Jane Hathaway, "Introduction" to *al-Jabartī's History of Egypt* (a selection of excerpts from Thomas Philipp and Moshe Perlmann (eds.), *ʿAbd al-Raḥmān al-Jabartī's History of Egypt: ʿAjāʾib al-āthār fīʾl-tarājim waʾl-akhbār* [Stuttgart: Franz Steiner Verlag, 1994]) (Princeton: Markus Wiener Publishers, 2009), xi–xxxiv.

On Thursday, the first of Muḥarram in the year 1123, the sun entered Pisces on the fourteenth of [the Coptic month of] Amshīr. On that day, Ismāʿīl Bey went down from [the governor's] *divan* in a military procession. On Wednesday, the fourteenth of Muḥarram, he set off on campaign from Būlāq, and on Friday, the sixteenth, the followers of the late Muṣṭafā Katkhudā al-Qazdaghlī gathered, and fifteen emirs from the notables of the Janissary regiment followed them to the ʿAzab barracks and sent word to the Janissary barracks "that we do not accept Frenk Aḥmad as *odabaşı* but that he should don the *ḍolama*[12] or become a *çorbacı*. If he doesn't accept one of these two conditions, then give us permission to go to any regiment we want." The people of the regiments supported them in this and said, "Frenk Aḥmad must be expelled from the office of *odabaşı*, and the eight soldiers who were previously expelled must return to their places in the regiments." They continued residing in the ʿAzab barracks. The Janissaries did not agree to those conditions. Gossip arose, and the troops began gathering, sometimes at the house of Qayṭās Bey the *daftardār* and sometimes at the house of Ibrāhīm Bey Bushnāq (the Bosniak). On Friday, the twenty-third of Muḥarram, everyone agreed that the eight soldiers would move to the ʿAzab regiment—they and those who had joined them: nearly 600 soldiers, of whom three had resigned from the rank of *katkhudā* and ten [from the rank of] *çorbacı*; the rest were [ordinary?] soldiers. They proposed this to the pasha.[13]

---

12 A dolman, i.e. a long robe signifying higher officer rank. Soldiers at the rank of *başodabaşı* and below wore knee-length trousers (Turkish and Persian *şālvār*, Arabicized to *shirwāl*).

13 *Akhbār al-nuwwāb*, fol. 69a:

"Wa-fī yawm al-khamīs ghurrat shahr al-Muḥarram sanat 1123, intaqalat al-shams bi-Burj al-Ḥūt fī rābiʿ ʿashar Amshīr. Wa-fī dhālika al-yawm nazala Ismaʿīl Bik bi-mawkib al-safar min al-dīwān. [fol. 70b] Wa-fī yawm al-arbiʿāʾ 14 Muḥarram safara min Būlāq, wa-fī yawm al-jumʿa sādis ʿasharihi ijtamaʿat atbāʿ al-marḥūm Muṣṭafā Katkhudā al-Qazdaghlī wa-tabiʿahum min aʿyān ūjāq al-Yangiçariyya khamsata ʿashara amīran bi-Bāb al-ʿAzab, wa-arsalū khabaran li-Bāb al-Yangiçariyya 'Annanā la-raḍiya [sic] Ifranj Aḥmad an yakūn ūda bāshī bal yalbas al-ḍulama aw yaṣīr jurbājī, wa-in lam yaqbal aḥad hādhayn al-sharṭayn, fa-aʿṭūnā ʿarḍanā li-nadhhab li-ayyi ūjāq aradnāhu.' Wa-kānat ahl al-ūjāqāt musāʿida lahum ʿalā dhālika, wa-qālū, 'Lā budda min ikhrāj Ifranj Aḥmad min al-ūdābāshiyya wa-radd al-thamāniyat anfār alladhīna nufiū sābiqan ilā maḥāllihim fi'l-ūjāq.' Wa'istamarrū muqīmīn bi-Bāb al-ʿAzab, fa-lam yuwāfiq al-Yangiçariyya ilā tilka al-shurūṭ, fa-ḥaṣala qīl wa-qāl, wa-ṣārat al-ʿaskar tāra tajtamiʿ bi-manzil Qayṭās Bik al-daftardār wa-tāra bi-manzil Ibrāhīm Bik al-Bushnāq. Fa-lamma kāna yawm al-jumʿa thālith ʿashri [sic] Muḥarram ajmaʿa raʾy al-jamāʿa ʿalā an yanqulū al-thamāniyat anfār ilā ūjāq al-ʿAzab, hum wa-man inḍamma ilayhim, wa-kāna naḥw al-sitt-miʾat nafar minhum thalātha nazalū [sic] al-katkhudāʾiyya wa-ʿashara jurbājiyya, wa'l-bāqī min al-anfār. Wa-ʿaraḍū dhālika ʿalā al-bāshā."

Al-Jabartī's rendition of these events, while similar overall, contains a number of telling differences:

> Muḥarram began on Thursday, corresponding to the fourteenth of the Coptic month of Amshīr and the seventh of the *rūmī* month of Shubbāṭ. On that day, the sun entered Pisces. And on that day Ismāʿīl Bey went out in a procession and passed through the middle of Cairo to Būlāq; he set off with the soldiers in the middle of Muḥarram. On Friday, the sixteenth, the party of Muṣṭafā Katkhudā al-Qazdaghli met, along with fifteen individuals from the Janissary leadership, and agreed that they did not accept Ifranj Aḥmad as *başodabaşı* but that he should don the *ḍolama* or become a *çorbacı* in the regiment, and that they did not agree to the expulsion from the regiment of any of the aforementioned officers but that they should go to any regiment they wished.
>
> The meeting was in the ʿAzab barracks, and the members of the six regiments supported them, and they also decided on the return of the eight soldiers whom they had thrown out of the Janissary barracks. The sanjak [beys] and the officers shuttled between them, and they began meeting, sometimes at the house of Qayṭās Bey the *daftardār* and sometimes at the house of Ibrāhīm Bey, the former pilgrimage commander. Then they all came to an agreement on the transfer of the aforementioned eight soldiers and those associated with them from the regiments to the ʿAzab barracks, and on the banishment of many soldiers from Cairo: three from the *katkhudās*, ten from the *çorbacıs*, and the rest from the Janissaries. They proposed this issue to the pasha.[14]

---

14 ʿAbd al-Raḥmān b. Ḥasan al-Jabartī al-Zaylaʿī al-Ḥanafī, *ʿAjāʾib al-āthār fī'l-tarājim wa'l-akhbār*, edited by Shmuel Moreh (Jerusalem: The Hebrew University of Jerusalem, 2013), 1: 45:

"Wa-istahalla al-Muḥarram bi-yawm al-khamīs al-muwāfiq li-rābiʿ ʿashar Amshīr al-qibṭī wa-sābiʿ Shubbāṭ al-rūmī. Wa-fī dhālika al-yawm intaqalat al-shams li-Burj al-Ḥūt. Wa-fīhi nazala Ismāʿīl Bik bi-mawkib wa-shaqqa min wasaṭ al-Qāhira ilā Būlāq wa-sāfara bi'l-ʿaskar fī muntaṣaf al-Muḥarram. Wa-fī yawm al-jumʿa sādis ʿasharihi ijtamaʿa ṭāʾifat Muṣṭafā Katkhudā al-Qāzdaghlī wa-maʿahum min aʿyān al-Yankiçariyya khamsata ʿashara nafaran, wa-ittafaqū ʿalā annahum lā yarḍawnā Ifranj Aḥmad bāsha ūdah bāshā fa-immā yalbas al-ḍulama aw yakūn çurbaçiyyan fi'l-ūjāq wa-in lam yarḍa bi-aḥad al-amrayn kharaja al-madhkūrīn min al-ūjāq wa-dhahabū li-ayy ūjāq shāʾū.

Wa-kāna al-ijtimāʿ bi-Bāb al-ʿAzab, wa-sāʿadahum ʿalā dhālika aṣḥāb al-bulukāt al-sitt wa-ṣammamū ayḍan ʿalā rujūʿ al-thamāniyat anfār alladhīna kānū akhrajūhum min Bāb al-Yankiçariyya. Wa-mashat al-ṣanājiq wa'l-ikhtiyāriyya baynahum wa-ṣārū yajtamiʿūn tāra bi-manzil Qayṭās Bik al-daftardār wa-tāra bi-manzil Ibrāhīm Bik amīr al-ḥājj sābiqan. Thumma ajmaʿa raʾy al-jamīʿ ʿalā naql al-thamāniyat anfār al-madhkūrīn wa-man inḍamma ilayhim min al-ūjāqāt ilā Bāb al-ʿAzab wa-an yakhrujū anfār kathīra min

Most obviously, al-Jabartī adds a *rūmī* date. While Coptic dates appear elsewhere in his chronicle, he ordinarily reserves them for events tied to the agricultural calendar, such as the annual Nile flood, and unusual astrological or meteorological occurrences.[15] Incidents related to climate, changes of season, and the cosmos were, as a matter of course, keyed to the Coptic calendar, a twelve-month solar calendar that regulated Egypt's agricultural year until the Gregorian calendar was adopted in the twentieth century. Much the same purpose was served in the Ottoman Empire's central lands by the *rūmī* calendar, an adaptation of the Julian calendar that started with the Prophet Muḥammad's Hijra to Medina, but that was likewise a twelve-month solar calendar. The Ottoman central administration adopted it as the dating system for fiscal matters in 1676.[16] It is exceedingly rare, however, for Egyptian chroniclers to cite this calendar; this is, in fact, one of only a handful of instances in al-Jabartī's chronicle in which a *rūmī* date occurs. The author of *Akhbār al-nuwwāb*, for his part, gives a *rūmī* date exactly once, when reporting a solar eclipse in 1708.[17] This fact makes one suspect that both chroniclers were using an external source of some kind, perhaps a rather bare-bones listing of events by Hijri date, but with corresponding Coptic and *rūmī* dates. The inclusion of *rūmī* dates likewise suggests a source in the Ottoman governor's administration since this might explain the allusion to a calendar employed in the Ottoman central lands.

Otherwise, al-Jabartī's account differs from that of *Akhbār al-nuwwāb* in being couched in a seemingly objective, third-person voice, with no attempt to reproduce the speech of the historical figures portrayed. He also seems less sure of the course of events, reporting an agreement to exile an unspecified number of soldiers from Cairo; here, it almost seems as if he were uncomfortable with the massive number—over 600—reported by *Akhbār al-nuwwāb*. But in fact, *Akhbār al-nuwwāb* did not claim that hundreds of soldiers had been exiled from Cairo: only the eight lower-ranking Janissary officers had been expelled. The 600 or so soldiers affiliated with them moved from the Janissary regiment to the ʿAzabs, causing a reversal in the numerical strength of these two rival regiments and swinging the conflict in the ʿAzabs' favor.

Miṣr manfiyyīn, minhum thalātha min al-katkhudāʾiyya wa-ʿashara min al-çurbaçiyya wa'l-bāqī min al-Yankiçariyya. Wa-ʿaraḍū fī sha'n dhālika li'l-bāshā."

15 See, for example, ibid., 1: 28, 35.

16 See Halil Sahillioğlu, "*Sıvış*-Year Crises in the Ottoman Empire," in *Studies in the Economic History of the Middle East*, edited by Michael A. Cook (London and New York: Oxford University Press, 1970), 230–254.

17 *Akhbār al-nuwwāb*, fol. 63a; Hathaway, "Sultans, Pashas, *Taqwīms*, and *Mühimmes*," 61.

The same basic narrative occurs in both the Turkish chronicle of Muḥammad b. Yūsuf al-Ḥallāq and the Arabic chronicle of Aḥmad Shalabī b. ʿAbd al-Ghanī. Al-Ḥallāq's chronicle is in general far more detailed than any of the other chronicles examined here. His version of the "rejection of Ifranj Aḥmad" episode runs as follows:

> On Thursday, the first of Muharrem in the year 1123, they [Ismāʿīl Bey and his troops] went to Būlāq in a great procession. After staying there for thirteen days, they proceeded from Būlāq to Rosetta by ship on the fourteenth of the aforementioned month, a Wednesday. On Friday the sixteenth, all the followers and hangers-on of the late Ḳāzdāğlı Muṣṭafā Ketkhüdā—along with fifteen high officers of the leaders of the Janissaries, some of them removed from the rank of *ketkhüdā*, some from the rank of *baş çavuş*, some *çorbacı*s, and peasant conscripts [fol. 270b] and [ordinary] soldiers totaling more than 600—went to the ʿAzab barracks. The ʿAzeban officers welcomed and accepted them. When they questioned them, saying, "What's the matter?" they said with one mouth, "We will no longer stay in the Janissary regiment." When asked the reason, they said, "As long as Frenk Aḥmed is *başodabaşı*, there is no position for us in that regiment. Let him don the *dolāma* or become a *çorbacı* or become a *çavuş* for the treasury of estates. If he doesn't accept one of these [options], give us all permission and we will move to the ʿAzab regiment. This is also the sultan's regiment." Ḥasan Ketkhüdā, the ʿAzab *ketkhüdā*, sent word to the beys, and the high officers of the six regiments brought [the news] to the ʿAzab barracks and informed [the beys] of the situation in a petition. They in turn in the same manner sent word to the Janissary barracks and informed them of the wishes of the soldiers who had left the regiment. "And the eight men who earlier, in 1122, with the knowledge of all of us, were expelled from the regiment should return to the regiment again and resume their positions."
>
> When this news reached the Janissary regiment, they all, with one mouth, said, "Impossible! We will neither accept these eight men back into our regiment [fol. 270a] nor remove Frenk Aḥmed from the office of *başodabaşı* just because a man from the ʿAzab side says so. Otherwise, give the soldiers in our regiment permission [to leave]; they can't do this!" After several exchanges of this sort, all the beys, the senior officers of the five [other] regiments, Qayṭās Bey the *defterdār*, Ibrāhīm Bey the former pilgrimage commander, and the beys associated with them intervened, but they could not restore order by any means. They then petitioned

the pasha, to no avail. Afterward they met in Qayṭās Bey's house and in the house of Ibrāhīm Bey the former pilgrimage commander, but nothing resulted. Then on Friday, the twenty-third of Muharrem, all the beys and the senior officers of the seven regiments met in the *defterdār* bey's house and petitioned the senior officers of the Janissaries [on the basis of] the aforementioned conversation. When it was not accepted, they all agreed to the following: "With the pasha's *fermān*, let some 600 soldiers' names be removed reciprocally from the Janissary register and added to the 'Azab regiment, and let the eight men who were previously exiled likewise be added to the 'Azabs." After which they dispersed. On Sunday, [fol. 271b], the twenty-fifth of the aforementioned month, the scribes, senior officers, and other leaders of the 'Azabs went to the governor's *divan* and got his *fermān*.[18]

---

18 Al-Ḥallāq, *Tārīkh-i Mıṣr-ı Ḳāhire*, fols. 270b–271a:

"Ve sene-i 1123 Muḥarrem'in ghurresinde yevmü'l-khemīs 'aẓīm alay ile Būlāḳ'a mütevvecih oldılar. On üç gün iḳāmetden ṣonra māh-i mezbūrun on dörtde yevmü'l-erbā'a Būlāḳ'dan sefīneler ile Reşīd'e revāne oldılar. Ve on altısında yevmü'l-cuma' merḥūm Ḳāzdāghlı Muṣṭafā Ketkhüdā'nın cemi'-i tevābi' ve levāḥiḳi ve Mustaḥfiẓān ocaghı a'yānından on beş ikhtiyār, kimi ketkhüdālıkdan munfaṣıl ve kimi baş çavuşlıkdan ve kimi çorbacı ve vācib re'āya [fol. 270a] ve neferāt fi-l-cümle altyüz adamdan mütecāviz 'Azeb ḳapusuna gitdiler. Ve 'Azebān ikhtiyārları hoş görüb, ḳabūl itdiler, ve 'Maṣlaḥatınız nedir?' deyü su'āl idince cümle bir aghızdan 'Biz şimden ṣonra Yeniçeri ocaghında durmazız.' Sebebinden su'āl idince, 'Mā dāmki Frenk Aḥmed başodabaşıdır ol ocakda bize dirlik yokdur; ya olur ki dolāma giysun, ya çorbacı olsun, yākhūd Beyt-i Māl çavuşı olsun, ve egher birisine rāżi olmazsa, cümlemizin 'arzımızı virsünler, 'Azeb ocaghına çıkarız. Bu dakhi pādişāhın ocaghıdır.' 'Azebler ketkhüdāsı Ḥasan Ketkhüdā beklere haber gönderdi, ve altı bölük ikhtiyārları 'Azeb ḳapusuna götürdi ve aḥvali 'arz idüb bildirdi. Anlar dakhi ol menvāl üzere Yeniçeri ḳapusuna haber gönderdiler, ocakdan çıkan yoldāşların murādlarını bildirdiler. 'Ve bundan aḳdem bin yüz yighirmi ikide cümlemizin ma'rifetiyle ocakdan ikhrāc olunan sekiz adamı tekrar ocagha rucū' idüb, herkes ola.'

Bu haber Yeniçeri ocaghına vardukda, cümlesi bir aghızdan 'Bu söz olmaz! Ne bu sekiz adamı bir dakhi ocaghımıza ḳabūl [fol. 271b] ideriz, ne Frenk Aḥmedi başodabaşlıkdan çıkarırız 'Azeb ṭarafından varan adam didighe çünkü. Bu iş olmazsa, ḳapumuzda olan yoldāşların 'arżlarını virin, anlar khayır ol[a]maz!' didiler. Birkaç kere böyle mürācā'at oldukdan ṣonra, cümle bekler ve beş bölük ikhtiyārları ve defterdār Qayṭās Bek ve sābiḳen emīrü'l-ḥac İbrāhīm Bek ve anlara munẓām bekler araya girüb, ber-vechle intiẓām olmiyub, ba'dehu paşaya 'arż eylediler. Ol dakhi müfīd olmadı. Ba'dehu Qayṭās Bek evinde ve emīrü'l-ḥac olan //sābiḳen// İbrāhīm Bek evinde cem'iyyet idüb, ber-vech ile mümkün olmadı. Ba'dehu yevmü'l-cuma' māh-i Muḥarremin 23 cümle bekler ve yedi bölük ikhtiyārları defterdār beghin evinde cem'iyyet idüb, Yeniçeri ikhtiyārlarına ol ẕikr olunan kelāmı 'arż eylediler, ber-vech ile ḳābil olmadılar ile olunca, cümlenin ittifāḳı bunun üzerine oldiki 'Paşanın fermāniyle altyüz ve ḳüşur yoldāşların esāmeleri müḳābelede Yeniçeri defterinden çıkarub, 'Azeb ocaghına ilḥāḳ eyleyeler, ve sābiḳen nefiy olunan sekiz adamı

Immediately noticeable is how intimately familiar al-Ḥallāq appears to be with the operations of Egypt's military and administrative cadres. This familiarity is evident, not only in the exhaustive detail in which he reports their activities, but also in the matter-of-fact way in which he includes officer ranks and military units (*baş çavuş, vācib reʿāya*) not even mentioned by any of the other chroniclers. Of all the chronicles examined here, his is most tightly keyed to the Hijri calendar. The passage quoted above cites five dates, all designated by the day of the Hijri month and the day of the week. Indeed, the passage would almost read as a rather tedious daily summary of military activity in Cairo but for the folkloric intrusion of first-person speech in the ʿAzab and Janissary barracks, as well as repetitive elements common to oral storytelling, most notably "they said with one mouth." In this passage, we have, it seems to me, a marriage of the *taqwīm*-based recital of events with a colloquial narrative tradition.

As for Aḥmad Shalabī's *Awḍaḥ al-ishārāt,* it covers these events in this manner:

> On Thursday the first of Muḥarram in the year 1123, Ismāʿīl Bey went in a great procession to Būlāq. On the fourteenth of Muḥarram, the soldiers set out from Būlāq. On Thursday, the group of Muṣṭafā Katkhudā al-Qazdaghlī met, and twenty of the leaders of the Janissaries followed them. They agreed that they did not accept Ifranj Aḥmad serving as *başodabaşı,* but that he should don the *ḍolamā* or they would make him a *çorbacı* in the regiment. If he didn't accept one of these two orders, "give us permission to go to any regiment we want." This talk was in the ʿAzab barracks. The six regiments aided them and resolved that [Ifranj Aḥmad would] don the *ḍolamā,* and they remained in the ʿAzab barracks determined to [pursue] the resolution that was previously mentioned. When they saw the situation, the sanjak beys and the aghas increased their efforts to make peace between them, and they began meeting, sometimes in the house of Qayṭās Bey and sometimes in the house of Ibrāhīm Bey Abū Shanab. Qayṭās Bey held the *daftardār*-ship. On Friday, the sixteenth of Muḥarram, they all reached agreement that the eight soldiers would move to the ʿAzab barracks, they and those who had joined

dakhi maʿen ʿAzebe ilḥāḳ oluna' deyü daghıldılar. Ve yevmü'l-eḥad, [fol. 271a] māh-i mezbūrun yighirmi beşinde, ʿAzeb kātibleri ve ikhtiyārları ve sā'ir aʿyān dīvāne çıkub, paşadan fermān aldılar."

> them: 600 men, including four *katkhudās* and ten *çorbacıs* and *odabaşıs*; the rest were [ordinary] soldiers of the Janissaries. They proposed this issue to the pasha.[19]

Unlike al-Jabartī and the author of *Akhbār al-nuwwāb*, Aḥmad Shalabī does not refer to a non-Hijri solar calendar at all. Meanwhile, his Hijri dates are less precise than those that appear in *Akhbār al-nuwwāb* and al-Ḥallāq's *Tārīkh-i Mıṣr-ı Ḳāhire*. The final agreement was apparently reached a week early, on 16 Muḥarram, whereas in both *Akhbār al-nuwwāb* and *Tārīkh-i Mıṣr-ı Ḳāhire*, the Ḳāzdāğlı group met on the 16th. If so, then the agreement on a plan of action was reached only on the 23rd. (Aḥmad Shalabī is vague on the date of the Ḳāzdāğlı meeting, noting only that it occurred on a Thursday, whereas *Akhbār al-nuwwāb* and al-Ḥallāq report that it took place on a Friday.)

Like al-Jabartī and al-Ḥallāq, Aḥmad Shalabī has the beys and the high regimental officers taking the initiative to make peace among the warring regimental factions. This is, then, an established part of the narrative tradition of the 1711 "revolution," even if *Akhbār al-nuwwāb* omits it. Unlike the author of *Akhbār al-nuwwāb*, who identifies the Qāsimī chieftain Ibrāhīm Bey simply as "the Bosniak," Aḥmad Shalabī calls him Abū Shanab ("moustachioed"), the *kunya* by which he is most commonly known in the Arabic chronicles of Egypt. Al-Jabartī and al-Ḥallāq use no identifying appellation, but simply point out that he is the former *amīr al-ḥajj*, or pilgrimage commander. Conceivably, both chroniclers could be alluding to the traditional pattern that the factional rivalry between the Faqārīs and the Qāsimīs followed, with a bey from one faction holding the post of *defterdār* and a bey from the other faction serving as

19 Aḥmad Shalabī, *Awḍaḥ al-ishārāt*, 228–229:

"Wa-fī yawm al-khamīs ghurrat Muḥarram sanat 1123, awkaba Ismāʿīl Bey bi-alāy ʿaẓīm ilā Būlāq, wa-fī rābiʿ ʿashar Muḥarram sāfara al-ʿaskar min Būlāq. Wa-fī yawm al-khamīs ijtamaʿat jamāʿat Muṣṭafā Katkhudā al-Qazdaghlī, wa-tabiʿahum ʿishrūn min aʿyān al-Yanjishariyya, wa-ittafaqū annahum lā yurīdūna bi-Ifranj Aḥmad an yaʿmal bāsh al-ūdabāshiyya, wa-annahu yalbas al-ḍulamā aw yajaʿalūnahu jurbajī fi'l-ūjāq wa-in kāna mā yarḍā bi-amr min al-amrayn, 'aʿṭūna ʿarḍanā li-nadhhab ilā ayyi ūjāq nurīduhu.' Wa-kāna hādhā al-kalām fī Bāb al-ʿAzab, wa-sāʿadathum al-bulūkāt al-sitt wa-ṣammamū ʿalā labs al-ḍulamā, wa-istamarrū bi-Bāb al-ʿAzab musammimīn ʿalā ʿazmihim alladhī taqaddama dhikruhu. Thumma anna al-ṣanājiq wa'l-aghawāt lammā ra'aw al-amr bi-yatazāyad mashū baynahum fi'l-ṣulḥ fa-ṣārat al-ṣanājiq wa'l-aghawāt yajtamiʿūna tāra bi-manzil Qayṭāz Bey wa-tāra bi-manzil Ibrāhīm Bey Abū Shanab, wa-kānat al-daftardāriyya maʿa Qayṭāz Bey. Fa-lammā kāna yawm al-jumʿa sādis ʿashar Muḥarram, ittafaqa ra'y al-jamāʿa ajmaʿīn annahum yanqulū ilā Bāb al-ʿAzab al-thamāniyat anfār wa-man inḍamma ilayhim, wa-kānū sitt mi'at rajul, minhum arbaʿa kawākhī wa-ʿashara jurbājiyya wa-ūḍabāshiyya, wa'l-baqiyya anfār al-Yanjishariyya. Wa-ʿaraḍū fī sha'n dhālika li'l-bāshā."

pilgrimage commander. This division of labor features prominently in an origin myth of the two factions that al-Jabartī reproduces early in his chronicle.[20] In this particular instance, the factional difference between the two beys appears to be largely irrelevant since the dispute concerns the regiments. Nonetheless, the conflict would soon expand to engulf the beys and would acquire a factional character, culminating in the murder of Ibrāhīm Bey Abū Shanab's comrade-in-arms, ʿIvāż Bey, and ultimately leading to the execution of the Faqārī Qayṭās Bey several years later. Here, then, these two chroniclers may arguably be indulging in a touch of foreshadowing.

As is well known, al-Jabartī, in his introduction to *ʿAjāʾib al-āthār*, adduces Aḥmad Shalabī's chronicle as one of his sources,[21] and there is no reason to doubt that his rendition of this episode is informed by its presentation in *Awḍaḥ al-ishārāt*. Nonetheless, Aḥmad Shalabī is only one of his sources for this account. Rather than relying exclusively on any one source for his narrative of events, al-Jabartī seems to be splicing together Aḥmad Shalabī's account with that of a source that remains unknown, yet must certainly be something very close to *Akhbār al-nuwwāb*. The latter clearly shares a calendrical source, as well as a basic narrative of events, with al-Ḥallāq's *Tārīkh-i Mıṣr-ı Ḳāhire*. They are four variations on a common narrative tradition, and in some sense they come together through al-Jabartī's editorial manipulations.

Of the four chronicles examined here, all follow a *taqwīm* in some manner. Al-Ḥallāq's *Tārīkh-i Mıṣr-ı Ḳāhire* is most tightly bound to the calendar while Aḥmad Shalabī's *Awḍaḥ al-ishārāt* is the least calendar-dependent. It strains credulity, however, to imagine an *urtext*, as yet undiscovered, consisting of a sort of diary in which the author carefully notes the date, then describes political, meteorological, and religious events in detail. Rather, there seems to have been some sort of official calendar or system of dating events in Ottoman Egypt, perhaps keyed to the recurring cycle of agricultural tasks (cutting the Nile dam, harvesting the clover) and religious holidays, perhaps both Muslim and Coptic Christian. Since the Coptic calendar was Egypt's functional agricultural calendar, citations of Coptic dates are hardly a surprise. Inclusion of *rūmī* dates seems out of place in Egypt, however, and may indicate the interference of a system of dating from the Ottoman central lands. In the hands of al-Jabartī, this dating system is not surprising since the chronicler would probably have had at least a passing familiarity with the histories of the official Ottoman court chroniclers (singular, *vaḳʿanüvīs*), above all through his father, Shaykh Ḥasan al-Jabartī (d. 1774), who was well-connected to the court

20 Al-Jabartī, *ʿAjāʾib al-āthār*, I: 25.

21 Ibid., I: 5.

of Sultan Muṣṭafā III (r. 1757–1774).[22] Accounts of governors' tenures could be "hung" on the framework of such a calendar, as could more elaborate accounts of rebellions and civil wars, such as the trauma of 1123/1711. The dates supplied the anchors for the narrative while also allowing other events, such as news of a comet or the arrival of an imperial order, to be inserted into the narrative.

Certainly, there must have been a vast trove of stories about the 1711 civil war, or "revolution," from a variety of vantage points and featuring a variety of heroes and villains.[23] We can imagine that these stories were initially narrated orally by different tellers (soldiers, shopkeepers, craftsmen, ulema) to different audiences (comrades-in-arms, students, wives, children). Perhaps they were even dramatized to an extent. The Damurdāshī chronicles provide some inkling of this sort of oral performance with their repeated oral prompts, notably *wa-li-narjiʿ ilā …* ("We now return to …") and *lahu maʿanā al-kalām* (roughly equivalent to "We'll get back to him later").[24] Even Aḥmad Shalabī's chronicle repeatedly employs such a prompt: *Fa-nẓur yā akhī ilā …* ("Now look, my brother, at …").[25] The *taqwīm*, even more than the governor's tenure, gave the chronicler a framework within which to order these events and, in a certain sense, a means of controlling them. Slotted into a calendar or framed within a rubric and inked-in borders, they become orderly "events of the year 1123" rather than transgressive disruptions of the social and political order.

5 Conclusion

From a broader standpoint, the 1711 revolution was in all likelihood seen as a turning point. It was the last time the Qāsimī faction triumphed over the rival Faqārīs and the last time a lower-ranking Janissary "boss" seriously challenged the higher officer echelons for control of the regiment. It was likewise the first time that the Ḳāzdāğlı household was publicly acknowledged as a coherent group with significant political and military influence. At the same time, all the sources considered here noted the beys' role in mediating the conflict between the Janissary and ʿAzab regiments. Al-Ḥallāq, Aḥmad Shalabī, and al-Jabartī, furthermore, pointed to a fundamental division between the beys

22 See al-Jabartī's necrology of his father: *ʿAjāʾib al-āthār*, I: 452–478, especially 463–465.

23 André Raymond analyzed the narrative sources for the 1711 upheaval from this perspective. See Raymond, "Une 'Révolution' au Caire," especially 97, 118–120.

24 For one example of each (out of many), see Aḥmad Katkhudā ʿAzabān al-Damurdāshī, *al-Durra al-muṣāna*, 104, line 10; 161, line 5.

25 See Hathaway, "Introduction" to *al-Jabartī's History of Egypt*, xxviii and 350 n. 43. This phrase also occurs in al-Jabartī's introductory sections; see *ʿAjāʾib al-āthār*, I: 23.

and the highest regimental officers, on the one hand, and the lower officers and the rank-and-file, on the other. This division determined, in no small part, how the events of 1711 played out. It would also loom large in Ottoman Egypt's future political culture: during the 1720s, the dominant military-administrative households were led by either beys or high regimental officers with the rank of *çavuş*, *çorbacı*, or *ketkhüdā*. The Ḳāzdāğlı household, founded by a Janissary *ketkhüdā*, ultimately outmaneuvered the bey-led households, then—beginning in the 1740s—came to dominate the rank of bey itself. By the late 1750s, its chiefs all held the rank of bey while high-ranking Janissary officers occupied a second rung in the household's leadership.[26]

Given the implications of the 1711 revolution and its aftermath, it is little wonder that a body of chronicles exist that culminate in these events. Both *Akhbār al-nuwwāb* and al-Ḥallāq's *Tārīkh-i Mıṣr-ı Ḳāhire* end within a few years of the events: *Akhbār al-nuwwāb* in 1126/1714, al-Ḥallāq's work in 1127/1715. I am inclined to think that the similar end dates of *Akhbār al-nuwwāb* and *Tārīkh-i Mıṣr-ı Ḳāhire* are more than pure coincidence, even if the former is not some sort of abridged translation of the latter. We tend to assume that all chroniclers, on the model of al-Jabartī, recorded events right up until their death or incapacitation.[27] This, however, was not the way that the official Ottoman court chroniclers worked. In one prominent example, the first official court historian (*vaḳʿanüvīs*), Muṣṭafā Naʿīmā (d. 1715), completed a version of the official Ottoman history that begins in 1000/1591 and ends in 1070/1660, decades before his own death.[28] Later court historians picked up the thread. Al-Ḥallāq and the author of *Akhbār al-nuwwāb* may have chosen to end their chronicles around 1714 because they had finished covering the upheaval that began with Ifranj Aḥmed's takeover of the Janissary corps and ended with the collapse of the fortunes, and ultimately the execution, of Qayṭās Bey, the Faqārī *defterdār* whose house became a meeting place for the disaffected Janissaries in the excerpts quoted above.[29] The closing line of *Akhbār al-nuwwāb* is telling in this regard: "I am stopping here [at] the year 1126."[30] It almost sounds as if the author is filling in details in a *taqwīm*-based frame and has decided to wrap up

26 See Hathaway, *The Politics of Households*, chapters 3, 5.

27 See Shmuel Moreh, "Editor's Introduction" (in Arabic) to *ʿAjāʾib al-āthār*, 1: 8, 16–18 (as Moreh explains, al-Jabartī stopped writing when his son Khalīl was killed in 1822).

28 Muṣṭafā Naʿīmā, *Tārīkh-i Naʿīmā* (*Ravżatüʾl-Ḥüseyn fī khulāṣati akhbāriʾl-ḥafīḳayn*), edited by Mehmet İpşirli, 4 vols. (Ankara: Türk Tarih Kurumu, 2007).

29 *Akhbār al-nuwwāb*, fol. 93a; al-Ḥallāq, *Tārīkh-i Mıṣr-ı Ḳāhire*, fol. 315b; Aḥmad Shalabī, *Awḍaḥ al-ishārāt*, 271. In al-Damurdāshī, *al-Durra al-muṣāna*, Qayṭās is blamed for ʿIvāż Bey's death; see 190, 200.

30 *Akhbār al-nuwwāb*, fol. 94a: "Aqifu hunā sana 1126."

his account. The *taqwīm*, this ending implies, continues, perhaps to be filled in by later chroniclers.

Bibliography

Aḥmad Shalabi b. ʿAbd al-Ghani. *Awḍaḥ al-ishārāt fī man tawallā Miṣr al-Qāhira min al-wuzarāʾ waʾl-bāshāt*, edited by A.A. ʿAbd al-Raḥīm. Cairo: Maktabat al-Khānjī, 1978.

Akhbār al-nuwwāb fī dawlat Āl ʿUthmān min ḥīn istawalā ʿalayhā al-sulṭān Salīm Khān. MS Topkapı Palace Library, Hazine 1623.

Ayalon, David. "The Historian al-Jabartī and His Background," BSOAS 23 (1960): 217–249.

Al-Damurdāshī, Aḥmad Katkhudā ʿAzabān. *Al-Durra al-muṣāna fī akhbār al-Kināna*. MS British Library, Or. 2073.

Al-Ḥallāq, Muḥammad b. Yūsuf. *Tārīkh-i Mıṣr-ı Ḳāhire*. MS Istanbul University Library, T.Y. 628.

Hathaway, Jane. "Sultans, Pashas, *Taqwīms*, and *Mühimmes*: A Reconsideration of Chronicle-Writing in Eighteenth-Century Ottoman Egypt," in *Eighteenth-Century Egypt: The Arabic Manuscript Sources*, edited by Daniel Crecelius. Claremont, CA: Regina Books, 1990.

Hathaway, Jane. *The Politics of Households in Ottoman Egypt: The Rise of the Qazdağlıs*. Cambridge: Cambridge University Press, 1997.

Hathaway, Jane. "Introduction" to *al-Jabartī's History of Egypt* (a selection of excerpts from Thomas Philipp and Moshe Perlmann (eds.), *ʿAbd al-Raḥmān al-Jabartī's History of Egypt: ʿAjāʾib al-āthār fīʾl-tarājim waʾl-akhbār* [Stuttgart: Franz Steiner Verlag, 1994]). Princeton: Markus Wiener Publishers, 2009, xi–xxxiv.

Hathaway, Jane. *A Tale of Two Factions: Myth, Memory, and Identity in Ottoman Egypt and Yemen*. Albany, NY: State University of New York Press, 2003.

Hathaway, Jane. *The Arab Lands under Ottoman Rule, 1500–1800*, with contributions by Karl K. Barbir. Harlow, Essex: Pearson/Longman, 2008.

Holt, P.M. "Al-Jabartī's Introduction to the History of Ottoman Egypt," BSOAS 25/1 (1962): 38–51.

Holt, P.M. *Egypt and the Fertile Crescent: A Political History, 1516–1922*. Ithaca: Cornell University Press, 1966.

Al-Jabartī, ʿAbd al-Raḥmān b. Ḥasan al-Zaylaʿī al-Ḥanafī. *ʿAjāʾib al-āthār fīʾl-tarājim waʾl-akhbār*, edited by Shmuel Moreh. Jerusalem: The Hebrew University of Jerusalem, 2013. 5 vols.

Moreh, Shmuel. "Editor's Introduction," in ʿAbd al-Raḥmān b. Ḥasan al-Jabartī al-Zaylaʿī al-Ḥanafī, *ʿAjāʾib al-āthār fīʾl-tarājim waʾl-akhbār*, edited by Shmuel Moreh. Jerusalem: The Hebrew University of Jerusalem, 2013, 1: 3–35.

El-Nahal, Galal H. *The Judicial Administration of Ottoman Egypt in the Seventeenth Century*. Minneapolis and Chicago: Bibliotheca Islamica, 1979.

Naʿīmā, Muṣṭafā. *Tārīkh-i Naʿīmā* (*Ravżatü'l-Ḥüseyn fī khulāṣati akhbāri'l-ḥafiḳayn*), edited by Mehmet İpşirli. Ankara: Türk Tarih Kurumu, 2007. 4 vols.

Penzer, N.M. *The Harem: An Account of the Institution as It Existed in the Palace of the Turkish Sultans, with a History of the Grand Seraglio from Its Foundations to Modern Times*. Philadelphia: J.B. Lippincott, 1936; 2nd ed. London: Spring Books, 1965; reprint New York: Dover Press, 1993.

Raymond, André. "Une 'Révolution' au Caire sous les Mamelukes: La crise de 1123/1711," *Annales Islamologiques* 6 (1966): 95–120.

Sahillioğlu, Halil. "*Sıvış*-Year Crises in the Ottoman Empire," in *Studies in the Economic History of the Middle East*, edited by Michael A. Cook. London and New York: Oxford University Press, 1970, 230–254.

The Sufi Personality of the Egyptian Historian ʿAbd al-Raḥmān al-Jabartī (1753–1825)

Michael Winter

1 Introduction

The chronicle *ʿAjāʾib al-āthār fiʾl-tarājim waʾl-akhbār* (The marvelous chronicles: biographies and events) has long been known to scholars. Of the many issues published, the edition that was most quoted was the one printed in Cairo (Būlāq), 4 vols., 1880. Shmuel Moreh of the Hebrew University devoted many years to, and recently completed, a critical new edition, based on several manuscripts, including the author's autographs, which the editor discovered in a number of libraries and collections.[1]

This new edition has both technical and graphic advantages. The huge index volume is detailed and easy to use. There are references to the Būlāq edition, which has been in use for 135 years and is still used today. The new index also has references to Arabic and European studies; this saves time and effort. Al-Jabartī's work is rich in information and insights. Among other things, it records the history of Egypt from 1688 to 1821, a period which includes the end of Mamluk rule, the Ottoman period, the three years under the French occupation, and the beginning of Muḥammad ʿAlī's rule.

An important topic in al-Jabartī's writing is religious life in Egypt, particularly Sufism. Other related issues regarding Ottoman Egypt at the time are the *mawlids* (saint days), the *ashrāf* or *sāda* (the Prophet's descendants), Sufi orders, and popular customs and beliefs, as well as al-Azhar, the ʿulamaʾ, and foreign communities in Egypt, especially the Turks and the Maghribis.

Al-Jabartī impresses by his inclination to justice, his deep understanding of his society, and by his beautiful Arabic style. The best parts of the *ʿAjāʾib* are those that depict events and persons that were nearest to the historian's own life. Even if he did not know them personally, at least he had heard about them from people who were older than he and who remembered them. This is natural and applies to chroniclers who authored several volumes about the history of their countries, although only the last volumes are direct and accurate.

1 ʿAbd al-Raḥmān b. Ḥasan al-Jabartī al-Zaylaʿī al-Ḥanafī, *ʿAjāʾib al-āthār fiʾl-tarājim waʾl-akhbār*, edited by Shmuel Moreh (Jerusalem: The Hebrew University, 2013), 5 vols.

 | DOI:10.1163/9789004459120_017

A good example is *Badāʾiʿ ʿal-zuhūr fī waqāʾiʿ al-duhūr* (The magnificent flowers regarding the chronicles of times) by Ibn Iyās, who was an eyewitness to the Ottoman conquest of Egypt in 1517.

A great historian like al-Jabartī had to use sources that had been written long before his time. *ʿAjāʾib al-āthār* begins in 1688. On the one hand, al-Jabartī did mention some contemporary historians who sent him materials for the chronicle—for example, Murtaḍā al-Zabīdī, his mentor and a famous scholar and philologist, and Muḥammad Khalīl al-Murādī, the Damascene historian who died in 1791 or 1792 and was therefore unable to cooperate with al-Jabartī as planned. On the other hand, al-Jabartī concealed the 18th-century sources he used to reconstruct that period. As Moreh notes in the introduction to his edition, al-Jabartī had no respect for the language of chronicles written by soldiers whose Arabic was not that of scholars. Moreh and other researchers pointed out that al-Jabartī did use the information he found in these writings, despite denying having done so. The most important of these sources was *Kitāb al-durra al-muṣāna fī akhbār al-kināna* (The book of the well-preserved pearl regarding the events in Egypt) by Aḥmad al-Damurdāshī (d. approximately 1756).[2] Other chronicles written in non-literary language and authored by soldiers including Musṭafā al-Qinālī and al-Farrāʾ were used by al-Jabartī in his chronicles of the mid-eighteenth century.

An interesting and important chronicle entitled *awḍaḥ al-ishārāt fī man tawallā Miṣr al-Qāhira min al-wuzarāʾ waʾl-bāshāt* (The clearest signs regarding ministers and pashas who governed Egypt) was written by al-Azhar scholar Aḥmad Shalabī (Çelebi) b. ʿAbd al-Ghanī. It covers the history of Egypt from the Ottoman conquest until 1737. Al-Jabartī relied heavily on this work, while claiming, "One of my friends borrowed it from me, but has not returned it. It must be considered as lost."[3]

There is no doubt that concealment of sources by an important historian is strange and embarrassing. It shows that even great men can have weaknesses.

As Moreh says, a large part of the second volume and the third and fourth parts of the chronicle are a great historiographical achievement. Al-Jabartī presented a panorama of persons, institutions, and dramatic events that had

---

2 Aḥmad al-Damurdāshī, *Kitāb al-Durra al-muṣāna fī akhbār al-kināna: fī akhbār mā waqaʿa bi-Miṣr fī dawlat al-Mamālīk*, edited by ʿAbd al-Raḥīm ʿAbd al-Raḥmān ʿAbd al-Raḥīm (Cairo: al-Maʿhad al-ʿIlmī al-Faransī liʾl-Āthār al-Sharqiyya, 1989).

3 Aḥmad Shalabī b. ʿAbd al-Ghanī, *Awḍaḥ al-ishārāt fī man tawallā Miṣr al-Qāhira min al-wuzarāʾ waʾl-bāshāt: al-mulaqqab bil-taʾrīkh al-ʿaynī*, edited by ʿAbd al-Raḥīm ʿAbd al-Raḥmān ʿAbd al-Raḥīm (Cairo: Maktabat al-Khānjī, 1978).

never been seen in Egypt. He understood the immensity of the French occupation and predicted that it was the beginning of an entirely new era.[4]

This paper aims at presenting the Sufi personality of al-Jabartī: how he regarded the movement as it was in his time, and which aspects he supported and what he opposed and despised. First, I will briefly review the development of Sufism in Ottoman Egypt until al-Jabartī's days.

2 Sufism in the Early Ottoman Rule: ʿAbd al-Wahhāb al-Shaʿrānī and Zakariyyā al-Anṣārī

Generally, Sufism in Egypt was leaning to Orthodoxy, meaning that it was faithful to orthodoxy and sharīʿa law, and that its mysticism was not far from the main approach of Muslim theology. In Egypt, as in other Muslim countries, there were movements and organizations that did not adhere to moral religious law and the practices of the shariʿa. Such movements were not recognized as Sufi at all. In the Turkish- or Persian-speaking regions, mystical movements were distant from normative Islam. The best example is the Bektāshiyya. Interestingly, the Mevleviyya or Khalwatiyya orders were considered orthodox in Istanbul, but not in Cairo.

The most important writer in sixteenth-century Egypt was a Sufi shaykh named ʿAbd al-Wahhāb al-Shaʿrānī (d. 973/1565),[5] who lived during the reign of Sultan Süleyman the Magnificent (*Kanuni*, the Lawgiver). His many writings represent Egyptian Sufism—orthodox, cautious, and moderate. He shows sincere concern for the common people. Like other Sufis of his milieu, al-Shaʿrānī struggled on two fronts: On the one hand, he was a scholar and attacked ignorant dervishes. He accused them of disrespecting the principles of the shariʿa and the ʿulama'. On the other hand, he condemned the ʿulama', especially the *fuqahā'* (jurisconsults), for their barren learning and for their lack of spiritual and moral dimensions, which only Sufism could provide.

Al-Shaʿrānī lived in a large Sufi *zāwiya* that was used for dwelling, prayer, and Sufi exercise. He was critical of al-Azhar, the great mosque-*madrasa*. He

4 Shmuel Moreh, *The Egyptian Historian ʿAbd al-Raḥmān al-Jabartī: His Works, Autographs, Manuscripts and the Historical Sources of ʿAjāʾib al-Āthār* (Oxford: Oxford University Press, 2014), 46.

5 Michael Winter, *Society and Religion in Early Ottoman Egypt: Studies in the Writings of ʿAbd al-Wahhab al-Shaʿrani* (Transaction: New Brunswick and London, 1982; paperback printing, 2007).

vehemently accused the ʿulamaʾ of neglecting the simple Muslims' religious needs and wasting time in debating among themselves judicial matters that had nothing to do with the essence of religion. Yet, as a young man, he had received an excellent Islamic education from Zakariyyā al-Anṣārī (d. 926/1520), the greatest teacher at the time. Al-Shaʿrānī was his student, assistant, and associate. Al-Anṣārī was the author of important works on religious subjects, and was committed to Azhari scholarship, as well as to Sufism. He also served as chief Shāfiʿī *qadi* for many years.

In 874/1469, there was a theological debate about ʿUmar b. al-Fāriḍ, the famous Egyptian mystic poet who lived in the thirteenth century. He was accused of *ḥulūl*, the belief in the fusion of the divine with creatures and people. Al-Biqāʿī, a Syrian scholar who was involved in such theological debates, led the attack against Ibn al-Fāriḍ. This was not a wise move, since the poet was an Egyptian icon who numbered among his defenders Sultan Qāyitbāy himself, along with several powerful emirs. Owing to his prestige, Zakariyyā al-Anṣārī was asked to write a *fatwā* about the poet and his ideas. At first, he tried to dodge the issue, since he was reluctant to attack a fellow *ʿālim*. Finally, having received supernatural hints, including a meeting with the ghost of the poet, he agreed. The essence of the *fatwā* was not original: only those who were experts in the terminology of the Sufis were qualified to judge their words and belief. Al-Biqāʿī escaped to Syria to avoid the wrath of the sultan.[6]

Ibn al-Fāriḍ was the contemporary of Muḥyīʾ al-Dīn b. ʿArabī, called *al-Shaykh al-Akbar* by his admirers. He was a great Arab mystic but was controversial and even accused of heresy. His doctrines of *waḥdat al-wujūd*, "the unity of existence," not distinguishing between God and his creatures, were more popular among the Turks than among the more legally minded Arabs—obviously with famous exceptions on both sides. The Ottoman sultans adopted the doctrines and writings of Ibn ʿArabī with a *fatwā* of Sultan Süleyman's *Şeyhülislâm*. Among the supporters of Ibn ʿArabī was ʿAbd al-Wahhāb al-Shaʿrānī, who was cautious and moderate and found an apologetic way to interpret the former's sayings favorably. We will return to Ibn ʿArabī when discussing al-Jabartī's Sufi attitudes.

6 Matthew B. Ingalls, *Subtle Innovation within Networks of Convention: The Life, Thought, and Intellectual Legacy of Zakariyyā al-Anṣārī (d. 926/1520)* (Ph.D. dissertation; Yale University, 2011), 71–76.

3 Muḥammad b. Abī al-Surūr al-Bakrī al-Ṣiddīqī: A Sufi Historian

Muḥammad b. Abī al-Surūr al-Bakrī al-Ṣiddīqī (d. 1676) was the most important chronicler of Egypt in the seventeenth century.[7] He belonged to a family of ʿulamaʾ and Sufis who were active in Egypt's religious and public life between the fifteenth and mid-twentieth centuries. The family was wealthy and aristocratic and maintained good relations with Ottoman representatives in Egypt. Hence al-Ṣiddīqī's enthusiastic support of the empire. By comparison, the timid al-Shaʿrānī only hinted at his disapproval of the Ottomans in his writings.

The Bakrī family claimed its origins from Abu Bakr al-Siddīq, the first caliph of Islam, and Ḥasan b. ʿAlī b. Abī Ṭālib, thus maintaining that they were *ashrāf*. In his history of the Ottoman Empire, from its rise until his own time, Ibn Abī al-Surūr enthusiastically praises the Ottomans. Naturally, he focuses on Egypt under Ottoman rule. He extols all the sultans, even Selim I the Grim, destroyer of Mamluk Egypt, whom Ibn Ṭūlūn and especially Ibn Iyās—eyewitnesses to the conquest of Syria and Cairo—painted in negative colors. Ibn Abī al-Surūr mentioned as good deeds the fact that Selim repaired the tomb of Ibn ʿArabī in Damascus and built a mosque and a *takiyya* next to it. Nevertheless, the majority of Arabs—remarkably the orthodox people of Damascus, where he was buried—rejected the great mystic's doctrines. On the other hand, most Turks believed in Ibn ʿArabī. The chief mufti of Kanuni Süleyman, Selim's son and successor, made it official by issuing a famous *fatwā*. The apologetic attitude towards defending the Ottomans against accusations of accepting saints of the past is also reflected in his mention of Hacı Bektaş, who later became the patron of the Janissaries. Ibn Abī al-Surūr wrote: "His tomb protects Muslims who were about to go on the *ḥājj*," adding, "In our days, several miscreants falsely attribute to him things that he is innocent of."[8]

All the sultans are presented as just and benign, but distant, figures. Selim I was the only sultan who went to Egypt. Ibn Abī al-Surūr divided his chronicle by the terms of the Ottoman governors, or viceroys, in Egypt. He met most of them personally and described their rule, with some exceptions, as just because they punished robbers and other criminals as well as religious individuals, some known by religious titles.[9]

7 Abdul-Karim Rafeq, "Ibn Abi al-Surur and His Works," *BSOAS* 38 (1975): 23–31; Muḥammad b. Muḥammad b. Abī al-Surūr, *al-Minaḥ al-raḥmānīyya fi'l-dawla al-ʿUthmāniyya*, edited by Laylā al-Ṣabbāgh (Damascus: Dār al-Bashāʾir, 1995).

8 Ibn Abī al-Surūr, *al-Minaḥ al-raḥmānīyya*.

9 Michael Winter, "The Islamic Profile and the Religious Policy of the Ruling Class in Ottoman Egypt," *Israel Oriental Studies* 10 (1980): 138–140.

By tradition and family connections, Ibn Abī al-Surūr was a believing Sufi. Yet, as far as we know, he did not write much about Sufism, unlike al-Shaʿrānī or the Syrian ʿAbd al-Ghanī al-Nābulusī (1641–1731). He reported some stories of miracles (*karāmāt*) that had happened in his family but that he had personally never experienced. On the other hand, al-Shaʿrānī wrote a lengthy book on miracles that had happened to him and also authored commentaries on Sufism, even on some difficult texts of Ibn al-ʿArabi.[10]

4 Sufi Families in the Position of *Naqīb al-Ashrāf*

The Bakrīs were considered descendants of the Prophet, and thus *ashrāf*. The *ashrāf* in Egypt, as in other Muslim countries, enjoyed certain social and financial privileges. Their chief was called *Naqīb al-Ashrāf*. Like other high office holders, he was appointed from Istanbul. He was in charge of the lists of *ashrāf* and took care that people who could not prove their ties to the house of the Prophet should not be included.

Toward the late seventeenth century, the office of *Naqīb al-Ashrāf* was transferred to local families of notables. These were the Bakrīs, the family of Abī al-Surūr al-Bakrī al-Siddīqī, the historian mentioned above. The second *ashrāf* family was al-Sādāt al-Wafāʾiyya, also aristocratic Sufis, who descended from Ḥasan b. ʿAlī. The Wafāʾis was a branch of the Shādhiliyya *ṭarīqa* that originated in North Africa. The order, which refrained from asceticism, was famous for its wealth, poets, and pompous gathering feasts where musical instruments were played and elegant clothes were worn—to the displeasure of the orthodox.

The Bakrīs were in charge of organizing the *mawlid al-nabī*, the Prophet's birthday, and the Wafāʾīs organized the *mawlid al-Ḥusayn*. The chief of the Wafāʾiyya was the rival of Shaykh al-Bakrī, although the latter usually enjoyed a higher religious and social position. The rivalry between the two houses was over the position of *Naqīb al-Ashrāf*.

It is important to mention that only when the *niqāba* passed to distinguished Egyptian families did the post become important in Egyptian public life, as al-Jabartī's descriptions prove. Historians before him had hardly mentioned the *nuqabāʾ* when they were Ottoman-appointed officials. This arrangement

10 ʿAbd-Wahhāb b. Aḥmad al-Shaʿrānī, *Laṭāʾif al-minan wa'l-akhlāq fī wujūb al-taḥadduth bi-niʿmat Allāh ʿalā al-iṭlāq, al-maʿrūf bi'l-Minan al-kubrā* (Cairo: ʿĀlam al-Fikr, 1976); ʿAbd al-Wahhāb b. Aḥmad al-Shaʿrānī, *Mukhtaṣar al-Futūḥāt al-Makkiyya, al-musammā Lawāqiḥ al-anwār al-Qudusiyya al-muntaqāt min al-futūḥāt al-Makkiyya*, edited by Muḥammad ʿAbd al-Qādir Naṣṣār (Cairo: Dār al-Iḥsān, 2016).

continued until the mid-twentieth century. There was a short interval when ʿUmar Makram received the *niqāba*. He was a strong and honest leader but was neither Sufi nor *ʿālim*. He acted as a tribune and led the people against oppression, especially the tyranny of Muḥammad ʿAlī. Al-Jabartī wrote of him with much admiration, which he indeed deserved.

As Muḥammad ʿAlī became the ruler of Egypt, the power of the *Naqīb al-Ashrāf* extended to *Shaykh mashāyikh al-ṭuruq al-ṣūfiyya*, the supreme shaykh of the Sufi *ṭarīqas*; that position was an innovation, since *niqābat al-ashrāf* had previously not been associated with Sufism. This link was formed only when the houses of al-Bakrī and al-Sādāt al-Wafāʾiyya were appointed to that post.

5 ʿAbd al-Ghanī al-Nābulusī and al-Azhar: Defending Sufism in Egypt

ʿAbd al-Ghanī al-Nābulusī (1641–1731) of Damascus was arguably the greatest Sufi shaykh in Ottoman Syria.[11] He was an original scholar who wrote many works on multiple topics. He was a true humanist and was a member of the Naqshbandi *ṭarīqa* that was widespread in central Asia and Anatolia but not popular in the Arab world. In the seventeenth century, there rose in the capital of the empire an influential anti-Sufi movement called Kadizadeli. Al-Nābulusī did not regard his mission as the propagator of the Naqshabandiyya but as the defender of all Sufi orders. He was a traveler and wrote descriptions, in particular of religious figures, institutions, and rites. His longest travelogue was entitled *al-Ḥaqīqa wa'l-majāz fi'l-riḥla ilā al-Shām wa-Miṣr wa'l-Ḥijāz* (The real and the imaginary regarding the travel to the Sham, Egypt, and the Hijaz).[12] He stayed for a long time in Egypt, visiting saints' tombs and meeting with ʿulamaʾ and Sufis. He described in a lively manner the Sufi rituals of the *dhikr*. Al-Nābulusī mentioned various *ṭarīqas*, all of them Arab and mostly definitely not orthodox. Yet, he joined some of the *dhikr* circles. He referred to three Turkish orders as follows: "We have seen in Egypt members of the Khalwatiyya, the Damurdāshiyya, and the order of Karīm al-Din al-Khalwatī.

11 The literature on al-Nābulusī is rich. See: Barbara Von Schlegell, *Sufism in the Ottoman Arab World: Shaykh ʿAbd al-Ghanī al-Nābulusī (d. 1143/1731)* (Ph.D. dissertation; Berkeley: University of California, 1997); Samer Akkach, *Letters of a Sufi Scholar: The Correspondence of ʿAbd al-Ghanī al-Nābulusī (1641–1731)* (Leiden-Boston: Brill, 2010).

12 ʿAbd al-Ghanī al-Nābulusī, *al-Ḥaqīqa wa'l-majāz fi'l-riḥla ilā al-Shām wa-Miṣr wa'l-Ḥijāz*, edited by Aḥmad ʿAbd al-Majīd Harīdī (Cairo: al-Hayʾa al-Miṣriyya al-ʿĀmma li'l-Kitāb, 1986).

They pronounce the sublime name (God's name) in a perfect way. Anyone who attributes to them infidelity is himself an infidel."[13]

It is important to mention that al-Nābulusī was an enthusiastic advocate of the mystical doctrine of Ibn ʿArabī and wrote commentaries on his writings and polemics against his adversaries.

6 The *Fitna* (Riot) of 1711

In Ramadan 1123 (October 1711), a violent anti-Sufi riot broke out in Cairo between Turks, who had been incited by a fundamentalist sermonizer, and Egyptian Sufis. The event was reported by Arab and Turkish chroniclers.[14] The crisis reveals ethnic tensions reflected in the attitudes towards Sufism of Turks who lived in Cairo and of the local Arab people. The preacher was called *softa* (a student of religion) in Turkish and *al-wāʿiẓ al-Rūmī* (the Turkish preacher) in Arabic. He did not speak only about Egyptian beliefs, institutions, and customs, but also about those that were common among the Turks. Wielding swords and cudgels, the Turkish mob attacked the Sufis who were practicing the *dhikr* at Bāb Zuwayla. Among the sweeping demands the preacher made was that dervish cloisters, such as the Gülşenî, Mevlevî, and the Bektaşi, be converted into *madrasas*, and that the Sufis be ejected. It is remarkable that in front of a Turkish audience in Cairo, the preacher attacked the very institutions that symbolized, more than any others, Turkish and Ottoman Sufism.

The Sufis called for the support of the ʿulamaʾ of al-Azhar, which the latter gave, just as they had seventeen years earlier. The preacher showed disrespect towards "Arab shaykhs," and the Egyptians spoke of "the rude and ignorant Turks." Since the crisis became an issue of law and order, the Mamluks drove away the preacher and punished the rioters.[15]

The *fitna* should caution us against ethnic generalizations and stereotypes. When the Turks attacked the Egyptian Sufis, they received the support of the orthodox ʿulamaʾ. The preacher's name remains unfamiliar, but it is known that he was influenced by the ideas of Birgivî Mehmet (d. 981/1573) and his followers in the Kadizadeli movement. By 1711, the movement had been suppressed by

---

13 Akkach, *Letters of a Sufi Scholar*. Karīm al-Din al-Khalwatī was the chief of the Khalwatiyya in the sixteenth century.

14 Al-Jabartī, *ʿAjāʾib al-āthār*, 1: 48–50; Michael Winter, *Egyptian Society under Ottoman Rule, 1517–1798* (London and New York: Routledge, 1992), 157–159.

15 Al-Jabartī, *ʿAjāʾib al-āthār*, 1: 48–50; Winter, *Egyptian Society*, 157–159.

the Ottoman Empire. It seems that the *fitna* was an aftershock of the Kadizadeli, but it can also be regarded as a forerunner of the Wahhabi movement.[16]

7 The Reformed Khalwatiyya Order in the Eighteenth Century

The most important development in Egyptian Sufism of the eighteenth century was the rise of the reformed Khalwatiyya order. As was mentioned above, the early Khalwatiyya that al-Shaʿrānī encountered was non-orthodox in its doctrines and in the ascetic regime that it forced on its novices. The doctrine of Ibn ʿArabī played a significant role in their education. It was difficult to attack the great mystic while Ottoman power was at its peak, and Sultans Selim I and Kanuni Süleyman supported the maintenance of his sepulcher in Damascus, as well as the complex that was built on it, and formally accepted his mystical theory.

The reformed Khalwatiyya turned into a perfectly orthodox movement, and the *ṭarīqa* became both respectable and popular among the ʿulamaʾ of al-Azhar. Almost all the ʿulamaʾ who served as Shaykhs al-Azhar in the eighteenth century were also practicing Khalwatīs. Al-Jabartī described the development and beliefs of the Khalwatiyya in detail.[17] Whether he relied on previous sources, or described the events and the personalities that he saw himself, he remained an enthusiastic adherent of the order. The orthodox-reformed Sufism that appeared in the Muslim world was represented in this *ṭarīqa*. Ottoman power weakened in some regions, including Egypt, and al-Jabartī and others allowed themselves the freedom to express their own opinions. Though the sultans themselves could not be criticized, expressions of censure against the Turks' behavior and beliefs were often strong and unrestrained.

Al-Jabartī was a devout Muslim and he praised the Khalwatiyya branch which he himself had joined, and which was called Karābāshiyya after the Turkish Shaykh who had founded it. Al-Jabartī quotes, in full agreement, the words of another Sufi: "It [this *ṭarīqa*] is an order which is buttressed by the noble shariʿa and the true religion. It does not impose (upon the devotees) anything unbearable. It is the best of the orders, since its specific *dhikr* is *lā ilāha illā Allāh* which, according to the noble Ḥadīth, is the best thing that a man can utter."[18]

---

16 The expression was suggested by Barbara Flemming, "Die vorwahhabische Fitna im osmanischen Kairo, 1711," *Ismail Hakki Uzunçarşil'ya Armaâan* (Ankara, 1976): 55–65.

17 Al-Jabartī, *ʿAjāʾib al-āthār*, 1: 294–304.

18 Ibid., 295.

The shaykh who instilled the new Khalwatiyya in Egypt was a Sufi from Damascus, Muṣṭafā b. Kamāl al-Dīn al-Bakrī (d. 1749), not related to the Egyptian Bakrīs. He traveled often to Egypt and authored many treatises and litanies. His close disciple, whom he appointed as his *khalīfa*, was Muḥammad b. Salīm al-Ḥifnī, or al-Ḥifnāwī (d. 1767), a distinguished scholar who was eventually Shaykh al-Azhar. He was strict and found it hard to admit new novices into the order. However, al-Bakrī ordered that all applicants be accepted, even women and Christians. According to hearsay, many of them eventually converted to Islam. He was seen as a saint endowed by moral and supernatural qualities. The Ottoman governor, Ragıp Paşa, said that as long as al-Ḥifnī lived, the country would remain peaceful and enjoy justice. Indeed, al-Hifni prevented the emirs from starting unnecessary battles. Nevertheless, he was poisoned. Al-Jabartī reported that the system had collapsed and had brought to power ʿAli Bey al-Kabīr, whom the ʿulamaʾ hated.[19]

8 Al-Jabartī's Attitude to Other Orders

Al-Jabartī greatly admired the Khalwatiyya, but he wrote biographies of members of other orders as well. One of the most active orders was al-Aḥmadiyya, named after al-Sayyid Aḥmad al-Badawī, a North African mystic who immigrated to Egypt in the thirteenth century. His sepulcher is in Tanta in the Delta and, on his saint's day (*mawlid*), is a destination for pilgrims. The *mawlid*—celebrated according to the Coptic (solar) calendar and not by the Muslim (lunar) one—was, and still is, a most popular public event in Egypt. Also other Egyptian *mawlid*s are set by the solar calendar. The devotees used to exercise the *dhikr* and ask for blessings from the saint. The ʿulamaʾ denounced the behavior of people during the *mawlid*s, especially the mingling of women and men, which at times led to sexual licentiousness. Al-Jabartī agreed with the ʿulamaʾ, but he himself visited Tanta and, while adoring the saint, did not admire his ignorant devotees. In other cases, he expressed his admiration for an *ʿālim* or a Sufi but denounced the circumstances in which interested parties, sometimes members of that saint's family, established a *mawlid* in his honor.

While criticizing the improper habits of the Egyptian Sufis, al-Jabartī vehemently attacked the Sufism of the Turks of Cairo, which he regarded as strange and blameworthy. He wrote several times: "The [Turks) are inclined to this kind of *dervishism*, which is Sufism without shariʿa." Among others, he wrote of a Sufi from Ṭāʾif who had come to Cairo: "He believes in *ḥulūl* and *ittiḥād*, the

19 Ibid., 302–304.

mystical theories of Ibn al-Fāriḍ and Ibn ʿArabī. Our Maghrebi masters [!] do not accept these things, since they adhere to the external meaning of the shariʿa. Yet the Turks (*ahl al-Rūm*) strongly believe in this Sufi and his doctrines."[20]

Al-Jabartī despised the Turkish dervishes of Cairo. He reported their roguery and tricks to control Sufi institutions, such as a Bektaşi *tekke* (or *takiyya*, Sufi center), and the case of an ignorant crook who tried to be appointed *Naqīb al-Ashrāf*. According to him, these swindlers frequently took advantage of the religious inclinations of the Ottoman governor.

The creation of Shaykh al-Sharqāwī's *mawlid* is an example of how a *mawlid* can be created through corrupt practices. ʿAbd Allāh b. al-Ḥijāzī al-Shāfiʿī al-Azharī al-Sharqāwī was an important scholar who was born in a small village in the Sharqiyya province and moved to the Azhar to study. When he wanted to join the Khalwatiyya, Shaykh al-Ḥifnī taught him the "first name" (of Allah). As a result, he lost his sanity and spent some time in a mental hospital. When his health improved, he returned to the *ṭarīqa* to live as an ascetic. His disciples and admirers sent him food and money and spent the nights performing *dhikr* and emitting religious cries. Eventually, his situation improved. Later, he was appointed Shaykh al-Azhar.[21]

However, al-Sharqāwī became greedy and bought a big house near al-Azhar. His wife, a Shaykh's daughter, took complete charge of the household, so that he did not move without her permission. She became wealthy by purchasing land, houses, shops, and bathhouses. They arranged a magnificent wedding for their son, to which the Ottoman governor contributed a generous sum of money. The shaykh established a *zāwiya* and had a tomb with a copula built for himself. Next to it was a large structure, which in the days of the Mamluks had been used as a *khānqāh*, a hostel for Sufis, and which had been renovated by the shaykh. When al-Jabartī visited the place, he was impressed by its beauty and size. However, there was an influx of residents, office holders, and maintenance personnel, which al-Jabartī considered to be outrageously wasteful. He thought that instead of these luxuries, al-Sharqāwī should have bequeathed his many biographies of Shāfiʿī scholars and his history books about recent events to his readers.

During the French occupation, al-Sharqāwī was appointed head of the *Dīwān* to act as an arbitrator for the Muslims. He became rich thanks to his high salary, and took control of estates of inheritance. After al-Sharqāwī's death (d. 1812), a guard was stationed at the sepulcher and called people to enter the *maqṣūra*, charging them an entrance fee. Then al-Sharqāwī's widow, his son,

20 Al-Jabartī, *ʿAjāʾib al-āthār*, 2: 237.

21 Ibid., 4: 159–163.

and their protégés introduced a false innovation (*bidʿa*) and named it a *mawlid*, coinciding with the *mawlid al-ʿAfīfī* which al-Jabartī regarded as objectionable. They obtained a decree from the Ottoman governor ordering the people of the town to attend the *mawlid*. Notables, too, were invited. Food was prepared and sweetmeats and drinks were served to the ʿulamaʾ and the shaykhs. The *mawlid* took place in cemeteries that soon became desecrated, and the whole event turned into a vulgar festival, with bonfires and much commotion.

Among the participants in the *mawlid* was the Maghribī ʿĪsawiyya group, which was infamous for its use of corrupt language. They beat drums and were noisily stamping their feet. Many more groups participated, each with its own rites. They ate inside the mosque, soiling it. The author added that the worst part was when the processions of dervishes arrived from the quarters. They carried candleholders, drums, and wind instruments. They chanted, using impure language and convincing themselves that this was *dhikr* and that God would reward them. Most of the participants had miserable occupations, and did not even have enough food for the next day. They borrowed money for candles and to pay drummers and other musicians. Those who joined them were all riffraff (*ḥarāfīsh*). They spend the nights sleepless and woke, dizzy and lazy, fooling themselves that they had served their God.

In his biography of Aḥmad b. Aḥmad al-Samālījī al-Shāfiʿī al-Aḥmadi (d. 1788), al-Jabartī described him as a jurist (*faqīh*), a great scholar (*ʿallāma*), a just man (*ṣāliḥ*), and Sufi Aḥmadī. He was a teacher in the tomb of the saint (*maqām*) al-Aḥmadī in Tanta. It was in the village of Samālīj in al-Manūfiyya, where he was born, that he memorized the Qurʾan. Later on, he moved to Cairo to study with several shaykhs. Then he went to Tanta, where he made his home. He taught and helped numerous students, issued *fatwās* and passed judgment on behalf of litigants who lived in the town. His name became famous as his legal opinion was widely respected. People came in droves to meet him.

From this short biography one can see that the shaykh was an orthodox Sunni, as well as a devoted practicing Sufi of the Aḥmadī order. Still, al-Jabartī counted that order as one of the blameworthy *ṭarīqa*s (the same duality is seen in the writings of al-Shaʿrānī). Finally, what is rather unusual in this biography is that the person described was the historian's personal friend and that he maintained close ties to the friend's family.[22]

---

22 Ibid., 2: 260.

9 Abū al-Anwār *khalīfa* of *al-Sajjāda al-Wafāʾiyya*: A Learned, Domineering, and Corrupt Sufi

9.1 *Rise to Office*

Al-Jabartī wrote an unusually long obituary of Muḥammad Abū al-Anwār al-Sādāt, the *khalīfa* of the *al-Sajjāda al-Wafāʾiyya*.[23] He was perhaps the most interesting Wafāʾī Shaykh, if not the most likable. The historian revealed many aspects of Egyptian society, pointing out how an ambitious and grasping individual could exploit his position as an influential Sufi shaykh. His claim to the position of *Shaykh al-Wafāʾiyya* was not strong, since he was a Wafāʾī only on his mother's side. When the male line of the family became extinct, he was quick to wear the *tāj*, the headgear of the order, to marry the mother of the deceased shaykh and to move into a house adjacent to the palace of the Wafāʾī *khalīfa*. He waited six more years until the death of his rival, who had been appointed to the post, and then, in 1082/1672, he rode with Shaykh al-Bakrī and the other Sufi shaykhs to the *khalwa ribāṭ* (Sufi center). Having performed the required religious ceremonies, he was invested by ʿAlī Bey, the de facto ruler of Cairo, with a robe of honor, and was appointed Wafāʾī *khalīfa*. He was more suited to the post than his brother Shaykh Yūsuf, although he was younger.

9.2 *The Scholar*

Abū al-Anwār did not neglect his role as a patron of learning and culture. He purchased many books for his library and invited ʿulamaʾ and poets who praised and flattered him, hoping to receive his gifts and to meet the emirs and notables who frequented his house. He studied with many teachers and Sufi shaykhs, and became a serious scholar and writer of books and commentaries. He was awarded many *ijāzāt* (personal diplomas granted by his teachers). While his masters belonged to various *madhhab*s, he himself was a Shāfiʿī.

Abū al-Anwār knew how to behave cleverly, with due modesty and politeness, toward shaykhs, colleagues, and notables. He adhered to the correct way of behavior, avoiding things that could harm their sense of honor. He kept busy reading, discussing religious and literary matters, and seeking the company of learned men, while lightening the time with anecdotes.

---

23 Ibid., 4: 185–195. In his opening sentence, he used superlatives such as the great scholar, the famous, the brilliant, the unique in his time. As will be seen, al-Jabartī used these words sarcastically. True, he was gifted and strong, but as al-Jabartī claimed, the shaykh was also selfish and cruel.

9.3 *The Corrupt Administrator*

Abū al-Anwār exploited his family's immense wealth. Al-Jabartī reports that their mansion resembled an emir's palace: it was elegant, had servants and gardens, and was spacious enough to entertain large numbers of guests.

Abū al-Anwār's treatment of his tenants was extremely cruel, worse than that of other *multazims*. He would add to their tax burden and had them arrested for months and whipped. He also cheated Shaykh al-Bakrī out of his trusteeship of the Ḥusayni shrine. The two had agreed to exchange the trusteeship of the Ḥusayni and al-Imām al-Shāfiʿī shrines, but according to al-Jabartī, Abū al-Anwār ended up keeping both positions. In addition, he got hold of other revenue-yielding trusteeships of the sepulchers of the holiest and most famous saints. In order to increase his prestige and income from *mawlid* al-Ḥusayn, he ordered the police to force shopkeepers to open their businesses at night and to light lamps throughout the fifteen nights of the *mawlid*, instead of only one night, as before. Over the years, he devoted all his efforts to amassing money, slave girls, and eunuchs. As he became richer and more powerful, he no longer condescended to participate in the religious ceremonies at al-Azhar, or even at the Wafāʾī center, but dressed like an emir rather than a man of religion, abandoning the *tāj* Sufi cup for a *qāwūq* (a kind of high felt hat) topped by a green turban that indicated a *sharīfi* origin.

The shaykh gained the post of administrator of religious endowments (*nāẓir*), including the shrines of Nafīsa and Zaynab (two famous holy women of *ahl al-bayt*); both had mosques in Cairo and other shrines that produced much income as people visited them, bringing sacrifices and votive offerings. The shaykh used to rob them of their income, and have their feet lashed with palm branches.

As a result, other keepers of shrines were afraid of him. He demanded all the incomes and goods they had accumulated. Fleecing keepers of shrines that were not wealthy, he contrived methods to humiliate and harm them and even personally arrested some of them. His hand also reached the notaries of the *qadi*'s house, interfering in their legal decisions regarding real estate about tombs or *waqf*, so that they now supported his interests. After our protagonist took control of Ḥusayn's shrine, he subdued al-Sayyid al-Badawī, the administrator of the shrine, taking his house, and evicting him. He destroyed the house and rebuilt it to use himself during the regular *mawlid* days.

Unwelcome innovations for these *mawlid* celebrations were introduced: processions of rabble playing drums and wind instruments and carrying torches. They belonged to lowly orders, like al-Aḥmadiyya and al-Saʿdiyya;

beat their drums while emitting flawed sounds; and gave repulsive titles to the shaykhs of their own orders.

Al-Jabartī went on with his descriptions of how the shaykh destroyed and reshaped at will his buildings and places of prayer and devotion. However, it is interesting to note that while no single administrator of a mosque or shrine managed to stop him, a throng of organized worshipers were finally able to oppose his plans—as happened during a struggle between the shaykh and worshipers, many of them Turkish traders from Khān al-Khalīlī and supported by Turkish Sufis, over a fountain or basin for ritual ablution (*mīḍa'a*). The crowd caused a public clamor, closed the gates, and disrupted the prayers. The shaykh abandoned his plan for a new *mīḍa'a* and turned it into a place where donkeys were tied up at a price, to be paid by their owners. The shaykh went on building luxurious houses and gardens. He also had a mosque built for his Friday prayers and a preacher's pulpit (*minbar*), because the communal mosques were too great a distance from his residence and he was reluctant to mingle with the common people. He liked good food and drinks, expensive clothes, perfumes and oils. He was arrogant, considered himself above others of his class, and avoided special prayers at al-Azhar during the night of *al-Miʿrāj*.

In one case, a group of local people and notables assembled at night in a private home to chat. Some of them amused themselves by imitating distinguished persons, but someone reported to Abū al-Anwār that he had been one of the people who had been ridiculed. He ordered all of them be brought to him, and be punished, humiliated, and beaten.

Once he quarreled with the Coptic secretary of *amīr al-balad*. He cursed him and gave him a brutal beating. When the secretary complained to his master, the latter answered: "What do you want me to do with a great shaykh who has beaten a Christian"?[24]

In sum, Abū al-Anwār's conduct lacked all integrity and good faith. He became like a commander of the police. He expected to be addressed with Ḥadīth sayings and exalted expressions. A famous preacher, al-Sayyid Ḥusayn al-Manzilāwī, prepared Friday sermons that the shaykh attended in the Ḥusayni Mashhad and in the *zāwiya* during the *mawlid*. The preacher described the shaykh as one who can unveil mystical things, remove sorrows, and forgive sins. Al-Jabartī reported that he himself had heard someone say cynically after the prayer, "All he needed was to tell the congregation to bow down in prayer to worship Shaykh al-Sādāt!"

24 Al-Jabartī, *ʿAjāʾib al-āthār*, 4: 191.

9.4 *His Social Life*

In the past, Abū al-Anwār had stayed away from the uneducated. Later on, things changed for the worse. His followers sought his company and his feasts, kissed his hands, and praised him in their poems, hoping to achieve fame through him and get acquainted with the emirs and other powerful persons who frequented his home. He became more and more arrogant as his guests flattered him with extreme expressions of humility. When a *mubāshir* (bureaucrat) or a *dhimmī* kissed his hand, he washed it to remove their touch and, refusing to reply with a Muslim greeting, he would only say, "Good, good."[25]

As he became richer and more powerful, he no longer condescended to participate in religious ceremonies at al-Azhar, or even at the Wafā'ī center. At the same time, he concentrated on strengthening his position. He did not pay the clerks their salaries according to the registers, made them feel that they were committing serious offenses, and imposed unjust taxes.

9.5 *Dealing with Rulers*

Al-Jabartī described Abū al-Anwār's skillful adjustment to the changing political conditions in Egypt. As an Ottoman province, Egypt was ruled by pashas who were appointed from Istanbul. Unlike the situation during the early Ottoman rule, when Istanbul held the reins quite firmly, in al-Jabartī's day, the city's influence was limited and the pashas were only symbolic figures. The real rulers were the Mamluks, with some significant hiatuses.

The first official Ottoman delegation mentioned reached Egypt in the years 1776–77, when al-Sādāt received Reisülküttab 'Abd al-Razzāq Efendi, one of the highest-placed Ottoman officials. Abū al-Anwār associated with him, extended invitations to him, and gave him gifts. At the same time, Mehmet Paşa was appointed governor of Egypt. The shaykh requested that his guest ask the pasha to help him restore the *zāwiya* of his ancestors. He invited the pasha to visit their tombs on the day of the regular annual *mawlid*, explaining that it was incumbent upon Muslims to visit the holy place. The shaykh was helped by Muḥammad Murtaḍā al-Zabīdī, the famous grammarian and lexicographer (and author of a dictionary, *Tāj al-'Arūs*), and a scholar of Ḥadīth. He was much respected by the Ottomans. The pasha wrote to the government about the *zāwiya*. Consequently, a decree was issued that fifty purses be taken from the Egyptian treasury to restore the building. The *zāwiya* was embellished with gold and marble. Another request was sent to Istanbul asking for more funds, since the work had been inadequate and a further fifty purses were approved.

---

25 Ibid., 185–195.

Abū al-Anwār built a large complex of houses adjacent to his palace. He also sent his *katkhudā* (chief steward) to the central government with letters asking the authorities to reduce the *mīrī* (government taxes) paid into the *Dīwān* each year by certain villages of his *iltizām*. Al-Jabartī noted that this steward was a swindler and did not forward the dues, but rather embezzled public money.

It is clear that our historian did not blame only the *katkhudā*, but his master too. However, al-Jabartī did not state the obvious, namely that Abū al-Anwār, who pleaded brazenly for funds from the government to restore the ancient *zāwiya* of his ancestors, had sufficient means to develop a big and luxurious real estate project and had the impudence to ask for more.

9.6 *Admiral Hasan Paşa's Intermezzo*

In 1786 the Ottomans attempted to reassert their direct rule in Egypt. This was done by an Ottoman fleet under the command of Admiral Cezayirli Hasan Paşa. At the time, two Mamluk emirs, Ibrâhîm Bey and Murâd Bey, established their control over Egypt. Hasan Paşa, the commander of the expeditionary force, moved to Cairo after defeating the duumvirs, who retreated to Upper Egypt.[26]

The *Dīwān* assembled to promulgate the reforms prepared by Hasan Paşa. The decrees aimed at a strict implementation of Muslim rules regarding Christians and Jews, among others.[27]

During his rule, Hasan Paşa confiscated the property of the evicted grandees. He also ordered that their women and children be seized, sold on the slave market, and their property confiscated for the treasury. Al-Jabartī reports that despite his unscrupulousness and despotism, Abū al-Anwār did not lack courage and was loyal to his friends. When the shaykhs objected to the atrocities that the paşa had committed, Abū al-Anwār said to him: "You have been sent to this land on the sultan's orders to establish justice and fight

---

26 The Ottoman effort, led by Hasan Paşa in 1786, to break the Mamluks' power and reassert direct control over Egypt is described by P.M. Holt, *Egypt and the Fertile Crescent 1916–1922: a Political History* (Ithaca: Cornell University Press, 1975), 99–101. It is very briefly discussed by al-Jabartī, *'Ajā'ib al-āthār*, 4: 188.

27 Similar orders were enforced by Ibrahim, Süleyman's Grand Vizier, in order to enforce order in Egypt. The document declares the Ottomans' intentions to enhance the status of Islam. See Michael Winter, "Egypt and Syria in the Sixteenth Century" in *The Mamluk-Ottoman Transition; Continuity and Change in Egypt and Bilād al-Shām in the Sixteenth Century*, edited by Stephan Conermann and Gül Şen (Bonn: Bonn University Press, 2017), 48–49.

oppression. Selling free women is wrong. Nobody has approved it." Hasan Paşa became angry, and ordered the secretary of his *Dīwān* to report to the sultan the names of those who had disobeyed his orders. Another shaykh said: "You can write whatever you like. We will sign our names ourselves." The paşa kept silent and desisted from his plan. However, he ordered the emirs' goods to be sequestrated. Ibrāhīm Bey left a sum of money for safekeeping with Abū al-Anwār, while Murād Bey left his money with Muḥammad al-Bakrī. Hasan Paşa sent solders to al-Bakrī to confiscate the money, and al-Bakrī handed it over. Conversely, Abū al-Anwār refused to give up Ibrāhīm Bey's money, saying that the owner was still alive, and the shaykh promised in writing not to give it up. The paşa's anger grew, and he was about to hit the shaykh but God protected him because he was upholding the truth. The paşa said: "In all the countries that I visited I have never seen a man who dared disobey my orders like this man; he has broken my heart."[28]

Hasan Paşa could no longer stay in Egypt, since the Ottoman Empire was on the brink of war with Russia, and he had to join the naval forces. The duumvirs resumed their power over Egypt until the invasion of Bonaparte. Murad Bey punished al-Bakri by imposing a heavy fine on him for surrendering his trust and took away his *iqṭā*ʿ (feudal estate). It is said that he had him poisoned.

Owing to Abū al-Anwār's loyalty to Ibrahim Bey, the friendship between them grew. The shaykh's position consolidated even more. Muḥammad al-Bakrī ceded the position of supervisor of Ḥusayn's shrine to him and sent him the registers of the *waqfs*. Al-Jabartī noted that the supervision of the shrine had been an issue for a long time, and that our shaykh had promised al-Bakrī to swap it for the position of al-Shāfiʿī's *waqf*. Yet, when the opportunity presented itself, he took control of the registers of the *awqāf*, since he desired both positions. As always, because he did not encounter any opposition from emirs or from other dignitaries, he sought even more power.

9.7 *The French Conquest*

When the French arrived in Egypt early 1798, they did not interfere with Abū al-Anwār; just the opposite, they respected him, released people who were attached to him, and accepted his intercessions. Their leader and grandees frequently visited his house and he planned banquets for them.

It should be mentioned that soon after entering Cairo in late July, the French commander, Bonaparte himself, asked Shaykh al-Bakrī about the forthcoming

28 Al-Jabartī, *ʿAjāʾib al-āthār*, 4: 188.

mawlid al-Nabī. Al-Bakrī apologized that, owing to the foreign occupation and the ensuing hardships, it could not be celebrated. Bonaparte insisted, however, and contributed a large sum of money. According to al-Jabartī, the Muslim feast became a festive event for the French, with drums, bands and fireworks.[29]

Al-Jabartī chronicled another *mawlid* that had been created during the French occupation. Its emergence was even stranger than that of al-Sharqāwī. A French captain, who was living in Husayn's shrine, ordered the inhabitants of the neighborhoods to keep shops and markets open in order to celebrate Ḥusayn's *mawlid*. He threatened that the doors of those who locked their businesses would be bolted shut and that the owners would be fined.

The initiator was the trustee of the *waqf* of Ḥusayn's mosque, who had fallen ill with a skin disease, probably venereal, and vowed that he would renew the *mawlid*, hoping that God would cure him. He used the *waqf* money, and started to organize the *mawlid*. He put candles and lamps in the mosque, and provided Qur'ans and popular prayer books for the readers. Many fanatics of the "irregular" Sufi orders came to celebrate, fouling the mosque and exhibiting utter disrespect for the site. The attendants took money and candles from the ignorant people, robbing them. This went on for more than ten years. Al-Jabartī pointedly concluded that the founder of the *mawlid* never changed his attitude.[30]

Al-Jabartī also reported that he had visited the residence of the French to see their crafts, paintings, drawings, and other marvelous creations. His impressions of French scientific innovations are famous. What is less known is that he followed Abū al-Anwār during this visit, an indication of the shaykh's standing with the French. This also shows the historian's close relations with him, despite (or because of) his opinion of him.[31]

During the French conquest of Cairo, there was a prolonged popular rebellion in reaction to a series of financial measures. The worst were the property taxes, which were demeaning since they invaded privacy, something even the Ottomans and the Mamluks had not done. Besides, there were also incredibly cruel actions, including executions.[32]

The fighting went on for thirty-six days. The rich had to contribute money to supply the Muslim warriors, since provisions did not arrive from outside. Abū al-Anwār had to contribute, like others, to his district. The French suppressed the uprising and took revenge on those who fought against them by taking their money rather than their lives. They jailed Abū al-Anwār, humiliated him,

29 Ibid., 3: 15.
30 Ibid., *'Ajā'ib al-āthār*, 3: 39.
31 Ibid., 4: 192.
32 Holt, *Egypt and the Fertile Crescent*, 157–158.

and demanded large sums of money. He blamed the oppressive rule of several emirs for causing this catastrophe with the French. When the Ottomans returned to Egypt with the help of the English, they put him in the Citadel, together with several other distinguished personalities, to prevent them from fomenting discord in town.

Finally, the French left Egypt, and Vizier Yūsuf Pasha took over control. Abū al-Anwār approached him to complain that he had been reduced to poverty by the French. The truth was that they had treated him better than they did other notables. The vizier and state officials, who had authority to organize events, were invited to his house. He returned to his previous arrogance and haughtiness. The vizier left the country after installing Hüsrev Paşa as the viceroy of Egypt. A struggle developed between his forces and the Mamluks, who had again established themselves in Upper Egypt. The advent of Muḥammad ʿAlī followed the anarchy resulting from the withdrawal of the French from Egypt. He was assisted by the people of Cairo and by ʿUmar Makram, *Naqīb al-Ashrāf*. For a while, he was a formidable *naqīb* and a popular tribune. He was neither Sufi nor *ʿālim* and earned his position thanks to powerful Mamluk emirs. Muḥammad ʿAlī rightly considered him to be too independent and exiled him from Cairo. Abū al-Anwār wanted the *niqāba* for himself, claiming that the office belonged to his family. He even managed to receive an appointment to this position from Istanbul but concealed it until the situation in Cairo was clarified.

He organized a petition to Istanbul against ʿUmar Makram, falsely accusing him of deleting names of *Ashrāf* from the register, replacing them with names of Copts, and giving them the salaries of the true *ashrāf*. The former *naqīb* was accused of plotting against the government and encouraging the English to attack Egypt. Other important ʿulamaʾ added their signatures to the petition. Only one honest mufti refused; according to al-Jabartī, he was dismissed from his office.[33]

Abū al-Anwār died in 1813. He was buried in the Qarāfa cemetery in a grave that he himself had prepared.[34]

33 Al-Jabartī, *ʿAjāʾib al-āthār*, 4: 194.

34 Ibid., 194–195.

10 The Transition to Abū al-Iqbāl, the Successor[35]

Abū al-Anwār was succeeded as *Shaykh al-Sajjāda al-Wafā'iyya* by his nephew, Aḥmad b. Yūsuf, his agnatic relative, who received the agnomen (*kunya*) Abū al-Iqbāl. Wearing the robe and the *tāj* (crown, a Sufi headgear), he rode to Muḥammad 'Alī Pasha to receive his approval. In the morning, he went to the *ribāṭ* where there was a *zāwiya*. The *ribāṭ* included an old *khalwa* in which the founding father of the order stayed a while upon his arrival from the Maghreb to Egypt. It became a tradition for everyone who assumed the rank of shaykh to enter the *khalwa* in the morning and stay there for a short while, to be inspired by the sanctity of his vocation. However, Abū al-Anwār had destroyed the wall of the *khalwa*, claiming that he was the "last of the saints" and that no one would ever be as fit as himself. Al-Jabartī noted sarcastically that he probably had a treaty and a pact for his special merits.

As the new *Shaykh al-Sajjāda al-Wafā'iyya* wanted to follow the old traditions, he entered the *khalwa*, followed by the greatest shaykhs and the members of the *ḥizb* (lit. a religious fraternity), and read parts of the holy texts. The people with him, including the personnel of the *Niqābat al-Ashrāf*, replaced the wall Abū al-Anwār had demolished with a screen. Afterwards, Abū al-Iqbāl moved with his relatives to the family house, to pray together according to the custom.

Muḥammad 'Alī Pasha sent a Katkhuda and some aides to seal the money safe. They seized the Coptic treasurer and house servants in order to find the hiding place of the valuables. Representatives of the family and well-known shaykhs went to the Citadel to plead for better treatment of the shaykhs' houses. They argued that the deceased had held a very high position with the rulers. The pasha replied:

> I did not disgrace their house and their positions. But it is known that the departed was a greedy person and hoarded money. His period of office was long, and he had been granted *iltizāmāt* and *iqṭā'āt*. He did not like his relatives, and did not leave anything for them. He dedicated whatever he possessed to his wife, a maid whose price is about two thousand piasters. He did not bequeath anything to his brother's children. It is unbelievable that a slave girl can possess everything alone, while the treasury has precedence, because of the expenses for the soldiers who have to fight the rebels, and needs of the *ḥaramayn* (Mecca and Medina), and the sultan's coffers. However, I am removing the seals out of respect for you.[36]

---

35 Ibid., 195–197.

36 Ibid., 4: 195–197.

The new Shaykh al-Sādāt and his household blessed the pasha, who presented him with a fur robe. It is remarkable that the *Niqābat al-Ashrāf* was separated and given to another person with all the paraphernalia of the office—the *shāwīsh*s (Turkish *Çavuş*) guards, the *bāsh shāwīsh*, and a general secretary. Sayyid Muḥammad al-Maḥrūqī, an influential person in the financial and commercial life of Egypt at the time, was appointed administrator of the Ḥusayni shrine, in place of the deceased.

In spite of the pasha's promises, officials came to the house of Abū al-Anwār the following day and broke its seals. They seized the man in charge of women's beverages and interrogated the builder in order to find the places where money and other valuable items had been hidden. Finally, after threatening to drown the widow in the Nile, the pasha's accountant took control of these funds. The pasha seized parts of the *iltizām* that had been registered in the woman's name. Afterwards, the resourceful al-Maḥrūqī asked the pasha to agree to marry off the widow to Abū al-Iqbāl, the new Shaykh al-Sādāt. The marriage produced offspring.

Abū al-Iqbāl settled down as *khalīfa* and shaykh over the *sajjāda*. With him lived his brother Yaḥyā, "May God add them success and happiness."[37]

11 Concluding Note

It is important to conclude this essay by explaining al-Jabartī's attitude to the doctrine and personality of Ibn ʿArabī, who was named *al-Shaykh al-Akbar* by his admirers. The great mystic was highly regarded by many Muslims (at the time, mostly Turks), but met with deep hatred and accusations of heresy by his opponents (primarily among Arabs, who were more legalistically minded). We have to emphasize that there were notable exceptions on both sides. Al-Jabartī did not mince words in his criticism of the mystic's religious attitudes nor did he discuss his ideas in depth. As has been mentioned above, al-Jabartī was a committed and enthusiastic Sufi, and a member of the reformed Khalwatiyya order. His biographies of Sufis are very vivid. However, the historian did not contribute to Sufi theology. By comparison, other distinguished Arab Sufis in the Ottoman period, particularly Zakariyyā al-Anṣārī, al-Shaʿrānī, and ʿAbd al-Ghanī al-Nābulusī, who were not historians but theologians of Sufism, wrote important works about Sufi thought, particularly regarding Ibn ʿArabī's doctrines and philosophy.

Al-Jabartī's ethnic generalizations, the paradigm of pro-Akbari Turks, and the anti-Akbari Arabs (and Maghribis) are inaccurate in some cases.

37 Ibid.

Bibliography

Akkach, Samer. *Letters of a Sufi Scholar: The Correspondence of ʿAbd al-Ghanī al-Nābulusī (1641–1731)*. Leiden-Boston: Brill, 2010.

Al-Damurdāshī, Aḥmad. *Kitāb al-Durra al-muṣāna fī akhbār al-Kināna: fī akhbār mā waqaʿa bi-Miṣr fī dawlat al-Mamālīk*, edited by ʿAbd al-Raḥīm ʿAbd al-Raḥmān ʿAbd al-Raḥīm. Cairo: al-Maʿhad al-ʿIlmī al-Faransī li'l-Āthār al-Sharqiyya bi'l-Qāhira, 1989.

Flemming, Barbara. "Die vorwahhabische Fitna im osmanischen Kairo, 1711," *Ismail Hakki Uzunçarşil'ya Armaâan* (Ankara, 1976): 55–65.

Holt, P.M. *Egypt and the Fertile Crescent 1916–1922: A Political History*. Ithaca: Cornell University Press, 1975.

Ibn ʿAbd al-Ghanī, Aḥmad Shalabī. *Awḍaḥ al-ishārāt fī man tawallā Miṣr al-Qāhira min al-wuzarā' wa'l-bāshāt: al-mulaqqab bil-ta'rīkh al-ʿaynī*, edited by ʿAbd al-Raḥīm ʿAbd al-Raḥmān ʿAbd al-Raḥīm. Cairo: Maktabat al-Khānjī, 1978.

Ibn Abī al-Surūr, Muḥammad b. Muḥammad. *al-Minaḥ al-raḥmānīyya fī'l-dawla al-ʿUthmāniyya*, edited by Laylā al-Ṣabbāgh. Damascus: Dār al-Bashā'ir, 1995.

Ingalls, Matthew B. *Subtle Innovation within Networks of Convention: The Life, Thought, and Intellectual Legacy of Zakariyyā al-Anṣārī (d. 926/1520)*. Ph.D. dissertation. New Haven: Yale University, 2011.

Al-Jabartī, ʿAbd al-Raḥmān b. Ḥasan al-Zaylaʿī al-Ḥanafī. *ʿAjā'ib al-āthār fī'l-tarājim wa'l-akhbār*, edited by Shmuel Moreh. Jerusalem: The Hebrew University, 2013. 5 vols.

Moreh, Shmuel. *The Egyptian Historian ʿAbd al-Raḥmān al-Jabartī: His Works, Autographs, Manuscripts, and the Historical Sources of ʿAjā'ib al-Āthār*. Oxford: Oxford University Press, 2014.

Al-Nābulusī, ʿAbd al-Ghanī. *al-Ḥaqīqa wa'l-majāz fī'l-riḥla ilā al-Shām wa-Miṣr wa'l-Ḥijāz*, edited by Aḥmad ʿAbd al-Majīd Haridi. Cairo: al-Hay'a al-Miṣriyya al-ʿĀmma li'l-Kitāb, 1986.

Rafeq, Abdul-Karim. "Ibn Abi al-Surur and His Works," BSOAS 38 (1975): 23–31.

Al-Shaʿrānī, ʿAbd al-Wahhāb b. Aḥmad. *Laṭā'if al-minan wal-akhlāq fī wujūb al-taḥadduth bi-niʿmat Allāh ʿalā al-iṭlāq, al-maʿrūf bi'l-minan al-kubrā*. Cairo: ʿĀlam al-Fikr, 1976.

Al-Shaʿrānī, ʿAbd al-Wahhāb b. Aḥmad. *Mukhtaṣar al-Futūḥāt al-Makkiyya, al-musammā Lawāqiḥ al-anwār al-Qudusiyya al-muntaqāt min al-futūḥāt al-Makkiyya*, edited by Muḥammad ʿAbd al-Qādir Naṣṣār. Cairo: Dār al-Iḥsān, 2016.

Von Schlegell, Barbara. *Sufism in the Ottoman Arab World: Shaykh ʿAbd al-Ghanī al-Nābulusī (d. 1143/1731)*. Ph.D. dissertation. Berkeley: University of California, 1997.

Winter, Michael. "The Islamic Profile and the Religious Policy of the Ruling Class in Ottoman Egypt," *Israel Oriental Studies* 10 (1980): 132–145.

Winter, Michael. *Egyptian Society under Ottoman Rule, 1517–1798*. London and New York: Routledge, 1992.

Winter, Michael. *Society and Religion in Early Ottoman Egypt: Studies in the Writings of 'Abd al-Wahhab al-Sha'rani*. Transaction: New Brunswick and London, 1982; paperback printing, 2007.

Winter, Michael. "Egypt and Syria in the Sixteenth Century," in *The Mamluk-Ottoman Transition; Continuity and Change in Egypt and Bilād al-Shām in the Sixteenth Century*, edited by Stephan Conermann and Gül Şen. Bonn: Bonn University Press, 2017, 33–56.

Encountering Modernity in the Late Nineteenth Century: Two Egyptian Accounts

Meir Hatina

1 Introduction

The nineteenth-century Middle East was caught up in a climate of gloom and distress. Europe no longer knocked on the gates of the East but encroached some of its territories, including in the heartland of the Arab orbit. Egypt was occupied by the British in 1882 and Algeria by the French a year later. Other areas, such as al-Sham (Greater Syria), witnessed a growing Western influence in terms of economic and missionary activities.

The resolve of political elites in Istanbul and Cairo to curb European colonialism and enhance their own authority not only took roots in administrative, economic, and educational institutions, but also permeated various ways of life, thought, and culture. One of the main repercussions was the remolding of the public sphere as a lively and rich arena of civic bodies and institutions with new voices, especially of academic graduates who had acquired organizational and communication skills and were exposed to Western culture.

These intellectuals, whose credo was worldly activism, sought to dismantle the monopoly of the old guard 'ulama' and Sufi shaykhs over society's norms and values and to instill civic virtues in young people. Religious beliefs and sociopolitical practices, which were thought to be an inherent part of a traditional cosmic order, became contested and debated.[1] A contributing factor was the well-developed printing press, which gave wide circulation to new ideas.[2]

---

1 On the fragmentation of religious authority, see Daphna Efrat and Meir Hatina (eds.), *Religious Knowledge, Authority and Charisma: Islamic and Jewish Perspectives* (Salt Lake City: University of Utah Press, 2014); Meir Hatina, *'Ulama', Politics and the Public Sphere* (Salt Lake City: Utah University Press, 2010), introduction.

2 Ami Ayalon, *The Arabic Print Revolution: Cultural Production and Mass Readership* (Cambridge: Cambridge University Press, 2016); Anthony Gorman (ed.), *The Press in the Middle East and North Africa 1850–1959: Politics, Society and Culture* (Edinburgh: Edinburgh University Press, 2018).

 | DOI:10.1163/9789004459120_018

However, modernity, as pointed out by scholars such as Lila Abu-Lughod, Walter Armbrust, Timothy Mitchell, Gregory Starret, and Benjamin C. Fortna,[3] was far from being a linear process of rationalism and emancipation in the Middle East. It was a much more hybrid process, in which Western cultural themes were contested while perceptions and legacies of the past endured or were even rejuvenated. This can also be inferred from the Arab renaissance (*Nahḍa*), the proponents of which sought to invigorate the Islamic-Arab heritage and align it with scientific analysis, humanism, progress, and nationalism. The *Nahḍa* served as a space of negotiation and transition of ideas and their meaning in the midst of political upheavals, religious-ethnic strives, and socio-economic transformations.[4]

This article seeks to add another layer to the discussion of modernization in the Middle East, as well as to the *Nahḍa* studies, by analyzing two (unexplored) Egyptian accounts that were written at the end of the nineteenth century, providing a close look at the encounter between Syrian society and Western modernity, with all its implications.[5] The first writer is Muḥammad al-Qāyātī (d. 1902), a graduate of al-Azhar in Cairo and head of a Sufi fraternity. He was tried and exiled to Syria for five years following his active involvement in the ʿUrābī revolt, 1881–1882, a protonational uprising that sought to depose

3 Lila Abu-Lughod, "Introduction: Feminist Longings and Postcolonial Conditions," in idem (ed.), *Remaking Women: Feminism and Modernity in the Middle East* (Princeton: Princeton University Press, 1998), 3–32; Walter Armbrust, *Mass Culture and Modernism in Egypt* (Cambridge: Cambridge University Press, 1996), mainly 1–10, 190–220; Timothy Mitchell, *Colonising Egypt* (Cambridge: Cambridge University Press, 1988), 161–179; Gregory Starret, *Putting Islam to Work: Education, Politics and Religious Transformation in Egypt* (Berkeley: University of California Press, 1998), mainly 15–18; Benjamin C. Fortna, *Imperial Classroom: Islam, the State, and Education in the late Ottoman Empire* (Oxford: Oxford University Press, 2002), 93–95.

4 For literature on the *Nahḍa*, see Albert Hourani, *Arabic Thought in the Liberal Age 1798–1939* (Oxford: Oxford University Press, 1962); Fruma Zachs and Sharon Halevi, *Gendering Culture in Greater Syria: Intellectuals and Ideology in the Late Ottoman Empire* (London: I.B. Tauris, 2015); Adel Beshara (ed.), *Butrus al-Bustani: Spirit of the Age* (Melbourne: Iphoenix Publishing, 2014); Peter Hill, "The First Arabic Translations of Enlightenment Literature: The Damietta Circle of the 1800s and 1810s," *Intellectual History Review* 25/2 (2015): 209–233; Jens Hanssen and Max Weiss (eds.), *Arabic Thought Beyond the Liberal Age: Towards an Intellectual History of the Nahda* (Cambridge: Cambridge University Press, 2016); Tarek El-Ariss (ed.), *The Arab Renaissance: A Bilingual Anthology of the Nahda* (New York: Modern Language Association, 2018); Wael Abu-ʿUksa, *Freedom in the Arab World* (New York: Cambridge University Press, 2016).

5 The two compositions are first mentioned, with excerpts, in my book, *ʿUlamaʾ, Politics and the Public Sphere*, 82–89.

the Khedive Tawfīq and end British and French influence over the country.[6] Al-Qāyātī recorded his impressions in a 1901 book called *Nafḥat al-bashām fī riḥlat al-Shām* (The scent of balsam on the journey to the Sham).[7]

The second author is ʿAbd al-Raḥmān Sāmī (d. 1892), a rich merchant from Minya (from the same district as al-Qāyāti), who was also in Syria at the time and recorded his impressions in a book (1890) entitled *al-Qawl al-ḥaqq fī Bayrūt wa-Dimashq* (The truth about Beirut and Damascus).[8]

The two compositions, which were a continuation of the rich Muslim travel literature found in *Bilād al-Shām*,[9] are mainly ethnographic documentations of landscapes, places, monuments, institutions, social groups, persons, customs, markets, manners, and smells. Beyond the rich information, which enables scholars to extract intriguing sociological insights, the two essays provide an important and comparative prism to monitor the challenges of modernity in the Middle East under increasing colonialism and the gradual transition from an imperial to a national era. Notably, the Ottoman-imperial perspective is hardly present in the two compositions, which rather highlight local-regional dynamics in the Arabic-speaking provinces of the empire. Still, both authors, al-Qāyāti and Sāmī, are members of Egyptian elites (ʿulamaʾ and merchants) and still committed to the empire, attesting to its ongoing political and cultural vitality.[10]

---

6 On the ʿUrābī revolt, see Alexander Schölch, *Egypt for the Egyptians: The Socio-Political Crisis in Egypt 1878–1882* (London: Ithaca Press, 1981); Juan R. Cole, *Colonialism and Revolution in the Middle East: Social and Cultural Origins of Egypt's ʿUrabi Movement* (Princeton: Princeton University Press, 1993).

7 Muḥammad al-Qāyātī, *Nafḥat al-bashām fī riḥlat al-Shām* (Beirut: Dār al-Rāʾid al-ʿArabī, [1901] 1981).

8 ʿAbd al-Raḥmān Sāmī, *al-Qawl al-ḥaqq fī Bayrūt wa-Dimashq*, new ed. (Beirut: Dār al-Rāʾid al-ʿArabī, [1890] 1981). The biographical details on Sāmī are quite scattered. It is known that he was the director of the Minya theatre troupe. ʿUmar Riḍā Kaḥḥāla, *Muʿjam al-muʾallifīn* (Beirut: Maktabat al-Muthannā, n.d.): 5: 139; Yūsuf Sarkīs, *Muʿjam al-maṭbūʿāt al-ʿArabiyya wa'l-muʿarraba* (Cairo: Maṭbaʿat Sarkīs, 1928), 2: 1279; Maryam Simāṭ, "al-Tamthīl al-ʿArabī," in *Taʾrīkh al-masraḥ al-ʿArabī*, edited by Fuʾād Rashīd (Giza: Wikālat al-Ṣaḥāfa al-ʿArabiyya, 2004), 51–53. The essay was regionally published in *al-Ahram*, August 20, 1915.

9 See, for example, Aḥmad Aybash, *Dimashq al-Shām fī nuṣūṣ al-raḥḥālīn wa'l-jughrāfiyyīn wa'l-buldāniyyīn al-ʿArab wa'l-Muslimīn* (Damascus: Wizārat al-Thaqāfa, 1998), 2 vols.

10 This observation corresponds with the new discourse which emerged in the early 1990s on Ottoman history in the Arab-speaking provinces between the seventeenth and nineteenth centuries. This discourse rehabilitated the Ottoman record of rule and cultural agency in these regions despite European colonialism and the rise of Arab and local nationalism. See e.g., Ehud Toledano, "The Arabic Speaking-World in the Ottoman Period: A Socio-Political Analysis," in *The Ottoman World*, edited by Christine Woodhead (London: Routledge, 2011), 453–466.

The two accounts differ in style. Though both were written in standard Arabic, al-Qāyātī's is rich, elegant, esthetic, and imbued with traditional terminology and phrases. In contrast, Sāmī's is simpler; it uses a more trivial and, in fact, more modern language. While al-Qāyātī used only *hijrī* dates, Sāmī gives only Gregorian dates, attesting to the authors' different educational backgrounds. More importantly, their different backgrounds dictated conflicting perceptions as to their encounter with European culture and its impact on the status of the other—women and religious minorities—in the polity. Hence the two compositions can be added to the intellectual corpus of the *Nahḍa*, its aspirations, and its dilemmas, by providing another prism about the ideological clash between ʿulamaʾ and laymen over cultural identity and moral authority in the late nineteenth-century Middle East.

2 Al-Qāyātī's Account: Restrained Modernity

Muḥammad al-Qāyātī (1838–1902) was deeply immersed in religious scholarship, Sufism, and politics. He was born in the village of al-Qāyāt, in the Minya province in Upper Egypt, into a family of religious dignitaries identified with the Shāfiʿī legal school.[11] Educated in al-Qāyāt, Muḥammad and his brother Aḥmad (d. 1890) moved to Cairo to study at al-Azhar under the patronage of renowned ʿulamaʾ such as Khalīfa al-Ṣaftī, Muḥammad al-Ashmūnī, Shams al-Dīn Muḥammad al-Inbābī, Muḥammad ʿIllaysh, and Muḥammad al-Khusrī. When his father died, Muḥammad inherited his position as head of the Qāyātiyya fraternity, choosing to return to his village, al-Qāyāt. His brother Aḥmad, who remained in Cairo, started teaching at al-Azhar after receiving a license to teach and transmit religious knowledge (*ijāza*). With the death of his patron, Shaykh al-Ṣaftī, Aḥmad was appointed *Shaykh Riwāq al-Fashniyya* in his place in 1876.[12] The life course of each brother, like that of other religious figures, was deeply affected by the ʿUrābī revolt.

Justifying his fraternity's alliance with the ʿUrābī movement which erupted in 1881, Muḥammad highlighted the external British threat that prompted the

11 For a biographical account of al-Qāyātī's family, see ʿAlī Mubārak, *al-Khiṭaṭ al-Tawfīqiyya al-jadīda li-Miṣr al-Qāhira* (Cairo, Būlāq: Dār al-Kutub, 1887–1889), 14: 95–97; Muḥammad al-Qāyātī, *Khulāṣat al-taḥqīq fī afḍaliyyat al-Ṣiddīq* (Cairo: Maṭbaʿat al-Islām, 1895), 43–49; Gilbert Delanoue, *Moralistes et politques musulmans dans l'Égypte du XIXe siècle, 1798–1882* (Cairo: Institut français d'archéologie orientale du Caire, 1982), 1: 314–323.

12 Al-Qāyātī, *Khulāṣat al-taḥqīq*, 49–51; ʿAbd al-Razzāq al-Bayṭār, *Ḥilyat al-bashar fī taʾrīkh al-qarn al-thālith ʿashar* (Damascus: Maṭbūʿāt al-Majmaʿ al-ʿIlmī al-ʿArabī, 1961–1963), 1: 204–205.

Egyptians to come to their country's defense, even to the point of self-sacrifice. In al-Qāyātī's view, "self-defense is the duty of every nation that is forced into war by another nation." This also explains the recruitment of 'ulama' and Sufi shaykhs, who, as al-Qāyātī stressed, would help dispel the curse hanging over the homeland by dint of prayers and sermons. He thus sought to deflect criticism made by Egyptian authorities, who claimed that the role of the 'ulama' was the study and propagation of religious knowledge, not intervention in politics. Al-Qāyātī confirmed that this was indeed the traditional role of the "holy vessels"; but, he contended, such a role was limited to ordinary times. It was not relevant in times of emergency, as was the case in Egypt at the time.[13]

The essence of al-Qāyātī's narrative regarding his order's motives for joining the 'Urābī cause was the defense of religion and homeland. Al-Qāyātī's argument revealed a multifaceted cultural world that recognized territorial pluralism in the context of a universal faith. It is no wonder that he portrayed Egypt as "the precious homeland" (*al-waṭan al-'azīz*) and the Ottoman Empire as "the house of the great caliphate" (*dār al-khilāfa al-'uẓmā*).[14]

The influence of the Qāyātiyya order on the events of the revolt was evident. The order's organizational infrastructure and membership, numbering some 4,000 persons, were mobilized to support the military effort. With the approach of the decisive confrontation with the British, the Qāyātī brothers, together with other 'ulama', appeared at the soldiers' assembly points—for example, at Tall al-Kabir and Kafr al-Dawwar—to inspire them with sermons and verses from the Qur'an and the ḥadīth. Similarly, *dhikr* ceremonies and the ritual repetition of names of Sufi saints were performed to ensure military success.[15] The participation of the Qāyātiyya order in the protest movement was described by the local authorities and the British as one of "the most serious cases" of rebellion.[16]

Following the suppression of the revolt in September 1882, Muḥammad and Aḥmad al-Qāyātī, like other 'ulama', were sentenced to exile. This, however, did not necessarily mean that they became strangers in alien lands or detached from productive intellectual work. On the contrary, exile became a second

13 Al-Qāyātī, *Nafḥat*, 5–9, 35, 169.

14 Ibid., 7, 35.

15 Latifa Muhammad Salim, *al-Quwwa al-ijtima'iyya fi'l-thawra al-'Urābiyya* (Cairo: al-Hay'a al-Misriyya al-'Amma li'l-Kitab, 1981), 367–368; Mīkhā'īl Shārūbīm, *Ta'rīkh Miṣr al-qadīm wa'l-ḥadīth* (Cairo: al-Matba'a al-Kubrā al-Amīryya, 1900), 323; al-Qāyātī, *Nafḥat*, 5–9; Ismā'īl Sarhank, *Ḥaqā'iq al-akhbār 'an duwal al-biḥār* (Cairo: al-Maṭba'a al-Amīriyya, 1895–1923), 2: 409; Ḥusayn Fawzī al-Najjār, *Aḥmad 'Urābī Miṣr li'l-Miṣriyyīn* (Cairo: al-Hay'a al-Miṣriyya al-'Āmma li'l-Kitāb, 1992), 181.

16 PRO, FO 881/4727/No. 56, Inclosure 4.

home for them, thanks to the intercultural and personal ties maintained with colleagues in the scholarly world throughout the Middle East—primarily a consequence of their shared experience at al-Azhar, which drew scholars and students from all parts of the Ottoman Empire. The Egyptian exiles were welcomed warmly by ʿulamaʾ in the Arabian Peninsula and Fertile Crescent, were given posts as preachers and educators, and devoted themselves to writing and molding the Islamic discourse of the time. Some even became involved in local politics.[17]

For the Qāyātī brothers, Beirut was a departure point for familiarizing themselves with the countries of the Fertile Crescent. In his *Nafḥat al-bashām fī riḥlat al-Shām*, Muḥammad al-Qāyātī described in detail their travels through Damascus, Beirut, Tripoli, Sidon, Jerusalem, Hebron, and Nablus, providing a fascinating portrait of the religious landscape and social composition of these cities.[18] Weaving in personal judgments based on his intimate knowledge of the Egyptian experience, al-Qāyātī thereby provided an additional prism for comparing Egypt with Syria in the age of modernization, along with tracing the cultural interaction between these two regions.

Al-Qāyātī's book focused on two main topics: the local elites, and social norms and customs. When describing the local elites, he highlighted the diversity of this stratum, which ranged from government officials and merchants to ʿulamaʾ and Sufi shaykhs. The two latter groups, who filled key posts

---

17 Thus, for example, Muḥammad Khalīl al-Hijrisī, who began teaching there soon after his arrival in Mecca, the destination of his exile, became acquainted with the Idrīsiyya Sufi order. Another *ʿālim*, ʿAbd al-Raḥmān ʿIllaysh, was exiled to Istanbul, but was soon suspected by the authorities of political subversion. He was subsequently imprisoned for two years in harsh conditions. Upon his release, he was exiled to the island of Rhodes, but after a while was permitted to settle in Damascus. ʿIllaysh's colleague in the ʿUrābī revolt, Muḥammad ʿAbduh, who was exiled to Beirut, eventually reached Paris, where he joined his mentor Jamāl al-Dīn al-Afghānī in editing the pan-Islamist and anticolonialist newspaper *al-ʿUrwā al-Wuthqā* (The firm bond). Upon ʿAbduh's return to Beirut in 1885, contact between him and the Qāyātī brothers intensified. They also introduced him to local Salafi circles close to ʿAbd al-Qādir al-Jazʾāirī, most notably ʿAbd al-Razzāq al-Bayṭār (d. 1917), scion of a renowned ʿulamaʾ family from Damascus that was prominent in the nineteenth century. See David Commins, *Islamic Reform* (Oxford: Oxford University Press, 1990), 31, 38–40; al-Hijrisī's books, *al-Jawhar al-nafīs ʿalā ṣalawāt Ibn Idrīs* (Cairo, Būlāq: al-Maṭbaʿa al-Miṣriyya, 1893); *Hādhā kitāb al-qaṣr al-mashīd fiʾl-tawḥīd* (Cairo: al-Maṭbaʿa al-ʿIlmiyya, 1896/1897); ʿAbd al-Ḥalīm Maḥmūd, *al-Madrasa al-Shādhiliyya al-ḥadītha* (Cairo: Dār al-Kutub al-Ḥadītha, 1968), 248–253; al-Qāyātī, *Nafḥat*, 8–11, 56–58, 198–202.

18 The large body of information in this work has also served local researchers in tracing social change in the Fertile Crescent in the nineteenth century. See, for example, Aḥmad Ṭarbīn, *Malāmiḥ al-taghyīr al-ijtimāʿī fī bilād al-Shām fiʾl-qarn al-tāsiʿ ʿashar* (Beirut: Maʿhad al-Inmāʾ al-ʿArabī, 1982).

in religious and cultural life, are analyzed in depth. Most of these figures, as revealed in biographical dictionaries as well, were educated in al-Azhar as members of the influential *Riwāq al-Shuwām*,[19] retaining a strong tie with the Azhar community after they returned to their birthplaces throughout Syria. This tie was reflected in their correspondence with Azharis about theological and legal issues, as well as about the roles of mysticism, grammar, literature, and poetry, while suitable local students were encouraged to become candidates for study there. Indeed, many of the ʿulama' who hosted the Qāyātī brothers during their travels were acquainted from their years as students together at al-Azhar. A number of them came from affluent families and were involved in commerce, thereby reinforcing the economic ties between Egypt and Syria.[20] These cross-regional Islamic networks were facilitated by developments in the second half of the nineteenth century such as improved roads, newly constructed railroads, the opening of the Suez Canal, and advances in

19 Faculty members and students from *Riwāq al-Shuwām* played an important role in the al-Azhar community and in some cases, were involved in local Egyptian politics—for example, during the French conquest and the ʿUrābī revolt. Several chose to make their home in Egypt permanently and held distinguished posts in the fields of education and the judiciary, including as Shaykhs al-Azhar. See Muṣṭafā Ramaḍān, "Riwāq al-Shuwām bi'l-Azhar ibbāna al-ʿaṣr al-ʿUthmānī," in *al-Muʾtamar al-duwalī al-thānī li-taʾrīkh bilād al-Shām 1517–1939* (Damascus: Jāmiʿat Dimashq, 1978), 17–97.

20 Al-Qāyātī, *Nafḥat*; Zakī Muḥammad Mujāhid, *al-Aʿlām al-Sharqiyya* (Cairo: al-Maṭbaʿa al-Miṣriyya al-Ḥadītha, 1949–50), vol. 2; Aḥmad Taymūr, *Aʿlām al-fikr al-Islāmī fi'l-ʿaṣr al-ḥadīth* (Cairo: Lajnat Nashr al-Muʾallafāt al-Taymūriyya, 1967); ʿAbd al-Raḥīm ʿAbd al-Raḥmān ʿAbd al-Raḥīm, "ʿAlāqat bilād al-Shām bi-Miṣr fi'l-ʿaṣr al-ʿUthmānī 1517–1798," in *al-Muʾtamar al-duwalī al-thānī li-taʾrīkh bilād al-Shām* (Damascus: Jāmiʿat Dimashq, 1978), 1: 275–292; Muḥammad Jamīl al-Shaṭṭī, *Aʿyān Dimashq fi'l-qarn al-thālith ʿashar wa-niṣf al-qarn al-rābiʿ ʿashar* (Damascus: Dār al-Bashāʾir, 1994); ʿAbd al-Hādī Najā al-Abyārī, *al-Wasāʾil al-adabiyya fi'l-rasāʾil al-aḥdabiyya* (Cairo: Maṭbaʿat al-Waṭan, 1883–1884); Bashīr Nāfiʿ, "Nashʾat al-ittijāhāt al-siyāsiyya fī Filasṭīn fi awākhir al-ʿahd al-ʿUthmānī," *Qirāʾāt siyāsiyya* (Winter 1995): 27–56. See also Abdul-Karim Rafeq, "The Ulama of Ottoman Jerusalem (16th–18th Centuries)," in *Ottoman Jerusalem: The Living City 1517–1917*, eds. Sylvia Aduld and Robet Hillenbrand (Jerusalem: Altajir World of Islam Trust, 2000), 1: 48–49; ʿAdil Manna, "Cultural Relations between Egyptian and Jerusalem ʿUlama' in the Early Nineteenth Century," *Asian and African Studies* 17 (1983): 139–152; Gabriel Baer, "Jerusalem Notables in Ottoman Cairo," in *Egypt and Palestine: A Millennium of Association*, edited by Amnon Cohen and Gabriel Baer (New York: St. Martin's Press, 1984), 167–175; Uri Kupferschmidt, "Connections of the Palestinian Ulama with Egypt and Other Parts of the Ottoman Empire," ibid., 182–185; Hourani, Albert Hourani, "The Syrians in Egypt in the Eighteenth and Nineteenth Centuries," in *Colloque international sur l'histoire du Caire* (Cairo: Ministry of Culture of the Arab Republic of Egypt, 1972), 221–222.

mass printing, which contributed to the proliferation of ideas in the Ottoman Middle East and beyond.[21]

Not only religious and cultural matters were discussed during the encounters between the Qāyātī brothers and their acquaintances, but politics were on the agenda as well. The state of affairs of Islam and of Muslims was reviewed, with resentment expressed at the "age of the traitors" (*dahr al-khuwwān*), as exemplified by the Egyptian leaders who were "struck with blindness" during the events of the ʿUrābī revolt.[22] In their struggle against foreign aggression, the Qāyātī brothers found they had much in common with notables who had played a similar role in other countries and who, following their defeat, had also made their home in the Syrian domain. These figures included ʿAbd al-Qādir al-Jazāʾirī of Algeria, ʿAbdallāh al-Kurdī of Iraq, and Ghulām Muḥammad Sirdār Akram of Afghanistan.

In his survey of local social customs, al-Qāyātī focused primarily on two cities—Beirut and Damascus. He described Beirut as an Islamic city in character, but with a government, army, and infrastructure based on the European model. He was particularly impressed by the high level of security and low level of crime in the city, which he explained as the products of well-organized governing systems and observance of the law by those in power and ordinary people alike. The situation, he pointed out, was different in Egypt, which was led by exploitative, despotic rulers who turned the law into a fraud and believed they were immune from deposition or dismissal.[23]

Regarding the ethnography of Beirut, al-Qāyātī noted that despite good neighborly relations with the Christian population, which constituted the majority and were linked with various European powers through commercial and patronage relationships, the Muslims displayed zeal for their religion and did not imitate the Christians. There was no suggestion of rebelliousness in their behavior, such as drinking wine or operating cafés selling alcoholic drinks or drugs.[24] Al-Qāyātī sketched a similar picture of other cities he visited, such

21 Cole, Juan R.I. "Printing and Urban Islam in the Mediterranean World 1890–1920," in *Modernity and Culture: From the Mediterranean to the Indian Ocean*, eds. Leila Tarazi Fawaz and Christopher A. Bayly (New York: Columbia University Press, 2002), 344–364; Mona Abaza, "Changing Images of Three Generations of Azharites in Indonesia," in *Islam: Critical Concepts in Sociology*, eds. Bryan S. Turner. (New York: Routledge, 2003), 4: 382–383; Liat Kozma et al. (eds.), *A Global Middle East* (London: I.B. Tauris, 2015).

22 Al-Qāyātī, *Nafḥat*, 25–31, 35–41.

23 Ibid., 42–46.

24 Ibid., 31, 52–53.

as Damascus, Sidon, Tripoli, and Jerusalem. In his view, loyalty to an Islamic lifestyle was a source of pride to the Muslim inhabitants.[25]

Al-Qāyātī's empathy for the Muslims in Beirut and for what he saw as their moral lifestyle was nevertheless interwoven with a certain disdain for their conduct during religious festivals and rites of celebration and mourning. For example, he noted that their reservoir of poems and songs marking the Prophet's birthday was limited and out of date, and that their reading of the Qur'an lacked precision and fluency. "The people of Beirut, and in effect of Syria generally, badly need precise, qualitative and tuneful Qur'an reciters," he declared, hinting at the rightful address to remedy these shortcomings—al-Azhar. He described the wedding ceremonies (*zaffa*) as lacking careful planning. This also applied to funeral services (*janāza*), in which the women did not cry out or shout, the men displayed no sorrow in their facial expressions, and the refreshments were mostly sweet, "in contrast to what is customary among the inhabitants of Egypt."[26]

Commenting on the attire of the Muslims of Beirut, al-Qāyātī noted that some of the men wore Western-style brimmed hat, jacket, and trousers, while others wore an Eastern robe, as was customary in Egypt. The traditional women's attire was varied and colorful, but revealed nothing of their bodies. This distinguished them from the Christian women, whose permissive and revealing manner of dress drew his criticism. In al-Qāyātī's view, the local Christian women emulated the European women in every way except language. He described them as offering their charms to wealthy and foolish men. Refuting the Christian premise that such behavior is a hallmark of civilized society, al-Qāyātī—revealing his opinion of modernity and alarmed by the violation the religious prohibition of imitating the infidel (*tashabbuh*)—[27] argued that such thinking strips religion of its moral content, of which one of the foundations is decency. "Those who seek prostitution blemish the attributes of religion," he asserted, quoting a comment by a member of a notable family of dignitaries in Beirut, Hasan Effendi Bayyuham, who also observed that "modernity is nothing but a diminishment of religion."[28]

Acknowledging that most Egyptian women did wear traditional attire, al-Qāyātī nevertheless stressed that some norms had been breached, since

25 Ibid., 60–88.

26 Ibid., 47–50.

27 Ibid., 50–52. On *tashabbuh* in Islamic legal discourse, see Youshaa Patel, "The Islamic Treatises against Imitation (*Tasabbuh*): A Bibliographical History," *Arabica* 65 (2018): 597–639.

28 Al-Qāyātī, *Nafḥat*, 14, 51–52.

they added adornments and decorations to their garments.[29] In his view, however, rejecting modernity did not mean disqualifying modern sciences, such as engineering, mathematics, or geography, or some knowledge of Western languages. He praised schools for girls that imparted knowledge of mathematics, reading, and sewing.[30] Al-Qāyātī's stance encompassed openness as to the right of women to acquire an education, although it was conditional on safeguarding the institution of the family and avoiding any challenges to male social supremacy. Such conservative views adhere to what could be termed "domestic ideology," and are also evident in al-Qāyātī's fierce attack on a widely debated book by Qāsim Amīn, *Taḥrīr al-mar'a* (Woman's emancipation, 1899).[31] In this book and in a subsequent one *al-Mar'a al-jadīda* (The new woman, 1900), Amīn, a French-trained jurist, advocated the abolition of polygamy and arranged marriages, the expansion of education for women, and the removal of the veil.[32]

Damascus, al-Qāyātī observed in his book, was less exposed to modernity than Beirut. Most of its buildings—with the exception of mosques, saints' graves, and old *madrasas*, which "are among the most beautiful in the landscapes of this world"—were made of mud and wood. The manners of its residents were exceedingly pleasing, to the point, al-Qāyātī felt, that the inhabitants tended to over-politeness and to over-welcoming guests, compared to what was the norm in Egypt. The women were typified by their quiet and modest behavior, which was also the case with Christian women, who generally did not adorn themselves in the pre-Islamic pagan (*jāhilī*) style, as they did in Beirut. Still, al-Qāyātī observed, the tendency to imitate European women was growing and thus also the potential for violating modesty (*sitr*)—one of the

29 Ibid., 34, 50–53.

30 Ibid., 53–56.

31 Delanoue, *Moralistes*, 1: 323.

32 Amīn's advocacy of women's rights also stemmed from pragmatic political considerations. In his view, the image of the woman defined the image of the nation—that is, the intellectual and social development of women, who constituted half the population, was closely bound up with the development of the nation. On Amīn's biography and thought and the debates this ignited, see Noëlle Baladi, *L'émancipation de la femme en Égypte* (Nantes: Éditions Amalthée, 2005); Juan Ricardo Cole, "Feminism, Class, and Islam in Turn-of-the-Century Egypt," *IJMES* 13/1 (1981): 387–407. However, Amīn's pioneering role in women's rights was revised in later works, mainly by Beth Baron (1994, 2016) which highlighted a flourishing field of journalism and literature dealing with the status and rights of women already in the early nineteenth century, preceding Amīn's 1890 *Taḥrīr al-mar'a.* Baron, *The Women's Awakening in Egypt: Culture, Society and the Press* (New Haven: Yale University Press, 1994); "Liberal Thought and the 'Problem' of Women, Cairo, 1890s," in Hanssen and Weiss (eds.), *Arabic Thought Beyond the Liberal Age*, 187–213.

shari'a imperatives—which often led to permissiveness and adultery. As the ḥadīth states, he noted: "Women are the devil's saboteurs."[33]

In describing the attributes of Muslims in the Fertile Crescent cities he had visited, particularly the careful observance of religion and preservation of social morality, al-Qāyātī drew an analogy with the Egyptian reality, directing blunt criticism at the social and political system there:

> Syria is the best Islamic land at this time, even though expertise in the Qur'an and [religious] knowledge is greater in Egypt. Still, indecent things are not as visible in public as in Egypt, for abhorrent deeds are well hidden, and one does not see special places for prostitutes as in the Land of Egypt. Nor does one see the smoking of hashish or addictions in the public space. You will find only relaxed patrons, sipping coffee and smoking tobacco in all the coffee houses throughout Syria. Therefore, neither a prince nor a common man nor an *'ālim* [sing. of 'ulama', a Muslim scholar] will hesitate to visit there, for there is nothing in these coffee houses to damage their virtue, like using drugs, drinking alcohol, or uttering vulgarities or obscenities, as mentally ill and crazed persons do.[34]

Al-Qāyātī was pessimistic about the prospect of the Egyptian rulers taking any steps to end such immoral manifestations and restore the dignity of Islam and its laws:

> If you question any one of the rulers of Egypt about this, he will reply: "This period is a period of freedom, and the European states would not want to relinquish this freedom." How can we use distant nations as an excuse—since they have no connection with what is happening in our countries and with our religious practices—to justify the abandonment of religious ritual, compassion, virtues and [religious] law. We do not believe that if we forbid our women and men to engage in abhorrent acts and behave wantonly and lawlessly in public, they [the Europeans] will

33 Al-Qāyātī, *Nafḥat*, 129–136, 140–142.

34 Ibid., 150–151. Al-Qāyātī's enumeration of forbidden practices in Egypt, such as imbibing alcoholic drinks or using hashish, is supported by Ehud Toledano's findings on the leisure activities of the lower strata. Toledano argued that the use of hashish as well as tobacco in coffee houses, and drinking alcoholic beverages in taverns (*khāmmāras*), seems to have been more common in mid-nineteenth-century Egypt than is generally believed. Toledano, *State and Society in Mid-Nineteenth-Century Egypt* (Cambridge: Cambridge University Press, 1990), 242–427.

> attack us for preventing this corruption, from which neither they nor we will derive any national or religious benefit whatsoever.
>
> Ultimately, the rulers and inhabitants of Egypt are still in love with the people of Europe and their ethics and customs, mimicking them to such an extent that they exceed them in these respects [...] May God have mercy of this generation. What would have happened if the Egyptian rulers forbade their fellow inhabitants—who are under their firm control—from performing indecent acts that are contrary to Islam—their religion and the religion of their fathers and forefathers? Would any of the foreigners force them to abandon the laws of their true religion? Absolutely not.[35]

The behavior of the Egyptian rulers, al-Qāyātī concluded, is even worse than that of the Christians in Europe:

> Some of the Europeans are not entirely devoted to religion or do not observe all its requirements, but they do not break its rules, belittle its ceremonies, or scorn its believers, as do the leaders of the Muslims now. If only these leaders could imitate the Christians in this, too, as they imitate them in their other customs. What a pity for Islam and for its believers to have such emirs, who think that imitation calls for complete scorn. We pray for God to inspire their understanding and banish their sick thoughts and low opinions of this true religion, the path of righteousness.[36]

Notably, al-Qāyātī's unfamiliarity with the West, which he never visited, contributed to his disdain—in contrast, for example, to Shaykh Rifāʿa Rāfiʿ al-Ṭahṭāwī a half-century earlier, who, as imam of one of Muḥammad ʿAlī's student missions to Europe, soon became an enthusiastic admirer of the new modern civilization and described it in his writings.[37]

While al-Qāyātī's narrative also reflected personal bitterness over the degradation and exile experienced by him and others involved in the ʿUrābī events, its strongest message was the censure expressed by a religious scholar of the

35 Al-Qāyātī, *Nafḥat*, 151–152.

36 Ibid., 152.

37 Al-Tahtawi, *An Imam in Paris: Account of a Stay in France by an Egyptian Cleric (1826–1831)*, trans. and introduction by Daniel Newman (London: Dar al- Saqi, 2011). See also John W. Livingston, "Western Science and Educational Reform in the Thought of Shaykh Rifaʿa al-Tahtawi," *IJMES* 28/4 (1996): 543–564; Israel Altman, *The Political Thought of Rifaʿah Rafiʿ al-Tahtawi: A Nineteenth-Century Egyptian Reformer* (Ph.D. dissertation; Los Angeles: University of California, 1976).

erosion of the status of Islam in its encounter with modernity. This explains his criticism of Muslim reformists' deconstruction of the age-old Sunni legal system. This took the form of challenging the authority of the *ṣaḥāba* (the Prophet's companions) and the validity of the *taqlīd* (reliance on the teaching of a *madhhab*), while expanding the boundaries of *ijtihād* (legal reasoning) and "public good" (*al-maṣlaḥa al-ʿāmma*) as a lever for reform in a range of national, social, or gender issues.[38] Al-Qāyātī argued categorically that the *ṣaḥāba* were among the best people created by God after the prophets. They were like "stars who illuminate the straight path" (*al-ṣirāṭ al-mustaqīm*) with a deep expertise in Islam and its ways. Casting aspersions on them was tantamount to undermining religion and automatically excluding such detractors from the community of believers.[39]

Moreover, al-Qāyātī warned, any defamation or deviation from the legal binding consensus (*ijmāʿ*) is *bidʿa* (disapproved innovation) and should be cast out. As for Sufism, which our author was affiliated with and which was attacked by reformists such as Muḥammad ʿAbduh, ʿAbdallāh al-Nadīm, Rashīd Riḍā, Jamāl al-Dīn al-Qāsimī, ʿAbd al-Ḥamīd al-Zahrāwī, and others as nurturing passivity and superstitions, al-Qāyātī made it clear that Sufism was one of the foundations of Islam. He defined it as a way to reach and be close to God (*al-waṣl wa'l-taʿarruf*). Its purpose is to strengthen our trust in God (*taqwā*) and fear of God (*waraʿ*), and to encourage us to walk the straight path.[40]

The extensive social documentation provided in Muḥammad al-Qāyātī's book illuminates the close and vibrant cultural links that existed between Egypt and the Syrian provinces in the second half of the nineteenth century. Against this background, al-Azhar stood out as a Middle Eastern beacon that attracted large numbers of students and scholars, despite the erosion of the institute's domestic status following Egyptian governmental reforms and the rivalry with religious centers such as Damascus and Istanbul.[41] Arab historians, among them the Egyptian ʿAbd al-ʿAzīz al-Shinnāwī and the Syrian Muṣṭafā Ramaḍān, defined the institution as second only to the *ḥājj* to Mecca in serving

---

38 Hatina, *ʿUlamaʾ, Politics and the Public Sphere*, chapter 4; Commins, *Islamic Reform*, chapter 5, 6.

39 Al-Qāyātī, *Khulāṣat al-taḥqīq*, 3, 39. Al-Qāyātī's criticism was also directed at the Shiʿis, who defamed the three most revered *ṣaḥāba*—Abū Bakr, ʿUmar, and ʿUthmān—for usurping ʿAlī's right to the caliphate. Ibid.

40 Al-Qāyātī, *Wasīlat al-wuṣūl fi'l-fiqh wa'l-tawḥīd wa'l-uṣūl* (Cairo: Maṭbaʿat al-Khayriyya, 1888), 6, 19–21.

41 See Uri Kupferschmidt, "Connections of the Palestinian Ulama with Egypt and Other Parts of the Ottoman Empire," in Cohen and Baer (eds.), *Egypt and Palestine*, 176–189; Mahmoud Yazbak, "Nabulsi Ulama in the Late Ottoman Period 1864–1914," *IJMES* 29 (1997): 78–79; Rafeq, "The Ulama of Ottoman Jerusalem," 48–49.

to unite the diverse areas of the Muslim world. In al-Shinnāwī's metaphoric depiction, "while the Kaʿba in Mecca served as the religious *qibla* (prayer direction), al-Azhar in Cairo provided the scientific learning *qibla*."[42] Al-Azhar's distinguished position as the focus of religious learning in the Muslim orbit was reflected not only in biographies by its non-Egyptian graduates, but also in religious guidance and legal opinions (*fatwās*).[43]

Locating al-Azhar within a broader network of scholarship constitutes a basis for widening the scope of research regarding the extent of the ties between Egyptian ʿulama' and their colleagues in Syria and elsewhere. Various studies have centered on Muḥammad ʿAbduh's sojourn in Beirut and his interaction with members of the Salafi reform movement.[44] However, ʿAbduh represented a minority viewpoint in al-Azhar in his time and therefore exerted only a limited ideological influence outside Egypt. As shown by Mona Abaza and Giora Eliraz, his reformist impact was actually more palpable in Southeast Asia, where it attracted a vast audience due to its inclusive message.[45] By contrast, Azharis with a more puritanical mindset became models for their colleagues in the Middle Eastern domain.[46]

Some of these Azharis were identified not only with Islamic jurisprudence, but also with Sufi culture, which was extremely popular in Syrian society, as indicated in Muḥammad al-Qāyātī's volume. Together with his brother Aḥmad, he was received with honor and esteem wherever he visited, in no small measure because of their affinity for Sufism.[47]

---

42 ʿAbd al-ʿAziz al-Shinnāwī, "Dawr al-Azhar fi'l-ḥifāẓ ʿalā al-ṭābiʿ al-ʿArabī li-Miṣr ibbāna al-ḥukm al-ʿUthmānī," in *Abḥāth al-nadwa al-duwaliyya li-ta'rīkh al-Qāhira* (Cairo: Dār al-Kutub, 1971), 2: 675–715.

43 See, for example, *al-Hilāl* 13 (April 1, 1899): 411–412. Al-Azhar's guidance was also sought also in distant Southeast Asia, as can be learned from a question addressed to its scholars, *al-Hilāl* 6 (1897–1898): 496.

44 See, for example Commins, *Islamic Reform*, 30–32; Albert Hourani, *Arabic Thought in the Liberal Age 1798–1939* (3rd. ed., Cambridge: Cambridge University Press, 1983), 130–160; Sylvia G. Haim, *Arab Nationalism: An Anthology* (Berkeley, CA.: University of California Press, 1962), 19–24; Bassam Tibi, *Arab Nationalism: A Critical Enquiry* (New York: St. Martin's Press, 1981), 78–90; Eliezer Tauber, *The Arab Movements in World War I* (London: Frank Cass, 1993), 23–33.

45 Abaza, "Changing Images," 383–391; Giora Eliraz, *Islam in Indonesia* (Brighton: Sussex, 2004), 1–25.

46 For example, on the issue of non-Muslims, see Meir Hatina, "*Fatwa*s as a Prism of Social History in the Middle East: The Status of Non-Muslims in the Nineteenth Century," in *Koexistenz und Konfrontation: Beiträge zur jüngeren Geschichte und Gegenwartslage der orientalischen Christen*, edited by Martin Tamcke (Hamburg: LIT, 2003), 51–74.

47 See, for example, his descriptions of Sufism in Damascus and Sidon. Al-Qāyātī, *Nafḥat*, 60–66, 112–116, 129–136.

3 ʿAbd al-Raḥmān Sāmī's Account: Cultural Rapprochement

Al-Qāyātī's account constituted a defiant manifesto highlighting the negative impact of modernity, and the notion of cultural rapprochement between East and West, on the Muslim community. A narrative more positive and open to modernity was provided by al-Qāyātī's contemporary, the Egyptian-born merchant ʿAbd al-Raḥmān Bay Sāmī. He, too, spent time in Syria at the end of the nineteenth century, recording his impressions in *al-Qawl al-ḥaqq fī Bayrūt wa-Dimashq*.[48] His arrival by ship from Istanbul to Syria in June 1890 was upon his doctors' advice that he change his environment and relax. And indeed, he found the calm he sought in Beirut and Damascus, which offered a mild climate; quiet, beautiful sites; and nice people.[49]

Sāmī's first stop was Beirut, where he was warmly welcomed by the mayor and city dignitaries, most of them merchants, waiting for him on the station platform—testimony to his craft and high social status. The sense of strangeness that accompanied him before his arrival dissipated quickly as he was invited to reside at the mayor's residence. Already in the opening pages of his book, Sāmī praised the respect and warmth he had received from people he had never met before, an impression that accompanied him throughout his stay in the city.[50]

Sāmī described the Beirut landscape in a variety of complimentary ways: "the flower of Syria" (*zahrat Sūriyā*) or "the city of knowledge and medicine" (*madīnat al-ʿilm wa'l-ṭibb*). Its streets, houses, municipal institutions, hospitals, pharmacies, and public gardens were depicted as having been built along the European model. Comparing it to Egyptian cities, he lamented Beirut's wide and clean streets and their lights at night, the aesthetic buildings, the numerous gardens—and, also located outside the city, the markets and the detached new houses.[51]

Sāmī placed special emphasis on Beirut's hospitals and its qualified doctors, who provided efficient treatment and served as gatekeepers of public health and hygiene, hence attesting to the city's advanced medicine. He also pointed out the many social welfare associations which extended services to the needy and the deprived, attesting to the city dwellers' altruism. As a man of letters he did not pass over the well-developed print and journalism culture, though noting in passing that some of the published journals, as in other countries,

48 Sāmī, *al-Qawl al-ḥaqq*.

49 Ibid., 5.

50 Ibid., 7–9, 112.

51 Ibid., 9–10, 23–24.

did not enjoy full freedom since they were supervised by the *Majlis al-Maʿārif* (Council of Education).[52]

As to the education system, he enumerated the large number of schools and colleges, most of them Christian, attesting to the city's status as a regional center for culture and intellectual production. The educational institutions were intended for boys and girls alike and attracted a large number of Syrian students, who thereby acquired useful vocational knowledge. Visiting some of the private schools, such as the American College, the al-Amīriyya, the al-Sulṭāniyya, and the Jesuit colleges, Sāmī praised not only their pleasant compounds and administrative management, but mainly their modern curricula and educational methods. He applied the same positive notions to governmental schools, hence leveling implicit criticism at the poor public education in his home country.[53] Beirut's educational system, Sāmī concluded, was the main drive for the significant progress of Beirut as a modern and cosmopolitan capital. Its schools

> championed a cultural revival (*nahḍa adabiyya*) that proved that in the East there are people who exploit every opportunity [for prosperity] offered by modern times and do not allow for stumbling blocks to impede progress. This century has already understood the pleasure to be found in science; thus you can see that most of their research topics revolve around science, prose, or poetry. They have many contacts within and outside the schools. And most members of these associations are young and well educated.[54]

Apparently, Sāmī was not particularly troubled by the fact that missionary groups generally sponsored such educational activity—a sensitive issue with those Muslim observers of the period who viewed missionaries as an additional arm of European colonialism in the destruction of local self-identity. From his point of view, this educational thrust was a welcome altruistic activity, as knowledge and the acquisition of it were among the merits of modern times.[55]

Sāmī provided some sociological insights into the human profile of these schools. Whereas in private schools, most of the pupils were from rich families, students in public schools came from the lower stratum of society, mainly from mountainous regions, and had to finance their studies by years of hard

52 Ibid., 16, 24, 29–30, 32.
53 Ibid., 11–13, 15.
54 Ibid., 12.
55 Ibid., 7–16, 22–24, 32.

work. However, their discipline and keen passion to acquire scientific knowledge enabled them to graduate and even to travel abroad to complete their higher education in Russia, Germany, France, England, or America. In their social conduct, they combined the best of European and Eastern norms and customs. "They do not have taverns for drinking beer, and there are only a few brothels and playhouses that lead people to the abyss of poverty and take from them the pleasure of being with their family and friends."[56]

Thus Sāmī, in contrast to al-Qāyātī's exclusive and reserved stance, took an inclusive approach as he viewed the adoption of European manners as a positive step and improvement on the human condition. Yet another section of the pedagogic system also praised by Sāmī was the institution of the boarding school, with the help of which charity associations granted education, health, and financial backing to poor pupils, some of whom were sent each year to neighboring countries to continue their studies.[57]

Moving from the institutional and educational realm to the population itself, Sāmī described Beirut society as diligent, innovative, industrious, and productive, and as an agent for the establishment of close encounters with the European economy and trade. "Among the Syrians," he applauded with pride, "there are some who proved that the Eastern man has the power of invention, just as the Western man does." Beirut society was also depicted as harmonious, with different classes intermingling, for example during holidays and celebrations, without distinction between rich and poor.[58]

> The people in Beirut are diligent. They get up before sunrise and work all day long. Everyone is at work, and rarely will you find idlers among them. In this city you have all the classes: wealthy businessmen and bank owners [...]; middle-class people, such as textile merchants and store owners; and working-class people, like craftsmen, tradesmen, and others. People of all classes live together, especially during the holidays, so you cannot tell who is rich or who is poor. All are diligent in their jobs despite the slowdown in the labor market. If it had not been for this, then poverty would have spread among them. All the residents are content with their work and do not seek to harm others, so that you will find that they hardly harass each other. Everyone lives in perfect harmony, as if

56 Ibid., 13.
57 Ibid., 15.
58 Ibid., 25–28, 33–34.

> they understood that every human being has a role in the world, and all together make up society.[59]

Sāmī also showed an empathetic and inclusive attitude toward the Christian members of society, with no mention of interethnic tensions between them and the Muslim population. He lauded the literary and intellectual accomplishments of such Christian writers as Nāṣīf al-Yāzijī and Buṭrus al-Bustānī, and highlighted the respect and affection that the Syrians displaying toward men of the pen in general, not just the clergy.[60] Additionally, he praised Christian women, who, like Muslim women, were mannerly and modest, and made a point of specifying their distinct and lofty merits:

> While Muslim women refrain from meeting guests, Christian women meet their visitors cordially and politely. They speak one or more European languages. Most of them have attended school and are familiar with the art of speaking like men. Some of them have written poems and have poetry collections (*dawāwīn*). I looked at a collection of speeches by members of the *Bākūra Sūriyya* [Syrian First Fruits] Association, and I can only praise the fruits of their diligence. Its women members compete with men in a number of ways. The wealthy have founded associations and established at their expense schools in which poor free girls are taught, such as the *Zahrat al-Iḥsān* Society and its school. This association is made up of the best [Christian] women in Beirut.
>
> I will also note with pride that one lady from the Syrian *Bākūra* Association in Beirut has collected a little money from her friends to devote two days a week to meeting in her home with women of limited capacity from all communities. Together with her friend, she educates them and teaches them how to take care of their homes and maintain high standards of cleanliness, and how to educate their children. She also reads them simple essays that they can understand and gives them the charity money she gathered from good people, or teaches them to sew and gives them the newly sewn clothes so that they walk away with thanks and praise [...] This illustrates how the women of Beirut are interested in science and are concerned about elevating its people.[61]

---

59 Ibid., 33–34.

60 Ibid., 18–19, 31–32, 37–38.

61 Ibid., 14.

Clearly Sāmī showed preference for such educated and involved types of women, thus revealing his critical stance with regard to the social backwardness of Muslim women.

Sāmī sketched a similarly pleasant and relaxed picture of Damascus, which he called "Paradise of the East" (*jannat al-mashriq*) and "the bride of the cities" (*ʿarūs al-mudun*).[62] Damascus is described as dynamic, and distinctive for its old and marvelous houses of worship, both mosques and churches, spectacular parks, and the cleanliness of its neighborhoods and roads, due in large measure to the abundance of water that reaches every home and byway in the city and its environs. Such public health and hygiene, Sāmī continued, was also the province of the countryside among the fellahin. As to the buildings and houses, in contrast to those in Beirut, they were attached dwellings, built of simple stones and woods.[63]

The local inhabitants largely spoke a high, elegant Arabic (*al-fuṣḥā*), and without exception and in all classes and sects were endowed with high standards of morals, virtues, and solidarity, and a warm attitude toward strangers who visit the city.[64] As in Beirut, Sāmī coded in detail the diligence, devotion, and attendance of the Damascenes to their crafts and daily activities, whether in the employ of the govern or as merchants, small artists, or laborers (*ʿummāl*). For men, women, and children alike, work was arduous and they worked hard from sunrise to late in the evenings. Nevertheless, they were diligent, never showing any laziness (*kasal*) and running their affairs wisely. This was also true of women who belonged to the lower stratum and who were very productive, working at home embroidering, weaving, and helping out to meet household expenditures.[65]

Sāmī also engaged in more general observations about Damascene women, which revealed his aesthetic tastes. He described them as among the most beautiful women in the East, praised their purchase of nice, colorful clothes and their hairdos, which often followed European fashion. When leaving the house for shopping or during holidays and festivals, Muslim women wore headscarves (*manādīl, mudawwarāt*). Moreover, when hosting relatives or other visitors, Muslim men and women were seated separately, whereas in the case of Christians and Jews, they sat together. Nevertheless, as Sāmī had observed earlier, none of the women, regardless of their creed, were spoiled and they were all diligent when working in the home. They were all visible in the public

62 Ibid., 59–61.
63 Ibid., 89–90, 95–99.
64 Ibid., 53–57, 65–67, 69, 71–72.
65 Ibid., 75–78.

sphere and the various city markets, wearing headscarves yet without hiding their beauty, which is a gift from God.[66]

From Sāmī's descriptions of Damascene women, in contrast to what he wrote about the women of Beirut, one perceives a more patriarchal society, where the private domain was still the main province of women, though the public sphere was also accessible to them. Here Sāmī's description matched that of al-Qāyātī's, though he did not share the latter's fear of the potential deterioration of public morality caused by women's exposure to modern modes of life and fashion.[67] Both authors confirmed the dignified character of the coffee shops (estimated by Sāmī to be around 120), mainly frequented by Muslims, pointing out that only a small number of taverns served alcohol to the scoundrels sitting there.[68]

Sāmī affirmed that Damascus was a known center of *tamaddun wa-ḥaḍāra,* i.e. of civilization, knowledge, and education, although the tone was set primarily by Christians, who were more intent than Muslims on promoting the modern sciences (such as mathematics, engineering, history, and geography) and foreign languages (mainly Ottoman Turkish, French, English, Greek, Armenian, and Syriac). They invested much energy and resources in education and established many schools. The outcome was that the majority of them was literate and knew foreign languages. By contrast, the Muslim schools were said to have been mainly devoted to religious and legal studies, training their students for positions in education and as mosque officials, side by side with government schools which offered training for the bureaucracy and other managerial fields. Nevertheless, in the case of girls' education, Sāmī observed subjective advancement not just in Christian milieus but also in Muslim and Jews ones. In addition, he also gave statistics dating to 1890 as to the number of schoolgirls and the general number of pupils: Christians—10 schools and 1,280 pupils; Muslims—12 schools and 20,000 pupils; Jewish—2 schools and 180 pupils.[69]

Sāmī depicted the social and ethnic mosaic of Damascus as multifaceted and impressive: Sunnis and Shiʿis, Druze, Allawites and Nuzirists, Christians and Jews, with religious differences never constituting an obstacle to harmony and brotherhood among Muslims, and between them and non-Muslims.[70] He noted that although Muslim-Christian harmony was upset in the wake of the

66 Ibid., 69–70, 78–80. On the city market, 91.

67 Note 36 above.

68 Sāmī, *al-Qawl al-ḥaqq*, 84–85, 93.

69 Ibid., 100–102.

70 Ibid., 13–14, 33–34, 53, 61–68, 73–78, 100–102, 105.

anti-Christian riots of 1860, which constituted a "black mark" (*nuqṭa sawdāʾ*) on the city's history, the situation reverted to its former orderly state as part of a general effort to preserve the unity of the homeland and attend to its welfare. Peace, love, and solidarity regained their supremacy. Quoting the inhabitants, Sāmī wrote: "We are separate in our faiths, but love unites us." He also pointed out that although Muslims and Christians continued, as had been customary until then, to live in distinct neighborhoods, there was a new and growing phenomenon of living together.[71] Sāmī attributed these fraternal ties between the denominational sectors of the city to material causes, such as employment opportunities, social support and welfare networks, a well-developed commerce, facilities for leisure activities and excursions, including numerous parks and nature areas (*muntazahāt*), which instilled tranquility in people's mind and souls.[72]

There is no doubt that Sāmī, as a merchant with financial resources, recognized the importance of material infrastructure and economic development not only as an impetus for the advancement of state affairs, but also as a means for easing tensions between religious and social groups. He did not support economic Darwinism and demonstrated social sensitivity, which he found in Syrian society and hoped to find in Egypt as well. His warm reception during his stay in Beirut and Damascus was a microcosm of the embracing nature of Syrians, Muslims, and Christians alike toward foreigners who entered their country. As a clear illustration of the positive role of Damascus (*akhlāq Dimashq*), Sāmī cited the Damascenes' support of Egyptians who had been tried and exiled to Syria following the suppression of the ʿUrābī rebellion, including the Qāyātī brothers. These exiles were enrolled in local institutions and their every need was met. Moreover, when Istanbul sought to deport some of the Syrian exiles suspected of political subversion, Syrian dignitaries annulled the decree and assured the sultan that they would guarantee that the exiles would avoid any involvement in politics.[73]

Muḥammad al-Qāyātī also shared Sāmī's view of the warm Syrian hospitality, as he had experienced it himself, but he referred mainly to Muslims, while demonstrating dissonance and aversion to the Christian population, missionary colleges, and the European culture they were identified with and which, in his view, threatened the viability of the indigenous Islamic identity. His aversion to the Christian civic emancipation that followed the Ottoman

---

71 Ibid., 73–74.

72 Ibid., 65–68, 104–105.

73 Ibid., 19–20.

reforms known as the Tanzimat (1839–1876)[74] was intertwined with a traditional disdain for Christian rituals in churches, such as pictures and statues, which, he wrote, distorted monotheism and would not serve any useful purpose on doomsday.[75]

4 Concluding Notes

Al-Qāyātī's and Sāmī's books provide two different perspectives of the relationship between tradition and modernity on the threshold of the twentieth century. For al-Qāyātī, the religious scholar, the values of science and modern culture embodied a threat to Islam and its superiority over other cultures. Hence, he accused the political elites of moral bankruptcy. For the Western-oriented Sāmī, these modern values were positive and desirable attributes of society. He urged the political elites to fortify them further. Though he avoided political statements, Sāmī did not conceal his frustration with the slow pace of modernity in the Arab-Muslim orbit, as can be inferred from his accounts of Syria's Muslim inhabitants (especially in Damascus) and of the status of Muslim women, in comparison to that of Christian women.

While al-Qāyātī focused on the socio-religious landscape of Syria, Sāmī concentrated on its sociological facets and structural landscape, signaling that the latter was the key to modern national development. Al-Qāyātī's descriptions are dry and imbued with resentment and anxiety, whereas Sāmī's are colorful, aesthetic, and complimentary. Having experienced revolt, suppression, and exile from his homeland, al-Qāyātī became a dissident. Sāmī, on the other hand, was affiliated with the elite and embraced the prevailing political order, both Egyptian and Ottoman, though eager to see more state activism in modernizing local Muslim societies.[76]

---

74 On the Tanzimat reforms and its impact on the status of non-Muslims in the Arab provinces of the Empire, see Bruce Masters, *Christians and Jews in the Ottoman Arab World: The Roots of Sectarianism* (Cambridge: Cambridge University Press, 2001), mainly chapter 5; Moshe Ma'oz, "Muslim Ethnic Communities in Nineteenth-Century Syria and Palestine: Trends of Conflict and Integration," *Asian and African Studies* 19 (1985): 283–307; also his "The Ulama and the Process of Modernization in Syria during the Mid-Nineteenth Century," *Asian and African Studies* 7 (1971): 77–88.

75 Al-Qāyātī, *Nafḥat*, 93, 98–99.

76 On dissident intellectuals, see John P. Nettl, "Ideas, Intellectuals and Structures of Dissent," in *On Intellectuals*, edited by Philip Rieff (New York: Doubleday, 1969), 53–122; Edward Shils, "The Intellectual and the Powers: Some Perspectives for Comparative Analysis," *Society and History* 1/1 (October 1958); 5–22.

The different social makeup and cultural orientation of the two narrators also dictated a different conception of the ʿulamaʾ and their role in the polity. Al-Qāyātī viewed them exclusively as men of religious learning within the Muslim community. Sāmī, by contrast, broadened this view to mean primarily men of learning equipped with Western knowledge—Muslim and Christian. In his view, they were the harbingers of renewal in the Middle Eastern milieu.[77] These differing conceptions reflected the vigorous contest over the preferred cultural and intellectual guidance of society.

Bibliography

Abaza, Mona. "Changing Images of Three Generations of Azharites in Indonesia," in *Islam: Critical Concepts in Sociology*, edited by Bryan S. Turner. New York: Routledge, 2003, 4: 382–418.

ʿAbd al-Raḥīm, ʿAbd al-Raḥīm ʿAbd al-Raḥmān. "ʿAlāqat bilād al-Shām bi-Miṣr fī'l-ʿaṣr al-ʿUthmānī 1517–1798," in *al-Muʾtamar al-duwalī al-thānī li-taʾrīkh bilād al-Shām*. Damascus: Jāmiʿat Dimashq, 1978, 1: 275–292.

Abu-Lughod, Lila. "Introduction: Feminist Longings and Postcolonial Conditions," in *Remaking Women: Feminism and Modernity in the Middle East*, edited by Lila Abu-Lughod. Princeton: Princeton University Press, 1998.

Abu-ʿUksa, Wael. *Freedom in the Arab World*. New York: Cambridge University Press, 2016.

Al-Abyārī, ʿAbd al-Hādī Najā. *al-Wasāʾil al-adabiyya fi'l-rasāʾil al-aḥdabiyya*. Cairo: Maṭbaʿat al-Waṭan, 1883–84.

Altman, Israel. *The Political Thought of Rifaʿah Rafiʿ al-Tahtawi: A Nineteenth-Century Egyptian Reformer*. Ph.D. dissertation; Los Angeles: University of California, 1976.

El-Ariss, Tarek (ed.). *The Arab Renaissance: A Bilingual Anthology of the Nahda*. New York: Modern Language Association, 2018.

Armbrust, Walter. *Mass Culture and Modernism in Egypt*. Cambridge: Cambridge University Press, 1996.

Ayalon, Ami. *The Arabic Print Revolution: Cultural Production and Mass Readership*. Cambridge: Cambridge University Press, 2016.

Aybash, Aḥmad. *Dimashq al-Shām fī nuṣūṣ al-raḥḥālīn wa'l-jughrāfiyyīn wa'l-buldāniyyīn al-ʿArab wa'l Muslimīn*. Damascus: Wizārat al-Thaqāfa, 1998. 2 vols.

Baer, Gabriel. "Jerusalem Notables in Ottoman Cairo," in *Egypt and Palestine: A Millennium of Association*, edited by Amnon Cohen and Gabriel Baer. New York: St. Martin's Press, 1984, 167–175.

77 Sāmī, *al-Qawl al-ḥaqq*, 31–32.

Baladi, Noëlle. *L'émancipation de la femme en Égypte*. Nantes: Éditions Amalthée, 2005.
Baron, Beth. *The Women's Awakening in Egypt: Culture, Society and the Press*. New Haven: Yale University Press, 1994.
Baron, Beth. "Liberal Thought and the 'Problem' of Women, Cairo, 1890s," in *Arabic Thought Beyond the Liberal Age: Towards an Intellectual History of the Nahda*, edited by Jens Hanssen and Max Weiss. Cambridge: Cambridge University Press, 2016, 187–213.
Al-Bayṭār, ʿAbd al-Razzāq. *Ḥilyat al-bashar fī taʾrīkh al-qarn al-thālith ʿashar*. Damascus: Maṭbūʿāt al-Majmaʿ al-ʿIlmī al-ʿArabī, 1961–1963. 3 vols.
Beshara, Adel (ed.). *Butrus al-Bustani: Spirit of the Age*. Melbourne: Iphoenix Publishing, 2014.
Cole, Juan R. *Colonialism and Revolution in the Middle East: Social and Cultural Origins of Egypt's ʿUrabi Movement*. Princeton: Princeton University Press, 1993.
Cole, Juan R.I. "Printing and Urban Islam in the Mediterranean World 1890–1920," in *Modernity and Culture: From the Mediterranean to the Indian Ocean*, edited by Leila T. Fawaz and Christopher Alan Bayly. New York: Columbia University Press, 2002. 344–364.
Commins, David. *Islamic Reform*. Oxford: Oxford University Press, 1990.
Delanoue, Gilbert. *Moralistes et politques musulmans dans l'Égypte du XIXe siècle, 1798–1882*. Cairo: Institut français d'archéologie orientale du Caire, 1982. 2 vols.
Eliraz, Giora. *Islam in Indonesia*. Brighton: Sussex, 2004.
Fortna, Benjamin C. *Imperial Classroom: Islam, the State, and Education in the Late Ottoman Empire*. Oxford: Oxford University Press, 2002.
Gorman, Anthony (ed.). *The Press in the Middle East and North Africa 1850–1959: Politics, Society and Culture*. Edinburgh: Edinburgh University Press, 2018.
Haim, Sylvia G. *Arab Nationalism: An Anthology*. Berkeley: University of California Press, 1962.
Hanssen, Jens and Max Weiss (eds.). *Arabic Thought Beyond the Liberal Age: Towards an Intellectual History of the Nahda*. Cambridge: Cambridge University Press, 2016.
Hatina, Meir. "Fatwas as a Prism of Social History in the Middle East: The Status of Non-Muslims in the Nineteenth Century," in *Koexistenz und Konfrontation: Beiträge zur jüngeren Geschichte und Gegenwartslage der orientalischen Christen*, edited by Martin Tamcke. Hamburg: LIT, 2003, 51–74.
Hatina, Meir. *ʿUlamaʾ, Politics and the Public Sphere*. Salt Lake City: Utah University Press, 2010.
Al-Hijrisī, Muḥammad Khalīl. *al-Jawhar al-nafīs ʿalā ṣalawāt Ibn Idrīs*. Cairo, Būlāq: al-Maṭbaʿa al-Miṣriyya, 1893.
Al-Hijrisī, Muḥammad Khalīl. *Hādhā kitāb al-qaṣr al-mashīd fīʾl-tawḥīd*. Cairo: al-Maṭbaʿa al-ʿIlmiyya, 1896/1897.

Hill, Peter. "The First Arabic Translations of Enlightenment Literature: The Damietta Circle of the 1800s and 1810s," *Intellectual History Review* 25/2 (2015): 209–233.

Hourani, Albert. *Arabic Thought in the Liberal Age 1798–1939*. 3rd ed., Cambridge: Cambridge University Press, 1983.

Hourani, Albert. "The Syrians in Egypt in the Eighteenth and Nineteenth Centuries," in *Colloque international sur l'histoire du Caire*. Cairo: Ministry of Culture of the Arab Republic of Egypt, 1972, 221–233.

Kaḥḥāla, ʿUmar Riḍā. *Muʿjam al-muʾallifīn*. Beirut: Maktabat al-Muthannā, n.d. 13 vols.

Kozma, Liat et al. (eds.). *A Global Middle East*. London: I.B. Tauris, 2015.

Kupferschmidt, Uri. "Connections of the Palestinian Ulama with Egypt and Other Parts of the Ottoman Empire," in *Egypt and Palestine*, edited by Amnon Cohen and Gabriel Baer. New York: St. Martin's Press, 1984, 176–189.

Livingston, John W. "Western Science and Educational Reform in the Thought of Shaykh Rifaʿa al-Tahtawi," *IJMES* 28/4 (1996): 543–564.

Maḥmūd, ʿAbd al-Ḥalīm. *al-Madrasa al-Shādhiliyya al-ḥadītha*. Cairo: Dar al-Kutub al-Ḥadītha, 1968.

Manna, ʿAdil. "Cultural Relations between Egyptian and Jerusalem ʿUlamaʾ in the Early Nineteenth Century," *Asian and African Studies* 17 (1983): 139–152.

Ma'oz, Moshe. "The Ulama and the Process of Modernization in Syria during the Mid-Nineteenth Century," *Asian and African Studies* 7 (1971): 77–88.

Ma'oz, Moshe. "Muslim Ethnic Communities in Nineteenth-Century Syria and Palestine: Trends of Conflict and Integration," *Asian and African Studies* 19 (1985): 283–307.

Masters, Bruce. *Christians and Jews in the Ottoman Arab World: The Roots of Sectarianism*. Cambridge: Cambridge University Press, 2001.

Mitchell, Timothy. *Colonising Egypt*. Cambridge: Cambridge University Press, 1988.

Mubārak, ʿAlī. *al-Khiṭaṭ al-Tawfīqiyya al-jadīda li-Miṣr al-Qāhira*. Cairo, Būlāq: Dār al-Kutub, 1887–89. 20 vols.

Mujāhid, Zakī Muḥammad. *al-Aʿlām al-Sharqiyya*. Cairo: al-Maṭbaʿa al-Miṣriyya al-Ḥadītha, 1949–50. 4 vols.

Nāfiʿ, Bashīr. "Nashʾat al-ittijāhāt al-siyāsiyya fī Filasṭīn fi awākhir al-ʿahd al-ʿUthmānī," *Qiraʾāt siyāsiyya* (Winter 1995): 27–56.

Al-Najjār, Ḥusayn Fawzī. *Aḥmad ʿUrābī Miṣr li'l-Miṣriyyīn*. Cairo: al-Hayʾa al-Miṣriyya al-ʿĀmma li'l- Kitāb, 1992.

Nettl, John P. "Ideas, Intellectuals and Structures of Dissent," in *On Intellectuals*, edited by Philip Rieff. New York: Doubleday, 1969, 53–122.

Patel, Youshaa. "The Islamic Treatises against Imitation (*Tasabbuh*): A Bibliographical History," *Arabica* 65 (2018): 597–639.

Al-Qāyātī, Muḥammad. *Wasīlat al-wuṣūl fī'l-fiqh wa'l-tawḥīd wa'l-uṣūl*. Cairo: Maṭbaʿat al-Khayriyya, 1888.

Al-Qāyātī, Muḥammad. *Khulāṣat al-taḥqīq fī afḍaliyyat al-Ṣiddīq*. Cairo: Maṭbaʿat al-Islām, 1895.

Al-Qāyātī, Muḥammad. *Nafḥat al-bashām fī riḥlat al-Shām*. Beirut: Dār al-Rāʾid al-ʿArabī, [1901] 1981.

Rafeq, Abdul-Karim. "The Ulama of Ottoman Jerusalem (16th–18th Centuries)," in *Ottoman Jerusalem: The Living City 1517–1917*, edited by Sylvia Aduld and Robet Hillenbrand. Jerusalem: Altajir World of Islam Trust, 2000, 1: 45–51.

Ramaḍān, Muṣṭafā. "Riwāq al-Shuwām bi'l-Azhar ibbāna al-ʿaṣr al-ʿUthmānī," in *al-Muʾtamar al-duwalī al-thānī li-taʾrīkh bilād al-Shām 1517–1939*. Damascus: Jāmiʿat Dimashq, 1978, 17–97.

Salim, Latifa Muhammad. *al-Quwwa al-ijtimaʿiyya fi'l-thawra al-ʿUrābiyya*. Cairo: al-Hayʾa al-Miṣriyya al-ʿĀmma li'l-Kitāb, 1981.

Sāmī, ʿAbd al-Raḥmān. *al-Qawl al-ḥaqq fī Bayrūt wa-Dimashq*. New ed., Beirut: Dār al-Rāʾid al-ʿArabī, [1890] 1981.

Sarhank, Ismāʿīl. *Ḥaqāʾiq al-akhbār ʿan duwal al-biḥār*. Cairo: al-Maṭbaʿa al-Amīriyya, 1895–1923. 3 vols.

Sarkīs, Yūsuf. *Muʿjam al-maṭbūʿāt al-ʿArabiyya wa'l-muʿarraba*. Cairo: Maṭbaʿat Sarkīs, 1928. 2 vols.

Schölch, Alexander. *Egypt for the Egyptians: The Socio-Political Crisis in Egypt 1878–1882*. London: Ithaca Press, 1981.

Shārūbīm, Mīkhāʾīl. *Taʾrīkh Miṣr al-qadīm wa'l-ḥadīth*. Cairo: al-Matbaʿa al-Kubrā al-Amīryya, 1900.

Al-Shaṭṭī, Muḥammad Jamīl. *Aʿyān Dimashq fi'l-qarn al-thālith ʿashar wa-niṣf al-qarn al-rābiʿ ʿashar*. Damascus: Dār al-Bashāʾir, 1994.

Shils, Edward. "The Intellectual and the Powers: Some Perspectives for Comparative Analysis," *Society and History* 1/1 (October 1958): 5–22.

Al Shinnāwī, ʿAbd al-ʿAzīz. "Dawr al-Azhar fi'l-ḥifāẓ ʿalā al-ṭabiʿ al-ʿArabī li-Miṣr ibbāna al-ḥukm al-ʿUthmānī," in *Abḥāth al-nadwa al-duwaliyya li-taʾrīkh al-Qāhira*. Cairo: Dār al-Kutub, 1971, 2: 667–715.

Simāṭ, Maryam. "al-Tamthīl al-ʿArabī," in *Taʾrīkh al-masraḥ al-ʿArabī*, edited by Fuʾād Rashīd. Giza: Wikālat al-Ṣaḥāfa al-ʿArabiyya, 2004, 51–53.

Starret, Gregory. *Putting Islam to Work: Education, Politics and Religious Transformation in Egypt*. Berkeley: University of California Press, 1998.

Al-Tahtawi, Rifaʿa Rafiʿ. *An Imam in Paris: Account of a Stay in France by an Egyptian Cleric, 1826–1831*. Trans. and introduction by Daniel Newman. London: Dar al-Saqi, 2011.

Ṭarbīn, Aḥmad. *Malāmiḥ al-taghyīr al-ijtimāʿī fī bilād al-Shām fi'l-qarn al-tāsiʿ ʿashar*. Beirut: Maʿhad al-Inmāʾ al-ʿArabī, 1982.

Tauber, Eliezer. *The Arab Movements in World War I*. London: Frank Cass, 1993.

Taymūr, Aḥmad. *Aʿlām al-fikr al-Islāmī fi'l-ʿaṣr al-ḥadīth*. Cairo: Lajnat Nashr al-Muʾallafāt al-Taymūriyya, 1967.

Tibi, Bassam. *Arab Nationalism: A Critical Enquiry*. New York: St. Martin's Press, 1981.

Toledano, Ehud R. *State and Society in Mid-Nineteenth Century Egypt*. Cambridge: Cambridge University Press, 1990.

Toledano, Ehud R. "The Arabic Speaking-World in the Ottoman Period: A Socio-Political Analysis," in *The Ottoman World*, edited by Christine Woodhead. London: Routledge, 2011, 453–466.

Yazbak, Mahmoud. "Nabulsi Ulama in the Late Ottoman Period 1864–1914," *IJMES* 29 (1997): 78–79.

Zachs, Fruma and Sharon Halevi. *Gendering Culture in Greater Syria: Intellectual and Ideology in the Late Ottoman Empire*. London: I.B. Tauris, 2015.

Shmuel Moreh's *Baghdad Mon Amour*: Autobiographical Works as Historical and Cultural Documents

Sigal Goorji

1 Introduction

The article examines Shmuel Moreh's memoirs, *Baghdād ḥabībatī* (Baghdad Mon Amour),[1] and the memoirs of other Iraqi Jews in order to try and clarify the relationship with their Arab neighbors and the history of Iraqi Jews, mainly from the 1930s and up to their immigration to Israel in the 1950s. As becomes apparent in these memoirs, the terrible June 1941 pogrom known as the *Farhūd* was a formative event that influenced and defined their identity. Autobiographies and memoirs are actually works of art that describe emotions and feelings of individuals in a specific space and time. Such documents, which are not written by historians, enrich history by providing a different perspective of a society's way of thinking and responses in a specific time period. The memories show that the religious difference between Jews (or other minorities) and their Muslim fellow citizens was especially sensitive in Iraqi society.

In the modern world and with the growth of philosophical, scientific, and secular theories such as psychoanalysis and existentialism, society has become less collectivistic as the emphasis has shifted to the individual. Because of this, literary forms, like diaries, memoirs, and autobiographies, are now widespread, becoming primary sources for historical research.

According to both the new cultural history and the history of sensibilities, the difference between past and present is not a difference of beliefs, values, and modes of representation, but a difference of perceptions and feelings.[2] Texts such as autobiographies, diaries, or memoirs can be used as tools that reveal how culture and thought deal with social and political issues. That is, by reading memoirs, we can learn how society is studied and how topics like religion, minorities, or gender are viewed.

We can therefore view Moreh's *Baghdad Mon Amour* as a kind of historical source written in an aesthetic, fictional style. Personal memory adds an

---

1 Shmuel Moreh, *Baghdād ḥabībatī: Yahūd al-ʿIrāq, dhikrayāt wa-shujūn* (Haifa: Maktabat Kull Shay', 2012).

2 Daniel Wickberg, "What Is the History of Sensibilities? On Cultural Histories, Old and New," *The American Historical Review* 112/3 (June 2007): 664.

 | DOI:10.1163/9789004459120_019

important dimension to the collective memory, especially if we add to Moreh's memoirs other autobiographies on the same events that are mentioned in his book, such as Anwar Shaul's *Qiṣṣt ḥayātī fī bilād al-rāfidayn* (The story of my life in Mesopotamia, 1980); Salman Darwish's *Kull shay' hādi' fī'i-'iyāda* (All quiet in the surgery, 1981); Salim Fattal's *Fī aziqqat Baghdād* (In the alleys of Baghdad, 2003); Violette Shammash's *Dhikrayāt min 'Adan: riḥla 'abra Baghdād al-Yahūdiyya* (Memories of Eden: A journey through Jewish Baghdad, 2008); Nissim Qazzaz's *Warrior and Scholar: Memoirs* (2010); and Meir Mu'allem's *A Fistful of Life: Memoirs of Iraq* (2011). These and other autobiographies often provide a clear, honest, and authentic picture of the cultural history of Iraqi Jewry.

2 Lost Paradise—Longing and Nostalgia

Moreh's academic research focuses on poetry, literature, theatre, and history, in each of which he has led to groundbreaking research. In addition, he himself is also a poet and writer. He started to write poems when he was eight years old.[3] In addition to poems, his literary work includes short stories and memoirs, all written in Arabic. The content of the poetry he wrote in Iraq was similar to that of the modernist poets of those days, poetry that expresses his inner world and emotions, and deals with philosophical questions, such as the meaning of life, the struggle for justice and equality, and women's rights.[4] The poetry he wrote after immigrating to Israel was melancholic and passionate, yet reflected not only a sense of isolation but also of optimism and a desire to be reunited with his father in Israel. His father immigrated to Israel only in 1962, after selling part of his wealth.[5]

Despite the fact that most of his research is written in English, Moreh has consciously chosen to write the bulk of his poems and his life story in his mother tongue, Arabic, which reflects his umbilical-cord connection to the Arabic language and culture. His memoirs, *Baghdad Mon Amour*, which are in fact an encyclopedia about Iraqi-Jewish culture and heritage and about Jewish-Muslim relations, reflect his love of homeland and the darkness of betrayal. It holds much love and much hatred. Through the memories, we

3 Shmuel Moreh, *Tilka ayyām al-ṣibā: majmū'a shi'riyya bi'l-lughatayn al-'Arabiyya wa'l-Inklīziyya* (Jerusalem: Association of Jewish Academics from Iraq, 1998), 6.

4 Shmuel Moreh, *Modern Arabic Poetry, 1800–1970: The Development of Its Forms and Themes under the Influence of Western Literature* (Leiden: Brill, 1976), 217–218.

5 Moreh, *Tilka ayyām al-ṣibā*, 63–67; Moreh, *Baghdād*, 62.

recognize the sensitive relationship between Jews and Muslims, which can blow up at any time whether the location of the events is Iraq, Israel, or London.

The author tells us his life story, following external events he has experienced and revealing his inner world. Through his writings, which by the author's own recognition are testimonies to history, he reopens and reexamines old wounds. They constitute the groundwork from which he scrutinizes the events that shaped his life and the lives of many Jewish immigrants from Iraq from a different point in time.

Moreh's *Baghdad Mon Amour* begins with a poem written in Arabic. In this poem, he engages in a dialogue with his mother, who symbolizes the Babylonian Jews, and talks about their longing for and betrayal of the motherland.[6] Since one's mother tongue is the language of one's soul and part of one's cultural identity, it seems that *Baghdad Mon Amour* is directed primarily at the Arab reader. Indeed, Moreh's stories, which began as articles in the electronic newspaper *Elaph*, quickly became serialized chapters that invited a flood of responses from Arab readers in general, and Iraqis in particular. In his dialogue with the Arab reader, Moreh wants to settle accounts with the Iraqi people and with fate. The interesting thing is that some of the respondents, especially the Iraqi ones, take responsibility for acts of hatred and persecution against the Jews of Iraq and ask for pardon, in the hopes that Iraqi Jews will return to help rebuild Iraq. The *Elaph* site contains numerous disputes among the respondents regarding this issue. Apparently, respondents of Iraqi origin often praise the writer and find in the suffering of Iraq today a punishment for past crimes against the Jews. Others try to divert the discussion into a discourse on the suffering of the Palestinians.[7]

Moreh was born in 1932, at the end of a period in the twentieth century known as the Golden Age of Iraqi Jews. King Fayṣal I, who was sympathetic to the Jews and visited their institutions, ruled Iraq between 1921 and 1933. The modernization that began taking root in Arab lands in the nineteenth century also affected the Jews. Hence, modern education within the framework of Jewish communal life increased, and—taught by European teachers—Jews began studying European languages, especially French and English, at Alliance and Shammash schools. Many Jews went on to study modern subjects, such as medicine, law, economics, and pharmacology, a trend that led them to adopt a new cultural identity. It should be noted that at the time, the question of identity and reshaping it according to criteria such as nationality and independence characterized intellectual discourse in the region. It was natural

6 Moreh, *Baghdād*, 3–4.

7 http://elaph.com/Web/ElaphWriter/2009/5/441337.htm (accessed: March 30, 2015).

that the Jews who were living in Iraq saw themselves as patriotic Iraqis closely connected to their beloved homeland. The motto "religion belongs to God and the homeland belongs to the people" (*al-dīn li'l-lāh wal-waṭan li'l-jamīʿ*) prevailed at the time in Arab society, and many Jews who saw Iraq as their beloved homeland adopted the motto out of desire to live in equality, harmony, and peace with the Muslim majority in their shared homeland.[8]

As noted above, the autobiographies and memoirs of Iraqi Jews describe this period as their Golden Age. In the 1930s, things started to change: After King Fayṣal's death in 1933, his son Ghāzī, who was under the influence of Arab nationalists, changed his approach to the Jews. Nazi propaganda began to seep into Iraq from 1933 onward, channeled through Ambassador Fritz Grover. Another reason for this change was the arrival in Iraq of Ḥājj Amīn al-Ḥusaynī, the Mufti of Jerusalem.[9] Increasingly, from 1929 onwards, many Palestinian and Syrian refugees fled to Iraq; most of them established and organized anti-Jewish clubs and societies in Baghdad.[10] The culmination of this incitement was the pogrom known as the *Farhūd*, which happened during the Festival of Shavuot (Pentecost) on June 1–2, 1941.[11]

Reading the memoirs of Jewish writers reveals the social sensitivities that affected the relations between Muslims and Jews at that time—despite the freedoms and equal rights all enjoyed. In his memoirs, ʿIzzat Sāsūn Muʿallim (d. 2004) describes relations of peace and brotherhood between Jews and Muslims in al-Dīwāniyya. Nevertheless, he notes the shadow cast over this relationship: Shiʿi Muslims regarded Jews as impure and there were cases when Muslim children provoked, beat, or cursed Jews, whether children or adults.[12] Hence, Jews still felt like second-class citizens. Hayim J. Cohen writes in his article on the *Farhūd*:

---

8 Shmuel Moreh and Lev Hakak, "Contemporary Literary and Scientific Activities by Jewish Writers from Iraq in Iraq and Israel," in *The Tree and the Branch: Studies in Modern Arabic Literature and Contributions of Iraqi-Jewish Writers*, edited by Olga Bramson (Jerusalem: Magnes Press, 1997), 297, 319–320 (in Hebrew); Reuven Snir, *Arabness, Jewishness, Zionism—A Clash of Identities in the Literature of Iraqi Jews* (Jerusalem: Ben-Zvi Institute, 2005), 42–77 (in Hebrew).

9 Sylvia G. Haim, "Aspects of Jewish Life in Baghdad under the Monarchy," *Middle Eastern Studies* 12/2 (May 1976): 191–192.

10 Hayim J. Cohen, "The Anti-Jewish '*Farhud*' in Baghdad, 1941," *Middle Eastern Studies* 3/1 (October 1966): 4, 6; David Qazzaz, *Mother of the Pound: Memoirs on the Life and History of the Iraqi Jews* (Tel Aviv: Maariv, 2006), 21 (in Hebrew).

11 See note 41 below.

12 ʿIzzat Sāsūn Muʿallim, *ʿAlā ḍifāf al-Furāt* (Shafā ʿAmr: al-Mashriq, 1980), 109–110.

> Jews were always the target of hooligans and youngsters, who might mock at them or hit them or snatch something belonging to them, and there were even cases of actual murder. But in general, all this should not be taken as a manifestation of hatred towards Jews, but as a means of humiliating them, and Jews were used to it.[13]

Similarly, Nissim Qazzaz writes in his work on the Jews of Iraq that after Iraq received its political independence, the Jews were categorized as equal Iraqi citizens, but in reality, they remained second-class citizens.[14] In short, the Jews knew that they were socially inferior to the Muslims and that they frequently had to give up their dignity in order not to clash with Muslims.

Shmuel Moreh's memoirs and the autobiographies of other Iraqi Jews reflect disappointment with their homeland. Despite their loyalty they were treated as second-class citizens, just for being Jews, whereas the Muslims felt confident and inherently superior. Despite the fact that in the public and economic fields, Jews felt at least partly on an equal footing with the Muslims, at the level of the individual, such as in schools and in the neighborhoods, things were different and insults were part of everyday life.

Moreh describes his childhood against the background of Jewish relationships with Muslim neighbors, and through these descriptions we can learn about the feelings of fear and anxiety experienced during encounters with Muslims: When he was three years old, he decided to try his luck as a "business man." Without his parents' knowledge, he took a tray of silver spoons and tried to sell them in the street. Some bystanders laughed at the young child and said, using a stereotype of the greedy and money-mad Jew: "These baby Jews! These have not hatched yet and they are already engaging in commerce."[15] One of the passersby took the tray with the spoons without leaving any money. Sami returned home, crying that he had been cheated. His parents panicked and thanked God that the Muslims had not harmed him physically. They reminded him not to go out alone in the street because Muslims could hurt him:

> Did I not tell you not to go outside? Both my parents were angry, and my mother said: Go to hell! Have I not told you already not to go out because the Muslims will beat you? It is God's miracle; we were lucky that the man does not strangle children and did not kill you. My father said: "You want

---

13 Cohen, "The Anti-Jewish," 4.

14 Nissim Qazzaz, *The Jews in Iraq after the Mass Immigration, 1951–2000* (Or-Yehuda: The Babylonian Jewry Heritage Center, 2002), 16 (in Hebrew).

15 Moreh, *Baghdād*, 20.

> me to kill you now? I told you a thousand and one times not to go out alone, in order not to be beaten."[16]

Another stereotype was that of the cowardly and weak Jew. When Moreh describes his first day at Saʿdūn Exemplary School, he notes that he and his brother Raymond were the only Jews there. When the Muslim pupils discovered that he was Jewish, they started to mock him, imitating a Jew afraid of rifles: "Abdālak Ḥisqīl [May I be your ransom (redeemer) Ḥisqīl (Yeheskel)], please tell me whether he fired the rifle or not?"[17] The pupils used the famous Jewish name Yeheskel to indicate the Jewishness of the person they were talking about. We can see how stereotypes were used in daily life: The Jew is such a coward and so paralyzed by fear that he cannot tell whether the rifle has been fired or not. After school, those pupils continued their provocations and drew their fingers across their necks to indicate that they would kill him. Moreh found himself coping with feelings of helplessness: "I felt unprotected, lost, and isolated—as orphans do."[18] However, he took up boxing, training with his older brother Jacob, and challenged the Muslim pupils to fight with him, in singles or in pairs. They were astonished at his bravery. They asked a Christian pupil to fight him. Moreh immediately tripped up his opponent and pushed him into a ditch behind them. When he asked who was next, they applauded him as a brave fighter.

As the Nazi and anti-Jewish propaganda in Iraq increased, the relationship between Muslims and Jews steadily deteriorated. Moreh recounts an incident involving his sister Gladys: On the evening of the Hebrew New Year, she proudly went to show her new golden dress to her grandmother. A Muslim woman stopped her and tore the dress, saying, "Now you can rejoice your feast."[19] His oldest brother Jacob received similar treatment: Muslim Shiʿi youths used to taunt Jews in the street and throw stones at them; in one case Jacob was the victim of an assault, returning home with blood streaming from his head.[20] Similar humiliation and harassment can be found in Gidʿon Shammash's memoirs. He writes about the influence of Nazi propaganda on the local population and about the events of the Arab Revolt between the years 1936–1939 in Palestine. He mentions that in the summer of 1937, as his father was strolling along with a friend, the friend suddenly began to curse the Jews and pulled out

16 Ibid., 20.
17 Ibid., 44.
18 Ibid., 45.
19 Ibid., 22.
20 Moreh, *Tilka ayyām al-ṣibā*, 18–19.

a gun in order to shoot his father, blaming the Jews for dispossessing the Arabs of their land in Palestine. The father asked, "What do we have in common with the Jews there?" The friend shoved Shammash's father aside and walked away from him forever.[21]

This shows how easy it was to threaten the Jews and harm them, leaving them unprotected. Despite the friendly relationships between the Jews and their neighbors, the Nazi incitement did manage to penetrate Iraqi society. In fact, social sensitivities rooted in religious differences acted like time bombs that could explode at any given moment, following even a slight change in mood. The Jews could do nothing but bribe their attackers, resign themselves to their unequal status, and tolerate the treatment they received from their Muslim neighbors.

These fragile relationships between Jews and Muslims in Iraq, as described in Moreh's *Memoirs*, are similar to the ones described in *Ṭalaʿa al-badr ʿalaynā* (The moon shone over our heads), the 1975 memoirs of the Egyptian writer and journalist Anīs Manṣūr (d. 2011). In this book, Manṣūr documents his childhood in his birthplace of al-Manṣūra. He describes the city as cosmopolitan, with Jewish and Christian minorities, so that already as a child, he became familiar with different religions and customs.[22] Manṣūr adds that his mother, who was of Christian-French ancestry,[23] preferred Christian neighbors, whom she perceived as goodhearted and generous.[24] He continues and writes that the wife of their householder was a German Jew. She was rich and kind, and her son Sāmī was Manṣūr's best friend. The books Sāmī brought him enriched Manṣūr's knowledge of literature and Western philosophy.[25] Manṣūr praises the dignity and generosity of his Christian neighbors, who cared for others and respected them, as opposed to his Muslim acquaintances.[26] There is indeed a basis to the German philosopher Nietzsche's observation that the social environment envelops us in outer shells of opinions and practices, and that in order to reach authenticity, we must remove the shells which institutions and conventions have imposed on us. Only then can one adopt new moral norms,

21 Gidʿon Shammash, *My Life's Journey in Iraq and Israel* (Jerusalem: Association of Jewish Academics from Iraq, 2011), 21–23 (in Hebrew).

22 Anīs Manṣūr's books, *Ṭalaʿa al-badr ʿalaynā* (Cairo: al-Maktab al-Miṣrī al-Ḥadīth, 1975), 20; *al-Baqiyya fī ḥayātī* (Cairo: Dār al-Shurūq, 1993), 49–51; *ʿĀshū fī ḥayātī* (Cairo: al-Maktab al-Miṣrī al-Ḥadīth, 1989), 112.

23 Manṣūr, *Ṭalaʿa al-badr*, 79; and his *ʿĀshū*, 147.

24 Manṣūr, *al-Baqiyya*, 45–46.

25 Ibid., 46–47.

26 Ibid., 46–50.

as one sees fit.[27] Hence, we might say that in Anīs Manṣūr's childhood, the authentic impression he received from his own experience with his Jewish and Christian friends, with whom he had strong ties, was different from the impression that society wanted to convey, namely that minorities, especially the Jews, are hated and regarded as enemies. Manṣūr dared to criticize Egyptian society in his book, *al-Baqiyya fī ḥayātī* (May I have a long life, 1993) and he asks:

> People say she is Jewish. What is the meaning of Jewish? What is the meaning of Christian? I do not know. But they are different people. How? I do not know. They do not go to mosques, but to the churches; they are not Muslims, but what's the difference? I do not know. But there is a strange thing that appears on the faces of the people and in their words when they talk of Christians or Jews, there is this kind of wonder, of condemnation, of pride, of fear, of hate, I do not know, and my mother doesn't say, but I notice that she feels good with these people who are different from us, and that's it![28]

It appears, therefore, that in spite of the neighborliness and friendship which characterized the residents in the neighborhood of Manṣūr, the sense of alienation and rejection of Muslims towards Christians and Jews did not change, even though the latter were loyal and contributed to Egypt's economy, culture, art, commerce, and press.[29] This was probably due to the condescending position of the monotheistic religions toward each other.[30] Each religion claimed that the key to the kingdom of heaven and eternal life lay in its hands. While Islam saw itself as setting the seal on monotheistic religions, the high percentage of the population suffering from ignorance and prejudice reinforced the feeling of rejection of minorities, especially the Jews, by Muslim society, as we can learn from the dialogue engaged in by Manṣūr and his uncles about his Jewish neighbors: His aunt exclaimed "save me God" (*aʿūdhu bi'l-lāh*) when Manṣūr told her about his Christian friend, and his uncle asked him what "Umm Barakāt," the mother of his Jewish friend Sāmī, looked like.[31] The uncle wondered how his nephew was "consorting with such people," but did not have an answer to Manṣūr's question, i.e. why it was forbidden to befriend Jews.

27 Jacob Golomb, *An Introduction to the Philosophies of Existentialism* (Tel Aviv: Broadcast University, 1990), 111.
28 Manṣūr, *al-Baqiyya*, 45–46.
29 Israel Gershoni, Orit Bashkin, and Liat Kozma (eds.), *Sculpting Culture in Egypt* (Tel Aviv: Ramot, 1999), 21–23 (in Hebrew).
30 Patricia Crone, *Pre-Industrial Societies* (Oxford: Blackwell, 1989), 93–94.
31 Manṣūr, *al-Baqiyya*, 49.

The uncle simply responded with a typical conservative Eastern saying, "That's the way it is." Another uncle became angry and accused his young nephew of heresy when he found him sitting on a bench with a Jew and a Christian, and asked him in front of his friends: "What is it? One Jew and one Copt and what are you, a Druze?" The uncle concluded with a warning: "Woe to you if I see you with them again!"[32]

These descriptions by Manṣūr reveal the deep prejudice about the nature of Jews and Christians within Muslim society. In spite of the friendly relations between Muslims and members of other creeds, hatred towards non-Muslims remains entrenched in Muslim beliefs. Manṣūr understood the danger of pasting labels on others, as he implies in his autobiography: "There is no difference between people of every color and religion, but why are people always ready to put imaginary barriers and false fears to shatter human relations, why? I do not know."[33]

In a similar vein, Moreh stresses in his memoirs that children are nurtured from an early age by everything their parents and society feed them. He describes how Muslim children used to visit the family home on Saturdays and ask whether there was a need to light the fire to heat up the food, but gradually the Jewish family started to feel that this relationship was getting more distant. One of the children, who regularly visited them on Saturdays to light the Shabbat stove, stood near the open door, terror-stricken. They called him to enter and light the fire, which was dying: "Daḥḥām, where were you? Please come and let us see you."[34] And he asked: "If I enter your house will you kill me? Will you butcher me?" He explained that the *al-Futuwwa* movement[35] had warned him not to enter Jewish homes because "Jews are slaughtering Muslim children on their holy days."[36]

We see how the Damascus blood libel becomes part of life in modern Iraq. The fact that the child comes close to but is afraid to enter the house illustrates his inner conflict. On the one hand is his belief that the Jews would not hurt him, and on the other hand there is a social, Nazi-inspired prohibition not to associate with Jews. It seems that these things were not strange to Iraqi Jews, who were used to such events, albeit they secretly hoped that they would

32 Ibid., 50–51.

33 Ibid., 50.

34 Moreh, *Baghdād*, 28.

35 *Al-Futuwwa* was a paramilitary youth movement. Stefan Wild, "National Socialism in the Arab Near East between 1933 and 1939," in *Hatred of Jews and the Farhud in Iraq*, eds. Shmuel Moreh and Zvi Yehuda (Or-Yehuda: The Babylonian Jewry Heritage Center, 1992), 35–36 (in Hebrew).

36 Moreh, *Baghdād*, 28.

not experience them again. Esther, the Morehs' cook, asks what else they will accuse the Jews of? Except for a sense of frustration and disappointment, and attempts to appease the child and explain to him that they are not killers, it does not seem that the Jews are able to change things. This is the pain and the betrayal that the Iraqi Jews experienced. Suddenly, out of the blue, their lives could be turned upside down without them being able to do anything about it. The frustration is clearly expressed in the words of Esther: "Woe to the *Futuwwa* that teaches him such awful and terrible things! They've ruined the poor child and poisoned his mind. What else are they going to accuse us of? Daḥḥām, don't be afraid! Jews do not kill anyone!"[37]

This was worse, according to Moreh, in Muslim neighborhoods where the majority was fanatic and poor. In these neighborhoods, where the socioeconomic conditions were low, people's frustration at times led to aggressive behavior towards minorities. The young Sāmī Moreh, who had been sent from the prestigious neighborhood al-Battāwīn to his aunt's house in a Muslim neighborhood, did not know the customs of the different places in this neighborhood and that it was forbidden for a Jew to hit a Muslim. When a barefoot Muslim boy asked him: "Hey Jew, what's with you standing here?,"[38] Moreh, who was accustomed to answering such questions with curses, replied: "You bastard, curse your father who brought you into the world and the mother who gave birth to you!"[39] The aunt had to act quickly in order to let the Muslim boy leave Moreh alone and not make things worse:

> It was the height of insolence for the child to enter my aunt's home and shout: "Your son cursed me; I have to beat him and educate him!" My aunt said to him: "Well, my son, forgive him for that, all the curses are on us!" I replied angrily: "No, on him! On him! Cursed be his father who brought him!" My aunt shouted: "Keep quiet! Do you think this is the al-Battāwīn neighborhood here? Do you want to cause us trouble?" My aunt offered the child candy and told him: "Forget about it, my son, it doesn't matter. He comes from al-Battāwīn, where Jews are friends with Muslims, not like here."[40]

37 Ibid., 31.
38 Ibid.
39 Ibid.
40 Ibid.

3 The *Farhūd*—The Shattering of a Dream

In his autobiographical writing, Moreh returns to his childhood experiences and the magical landscapes of Iraq in an attempt to reconstruct and clarify his past both to himself and to his readers, to confront and reshape it in order to redefine his self-identity in the present. His memoirs and those of his contemporaries illustrate how Jewish society knew deep down that they must avoid provoking the anger of their Muslim neighbors. Although most of the time it seemed that they did have good neighborly relations, there were social sensibilities based on religious differences that could be affected by political or social changes.

One of the formative events of the story of the Jews of Iraq was the brutal and terrible pogrom known as the *Farhūd*. These were riots carried out by Muslims against Jews during the Jewish holiday of Shavuot in June 1941[41] during which 179 Jews were murdered.[42] Conversations with Iraqi Jews and a perusal of their memoirs indicate that the *Farhūd* was a decisive turning point in the history of Iraqi Jewry.

Moreh notes that the *Farhūd* was a "slap in the face," which caused the Jews of Iraq to understand that their hope for a future of brotherhood and equality had ended.[43] What also shocked him was that none of the Arab intellects and writers bothered to write about this event, except as brief footnotes.[44]

In his memoirs, he writes that on the day the *Farhūd* started, a Muslim neighbor, who loved their family because Moreh's mother had helped him find a job and helped his two wives with dresses and advice on how to raise and take care of their children, warned the head of the family not to leave the house that day and advised him to stand outside his house with a knife to protect his family from the rioting mob. Moreh mentions the shots they heard being fired far from his home and the terrible screams from his uncle's home. Luckily, the attempt to break into the house of his uncle, who had beautiful young daughters, failed. The uncle expressed his disappointment with his homeland and

---

41 Cohen, "The Anti-Jewish," 5–6, 10–17; Shmuel Moreh, "The Pogrom of June 1941 as Reflected in the Literature of Jews from Iraq in Israel," in Moreh and Yehuda (eds.), *Hatred of Jews*, 187.

42 Snir, *Arabness*, 247; Muʿallim, *ʿAlā ḍifāf*, 158; Salim Fattal, *In the Alleys of Bagdad* (Jerusalem: Karmel, 2003), 121 (in Hebrew).

43 Moreh, *Tilka ayyām al-ṣibā*, 8–19; and his "The Pogrom," 189, 209; Moreh and Hakak, "Contemporary," 301; Mu'allem, *On the Banks*, 111; Tamar Morad, Dennis Shasha, and Robert Shasha (eds.), *Iraq's Last Jews* (New York: Palgrave Macmillan, 2008), 14.

44 Moreh, *Tilka ayyām al-ṣibā*, 18–19; and his "The Pogrom," 189, 209.

said sarcastically: "By God, what a rich reward I've received! I worked for them at the police and the train station, and they reward me like this!"[45]

Moreh uses the following words in his descriptions: "A scary shot," "terrible shouting," "quiet and deep silence," "stress and insomnia."[46] They indicate the feelings of fear, insecurity, and helplessness the Jews experienced during the *Farhūd*, as well as the sense of disappointment with their Muslim friends. Another event that influenced Moreh, and which he documented it in his memoirs, was the story of his classmate Morris. This boy witnessed the *Farhūd* at close range: he saw how his mother and sister were raped and how his father was murdered trying to protect them. Morris also witnessed the amputation of a baby's feet in order to take his bracelets.

When Moreh heard these stories, he spent sleepless nights. They explained why Morris could no longer sing the Iraqi national anthem and why, when he held the Iraqi flag, he hissed through his lips and wished for it to be erased.[47] It seems that for many Jews, especially those who had witnessed it firsthand, the *Farhūd* was a formative event that changed their attitude towards their homeland, Iraq. Ovadia Goorji's (d. 2013) documentation of the *Farhūd* recounts how, when he was fifteen years old, the minibus in which he, his mother, and his brother were traveling was stopped by an Arab mob. The mob demanded that the driver to force all the Jews to get off the bus so that they could be slaughtered. One of the passengers pretended to be an Arab and, pushing away the rioters, told the driver: "Drive or we will all die here because of the Jews." Ovadia was terrified. He jumped out of the window and started running towards the road, with an angry crowd chasing him. He was wounded but was saved by a police officer who was horrified to see a wounded child and took him to the police station until things quieted down. His mother was sure that her younger son had been murdered. She crossed the road, crying, and was hit by a car.[48] In his recounting of these events, Ovadia repeatedly claimed that it was this event which marked his dream to live in his homeland, equal to the Muslims. However, he recognized that the Jews no longer had any confidence in Iraq. He decided to join the resistance, knowing that as soon as he could, he would escape from Iraq.

Nissim Qazzaz (b. 1930), whose father was murdered at the very same place where Ovadia had been injured, reached a similar decision. His father was

---

45 Moreh, *Baghdād*, 40–41.

46 Ibid., 41.

47 Ibid., 53–55.

48 Zvi Yehuda, "A Selection of Documents on the Pogrom of June 1941," in Moreh and Yehuda (eds.), *Hatred of Jews*, 227–229.

traveling in one of the minibuses that the mobs tried to stop.[49] In his memoirs, Nissim describes the nightmares that haunted him after his father was murdered. His lifestyle changed radically: The family stopped celebrating holy days, the abundant food that had always been on the table became scarce. From being an excellent pupil, he started to fail. In 1944, at the age of fourteen, he joined the underground in order to immigrate to Israel. He fulfilled his dream in 1946 and joined his three brothers, who had already emigrated.[50]

Like Ovadia and Nissim, Gid'on Shammash (b. 1929), who had also witnessed the *Farhūd*, decided to join the Zionist underground. His father was almost killed, but Shammash's begging and pleading to the outlaw who wanted to shoot him saved his live. Gid'on describes how his family tried to block the entrance to their home to rioters. He describes the feeling of helplessness that overwhelmed the family. He notes that the vilest act was the cutting off of a baby's leg, apparently the same baby that Moreh mentioned in his memoirs.[51] According to Gid'on, the *Farhūd* profoundly shocked the Jews of Baghdad and left a deep wound in the heart of the Jewish community. It was a formative event that, a decade later, determined the fate of the entire Iraqi exile that immigrated to Israel. On a personal level, Gid'on writes that he stopped believing that his future was in his native land, as did many Jews.[52] Salim Fattal (b. 1930) writes in his autobiography that Muslim officers were prepared to guard their houses against the rioters in exchange for money.[53] He describes Jewish families who were helpless and were not guaranteed equal rights as their Muslim neighbors.[54] The pogrom of 1941 aroused in him strong feelings that his existence as a Jew was worthless: "One common thread connects all the murders that were committed then in Baghdad and in the Arab world: 'Jews! You have no place among us.'"[55]

Similarly, in his autobiography, David Qazzaz (b. 1923) describes the *Farhūd* as a deep emotional trauma.[56] He decided to write a novel against the background of that "night of terror," based on real events and characters. But when he presented it to two of his friends, they advised him not to publish the novel because "Muslims do not want to be reminded of their sins and the Jews do

---

49 Ibid., 225–227.
50 Nissim Qazzaz, *Warrior and Scholar* (Jerusalem: Rubin Mass, 2010), 107–116 (in Hebrew).
51 Shammash, *My Life's*, 36–38.
52 Ibid., 38.
53 Fattal, *In the Alleys*, 115–116.
54 Ibid., 121.
55 Ibid., 307.
56 Qazzaz, *Mother*, 224.

not want to relive the pain."[57] This response was similar to the one Yitzhak Bar-Moshe received when he informed his Muslim friend about his intention to write about the *Farhūd*. The novel remained in Iraq after he immigrated to Israel in 1950 and was never published.[58] Similar to what the authors mentioned above wrote, he wrote that life after the traumatic event could be compared to recovery from an earthquake and that the future was expected to be even worse.[59]

The writer and poet Ezra Morad (b. 1933) describes his disappointment with his Muslim neighbors, who sang songs that praised the murders and the desecration of women during the *Farhūd*.[60] In his Poem "*Farhūd* 1941" he writes that since the *Farhūd* the hearts of the people are burning because something has changed and they long for another, more tolerant Iraq.[61] *Kinnorot Bavel* (The violins of Babylon), the autobiography of Avner-Yaacov Yaron (b. 1933), expresses feelings of pain and lack of faith in the possibility of an equal life and of brotherhood in Iraq. He felt that life in Baghdad was like life in exile because there was no national or social solidarity, which is the main reason he decided to emigrate and move to Israel. Although his Muslim friends sympathized with him, he keenly felt the absence of national honor of the Jewish people. He notes that it was not pleasant to live in a regime that did not allow Jews any hope of freedom, growth, and development.[62] According to Yaron, the *Farhūd* carried a kind of historical message to the Jews in Iraq, warning them that if they did not rouse themselves, they would be led to the slaughter as had happened to the Jews of Europe, and that if they wanted to live they should think of a homeland of their own.

In fact, the *Farhūd* marked the shattering of the illusion that "religion belongs to God and the homeland belongs to the people," a slogan King Fayṣal I borrowed from the Egyptian national leader, Saʿd Zaghlūl, in an attempt to unite Muslims and Copts in a joint campaign to achieve independence from the British. The years that followed were lucrative for Jewish merchants in Iraq, but Jews continued to be subjected to condemnation, fights, insults, and negative comments. Since they were a minority within a Muslim majority, their hands were tied, and they had to accept their inferior status in their homeland. The central message of these memoirs seems to be that the spilling of Jewish blood

---

57 Ibid., 231.

58 Ibid.

59 Ibid.

60 Ezra Morad, *Childhood Scenery from My Father's Home* (Jerusalem: Association of Jewish Academics from Iraq, 2012), 219–222 (in Hebrew).

61 Ibid., 220.

62 Avner-Yaacov Yaron, *Violins of Babylon* (Tel Aviv: Miksam, 2007), 1: 9.

was permitted because it was Jewish blood. Since they were highly vulnerable, Jews were forced to forego their dignity and remain silent; they constantly had to appease the Muslim, so as to receive his protection (as *dhimmīs*) and stave off his anger. Although there were periods of brotherhood and friendship between Muslims and Jews (or other minorities), the latter were always aware that this relationship could be shattered at any given moment.

In his wide-ranging book *Arabness, Jewishness, Zionism*, Reuven Snir writes that the religious norms of Jewish and Arab cultures prevented the vision of one Arab culture in Iraq from being realized, despite its secular trends.[63] When one reads the memoirs of Iraqi Jews, it becomes clear that there has always been social tension between Jews and Muslims in Iraq, based on religious differences. There were times when it was latent and there were times when it exploded. In the poem that opens his memoirs, Shmuel Moreh clearly expresses this tension: "How will I return? For whom shall I return? For we are Jews!"[64]

4 Identity—Being a Babylonian Jew Outside Iraq

Baghdad Mon Amour deals with the sense of alienation and separateness that Moreh felt in Iraq and elsewhere: In elementary school he was called "Jew," while in Israel he was called "Iraqi" or "Iraqi poet," and during his studies in London, the Arab students he met refused to have any contact with him. They took care to warn all Arab students against the Israeli student who had come from Iraq. They were told not to talk to him as he could very well be a spy.[65]

Moreh's stories demonstrate the negative attitude towards Iraqi Jews even outside Iraq. In his memoirs, he chronicles his study period in London, including a conversation he had with British-Jewish students. At the time, Golda Meir had come to London in an attempt to encourage Jewish immigration from Europe to Israel in order to safeguard the majority of Ashkenazi Jews from the "black and illiterate" Jews who had emigrated from Arab countries to Israel.[66] However, his fellow students were surprised to find that he and his two brothers were of Iraqi origin, were not black, and were actually writing doctoral theses in London and being praised for the excellence of their education.[67]

63 Snir, *Arabness*, 415, 515.
64 Moreh, *Baghdād*, 4.
65 Ibid., 199–200.
66 Ibid., 199.
67 Ibid.

The British hinted at the feeling of superiority that the European Jews had towards Jews from Arab countries. These words exacerbated the sense of alienation Iraqi Jews felt in Israel. While in Iraq one was at fault for being Jewish, in Europe and Israel one was at fault for being of Iraqi origin.

On the one hand, throughout his writing we perceive Moreh's longing for his homeland and its landscapes, but on the other hand, we can also sense that he feels a deep emotional connection with Israel. Moreh is aware of the difference between life in a democratic State of Israel, which enables strangers to express their opinions, however extreme these may be, and life in Iraq, which is always monitored and where a sword of Damocles seems to be hovering above them permanently.[68]

Baghdad Mon Amour and other memoirs are the artistic representation of the social world as individuals remember it. Their authors write about things and events that have shaped their identity. Reviewing the Iraqi Jews' memoirs teaches that the *Farhūd* marked a turning point in their thinking and was a formative event in their lives. Those who were hurt directly by the *Farhūd* clearly knew that they could no longer live in Iraq—as did some who had not experienced the *Farhūd*. Most Iraqi Jews left Iraq in the 1950s. Others, however, chose to stay in the country, still hoping for true equality. History ultimately indicated that their hope turned out to be wishful thinking. Eventually most of the Jews who remained in Iraq left in the 1970s, so that today, in the twenty-first century, very few Jews are still living in Iraq. The last head of the Jewish community was Naji Gabriel (1936–2012).

In order to understand the social history of the Jews in Iraq, we must understand their mentality, which means the social sensitivities in Iraqi society as they are uncovered in memoirs that reflect the era and its social customs. As these memories teach, religion was one of the most prominent sensitivities of life in Iraq and in other Arab countries, and the main barrier to being, or at least feeling, equal. They document personal moments, words, and feelings, which cannot be found in historical writings that document the *Farhūd* but not the interpersonal feelings and relationships behind it. The authors mentioned in this study describe the *Farhūd* and life in Iraq in light of their own experiences in such a way that the reader cannot ignore the feelings they convey—the very thing that is lacking in history books. Personal memoirs like these add important elements to our understanding of history, such as mentality, customs, atmosphere, and interpersonal encounters.

68 Ibid., 353.

Bibliography

Cohen, Hayim J. "The Anti-Jewish 'Farhud' in Baghdad, 1941," *Middle Eastern Studies* 3/1 (October 1966): 2–17.

Crone, Patricia. *Pre-Industrial Societies*. Oxford: Blackwell, 1989.

Fattal, Salim. *In the Alleys of Bagdad*. Jerusalem: Karmel, 2003 [in Hebrew].

Gershoni, Israel, Orit Bashkin, and Liat Kozma (eds.). *Sculpting Culture in Egypt*. Tel Aviv: Ramot, 1999 [in Hebrew].

Golomb, Jacob. *An Introduction to the Philosophies of Existentialism*. Tel Aviv: Broadcast University, 1990.

Haim, Sylvia G. "Aspects of Jewish Life in Baghdad under the Monarchy," *Middle Eastern Studies* 12/2 (May 1976): 188–208.

Manṣūr, Anīs. *Ṭalaʿa al-badr ʿalaynā*. Cairo: al-Maktab al-Miṣrī al-Ḥadīth, 1975.

Manṣūr, Anīs. *ʿĀshū fī ḥayātī*. Cairo: al-Maktab al-Miṣrī al-Ḥadīth, 1989.

Manṣūr, Anīs. *al-Baqiyya fī ḥayātī*. Cairo: Dār al-Shurūq, 1993.

Morad, Ezra. *Childhood Scenery from My Father's Home*. Jerusalem: Association of Jewish Academics from Iraq, 2012 [in Hebrew].

Morad, Tamar, Dennis Shasha, and Robert Shasha (eds.). *Iraq's Last Jews*. New York: Palgrave Macmillan, 2008.

Moreh, Shmuel. *Modern Arabic Poetry, 1800–1970: The Development of Its Forms and Themes under the Influence of Western Literature*. Leiden: Brill, 1976.

Moreh, Shmuel. "The Pogrom of June 1941 as Reflected in the Literature of Jews from Iraq in Israel," in *Hatred of Jews and the Farhud in Iraq*, edited by Shmuel Moreh and Zvi Yehuda. Or-Yehuda: The Babylonian Jewry Heritage Center, 1992, 13–26 [in Hebrew].

Moreh, Shmuel. *Tilka ayyām al-ṣibā: majmūʿa shiʿriyya bi'l-lughatayn al-ʿArabiyya wa'l-Inklīziyya*. Jerusalem: Association of Jewish Academics from Iraq, 1998.

Moreh, Shmuel. *Baghdād ḥabībatī: Yahūd al-ʿIrāq, dhikrayāt wa-shujūn*. Haifa: Maktabat Kull Shay', 2012.

Moreh, Shmuel and Lev Hakak. "Contemporary Literary and Scientific Activities by Jewish Writers from Iraq in Iraq and Israel," in *The Tree and the Branch: Studies in Modern Arabic Literature and Contributions of Iraqi-Jewish Writers*, edited by Olga Bramson. Jerusalem: Magnes Press, 1997, 296–345 [in Hebrew].

Muʿallim, ʿIzzat Sāsūn. *ʿAlā ḍifāf al-Furāt*. Shafā ʿAmr: al-Mashriq, 1980.

Qazzaz, David. *Mother of the Pound: Memoirs on the Life and History of the Iraqi Jews*. Tel Aviv: Maariv, 2006 [in Hebrew].

Qazzaz, Nissim. *The Jews in Iraq after the Mass Immigration, 1951–2000*. Or-Yehuda: The Babylonian Jewry Heritage Center, 2002.

Shammash, Gidʿon. *My Life's Journey in Iraq and Israel*. Jerusalem: Association of Jewish Academics from Iraq, 2011 [in Hebrew].

Snir, Reuven. *Arabness, Jewishness, Zionism—A Clash of Identities in the Literature of Iraqi Jews*. Jerusalem: Ben-Zvi Institute, 2005 [in Hebrew].

Wickberg, Daniel. "What Is the History of Sensibilities? On Cultural Histories, Old and New," *The American Historical Review* 112/3 (June 2007): 661–684.

Wild, Stefan. "National Socialism in the Arab Near East between 1933 and 1939," in *Hatred of Jews and the Farhud in Iraq*, edited by Shmuel Moreh and Zvi Yehuda. Or-Yehuda: The Babylonian Jewry Heritage Center, 1992, 28–66 [in Hebrew].

Yehuda, Zvi. "A Selection of Documents on the Pogrom of June 1941," in *Hatred of Jews and the Farhud in Iraq*, edited by Shmuel Moreh and Zvi Yehuda. Or-Yehuda: The Babylonian Jewry Heritage Center, 1992, 211–313 [in Hebrew].

Index

Abbasids, Abbasid Caliphate 116, 249
ʿAbd al-Munʿim, Tāmir 218
ʿAbd al-Nāṣir, Jamāl 163–164, 164n13, 164n14, 166–165
ʿAbduh, Muḥammad 293n17, 300–301
Abū al-Anwār al-Sādāt, Muḥammad 276–285
Abū Bakr (first Caliph) 12, 35, 40, 300n39
Abū Tammām 32, 35, 37–38, 43
adab (literature) 21, 111, 111n8, 114, 116n26, 121n40, 129
Adab Ayyām al-ʿArab 31
ʿAdnān, Ṭāhā 230, 232
al-Afghānī, Jamāl al-Dīn 293n17
al-Aḥmadi, Aḥmad b. Aḥmad al-Samālījī al-Shāfiʿī 275
Aḥmadīyya (Sufi order) 273, 277
Akram, Ghulām Muḥammad Sirdār 295
al-ʿAlamī, Sīdī Qaddūr 57–58, 64
al-Albānī, Nāṣir al-Dīn 130, 132n20, 138
Aleppo 250
Algeria, Algiers 20, 73, 78, 288, 295
ʿAli Bey al-Kabīr 273
Allawites 307
Amīn, Qāsim 297, 297n32
Amīr al-ḥajj (pilgrimage commander) 251, 258
Amman 7, 74
al-Anṣārī, Zakariyyā 266–267, 285
al-ʿAqīq 35n11
The Arab-Israeli conflict 63n29
The Arab Poets' Association 10
ʿĀrif, ʿAbd al-Salām 73
Aristotle 31
al-Arnāʾūṭ, Nāṣir al-Dīn 129
Asad (tribe) 12, 33–38, 35n11, 40, 42, 45
al-Ashmūnī, Muḥammad 291
ashrāf (the Prophet's descendants) 264, 268–270, 283
ʿĀshūrāʾ 179, 182, 180–190
Atatürk, Mustafa Kemal 247
Ayyām al-ʿArab 31
ʿAzab 250–257, 260
al-Azhar 164, 264–266, 270–274, 277–279, 289, 291, 293–294, 296, 300–301
ʿAzīza, Muḥammad 191–192

Babylon 142, 148, 156, 157n57
al-Badawī, al-Sayyid Aḥmad 273, 277
Baghdad 1, 6–9, 23, 72, 145, 149, 155–156, 158, 183, 318, 327–328
al-Bakrī, Muṣṭafā b. Kamāl al-Dīn 273
Ballas, Shimon 145
Banū Nabhān b. ʿAmr b. Aws 12, 32
Banū ʿUqayl 35n11
Basra 72–73
al-Battāwīn (Baghdad's central Jewish neighborhood) 1, 7, 324
al-Bayṭār, ʿAbd al-Razzāq 293n17
Beirut 73, 85, 290, 293, 293n17, 295–297, 301–308
Bektāshiyya (Sufi order) 266
bidʿa (disapproved innovation) 275, 300
Bildiyyīn (Jewish converts to Islam in Morocco) 59, 60n10, 61n13, 66n38
al-Bustānī, Buṭrus 305
Būziyān, Fāṭima 229–230

Cairo 7, 16, 19, 73–74, 111–112, 121n37, 121n39, 131, 162–163, 167–168, 194, 196–198, 201, 204, 206–207, 217, 248, 250, 253–254, 257, 271, 273–277, 280, 282–283, 288–289, 291, 301
  Qalʿat al-Jabal 111, 120
  Sayyida Zēnab 199, 201, 213
The Cairo Genizah 197
Chodzko, Alexander 192
Christian, Christians 5, 7, 19, 102 115n22, 194, 202, 259, 273, 278, 280, 295–297, 299, 303, 305–310, 320–323
Copts 202–203, 283, 328

Dafterdār, defterdār (chief financial officer) 251, 255–256, 258, 261
Damascus 13–14, 50–51, 53, 73–74, 126, 127n2, 128–139, 163, 180, 182, 268, 270, 272–273, 290, 293n17, 295–297, 300, 301n47, 302, 306–310
  The Damascus blood libel 323
Damurdāshī (chronicles) 247–250, 260
al-Damurdāshī, Aḥmad 265
Damurdāshiyya (Sufi order) 270
al-Dānā, Nadā 227–228

Darwīsh, Maḥmūd 45
Darwish, Salman 316
al-Dawsī, Ṭufayl b. ʿAmr 32
dhikr (Sufi ritual) 270–275, 292
Dhuhl 43–44
Druze 95, 308, 323

Faraj, Bahjat 219
Farhūd (1941 riots against Jews in Iraq) 5, 5n11, 7, 7n19, 315, 318, 325–328, 330
Fattal, Salim 316, 327
Fatwā (legal opinion) 59, 104, 267–268, 275, 301
Fayṣal I (king of Iraq) 5, 317–318, 328
Fez 59n7, 63n27
al-Find al-Zimmānī (aka Shahl b. Shaybān) 43–44
Firdawsī 180
fitna (civil strife) 271–272
Frenk Aḥmad / Ifranj Aḥmad 248, 250–252, 252n13, 253, 253n14 255, 256n18, 257, 258n19, 261
fuqahā' (jurisconsults) 266
al-Futuwwa (Iraqi paramilitary youth movement) 323, 323n35

Ghānim, Fatḥī 162
ghazal (love poetry) 237
Ghāzī (king of Iraq) 32, 318
al-Ghīṭānī, Jamāl 161–176, 218
Goorji, Ovadia 326
Grover, Fritz 318

Ḥabībī, Emile 163
al-Ḥallāq, Muḥammad b. Yūsuf 248–251, 255, 257–261
al-Hamadhānī, Badīʿ al-Zamān 114
Ḥanafī (legal school) 248
al-Ḥarīrī, al-Qāsim b. ʿAlī 114
Hārūn al-Rashīd 116n26
Hasan Paşa (Ottoman Admiral) 280–281
al-Ḥifnī (al-Ḥifnāwī), Muḥammad b. Salīm 273–274
Hijaz 33n6, 126n1, 133, 270
al-Hijrisī, Muḥammad Khalīl 293n17
The Holy land 14, 126, 128, 128n7, 129–130, 130n15, 131, 133–135, 139
ḥulūl (Sufi doctrine) 267, 273
Ḥusayn (grandson of Prophet Muḥammad) 14, 179–185, 188–192, 269, 277–278, 281–282, 285
al-Ḥusaynī, Ḥājj Amīn 318
Hüsrev Paşa (Ottoman viceroy of Egypt) 283

Ibn ʿAbd al-Ghanī, Aḥmad Shalabī 247, 249–251, 255, 257–260, 265
Ibn Abī al-Surūr, Muḥammad al-Bakrī al-Ṣiddīqī 268–269
Ibn Abī Ṭālib, Ḥasan b. ʿAlī 133, 268
Ibn ʿArabī, Muḥyī al-Dīn 166, 166n22, 175, 267–268, 271–272, 274, 285
Ibn ʿAsākir 132
Ibn Falīta 110, 110n4, 110n5, 111, 119n34
Ibn al-Fāriḍ, ʿUmar 267, 274
Ibn Ḥabīb, Muḥammad 50, 130n15, 134–135, 135n32, 136, 138–139
Ibn al-Ḥakam, Unayf 12, 32–33, 35–41, 44
Ibn Ḥātim, ʿAdī 40
Ibn Iyās, Muḥammad b. Aḥmad 164, 265, 268
Ibn Mawlāhum, Muḥammad 112, 112n13
Ibn Maymūn, Muḥammad b. al-Mubārak 32, 36n12
Ibn al-Murajjā, al-Musharraf 126n1, 127, 137n39
Ibn Rifāʿa, al-Ḥārith 35n11
Ibn Taghrī Birdī, Abū al-Maḥāsin Yūsuf 249
Ibn Ṭūlūn, Shams al-Dīn 13, 51–52, 52n9, 53, 268
Ibn ʿUthmān, Muḥammad 111
Ibn Yaḥyā, Abū Mikhnaf Lūṭ 184
Ibrāhīm (Ibrâhîm) Bey Abū Shanab (Mamluk emir) 252–253, 256, 256n18, 257–258, 258n19, 259, 280–281
Idrīs, ʿAbd al-Nūr 236–237
Idrīs, Yūsuf 162
Idrīsiyya (Sufi order) 293n17
ijāza (license to teach and transmit religious knowledge) 291
ijmāʿ (legal binding consensus) 300
ijtihād (legal reasoning) 300
al-Ilbīrī, Abū Isḥāq 58
ʿIllaysh, ʿAbd al-Raḥmān 293n17
ʿIllaysh, Muḥammad 291
iltizām (tax farm) 251, 280, 284–285

al-Inbābī, Shams al-Dīn Muḥammad 291
Internet 15, 195n3, 198, 206, 224–240, 242
Iraq 2–4, 4n8, 5–7, 10, 14, 23, 69, 73, 78–81, 133, 142–143, 143n5, 143n7, 144, 146–147, 147n20, 148–149, 149n24, 150–152, 155–158, 179, 189–190, 295, 316–321, 323, 325–326, 328–330
Israel 1–3, 3n4, 6, 9–10, 14, 16, 23, 54, 64, 91, 142–157, 157n57, 158–159, 162, 165–167, 315–317, 327–330
Isrāʾīliyyāt ("Israelite" fabricated ḥadīths) 129, 132
Istanbul 16, 247–248, 266, 269, 279–280, 283, 288, 293n17, 300, 302, 309
ʿIvāż Bey 259, 261n29

al-Jabartī, ʿAbd al-Raḥmān 3, 15–16, 18, 21–23, 251, 253–254, 258–261, 261n27, 264–267, 269–270, 272–276, 276n23, 277–285
Jād, Nihād 217
jāhiliyya (the pre-Islamic period) 41
al-Jāḥiẓ, ʿAmr b. Baḥr 110n3, 114, 119n34
al-Jazʾāirī, ʿAbd al-Qādir 293n17
Jericho 49n1, 50–51, 53, 128, 128n7, 128n9, 129, 130n15
Jerusalem (Bayt al-Maqdis) 7, 9, 50–51, 57, 62, 62n18, 63, 126, 126n1, 127, 127n3, , 128, 128n7, 128n9, 129–130, 130n15, 132, 132n22, 133, 134n29, 135, 135n33, 136, 136n37, 137, 137n39, 138, 138n39, 139, 139n42, 155, 158
Jews 2, 5, 5n11, 6–7, 10, 12, 23, 53, 58–59, 59n7, 60, 60n10, 61, 61n15, 62, 62n21, 63, 63n27, 64, 64n30, 66n39, 142–143, 143n5, 144–146, 148–150, 156–158, 194, 280, 307–308, 315, 317–330
  Ashkenazi 14, 62n20, 329
  Baghdadi Jews 144, 148
  Iraqi/Babylonian Jews 1, 3, 4n8, 5n11, 6–7, 7n18, 8, 10, 16, 22–23, 142–143, 143n5, 144, 146, 149, 315–319, 323–325, 329–330
  Mizrahi/Sephardi 3, 3n5, 9, 14, 20, 149
Jordan 51, 63, 128n7, 130n15, 133, 136
Joseph ha-Nagid Ibn Naghrela 58

Kaʿba 128n9, 301
Kadizadeli (anti-Sufi movement established in Istanbul) 270–272
Karbala 14, 179, 182–183, 190
Kāshānī, Muḥtasham 185
Kāshifī, Ḥusayn Vāʿiẓ 184
al-Kātib, ʿAlī b. Naṣr 110
al-Kātib, ʿAlī b. ʿUmar al-Qazwīnī 110n6
al-Khafājī, Muḥammad ʿAlī 191–192
khalwa (place of seclusion) 276, 284
al-Khalwatī, Karīm al-Din 270, 271n13
Khalwatiyya (Sufi order) 266, 270, 271n13, 272–274, 285
khānqāh (Sufi lodge) 274
al-Kharrāṭ, Idwār 162
khayāl al-ẓill (shadow theater and puppets) 2–3
al-Khayālī, Muḥammad b. Mawlāhum 112, 112n13
Khayrbāy 250
al-Khusrī, Muḥammad 291
Kīwān, Suhayl 233–234
Kufa 179, 192
al-Kurdī, ʿAbdallāh 295

Lebanon 53, 73, 145–147, 189
Libya 73

madhhab (legal rite, school) 276, 300
Maghāzī (the expeditions and raids organized by the Prophet) 32
Maḥfūẓ, Najīb 161–163
Makram, ʿUmar 270, 283
al-Malāʾika, Nāzik 19
Mamluks 271, 274, 279, 280n27, 282–283
Manṣūr, Anīs 321–323
maqātil (Arabic genre of literature) 184
al-Maqdisī, Shihāb al-Dīn 128n9, 137
majlis (Persian plays) 180, 182–183
al-Maqrīzī, Taqī al-Dīn Aḥmad b. ʿAlī 118n31, 165, 249
Marj Dābiq 250
mawlid(s), (saint's day commemoration) 264, 273–275, 282
mawlid al-Ḥusayn 269, 277–279
mawlid al-nabī 269, 282
Mayyāra, Abū ʿAbd Allāh Muḥammad 59

Medina (Yathrib) 12, 33–34, 35, 40, 126, 126n1, 129, 132, 137–138, 191, 254, 284
Mecca 33n6, 50n4, 62n18, 126, 126n1, 129, 132, 137–138, 284, 293n17, 300–301
Meḥmed IV (Ottoman Sultan) 250
Mevleviyya (Sufi order) 266
Michael, Sami 145, 145
Morad, Ezra 328
Morocco 13, 57, 59, 63n26, 64n30
Moscow 73–74
Moses (the Prophet) 13, 49, 49n1, 50–54, 54n16, 54n17, 126n1, 128, 128n9, 129–130, 230
Mu'allim, 'Izzat Sāsūn 318
Mu'allem, Meir 316
Mubarāk, 'Alī Pasha 165
Muḥammad (the Prophet) 12–13, 33–35, 35n11, 40, 54, 54n18, 55, 62n18, 64n30, 128n9, 130, 135, 137, 179, 184, 188, 254, 264, 269, 296
Muḥammad 'Alī (ruler of Egypt) 264, 270, 283–284, 299
al-Munajjid, Ṣalāḥ al-Dīn 127, 129, 138
Murâd Bey (Mamluk emir) 180
al-Murādī, Muḥammad Khalīl 265
murū'a (the sum of the physical and moral qualities of a man) 31, 111
Musaylima 40
Muṣṭafā III (Ottoman Sultan) 260

Nablus 50–51, 134–135, 135n32, 136, 136n37, 139, 293
al-Nābulusī, 'Abd al-Ghanī 129, 269–271, 285
al-Nadīm, 'Abdallāh 300
Nahḍa (Arab renaissance) 2, 2n1, 5, 289, 289n4, 291
nahḍa adabiyya (cultural revival) 303
Na'īmā, Muṣṭafā 261
Nakba (1948 Palestinian catastrophe) 6, 45
Naqīb al-ashrāf (chief of the Prophet's descendants) 269–270, 274, 283
Naqqāsh, Samīr 14, 142, 144–149, 151–153, 154n48, 155, 157n57, 158–159
Naṣr Allāh, 'Ayda 235
Nijm, Aḥmad Fu'ād 220
Nostradamus 96–101, 104–105
Nuzirists 308

Orwell, George 163–165
Ottomans 22, 163, 175, 268, 280, 280n27, 282–283

Palestine 50–51, 53, 126, 127n2, 128n7, 128n9, 130n15, 131–134, 134n29, 136, 136n35, 139, 156–157, 320–321

Qāḍī (judge) 248
Qāḍī 'askar (chief judge) 248
Qāḍī *al-quḍāt* (chief judge) 248
Qānṣawh al-Ghawrī (Mamluk Sultan) 250
Qāsim, 'Abd al-Karīm 73
al-Qāsim, Samīḥ 13, 91–105
al-Qāsimī , Jamāl al-Dīn 300
al-Qāyātī, Aḥmad 291–292, 301
al-Qāyātī, Muḥammad 289–293, 295–298, 298n34, 299–302, 304, 307, 309–310
Qāyātiyya (Sufi order) 291–292
Qāyitbāy (Mamluk Sultan) 267
al-Qazdaghlī, Muṣṭafā Katkhudā 252, 252n13, 257, 258n19
Qazzaz, David 316, 327
Qazzaz, Nissim 319, 326–327
al-Qinālī, Musṭafā 265
Quḍā'a (tribe) 35

al-Rab'ī, Abū al-Ḥasan 'Alī b. Muḥammad 127, 129, 132
Rabī'a (tribe) 43
al-Rāḍī, 'Abd al-Majīd 76
Rāshid, Ḥusayn 232
al-Ramlī, Lenīn 216
ribāṭ (Sufi center) 276, 284
Riḍā, Rashīd 300
ridda wars (series of military campaigns launched by the Caliph Abu Bakr against rebel Arabian tribes, 632–632) 40
Riyadh 226

Sāda (the Prophet's descendants) 264
ṣadaqa (alms-giving) 34
al-Sādāt, Anwar 166
al-Ṣaftī, Khalīfa 291
ṣaḥāba (the Prophet's companions) 35, 300, 300n39
Sāmī, 'Abd al-Raḥmān 290, 290n8, 291, 302–310

Sanājla, Muḥammad 232, 238, 240–241
al-Ṣāniʿ, Rajāʾ 226
al-Sayyāb, Badr Shākir 19, 78, 80
Sefrou (Morocco) 13, 57, 59n7, 63n27
Selim I (Ottoman Sultan) 249–250, 268, 272
Shādhiliyya (Sufi order) 269
Shāfiʿī (legal school) 267, 274, 276, 291
al-Shāfiʿī, Muḥammad b. Idrīs 132n22, 277, 281
al-Shām (Greater Syria) 53, 131, 290
Shammash, Gidʿon 320–321, 327
Shammash, Violette, 316
al-Shanfarā 93–95
al-Shaʿrānī, ʿAbd al-Wahhāb 266–269, 272, 275, 285
sharīʿa (Islamic law) 266
al-Sharqāwī, ʿAbd Allāh b. al-Ḥijāzī al-Shāfiʿī al-Azharī 274, 282
al-Sharqāwī, ʿAbd al-Raḥmān 191
Shaul, Anwar 316
Shaykh al-Azhar (rector of al-Azhar) 273–274
Shaykh mashāyikh al-ṭuruq al-ṣūfiyya (supreme shaykh of the Sufi orders) 270
Shiʿis, Shiʿism 12, 179–180, 184, 189, 191–192, 300n39, 308
Shimr 182, 185
al-shiʿr al-ḥurr (free verse) 2, 19
al-Shirbīnī, Yūsuf b. Muḥammad 117n30, 195n3
Sufi, Sufis 13, 16, 165–166, 175–176, 264, 266–278, 282–285, 288–289, 292–293, 293n17, 301
Sufi literature 163
Sufism 16, 264, 266–267, 269–273, 285, 291, 300–301, 301n47
Süleyman the Magnificent, Kanuni Süleyman (Ottoman Sultan) 266–268, 272, 280n28
Sunna 58
Sunnis 191–192, 308
Syria 13–14, 16, 51, 53, 73, 126, 126n1, 127n2, 128n7, 130n15, 131, 133–134, 136, 139, 250, 267–268, 270, 288–290, 293–294, 298, 301–303, 306, 310

al-Ṭabarī, Muḥammad b. Jarīr 40n18, 249
al-Ṭahṭāwī, Rifāʿa Rāfiʿ 299
al-Tamartāshī, Ṣāliḥ b. Aḥmad 129, 131–132, 136, 139

takiyya (Sufi center) 268, 274
taqlīd (adherence to a school of law) 300
tārīkh (history, historiography) 15
ṭarīqa, ṭarīqas (order in Sufi terminology) 269–270, 272, 274–275
Ṭasm, Ṭasam (tribe) 39n16, 41n21
Tawfīq (Khedive of Egypt) 165, 290
Ṭayyiʾ (tribe) 12, 32–33, 33n6, 34–42, 45
taʿziya (Shiʿi mourning rituals in Iran) 14, 179–186, 188–192, 192n12
Tanzimat (Ottoman reforms) 309, 309n76
Tel Aviv 153, 155
al-Tīfāshī, Aḥmad b. Yūsuf 110–111, 119n34

ʿulamāʾ 16, 264, 266–268, 270–273, 275–276, 283, 288, 290–293, 293n17, 294, 298, 301, 310
al-ʿUlaymī, Mujīr al-Dīn al-Ḥanbalī 53
ʿUmar (second Caliph) 62n19, 308n39
al-ʿUmarī, Muqbil Aḥmad 238
Umayyads, Umayyad Caliphate 126, 180
The ʿUrābī revolt 1881–1882 (in Egypt) 289, 290n6, 291–292, 293n17, 294n19, 295, 299, 309
ʿUthmān (fourth Caliph) 300n39

al-Yaʿlāwī, Muḥammad 31
Yaron, Avner-Yaacov 328
Yazīd (Umayyad Caliph) 179–180, 182, 185, 191
al-Yāzijī, Nāṣīf 305
Yemen 33n6, 73–75, 110n4, 132, 138n39
Yusuf (Prophet) 99
Yūsuf, Saʿdī 13, 69, 72–86, 88

waḥdat al-wujūd (the unity of existence) 267

al-Zabīdī, Murtaḍā 121n39, 265, 279
Zaghlūl, Saʿd 328
al-Zahrāwī, ʿAbd al-Ḥamīd 300
zakāt (alms) 34–35, 40
zāwiya (Sufi lodge) 266, 274, 278–280, 284
Zayd al-Khayl 34, 40
Zion, Zionism, Zionist movement 9–10, 142–143, 148, 157, 327
ziyāra (pilgrimage to venerated tombs) 49, 50n4

Printed in the United States
by Baker & Taylor Publisher Services

Printed in the United States
by Baker & Taylor Publisher Services